Models developed with *eXpress*™ by DSI
2013 FORD F150 1St Generation Model

Software Model developed in the U.S.A. by Model Path LLC

Printed in the U.S.A
Copyright © Pending

WIRING DIAGRAMS & SCHEMATICS 2013 FORD F150 Volume 1
ISBN: 979-8-218-75232-3

Steve Ghazi
Model Path LLC

Example Charging Systems

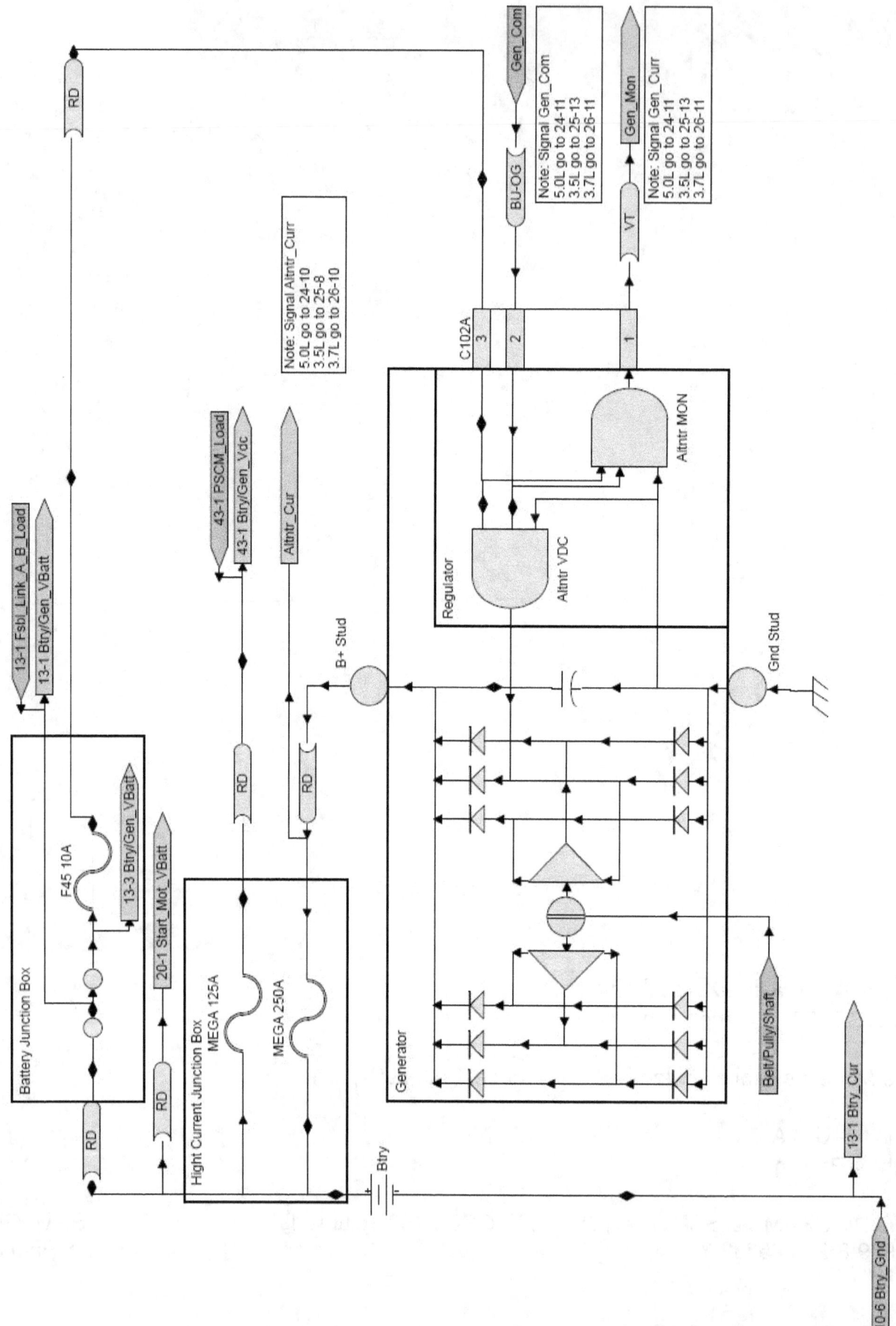

Example Power Distribution

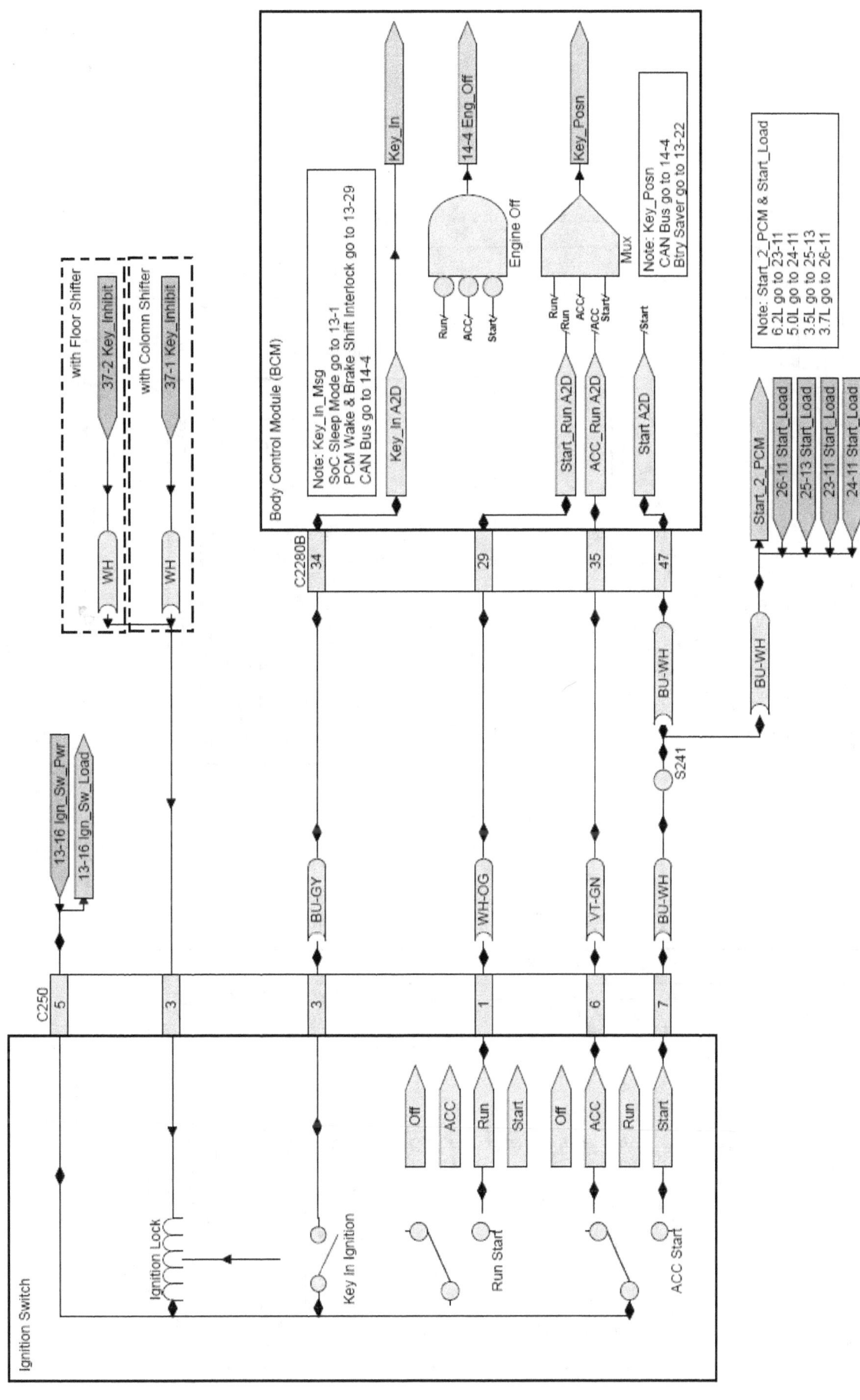

Example Module Communications

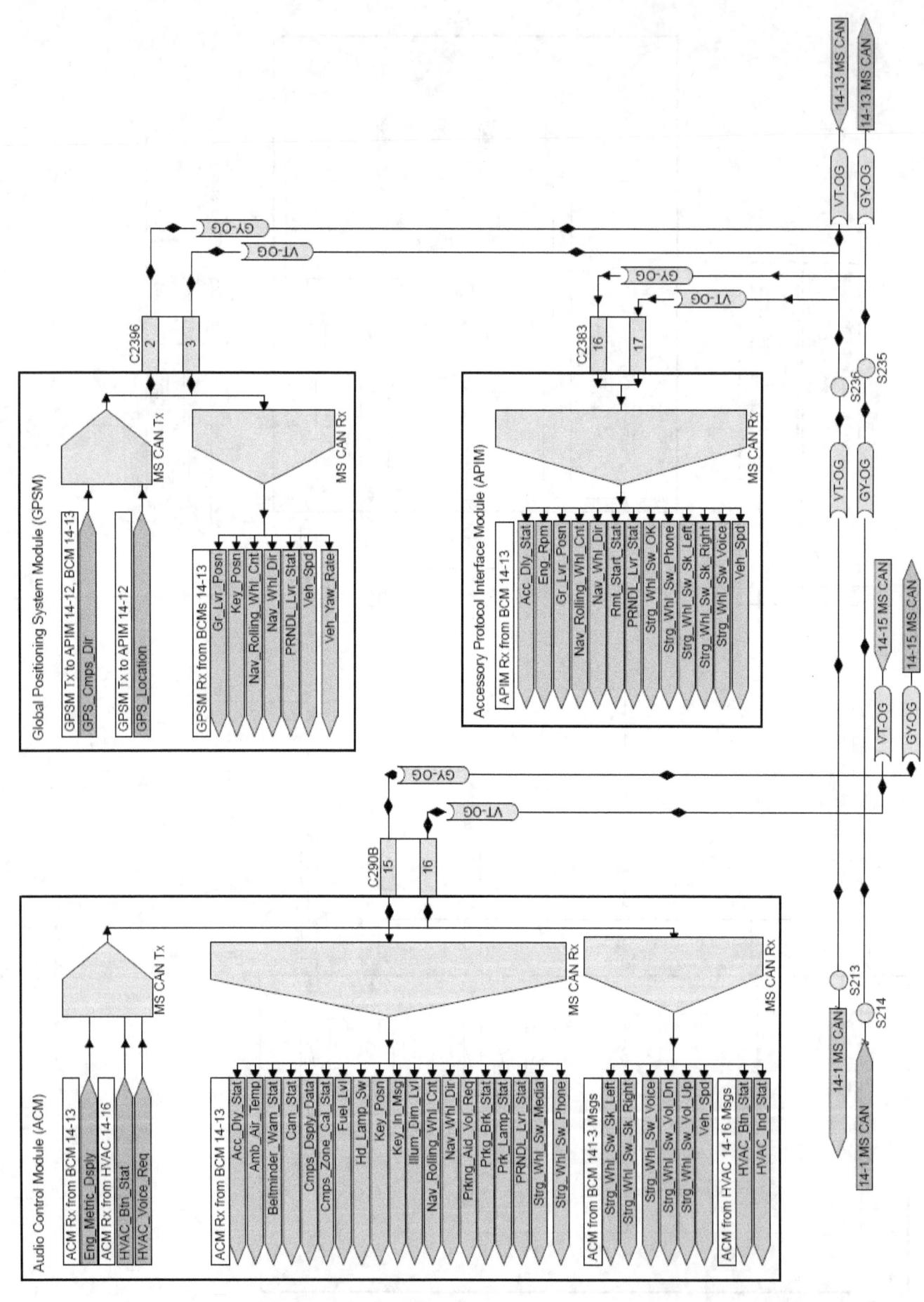

Example: Starting System

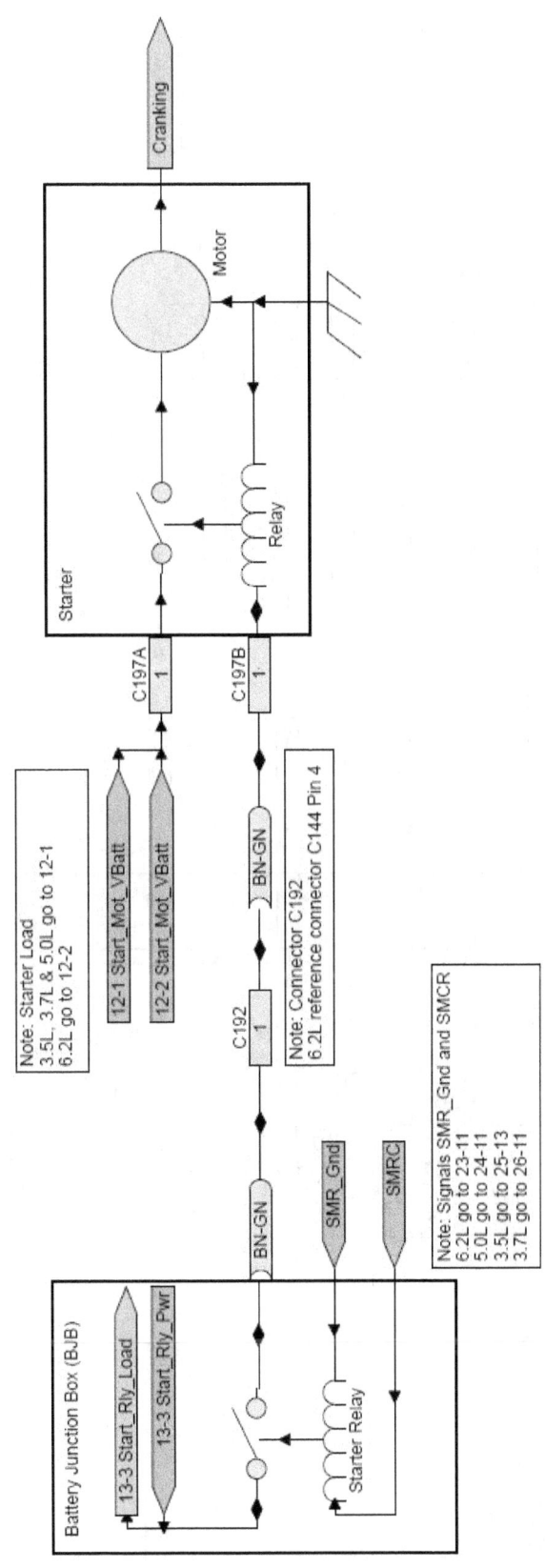

Example Powertrain Control Module

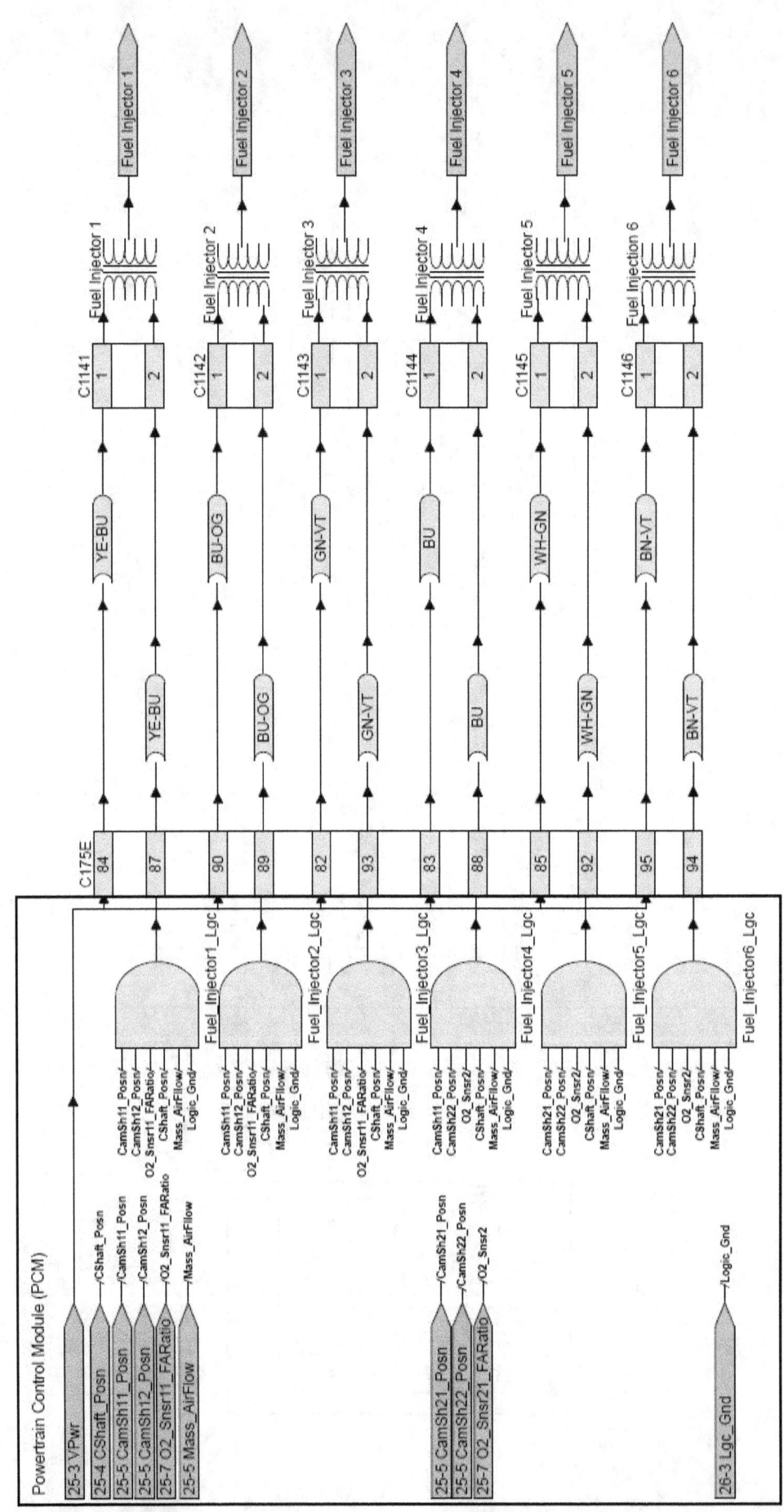

Example Transmission

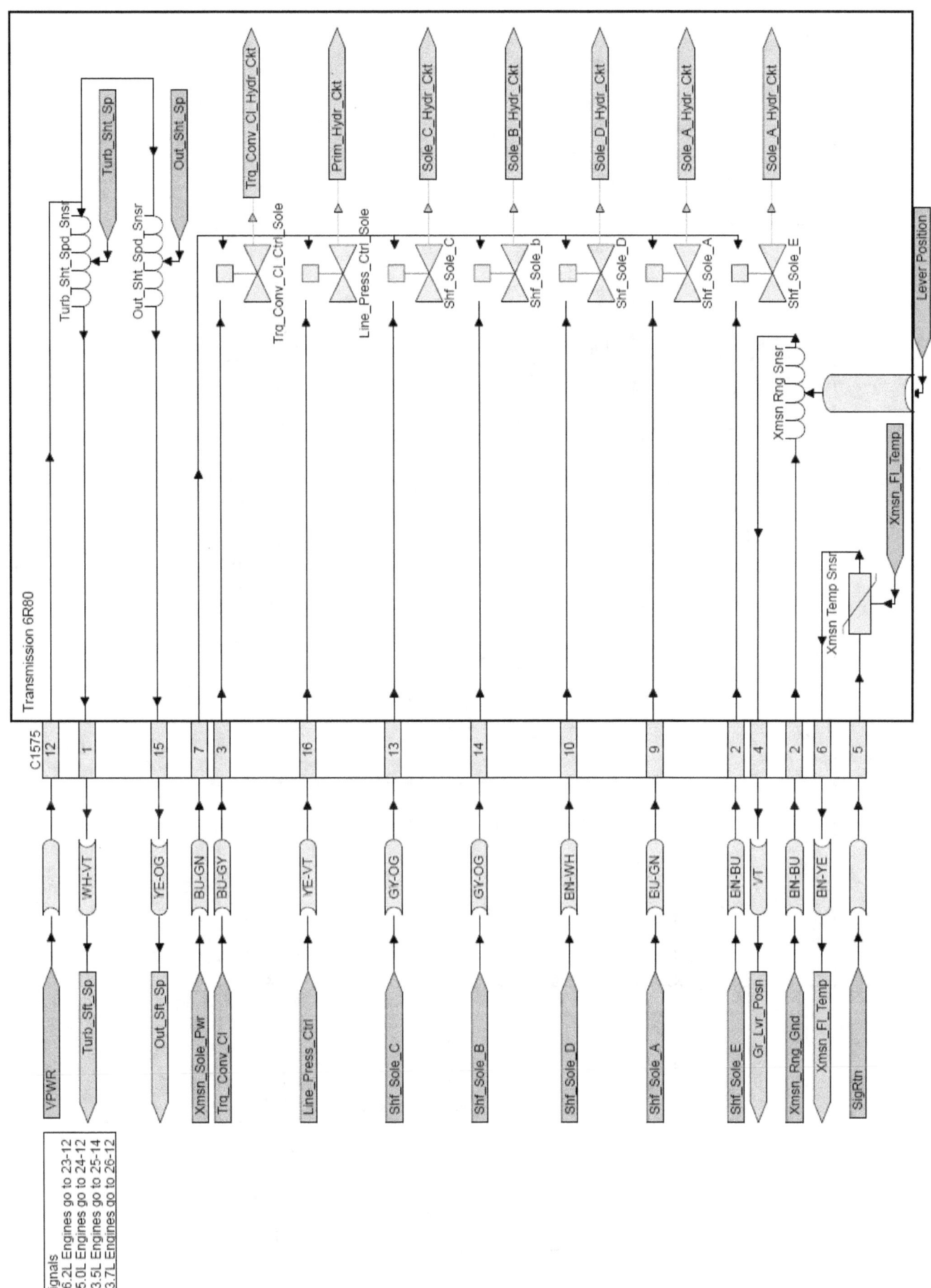

Example Transfer Case Control Module

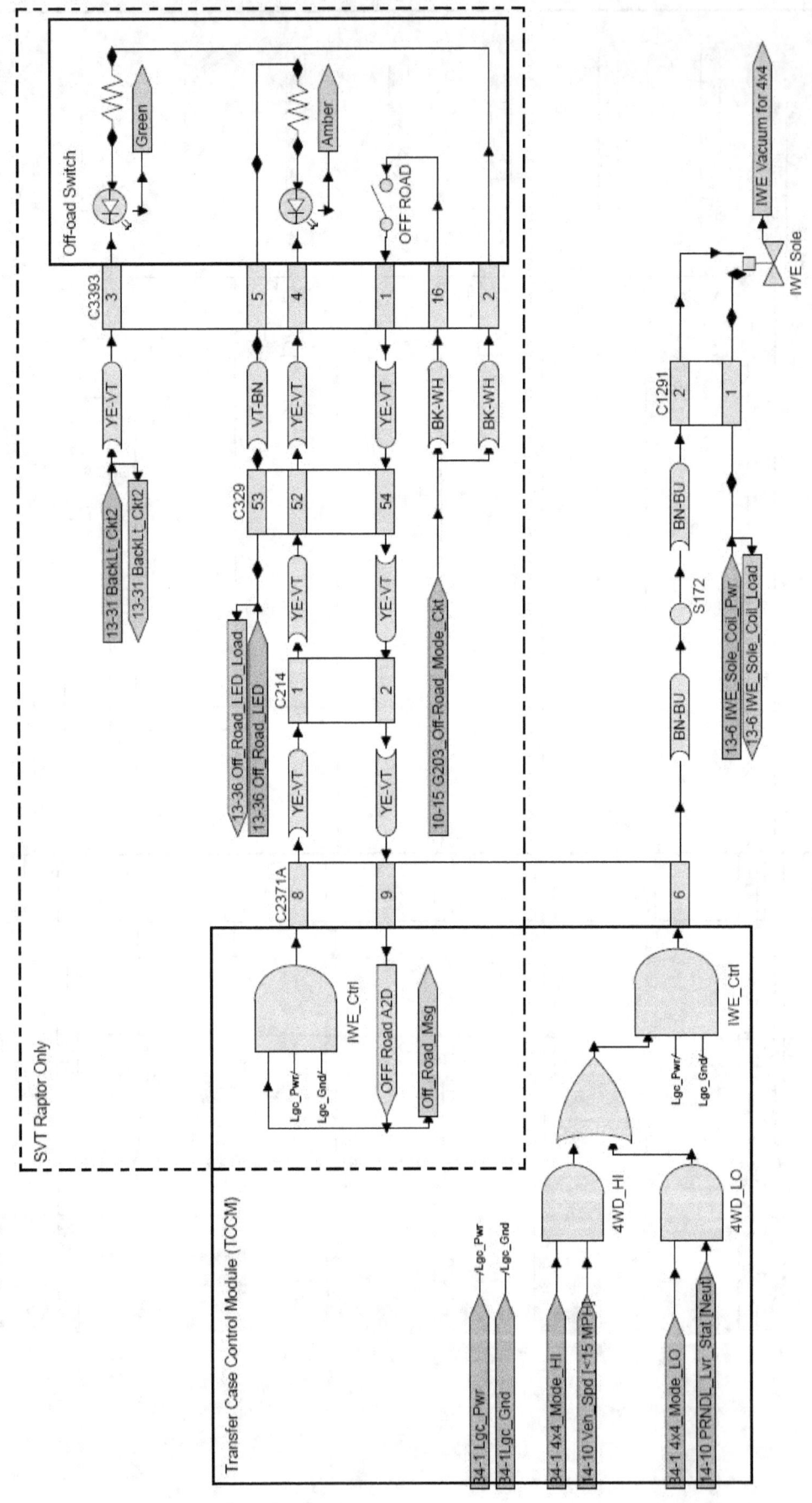

Table of Contents

Acknowledgements 1
Introduction 1
How to use this manual 2
10 Grounds 5
12 Charging Systems 24
13 Power Distribution 26
14 Module Communications 63
20-1 Starting System 84
23 Powertrain Control Module (PCM) for 6.2L Engines 85
24 Powertrain Control Module (PCM) for 5.0L Engines 97
25 Powertrain Control Module (PCM) for 3.5L Engines 109
26 Powertrain Control Module (PCM) for 3.7L Engines 123
30 Transmission Controls 6R80 135
31 Steering Column Control Module (SCCM) 137
33 Engine Cooling Fans 139
34 Transfer Case Control Module (TCCM) 140
37 Brake Shift Interlock 144
42 Anti-Lock Braking System Module (ABSM) 146
43-1 Power Steering Control Module – Steering Gear 149
44-2 Horn Circuit 150
44-4 DC / AC Inverter Module – AC Outlet 151
46 Occupant Classification Module (OCM) & Restraint Control Module (RCM) 152
54 Electronic Manual Temperature Control (EMTC) System 160
55 Electronic Automatic Temperature Control (EATC) System 165
56-1 Heated Windows Rear Defrost Grid 169
60 Instrument Panel Cluster (IPC) 170
71-7 Steering Column Control Module – Instrument Panel Dimmer Switch 176
81 Wipers & Washers 177
85 Headlamp Assemblies 179
89 Interior Lighting 182
90 - 93 Exterior Lighting 187
95 Trailer Electrical 192
100 Power Windows 196
101-1 Overhead Switch Console and Roof Opening Module 201
109-1 Power Running Board Module and Motors 202

110 Power Door Locks	203
112-1 Passive Anti-Theft Transceiver	207
118-1 Tire Pressure Monitor Module (TPMM)	208
119 Climate Control Seating	209
120 Power Seats	215
123 Memory Settings	217
124, 127 Power Mirrors	222
128-2 Steering Column Tilt and Telescoping Motors	230
130 Audio Control Module (ACM)	231
131 Parking Aid Module (PAM) & Cameras	246
140 SVT Raptor	249
141-2 Telematics Module	251
Abbreviations	252

Acknowledgements

All rights reserved. No part of this book may be reproduced or transmitted in any form or by any means, electronic or mechanical, including photocopying, recording or by any information storage or retrieval system, without permission in writing from copyright holder.

While every attempt is made to ensure that the information in this manual is correct, no liability can be accepted by the authors or publishers for loss, damage or injury caused by errors in, or omissions from, the information given.

The illustrated Model-Based Diagrams depict dependency flows of input signals that produce output functions. They conceptually represent electrical systems but do not always follow traditional electrical flow.

"Ford" and the Ford logo are registered trademarks of Ford Motor Company is not a sponsor or affiliate of Model Path LLC and is not a contributor of this manual.

"DSI international inc" and DSI Logo are registered trademarks of DSI international inc. is not a sponsor or affiliate of Model Path LLC and is not a contributor to this manual.

Introduction

The diagrams in this manual are print-outs from the *eXpress*™ modelling software by DSI International and are to be used as supplemental references to Original Equipment Manufacturer's manuals. A software model was created to emulate the electrical, mechanical, software, data bus interactions and their resultant functions.

Volume1 lays out the signal flow from origination to termination, with digital logic to simplify software and electronic functions.

Volume2 will lay out optimized troubleshooting.

How to use this manual

Symbol	Interpretation
123-1 Drvr_Seat_Mdl_Pwr / 123-1 Drvr_Seat_Mdl_Load	Bi-directional signal flow with Output and Input Continuation flags
ClockSpring	Clockspring, a physical medium for signal flow through a rotating device, such as a steering wheel.
with Floor Shifter / WH / 37-2 Key_Inhibit / with Colomn Shifter / WH / 37-1 Key_Inhibit	Dotted line Box, indicating difference in configuration
C316 / 14	Connector, a physical medium representing a plug and jack, example C316 is the connector reference, 14 is the pin reference.
Function References	Function References, do not have _ between key words, versus Signal_References, have underscores between key words.
(ground symbol)	Ground input originating, (Start of signal flow)
10-2 G101_Ckt	Input flag continuation, formatted with diagram sheet and signal name indicating where this signal continued from.

Symbol	Interpretation
Engine Vibration (KS2)	Input Flag originating, formatted without sheet references and without underscores (_) between key words.
(Logic AND symbol)	Logic AND, requires all inputs to produce output signal.
(Logic OR symbol)	Logic OR, requires any of inputs to produce output signal.
F11 30A	Fuse, with Fuse reference, current rating, with bi-directional net for signal flow. Fuses are modelled with bi-directional nets for output and feedback. The output is the power and the feedback is the current draw.
⟶	Net, a conceptual medium for signal flow.
⊣⟶	Not Connected two nets crossing at 90 degrees.
G100_PCM — Note: G100_PCM Signals 3.5L PCM go to 26-3, 3.7L PCM go to 25-3, 5.0L PCM go to 24-3, 6.0L PCM go to 23-3	Output flag with note, indicating the multiple sheets this signal continues to.
10-3 G101_Ckt	Output flag continuation, formatted with 10-3 indicating the diagram sheet to where the signal continues to
Fog Light RS	Output flag terminating, without a sheet reference, with function name, Functions names are without "_" between keys word
Signal_References	Signal References, have underscore "_" between key words, versus Function References do not.

3

Symbol	Interpretation
PCM Pwr Relay	Relay, the coil on the bottom when energized provides a electromagnetic field to close the contact on the top. The contact on the top has a dependency provide by the coil.
S154 → BK-GY / BK-GY	Splice, indicating a split in the signal flow.
BK-YE	Wire, a physical medium for signal flow. Lettering indicates color coding. BK is black with YE yellow striping.

10 Grounds
Grounds G100, G112 **10-1**

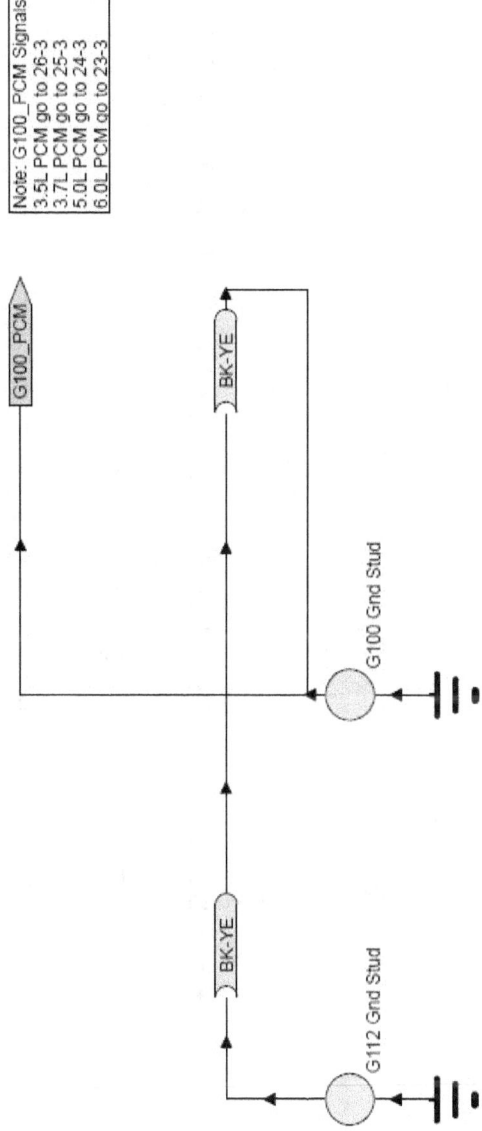

10-2 Grounds G101

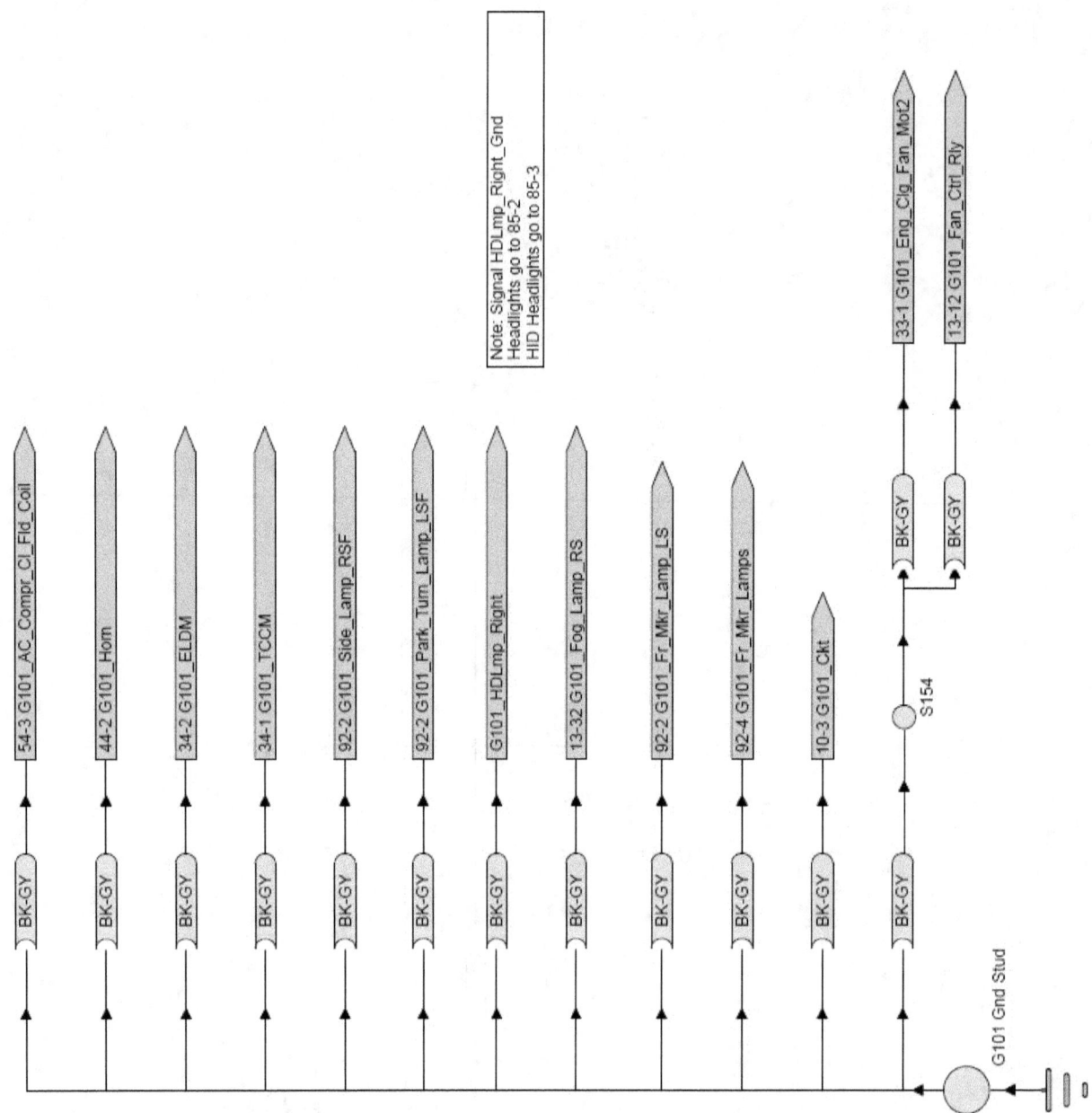

Grounds G101 **10-3**

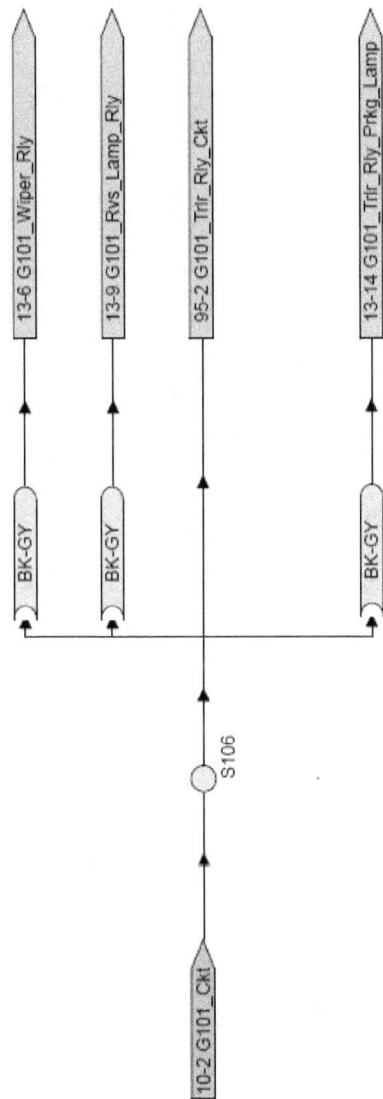

10-4 Grounds G102

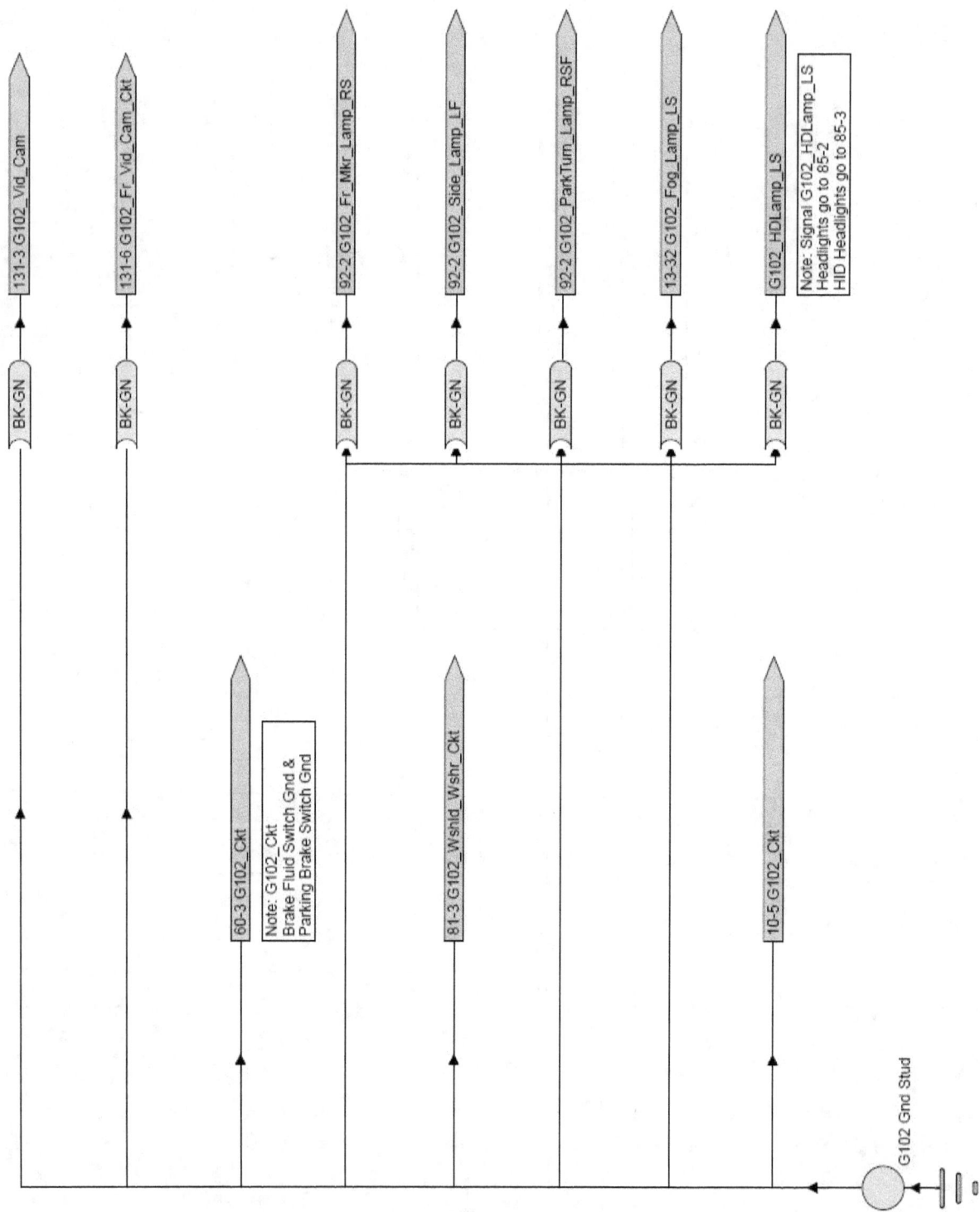

Grounds G10 **10-5**

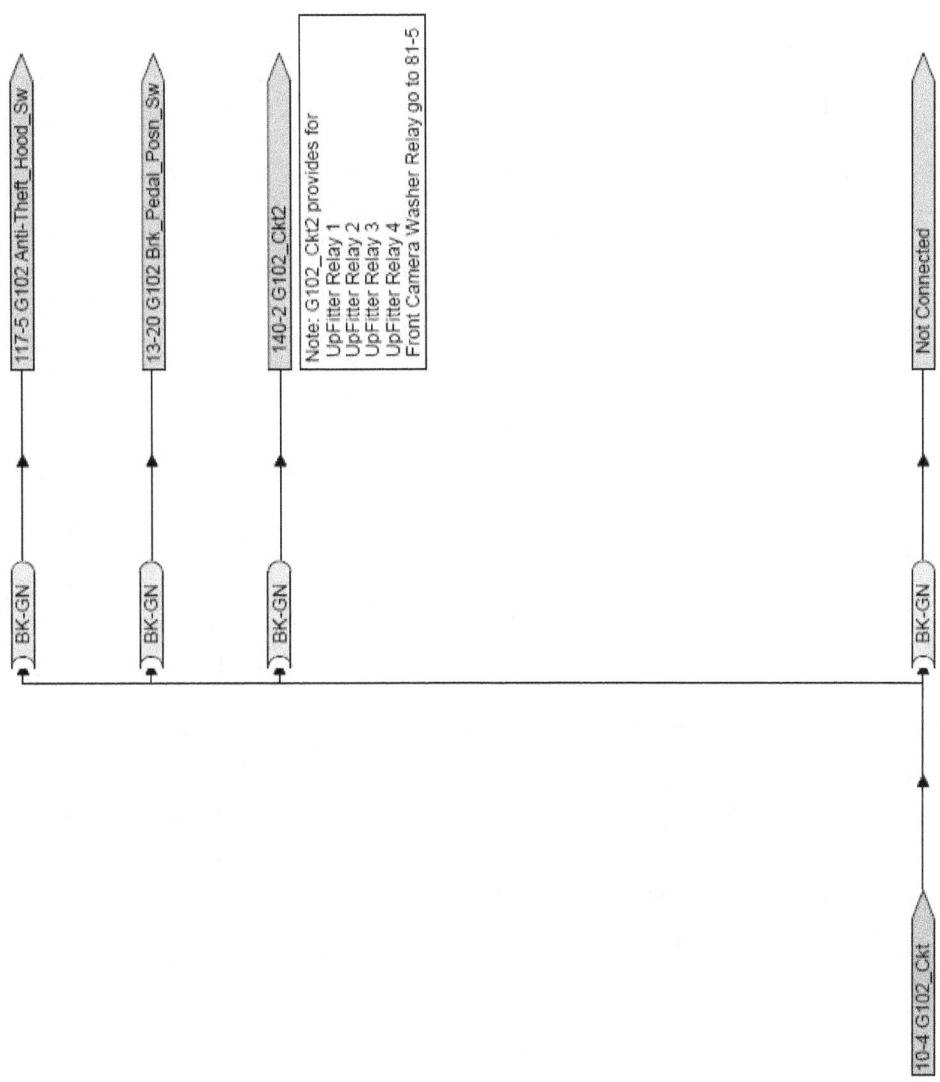

10-6 Grounds G103, G104, G105, G109, G106, G107, G108

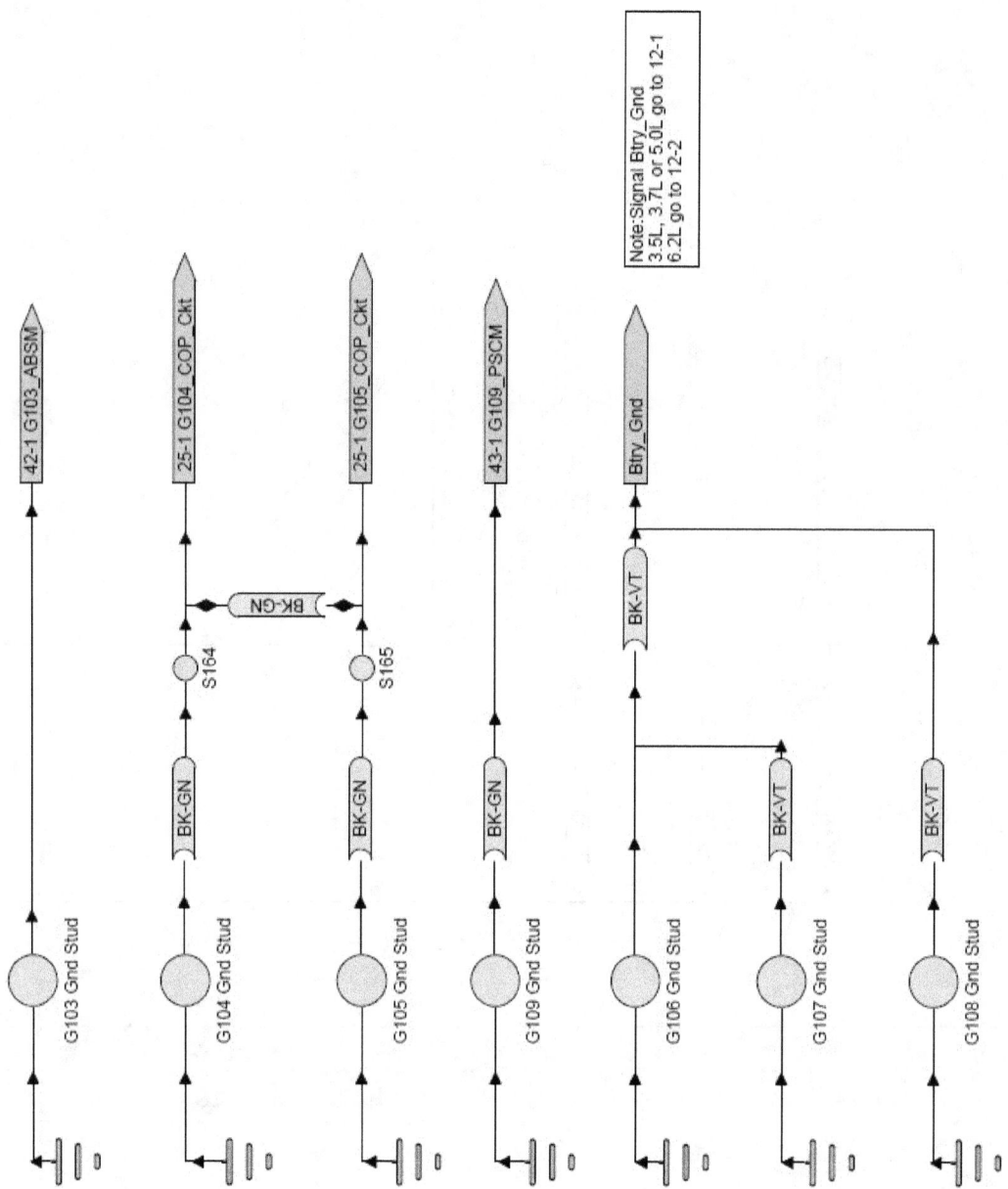

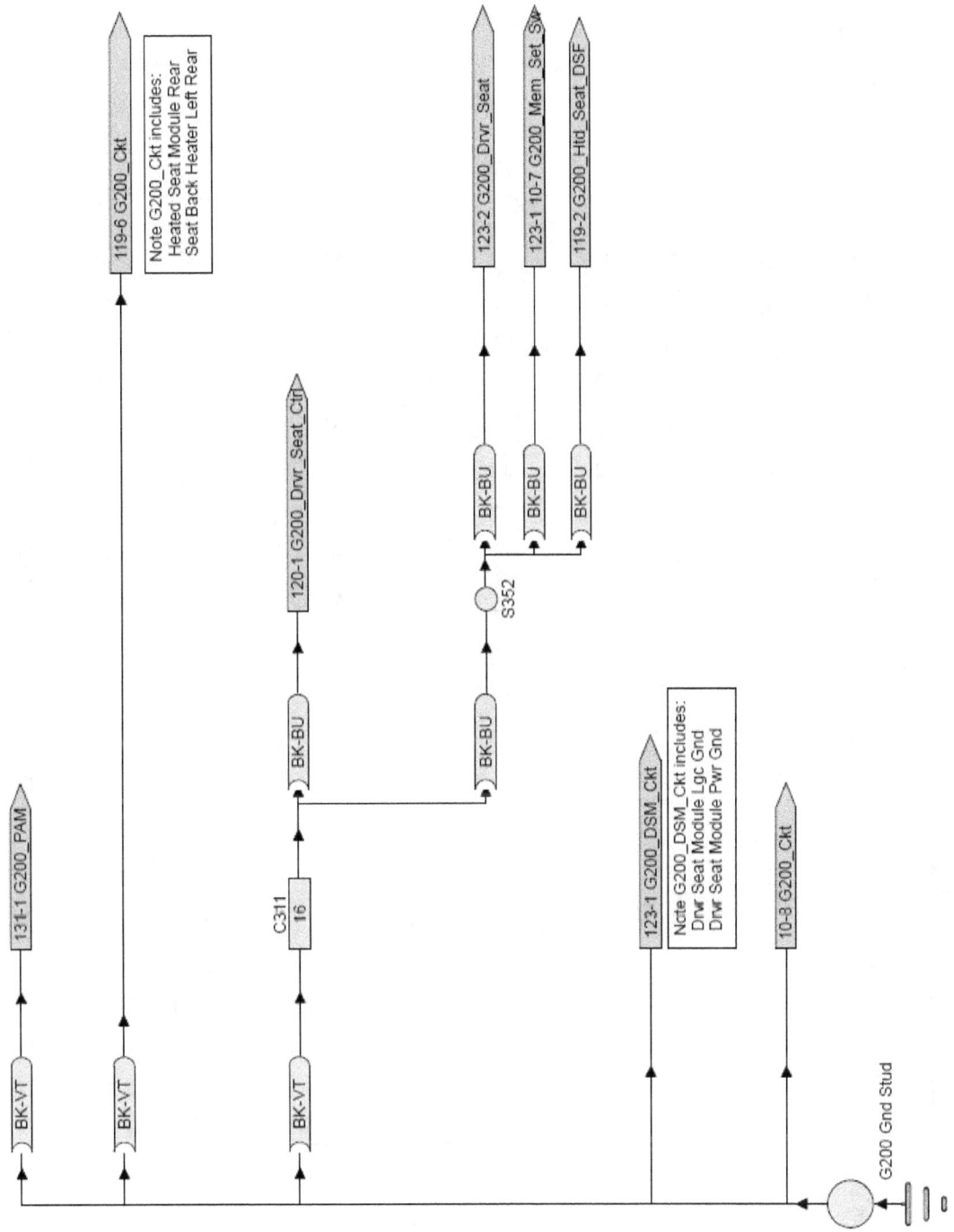

10-8 Grounds G200

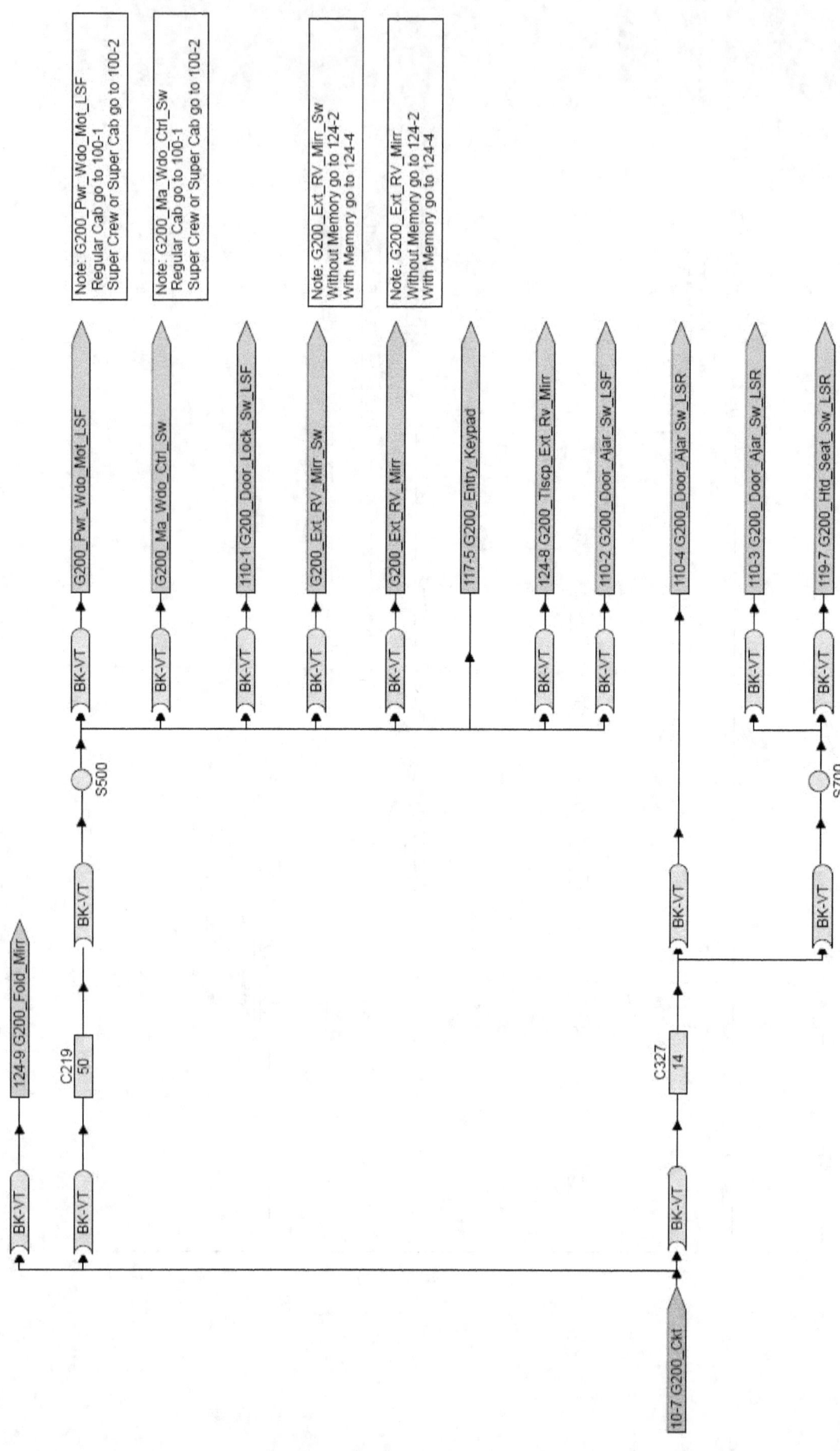

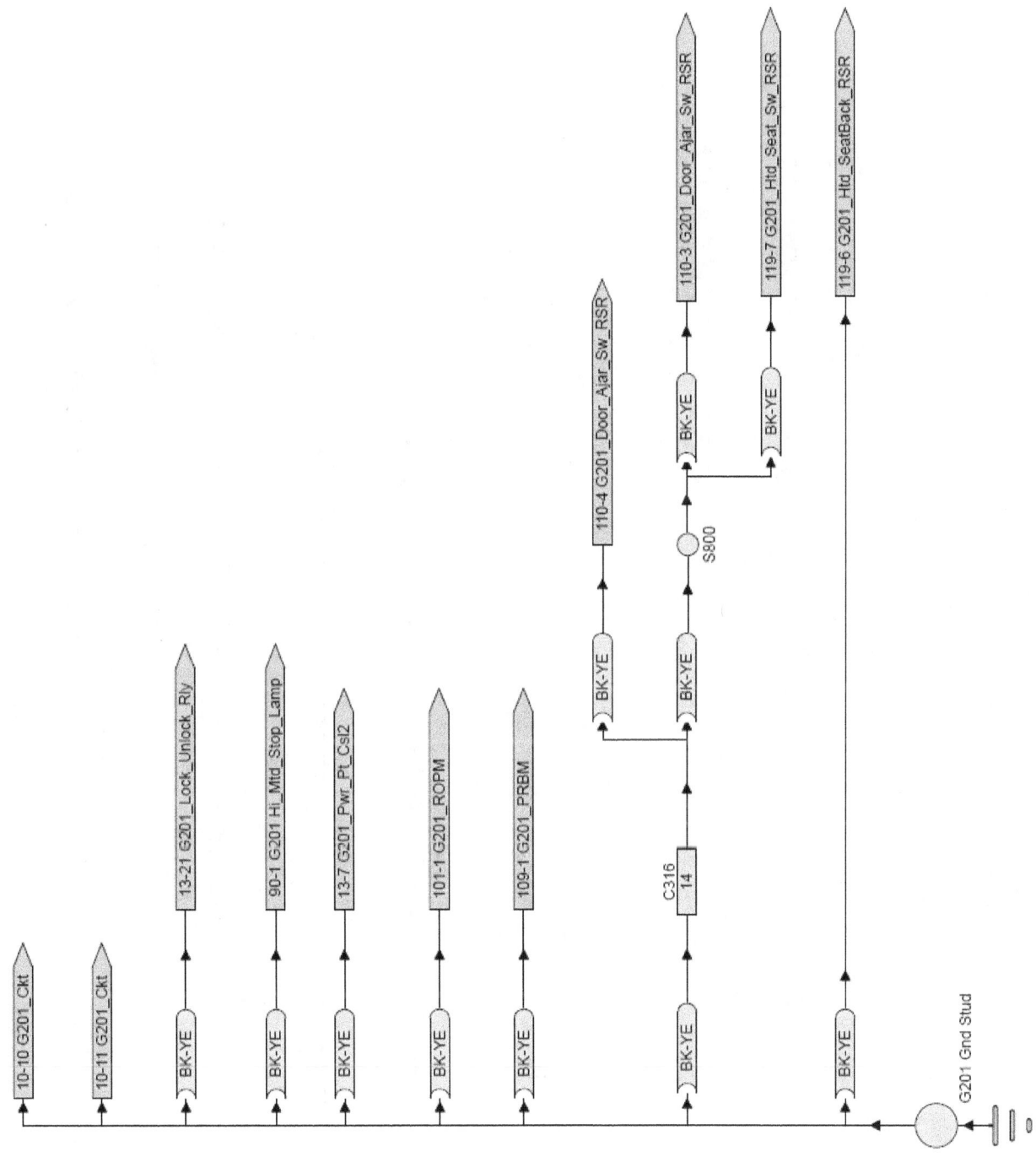

10-10 Grounds G201

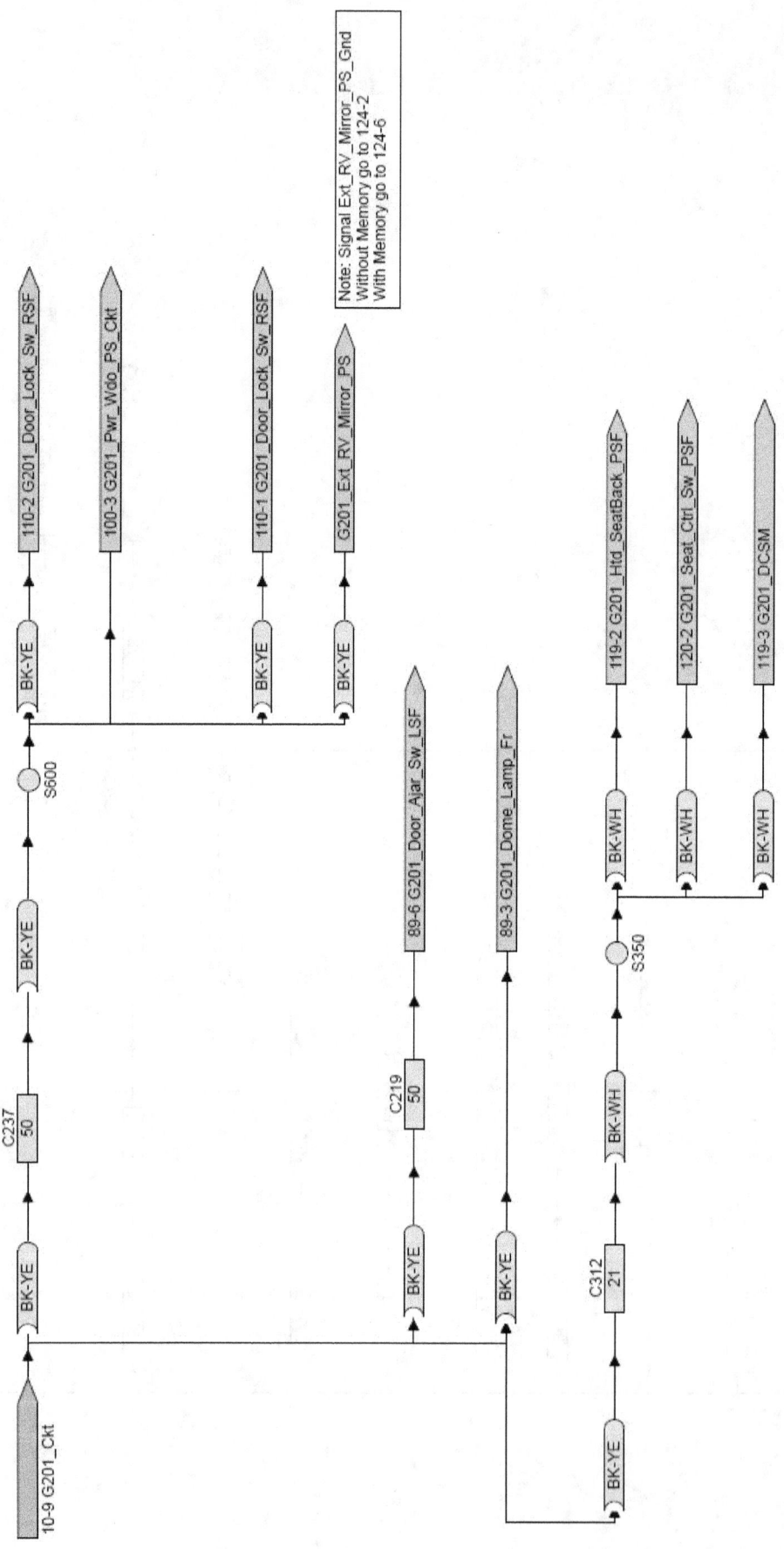

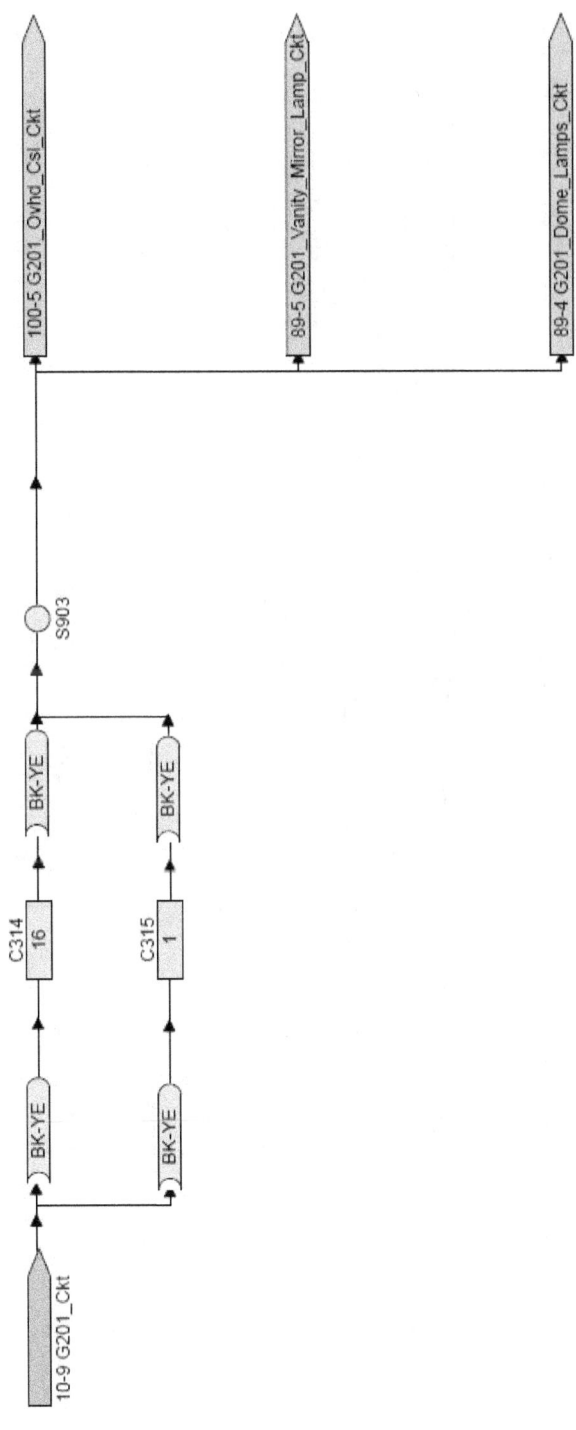

10-12 Grounds G202

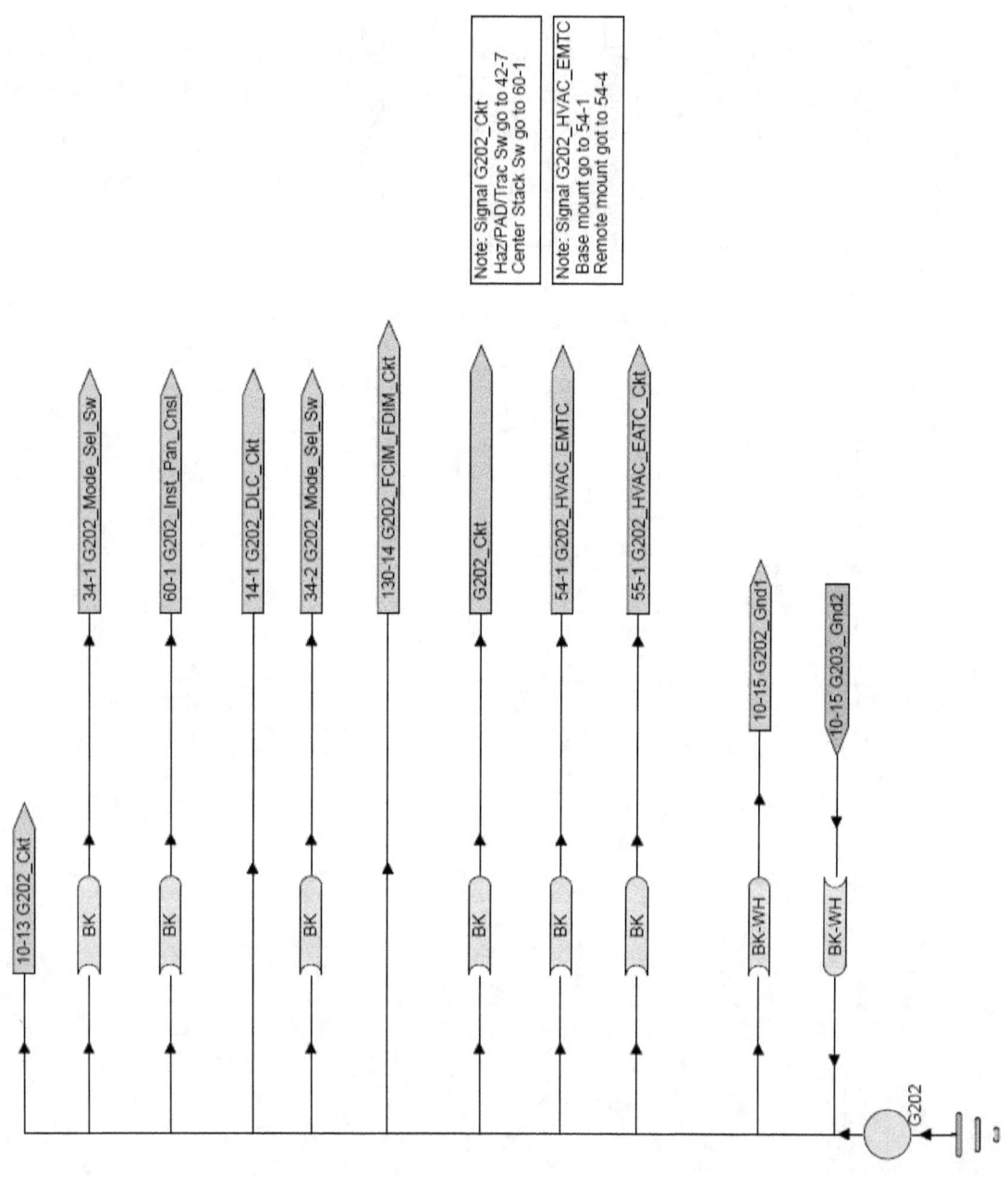

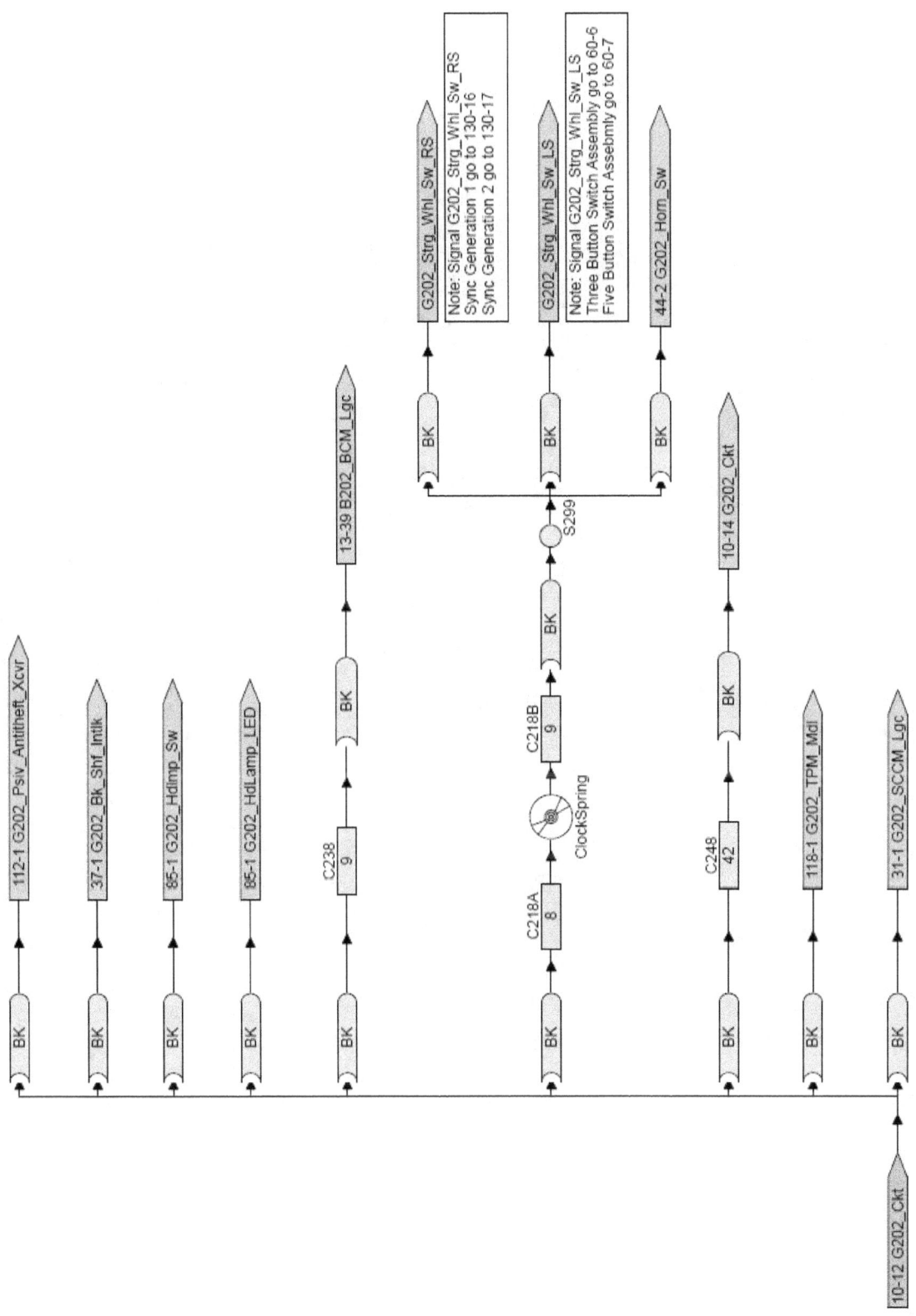

10-14 Grounds G202

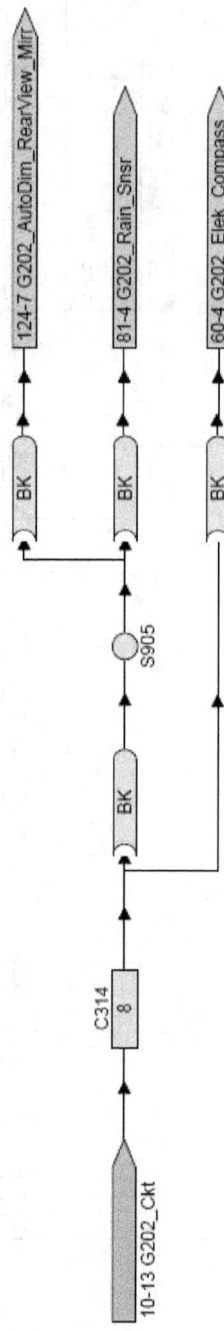

Grounds G203 10-15

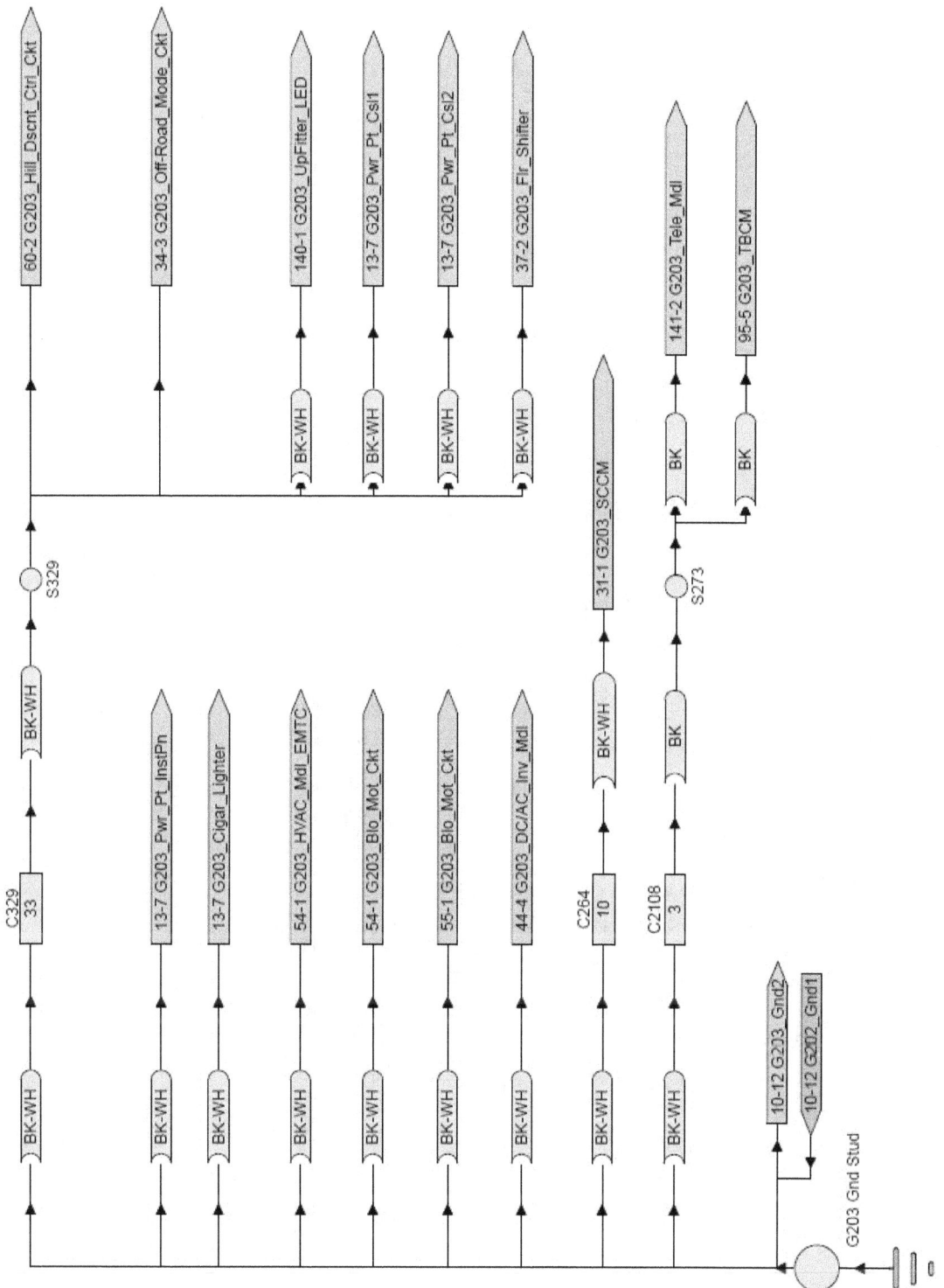

10-16 Grounds G204

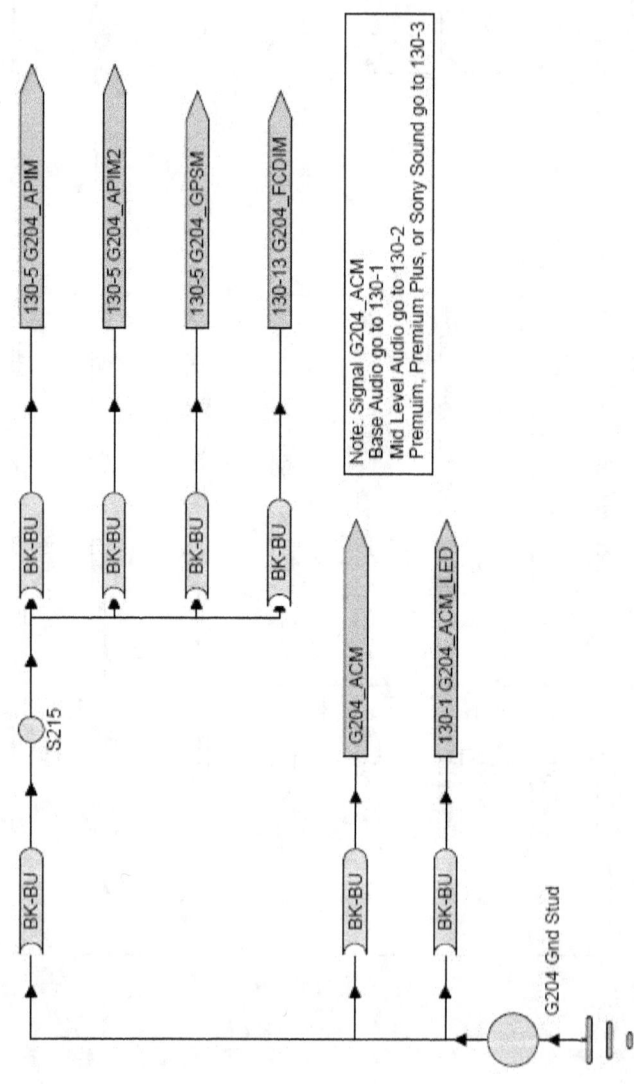

Grounds G300 **10-17**

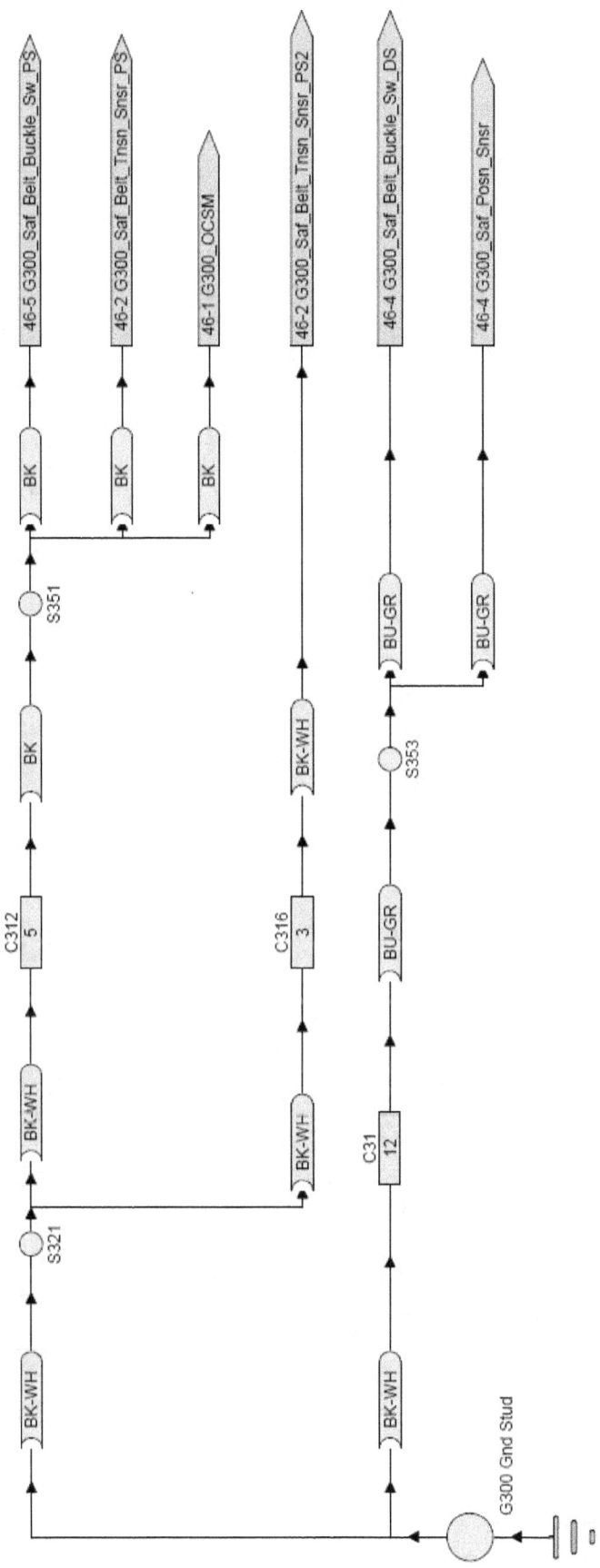

10-18 Grounds G301, G400

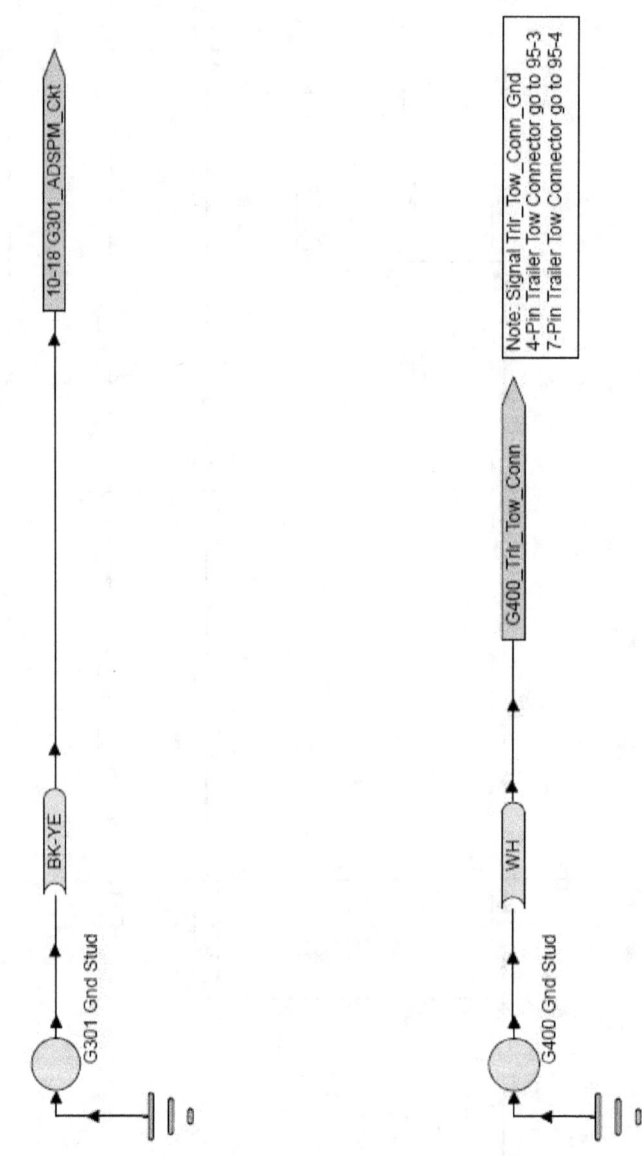

Grounds G401 **10-19**

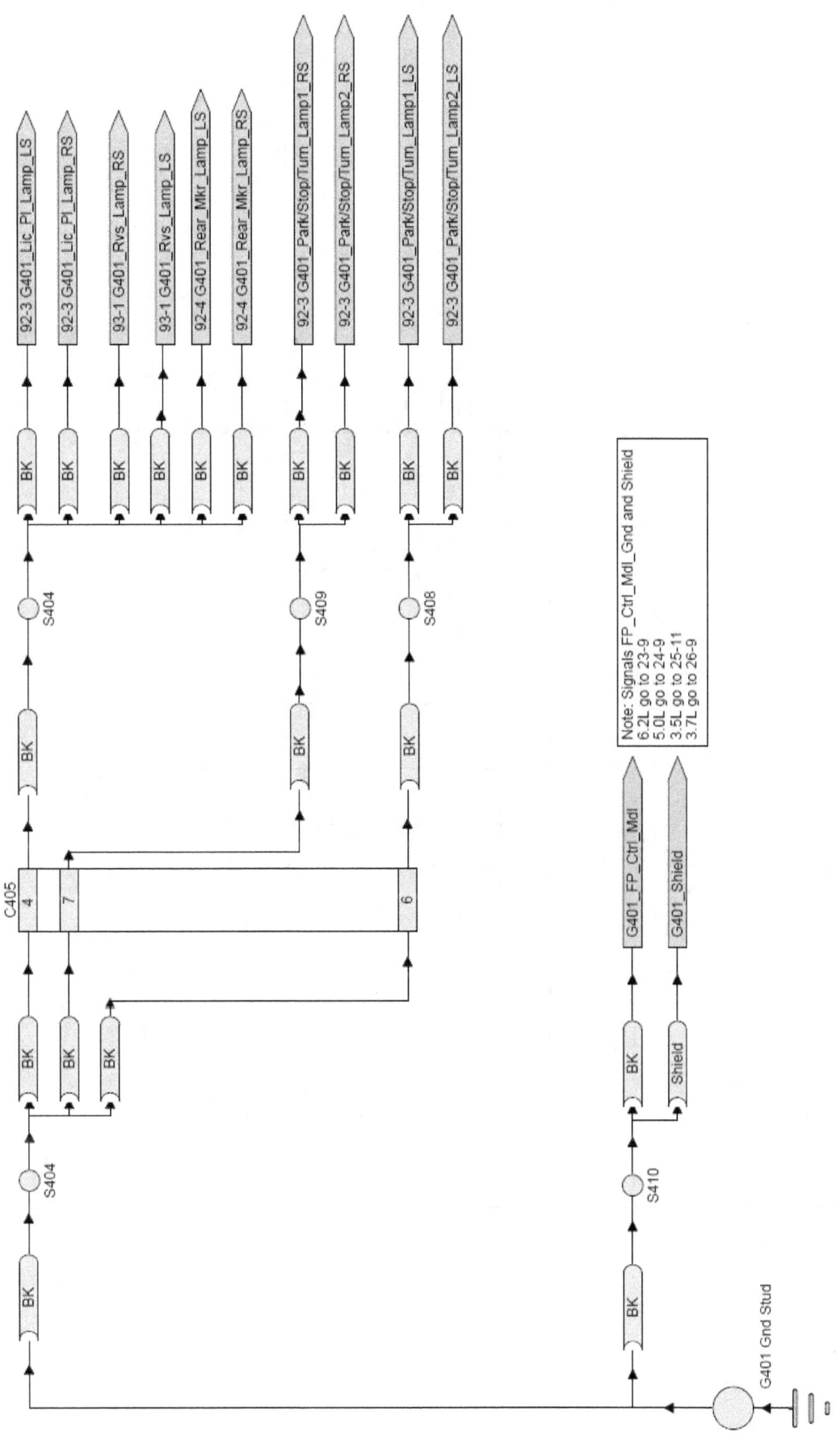

12 Charging Systems

12-1 Charging System for 3.5L, 3.7L & 5.0L Engines

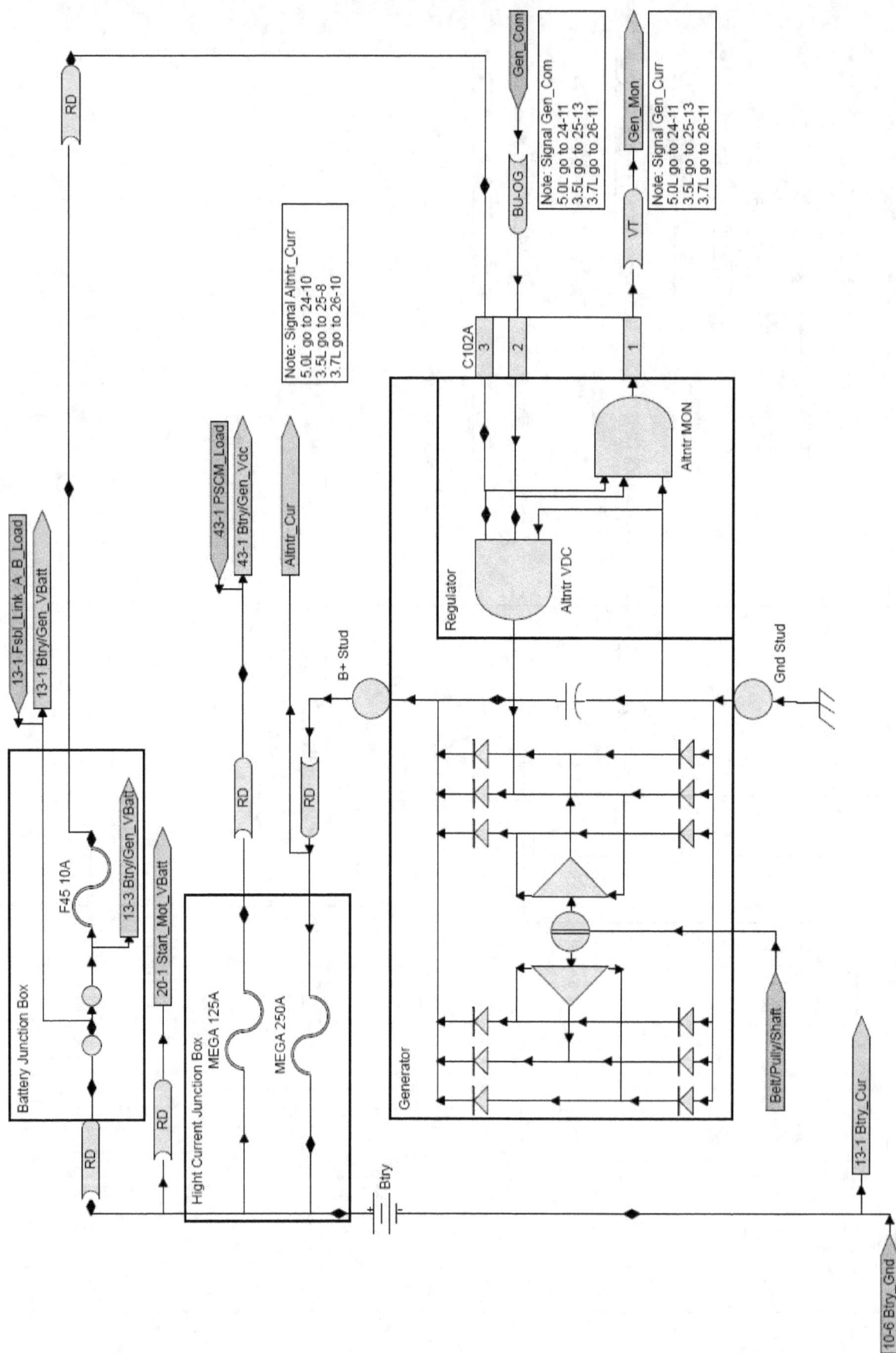

Charging System for 6.2L Engine 12-2

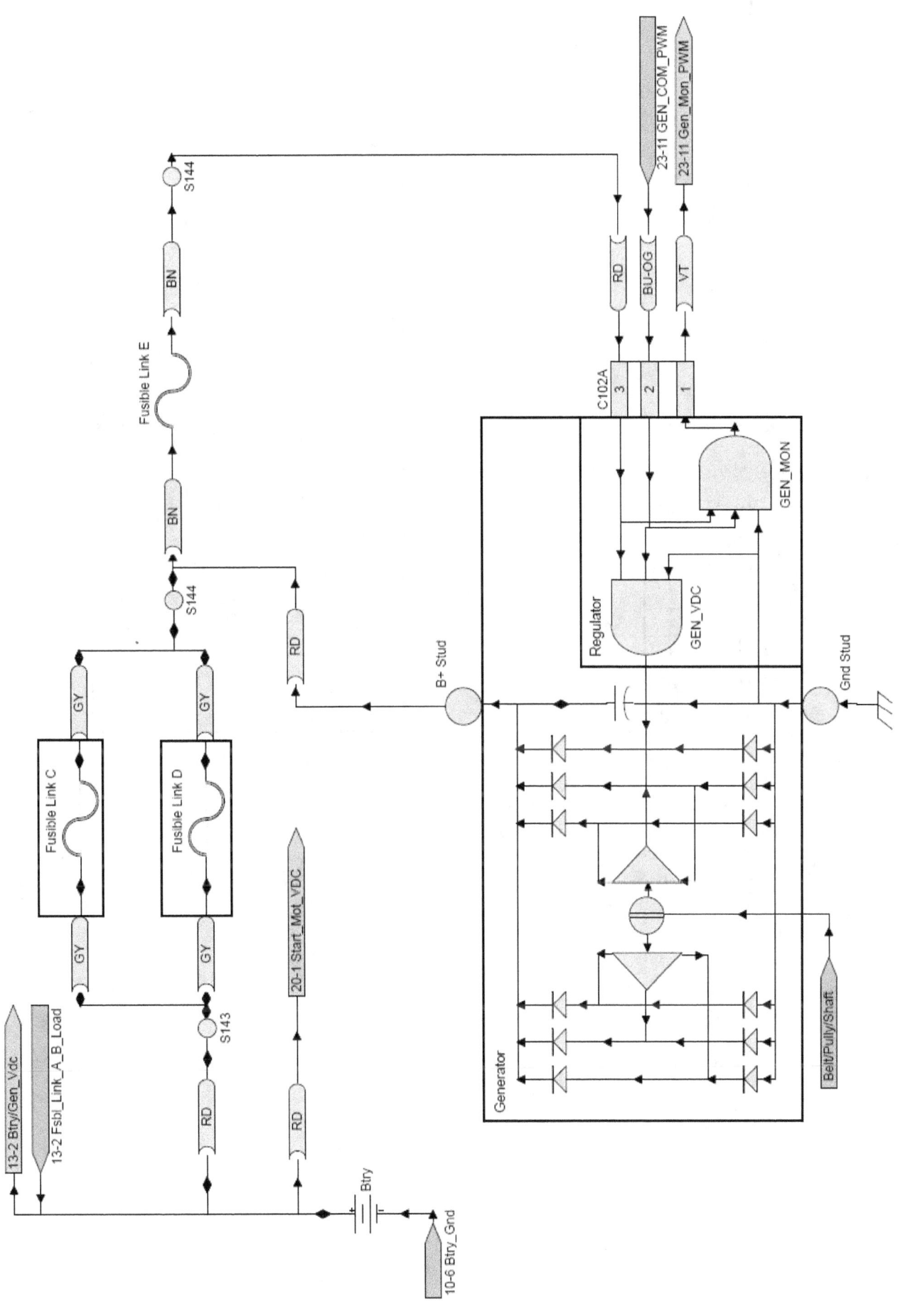

13 Power Distribution

13-1 Power Distribution BCM for 3.5L, 3.7L & 5.0L Engines

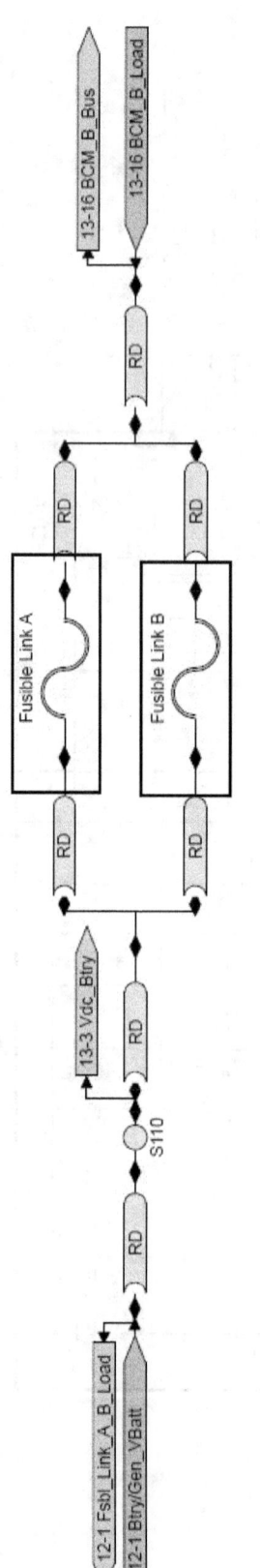
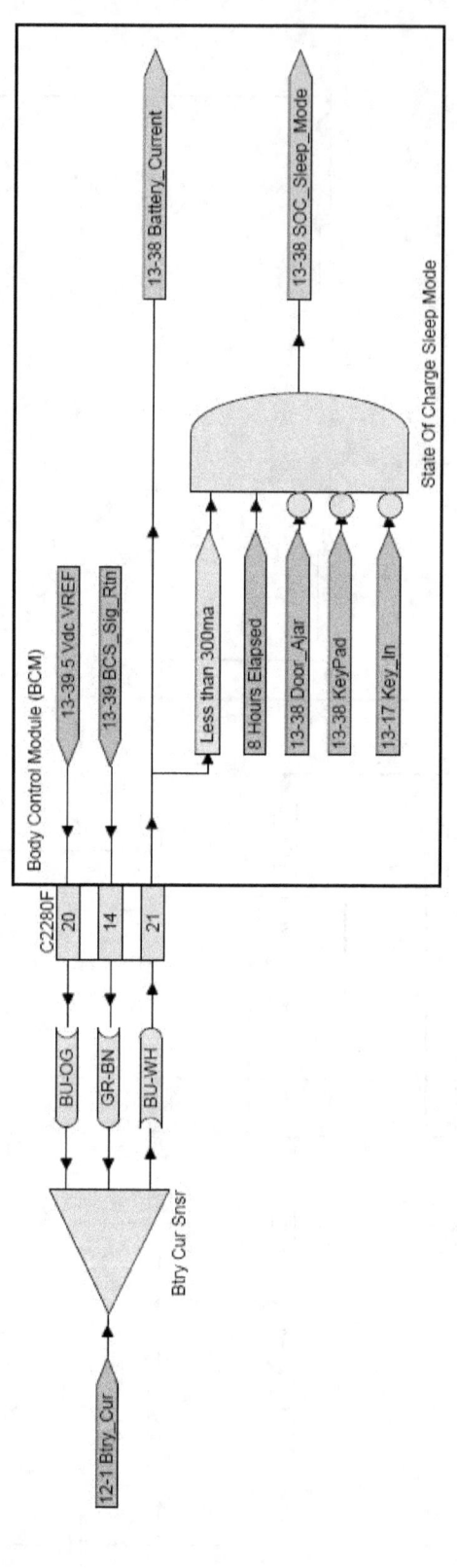

Power Distribution for 6.2L Engines 13-2

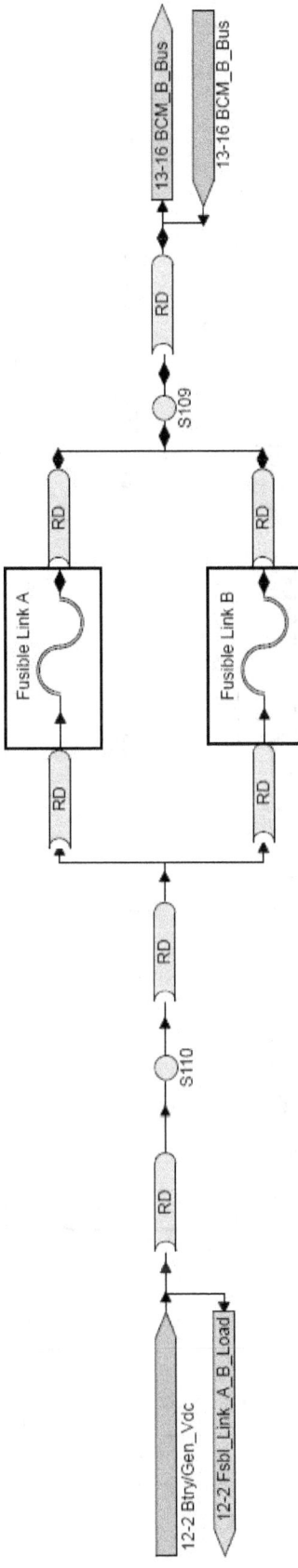

13-3 Power Distribution BJB F11, F14, F17, F20, F13, F21

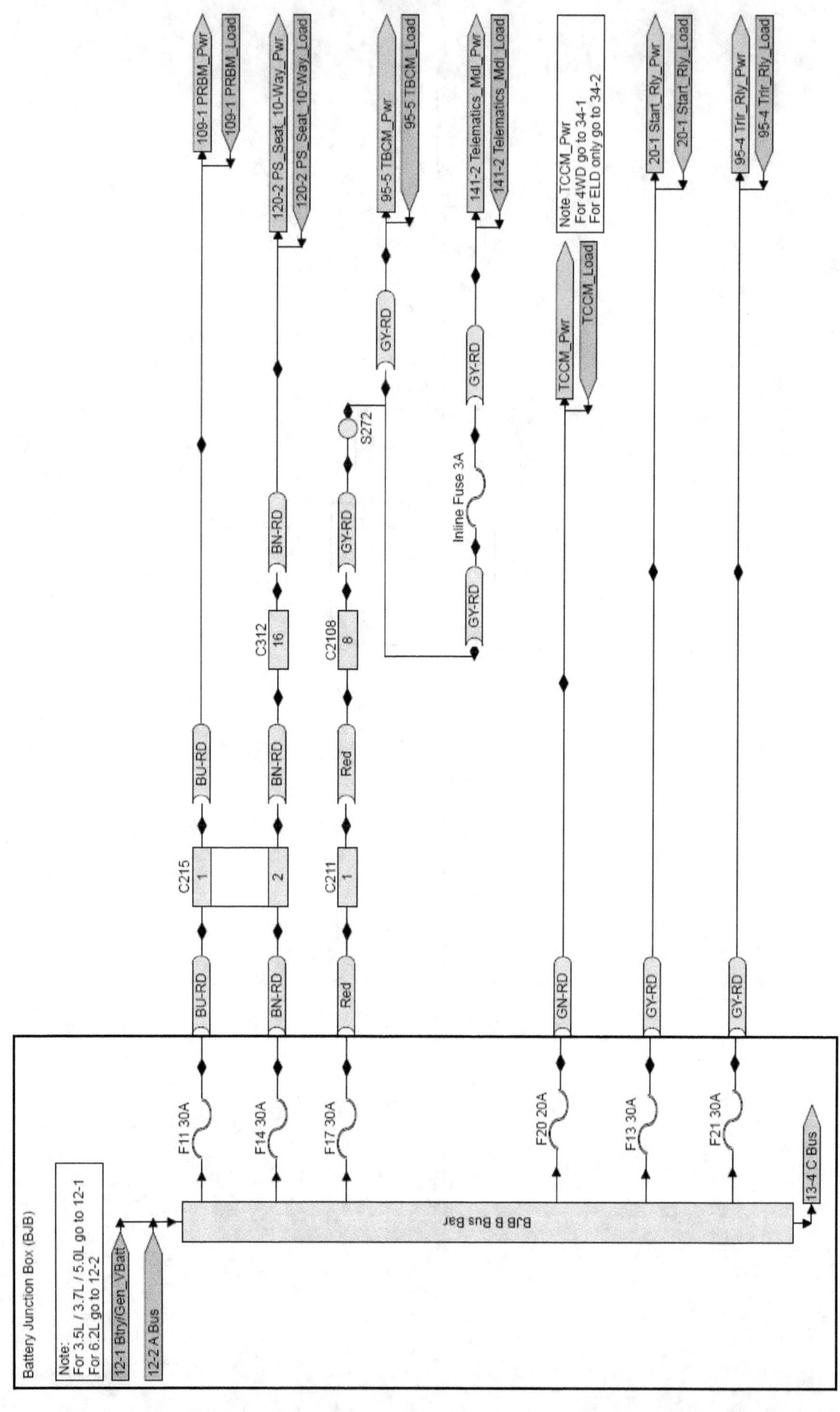

Power Distribution BJB F27, F16, F35 **13-4**

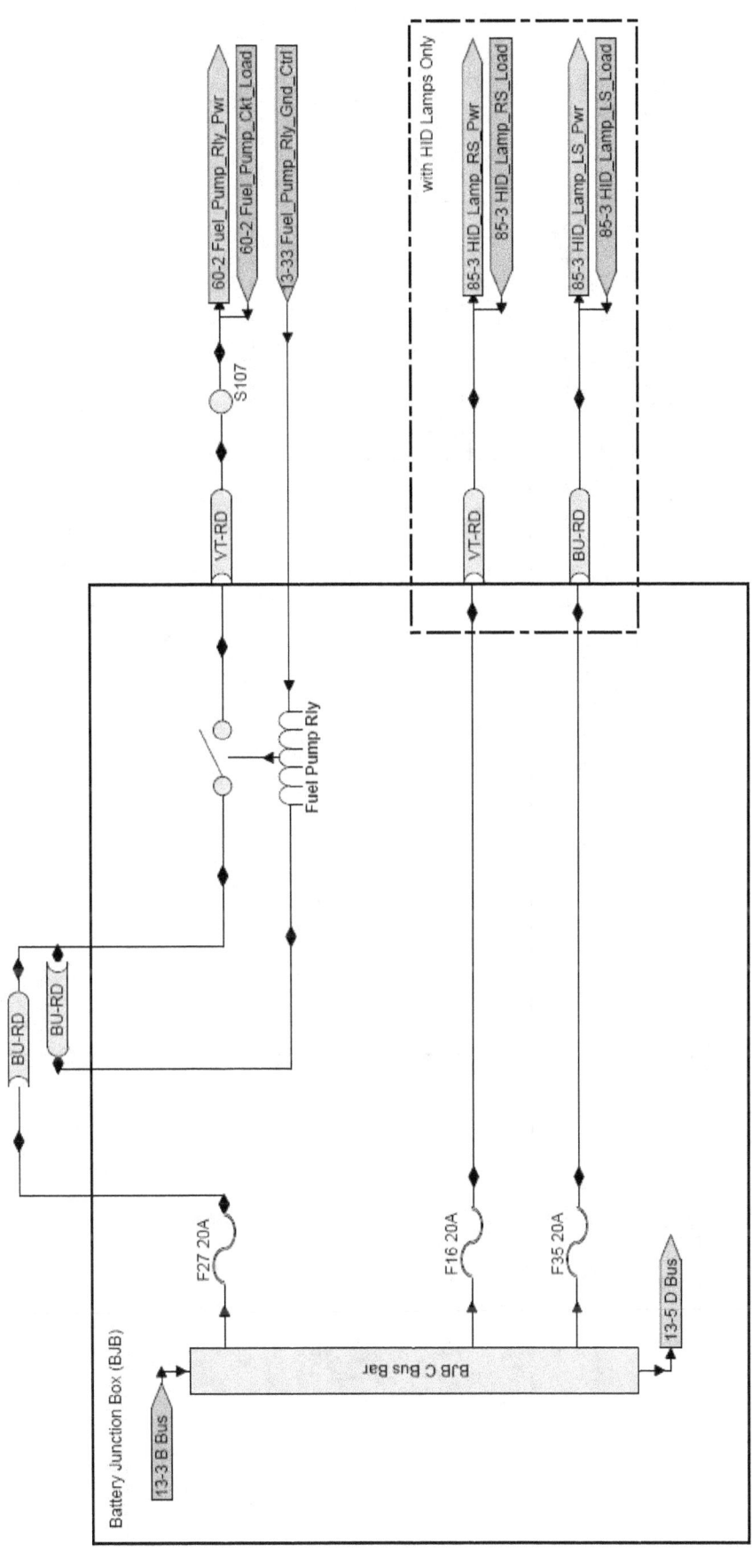

13-5 Power Distribution BJB F26, F34, F33, F76, F77, F75

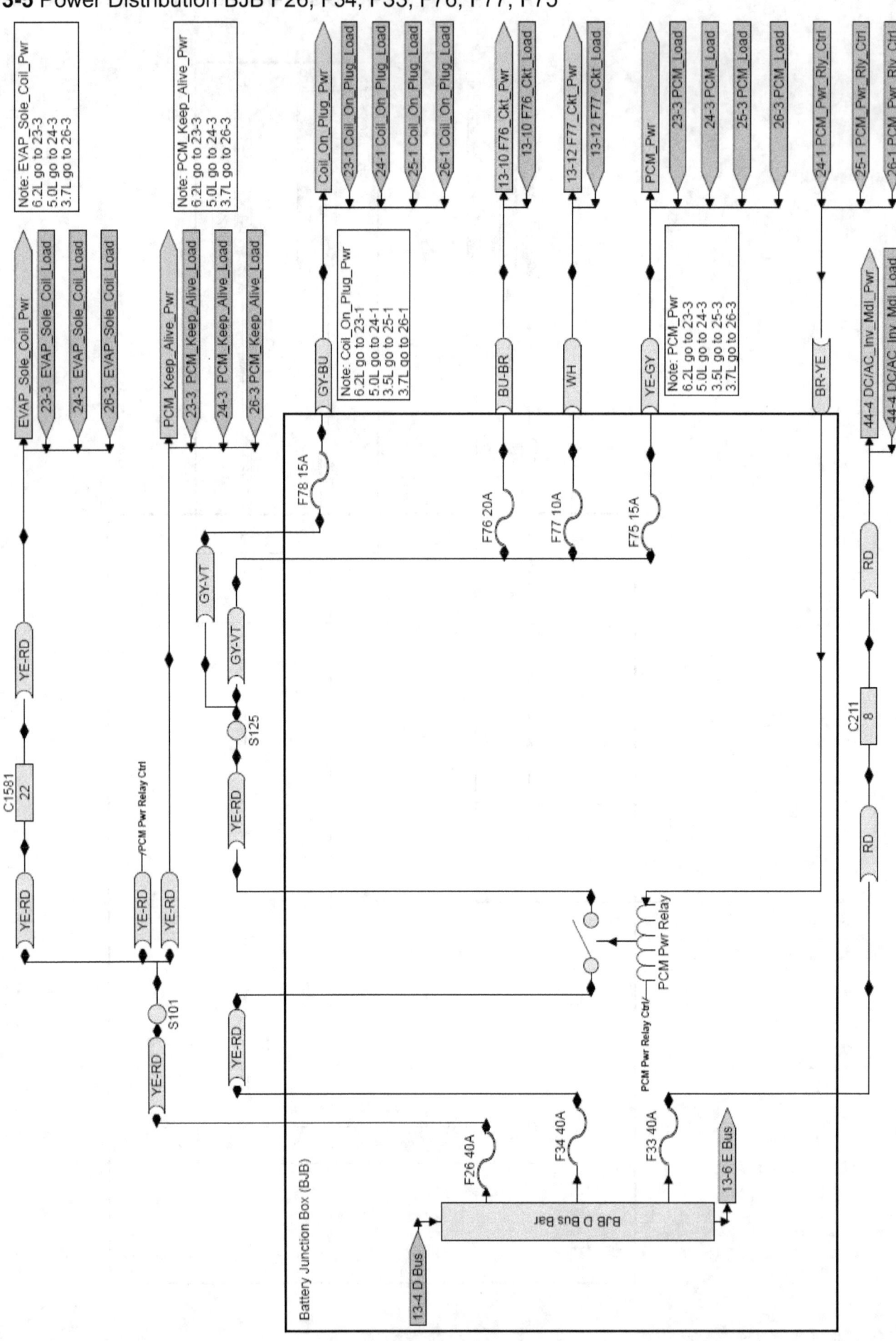

Power Distribution BJB F49, F44, F29, F36, F47 13-6

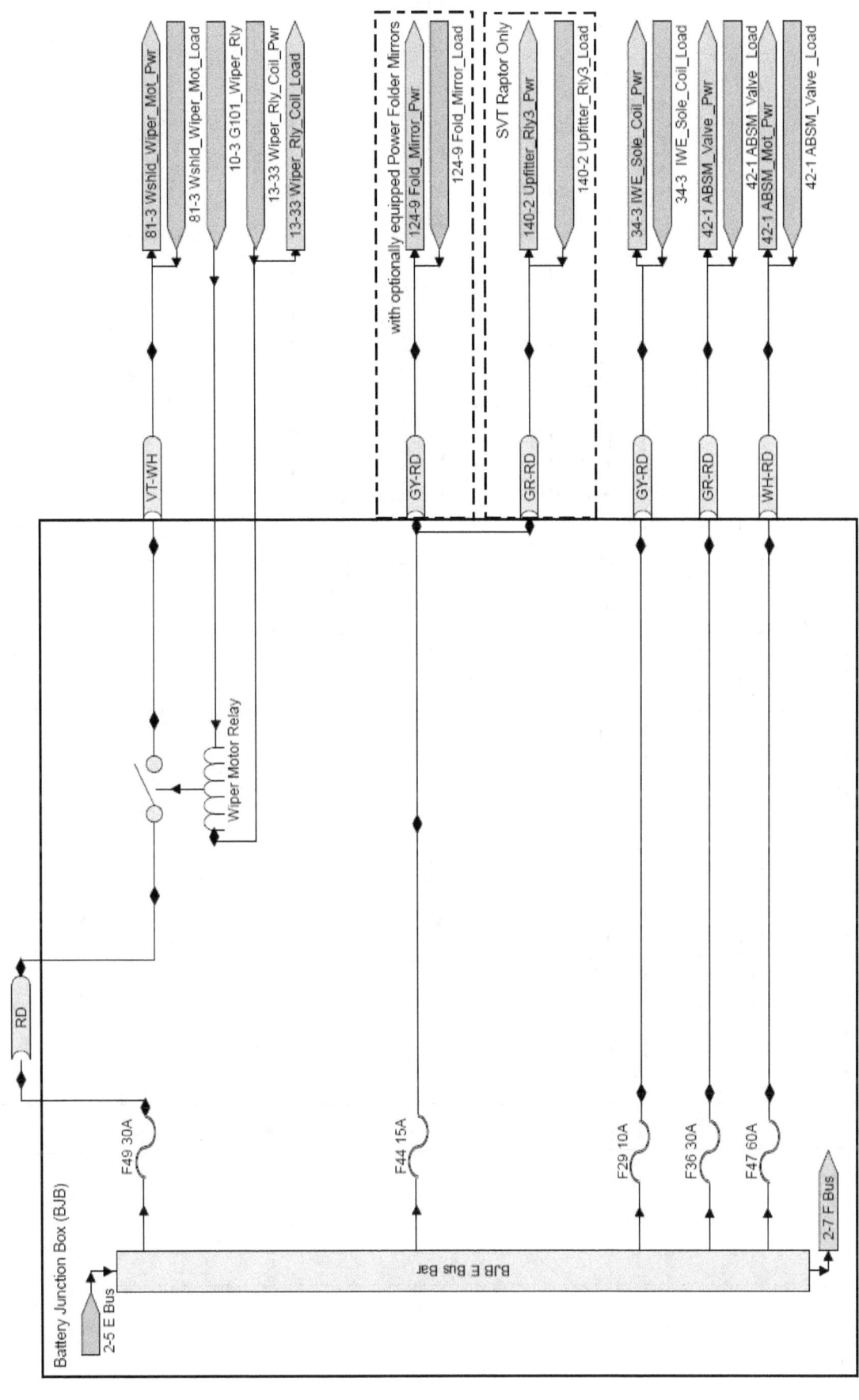

13-7 Power Distribution BJB F49, F44, F29, F36, F47

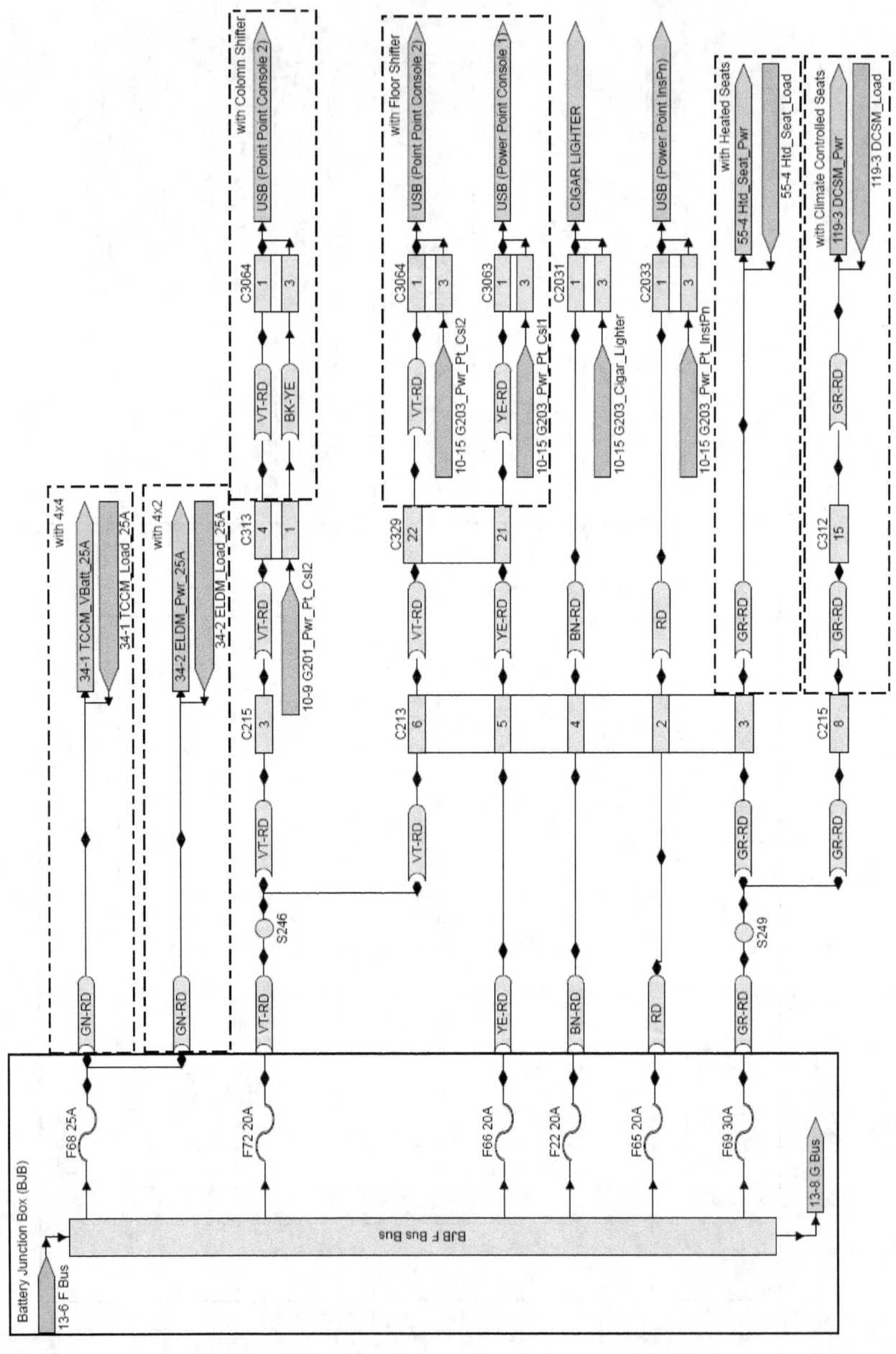

Power Distribution BJB F74, F30, F51, F48 13-8

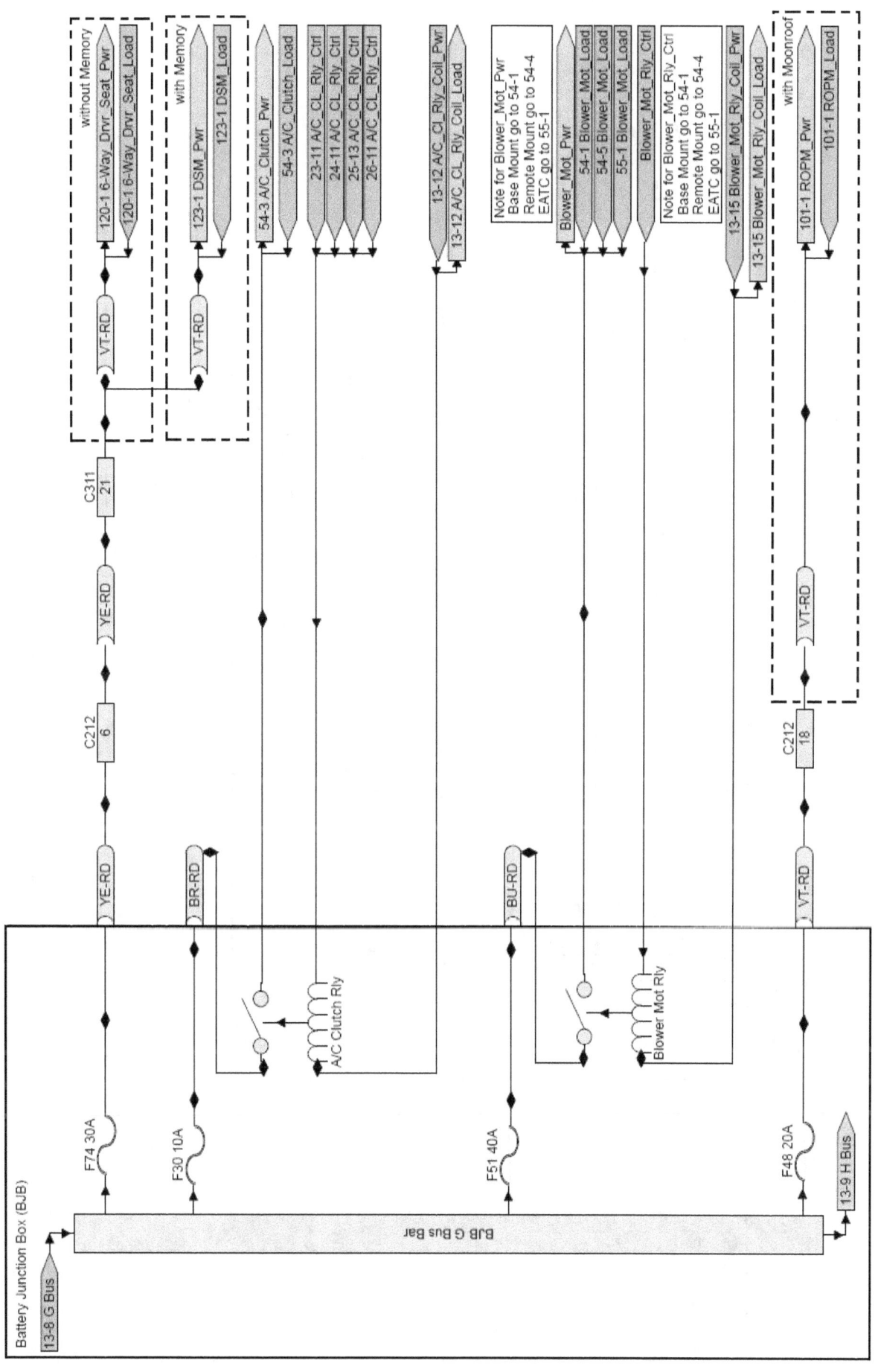

13-9 Power Distribution BJB F43, F32, F46, F56

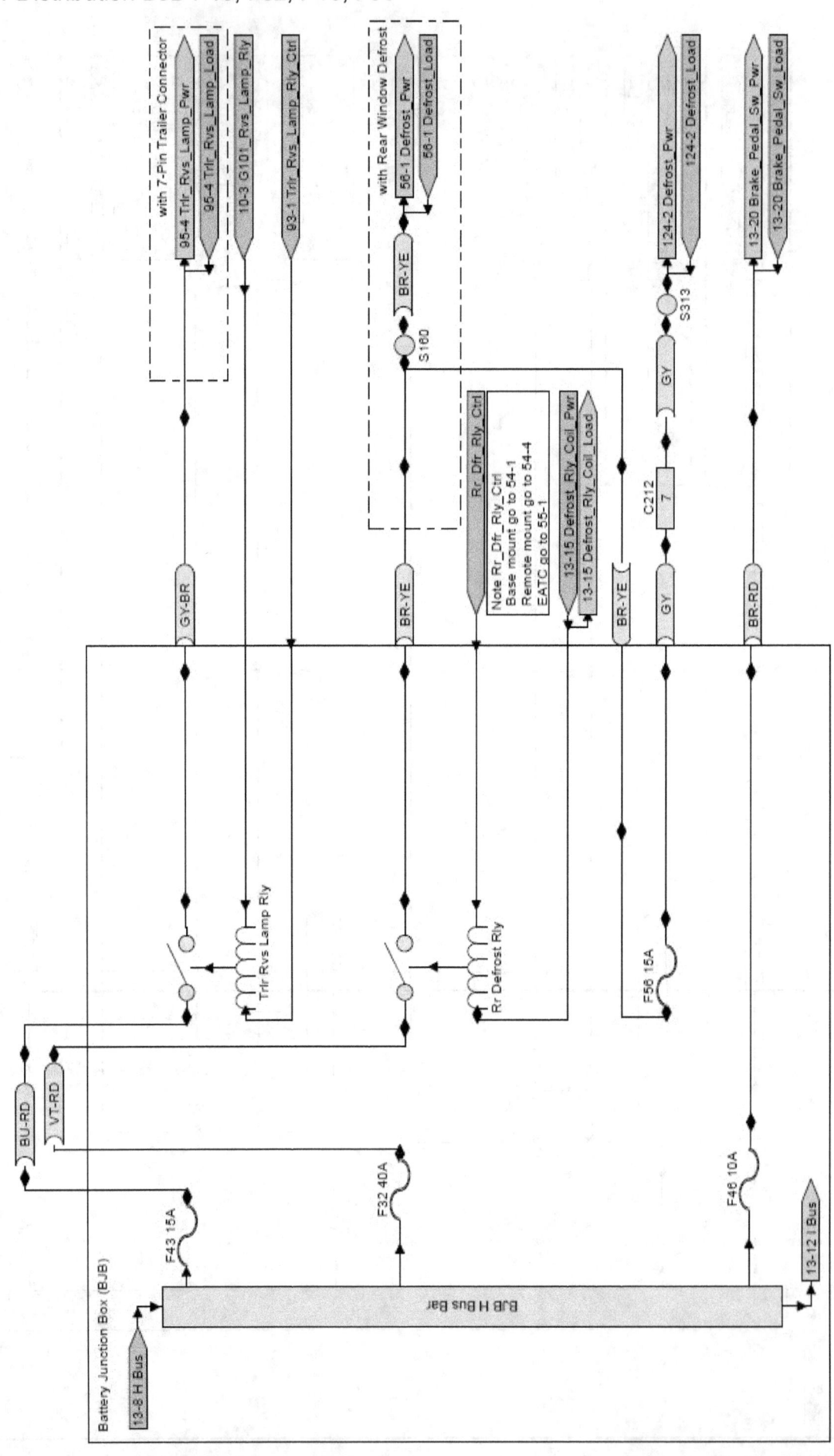

Power Distribution BJB F76 Ckt **13-10**

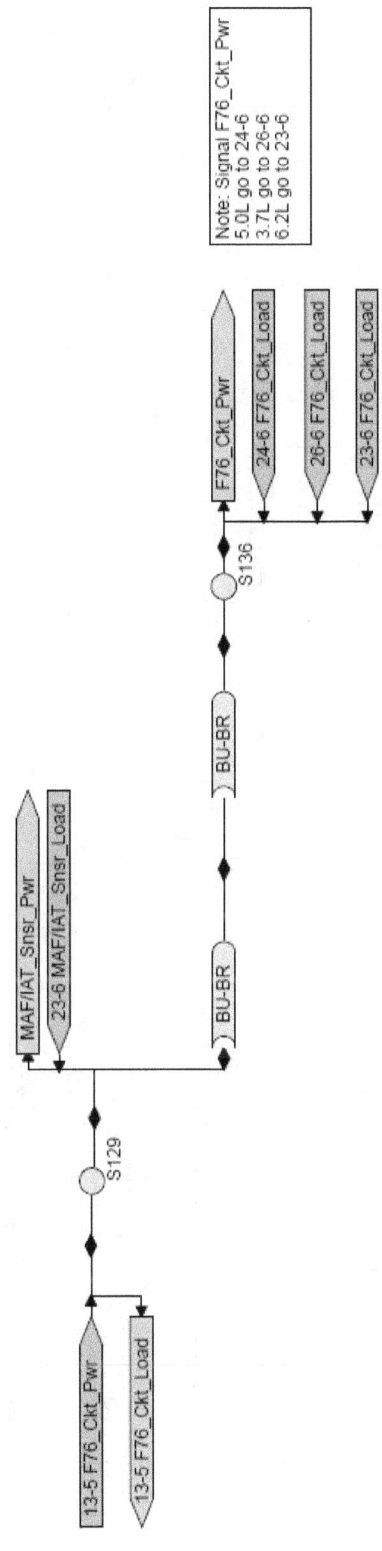

13-12 Power Distribution BJB F15, F63, F12

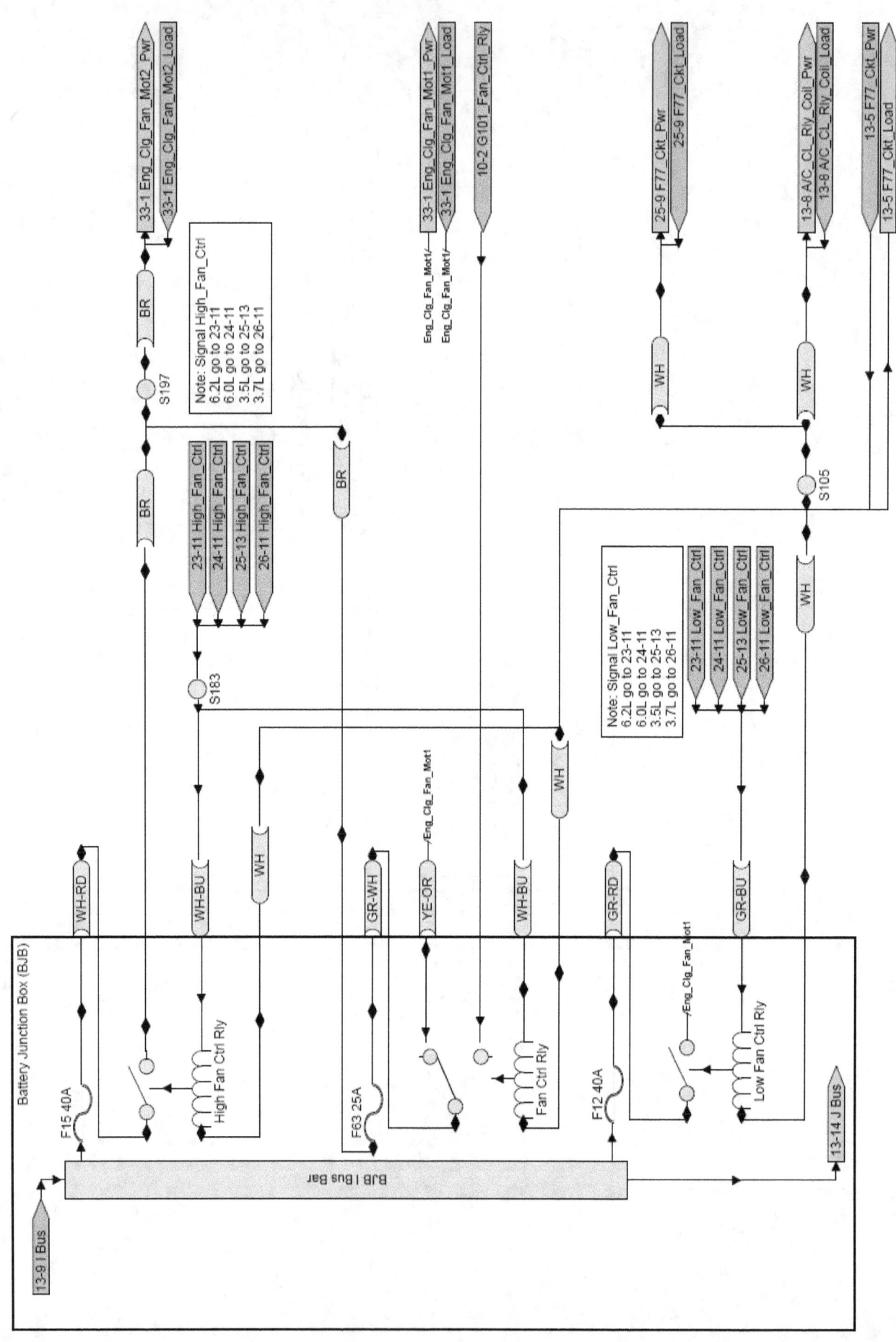

Power Distribution BJB F31, F42, F67, F73, F71 13-14

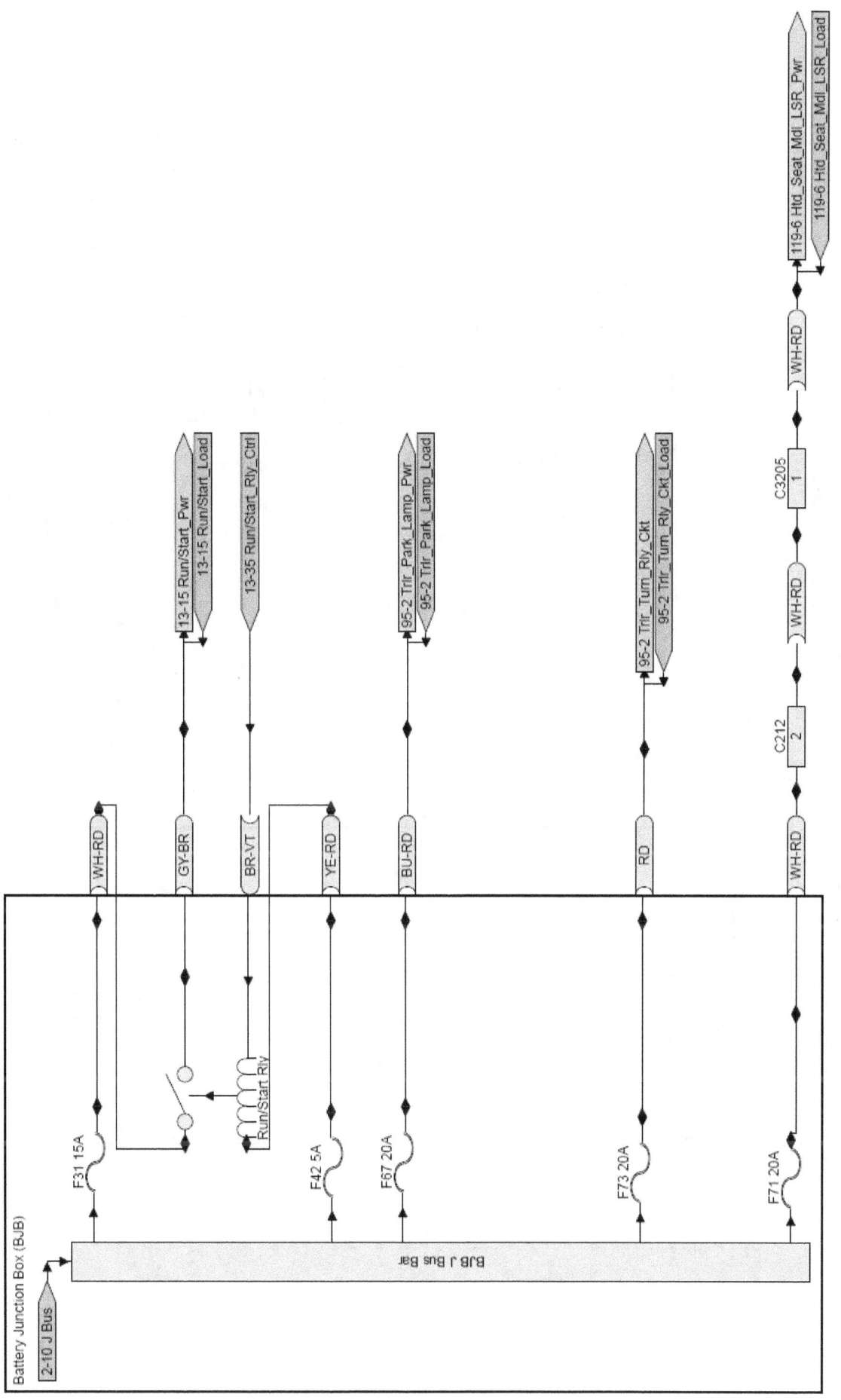

13-15 Power Distribution BJB F53, F54, F52

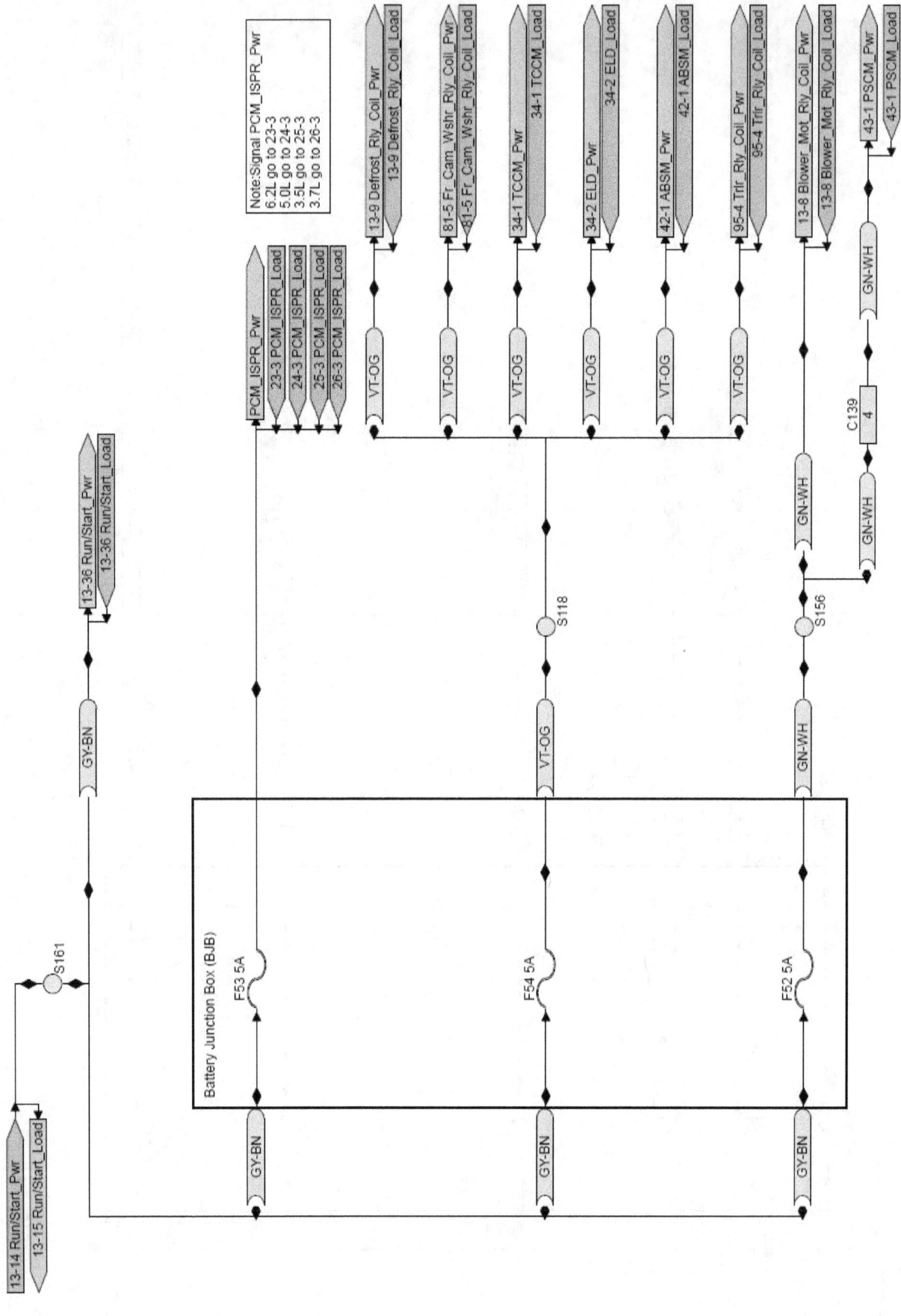

Power Distribution BCM F11, F24, F28, F29 **13-16**

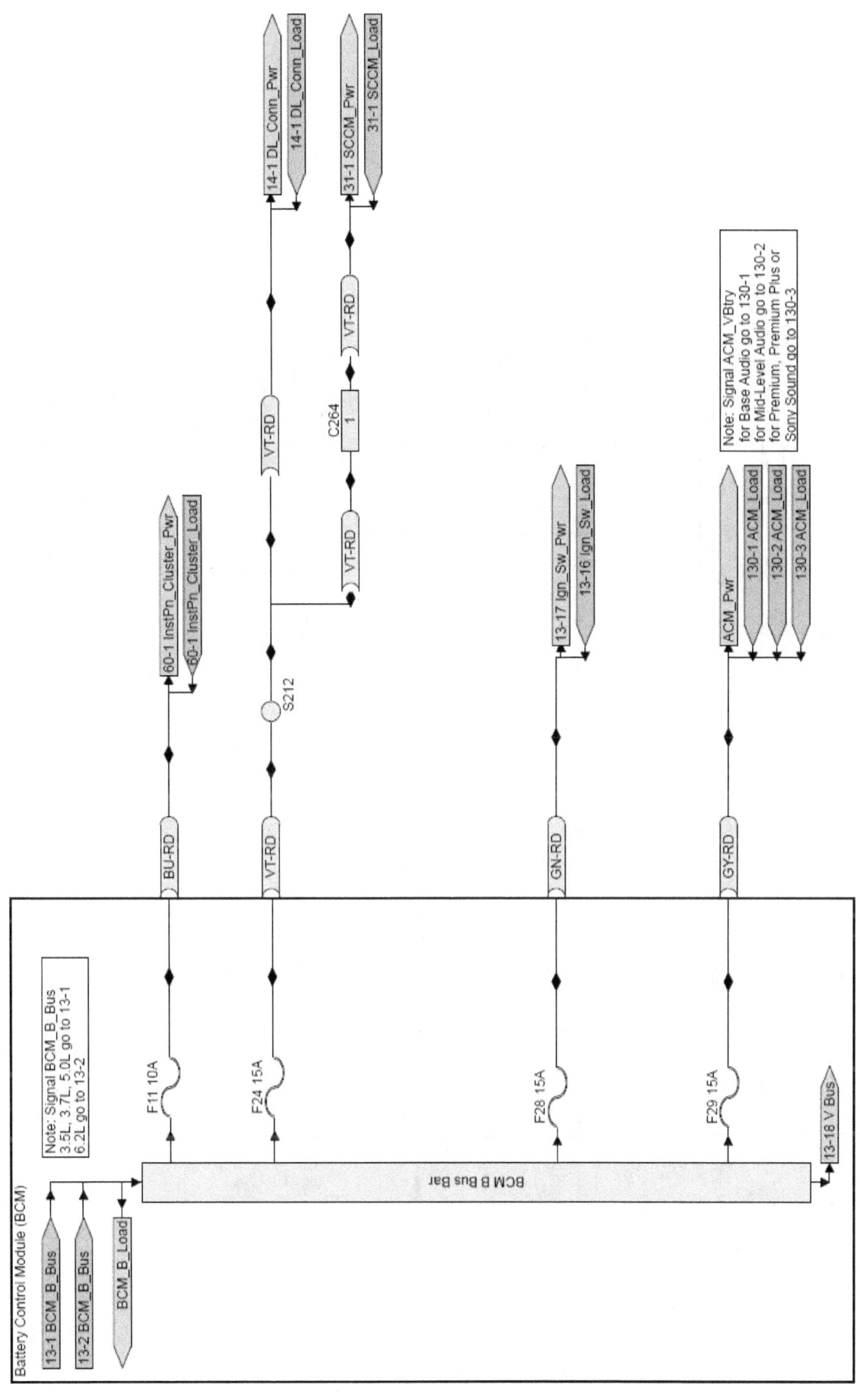

13-17 Power Distribution BCM & Ignition Switch

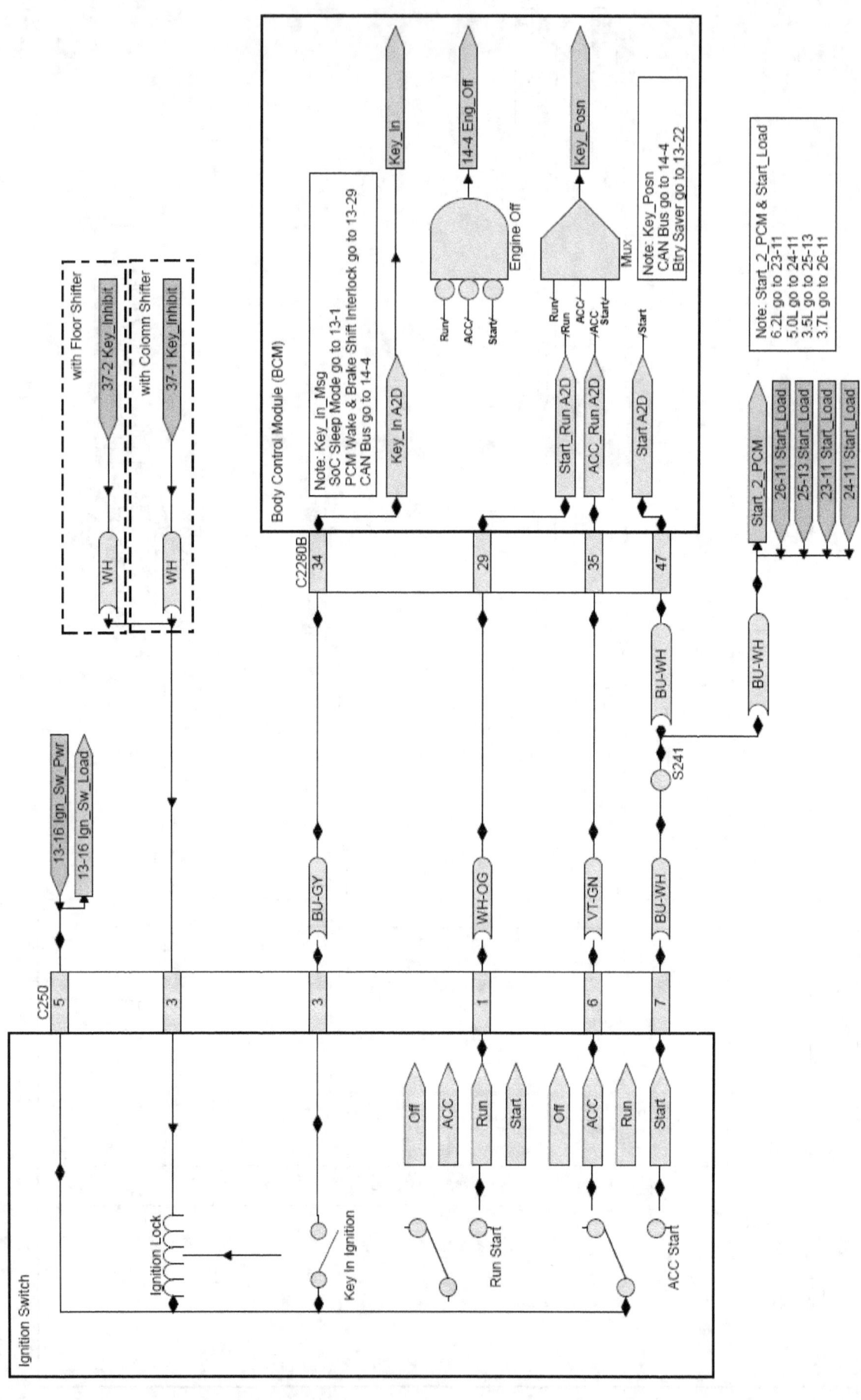

Power Distribution BCM F46, F23, F9 **13-18**

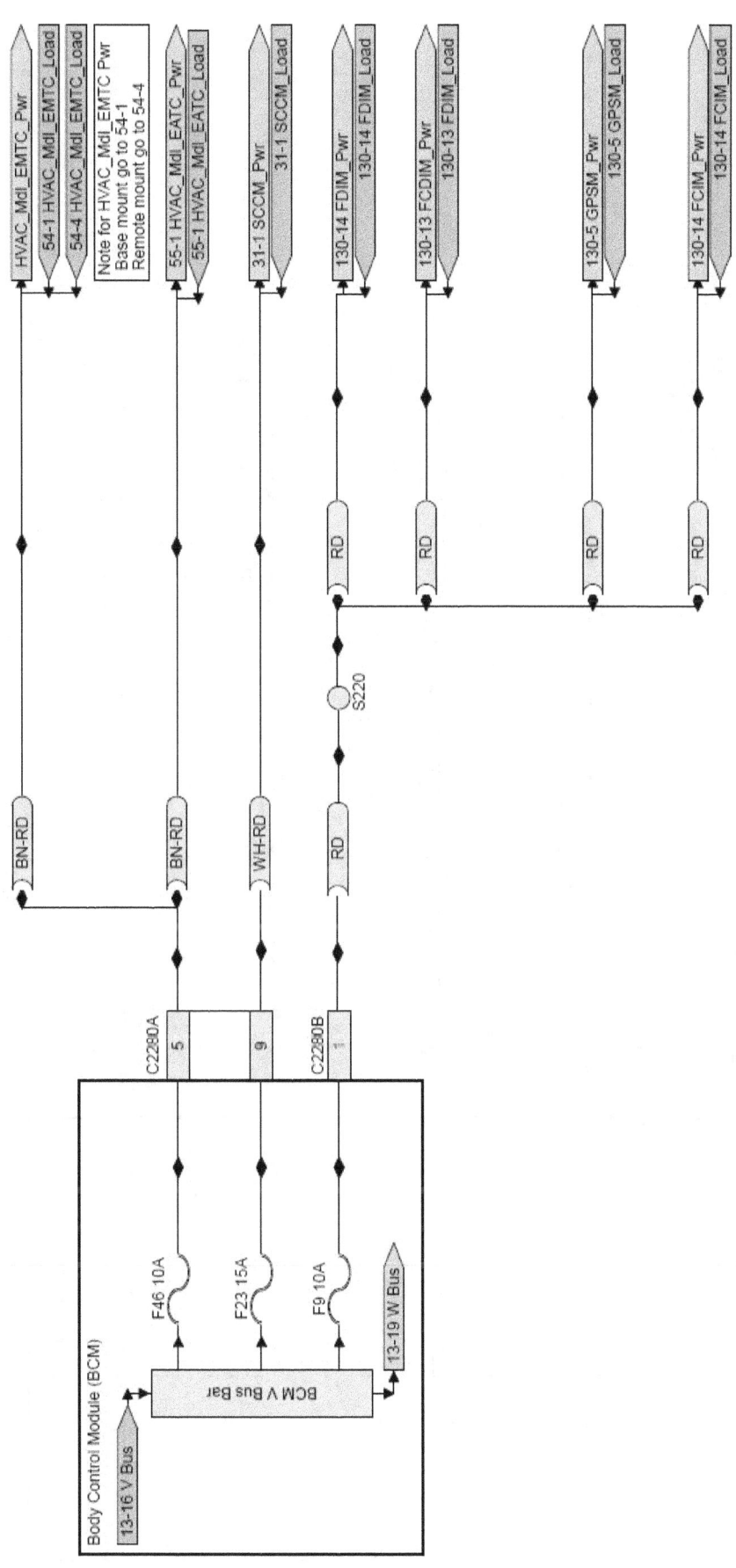

13-19 Power Distribution BCM F26, F1, F2, F3, F5, F7

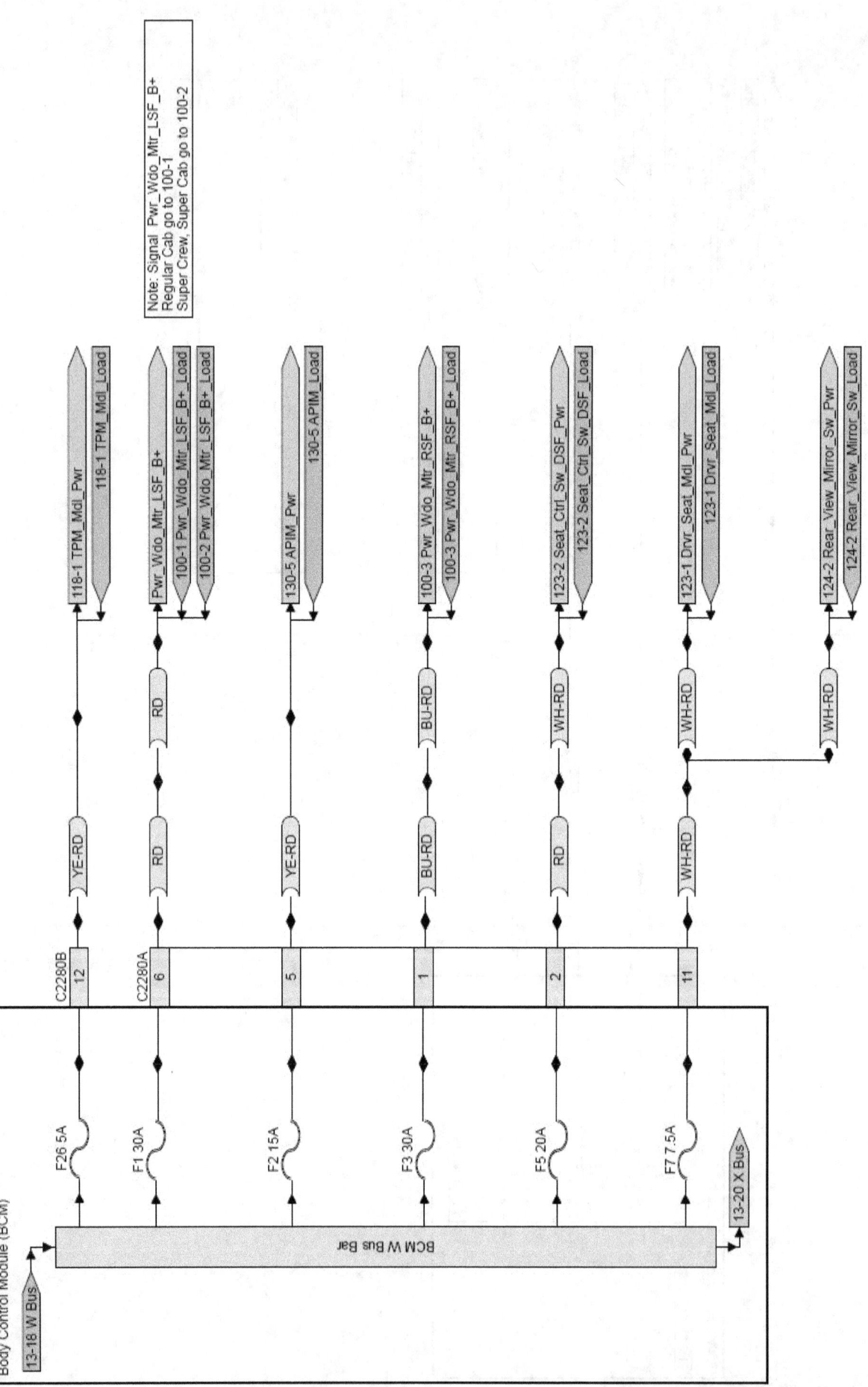

42

Power Distribution BCM F31, F19 & Brake Pedal Position (BPP) 13-20

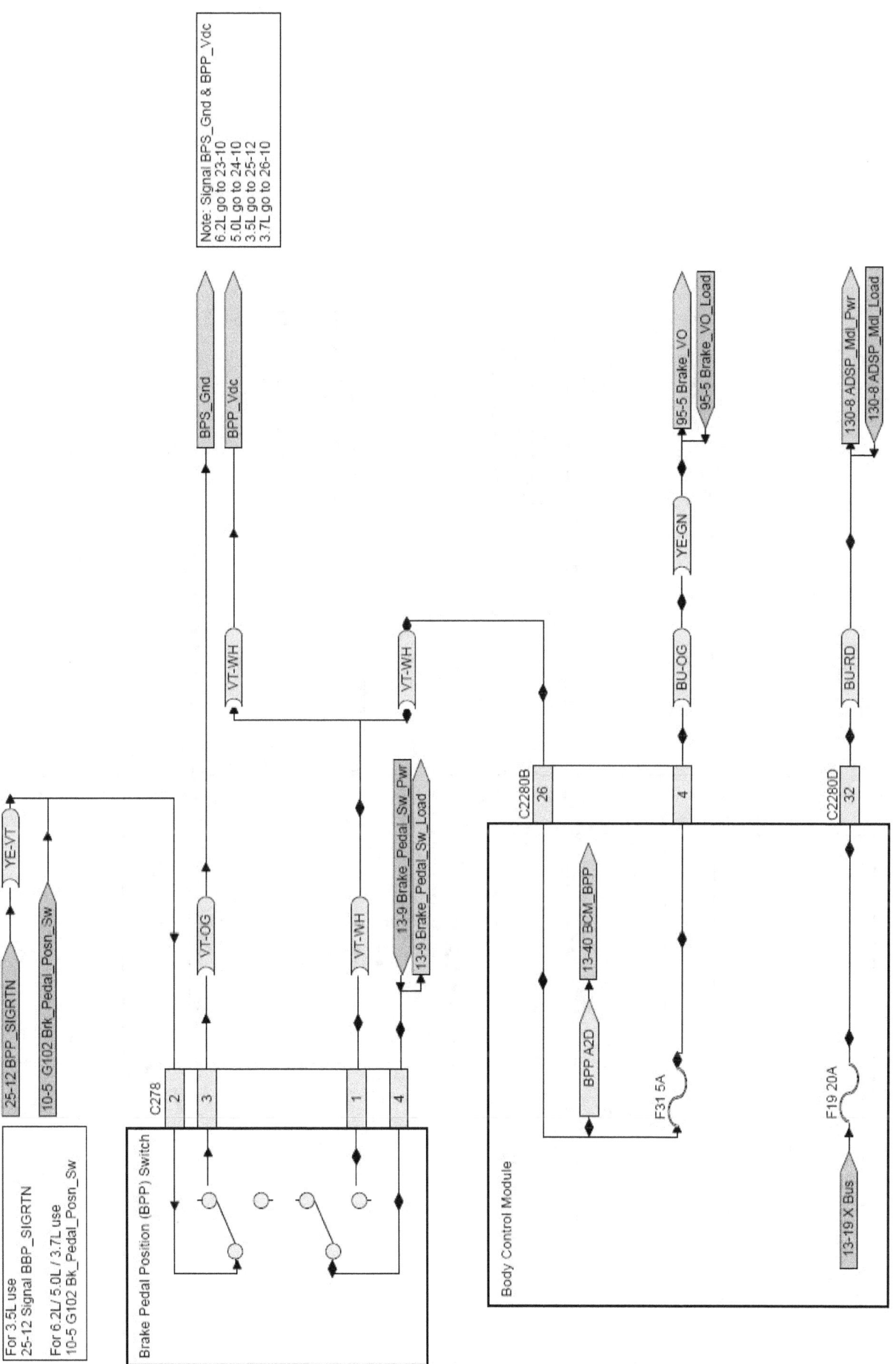

13-21 Power Distribution BCM F20

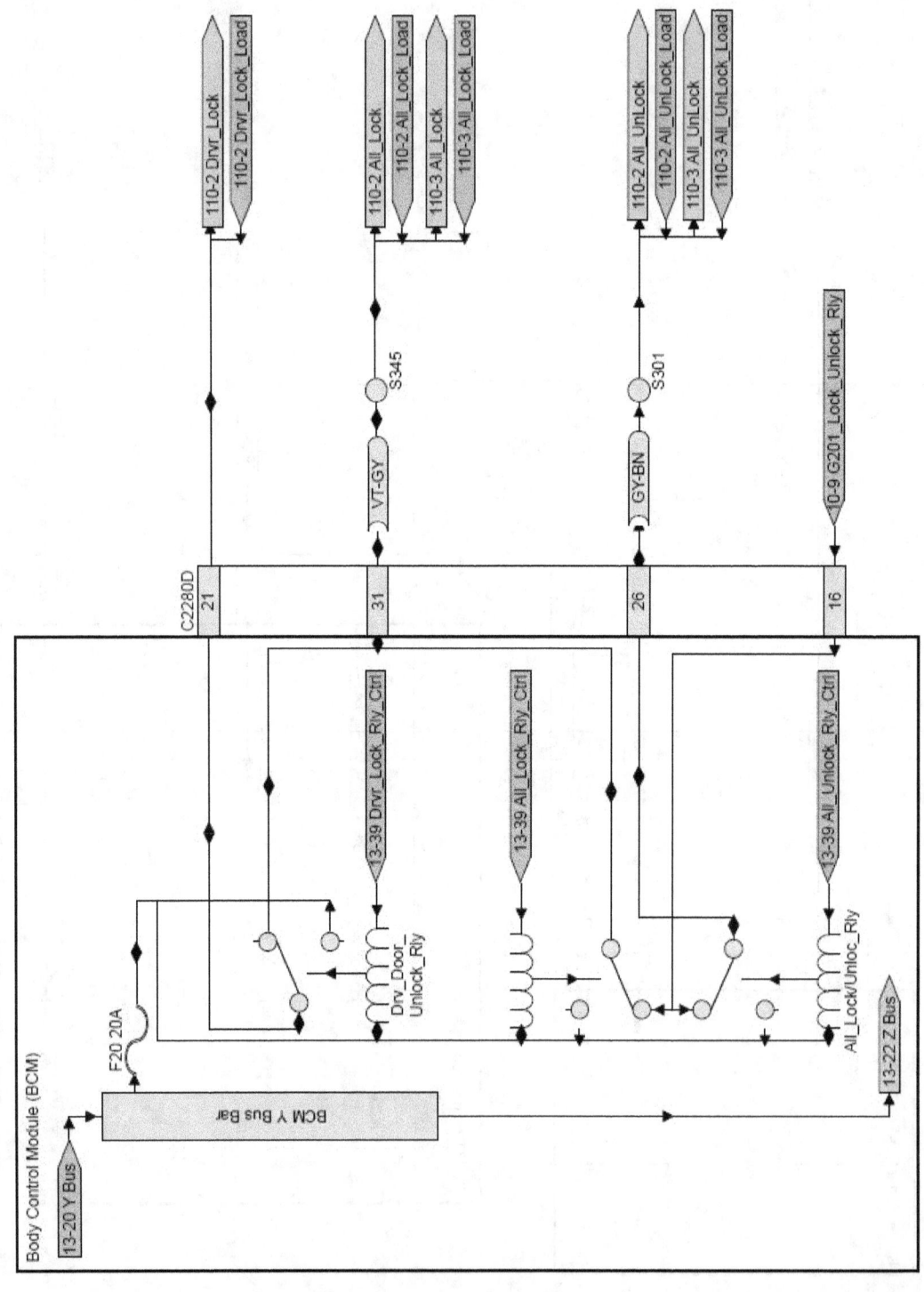

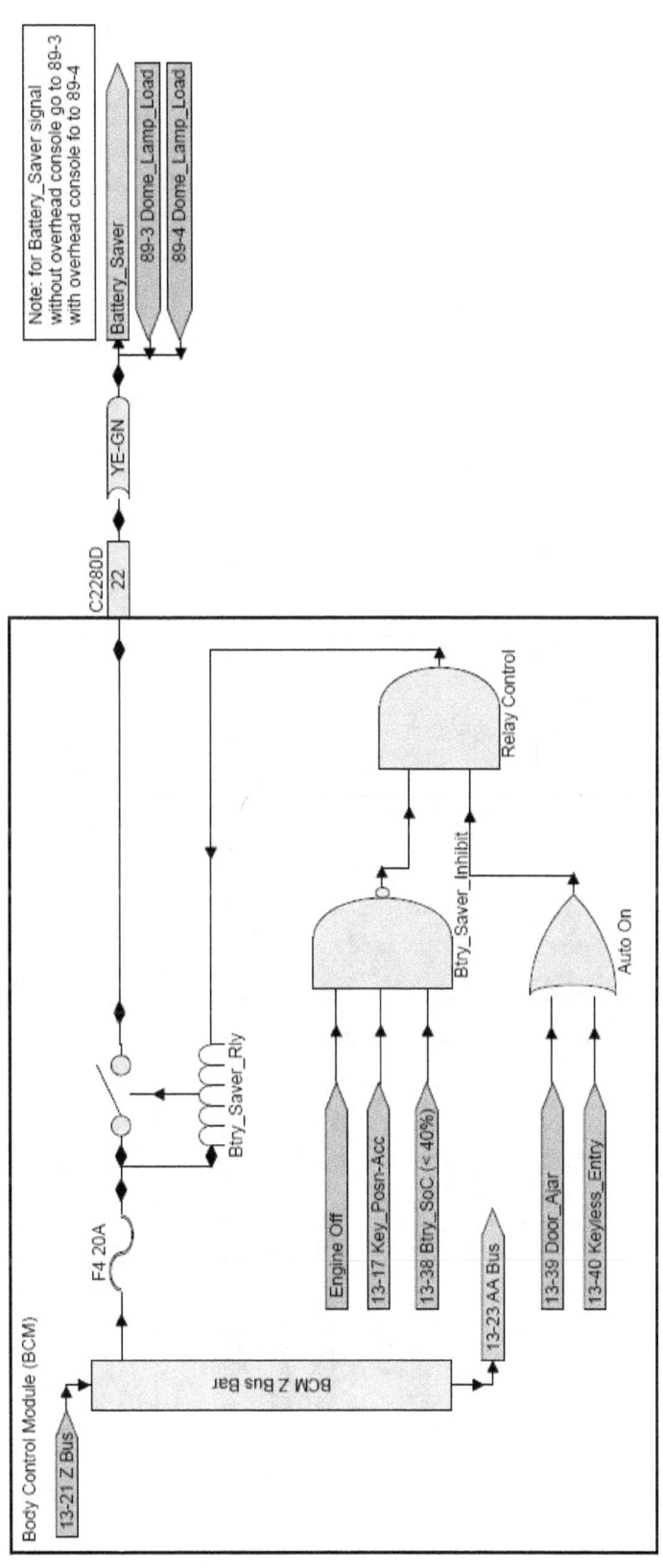

13-23 Power Distribution BCM Park Lamp Ckt

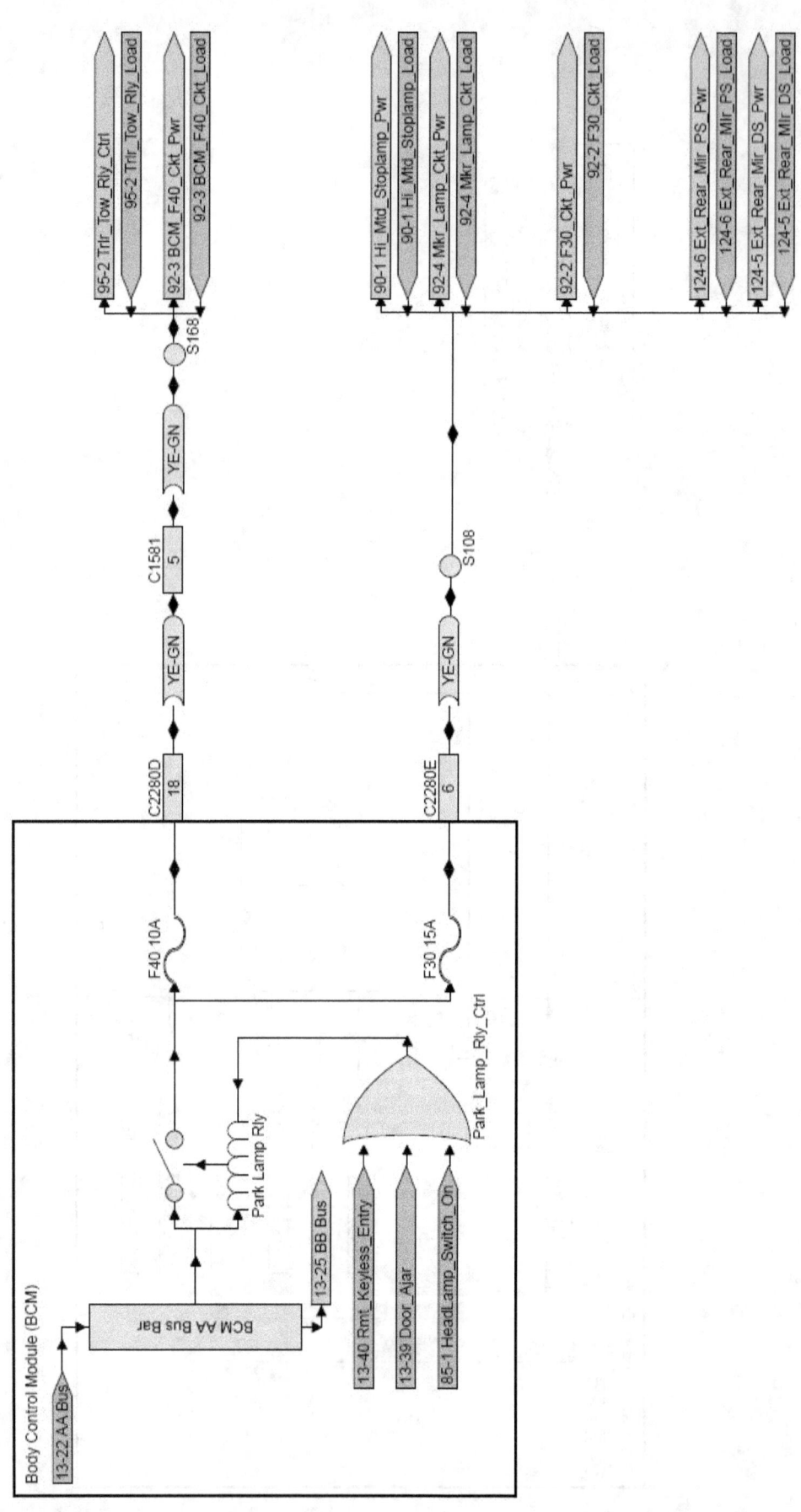

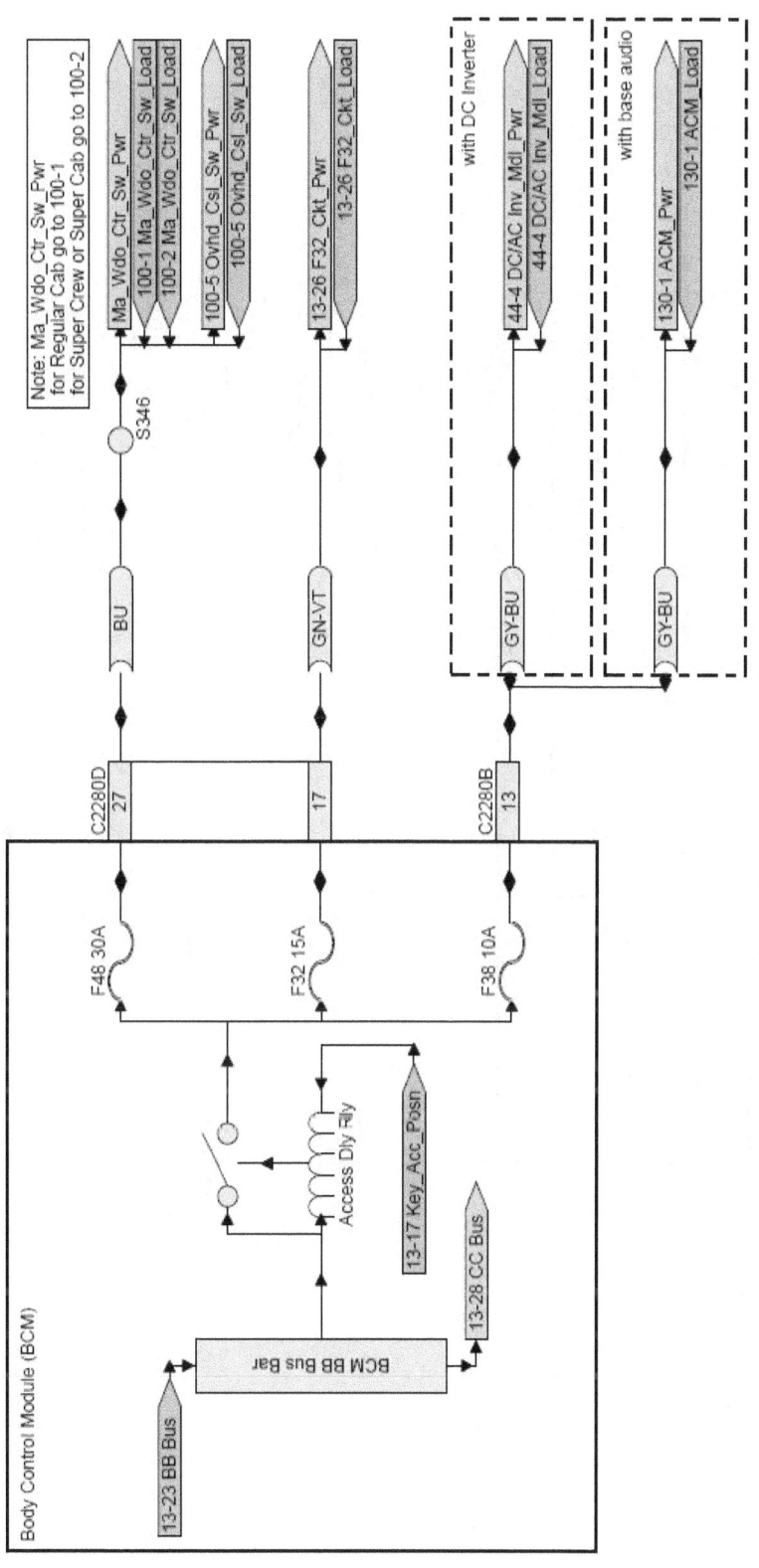

13-26 Power Distribution BCM F32 Ckt

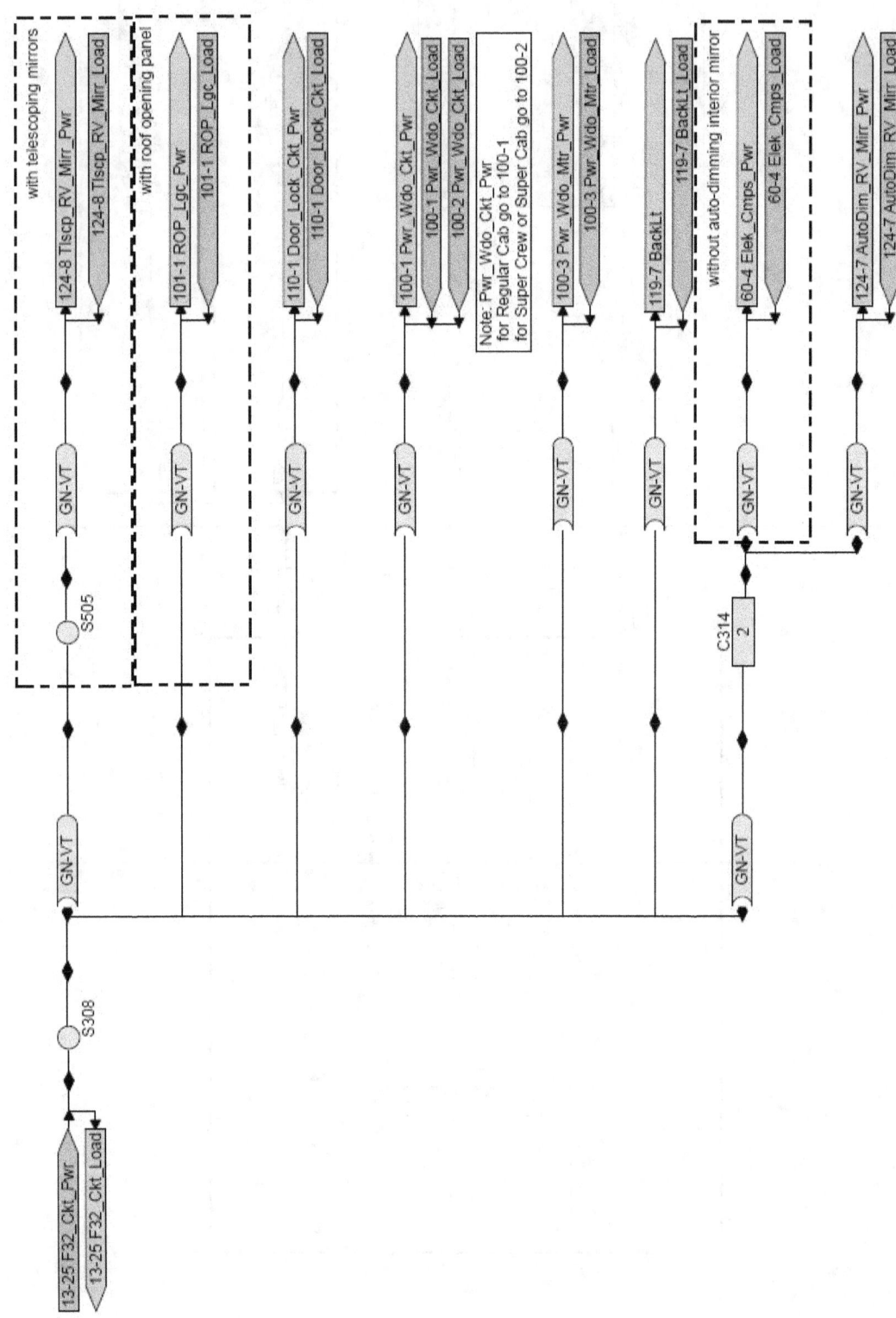

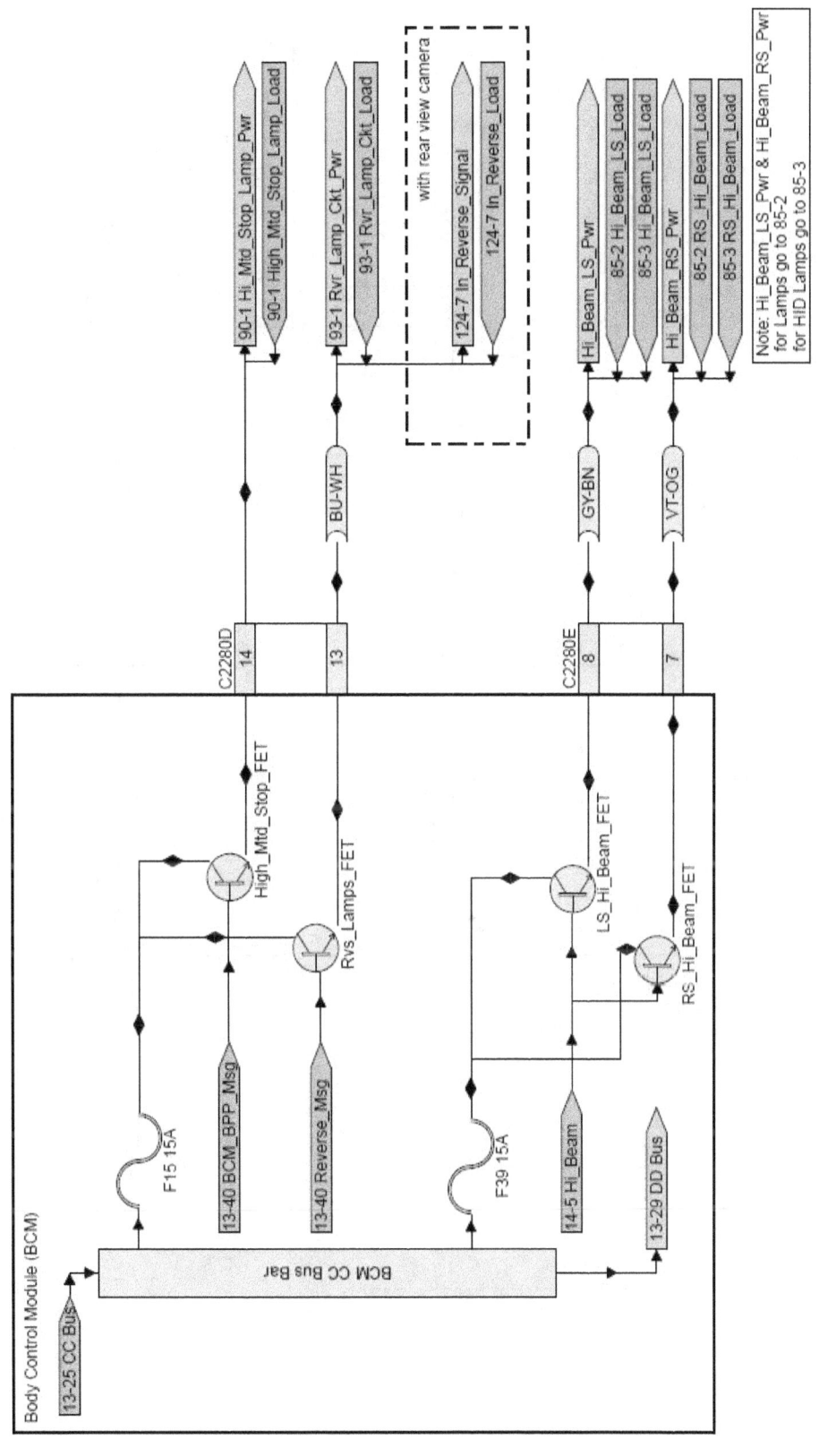

13-29 Power Distribution BCM F18

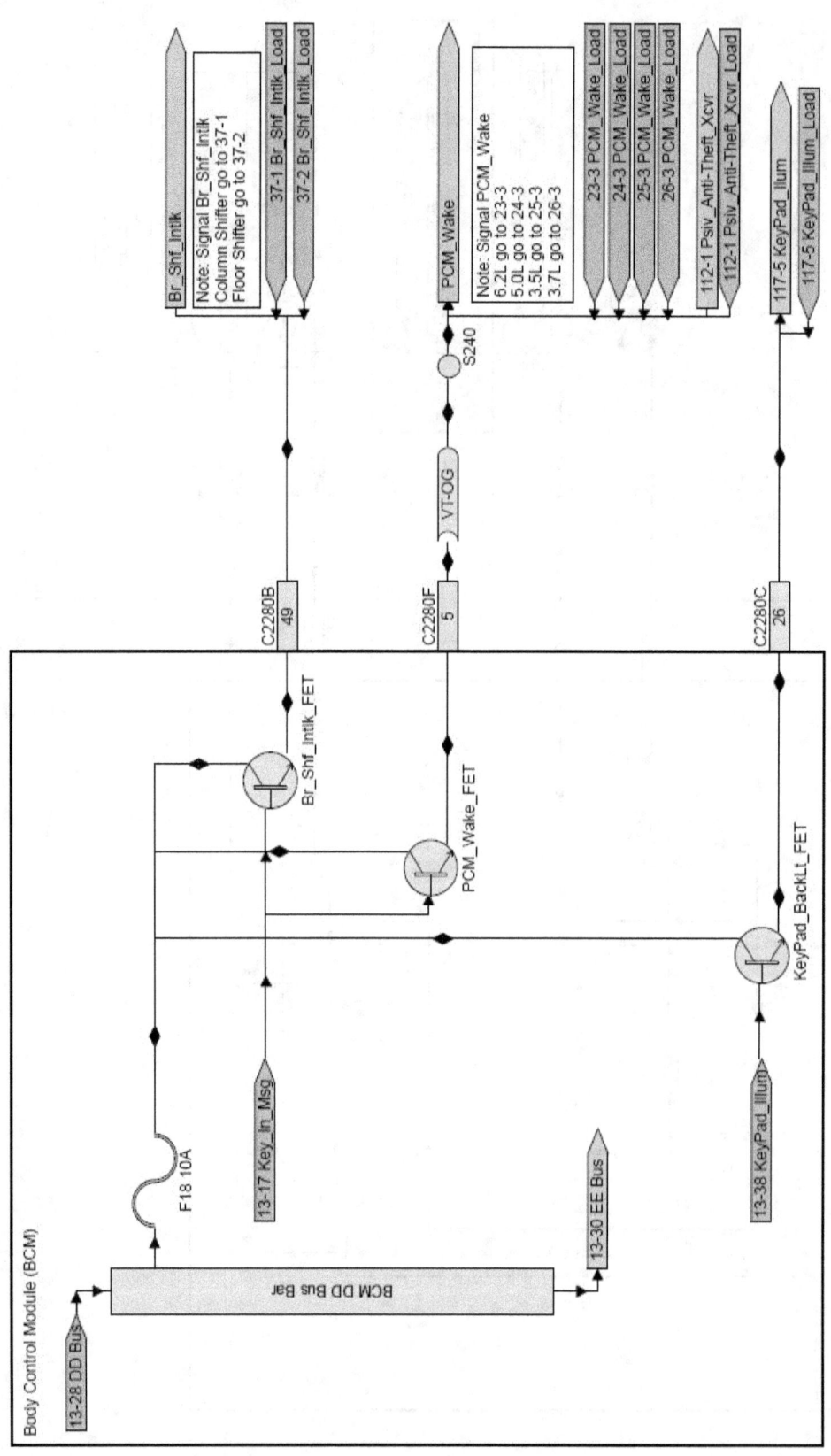

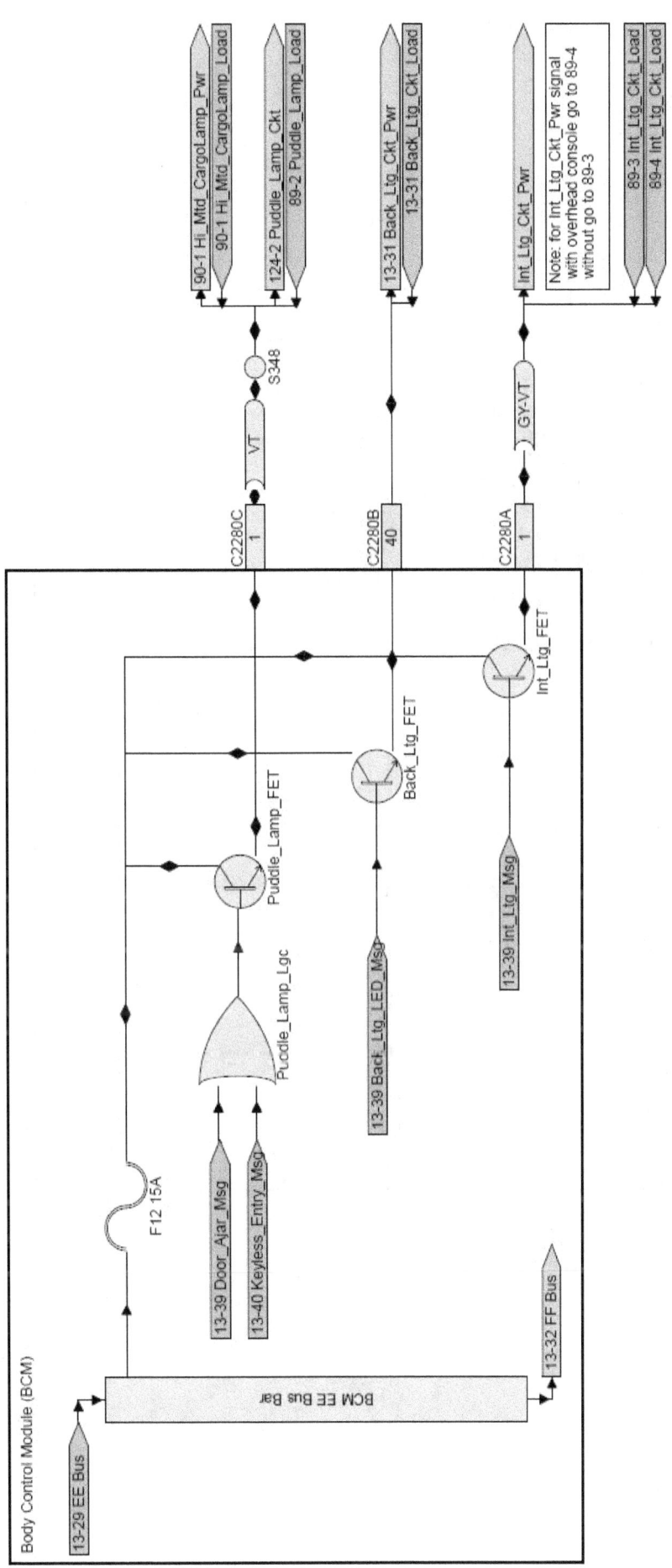

13-31 Power Distribution BCM F12 Back Ltg Ckt

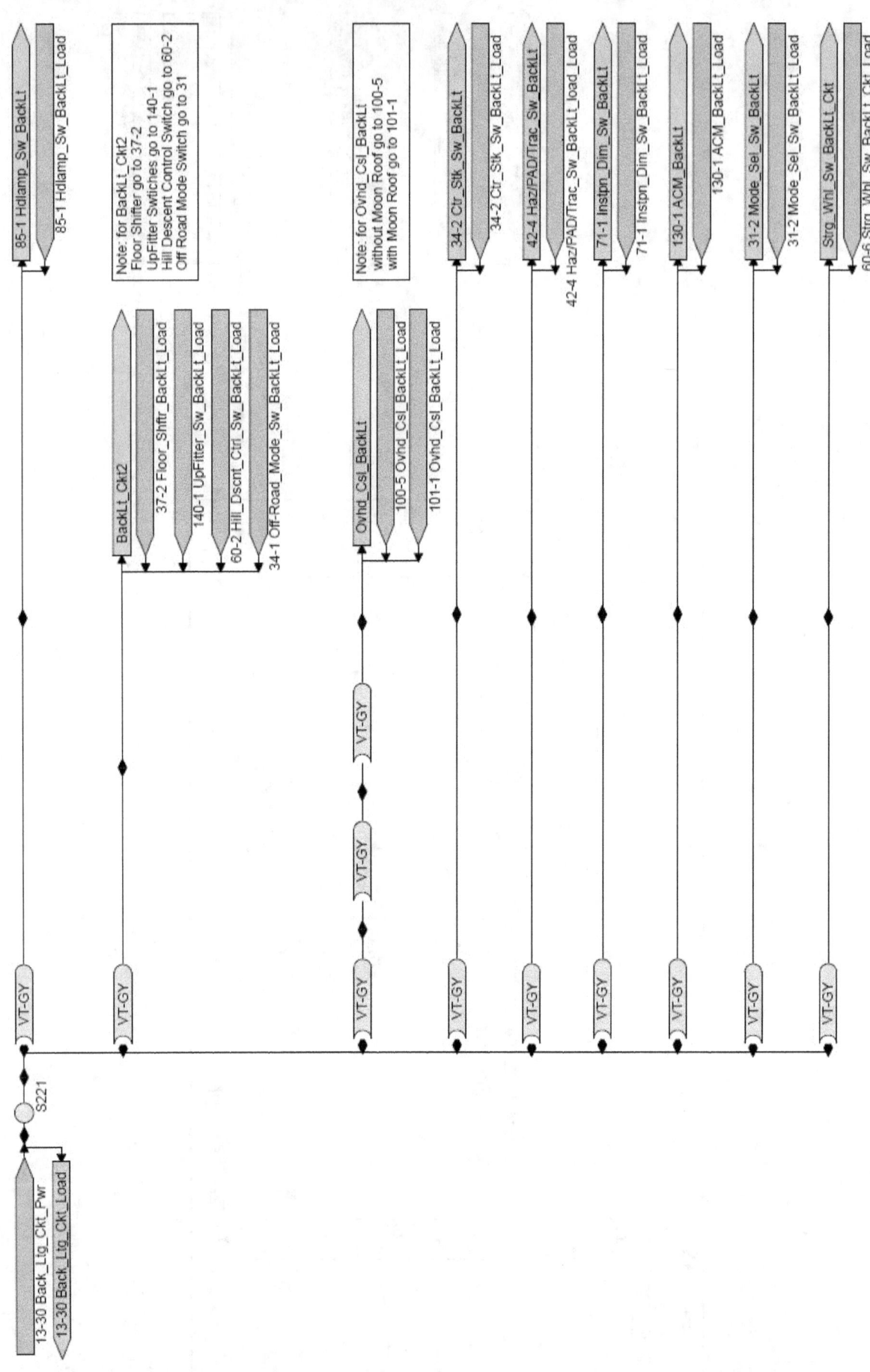

Power Distribution BCM F22, F47 **13-32**

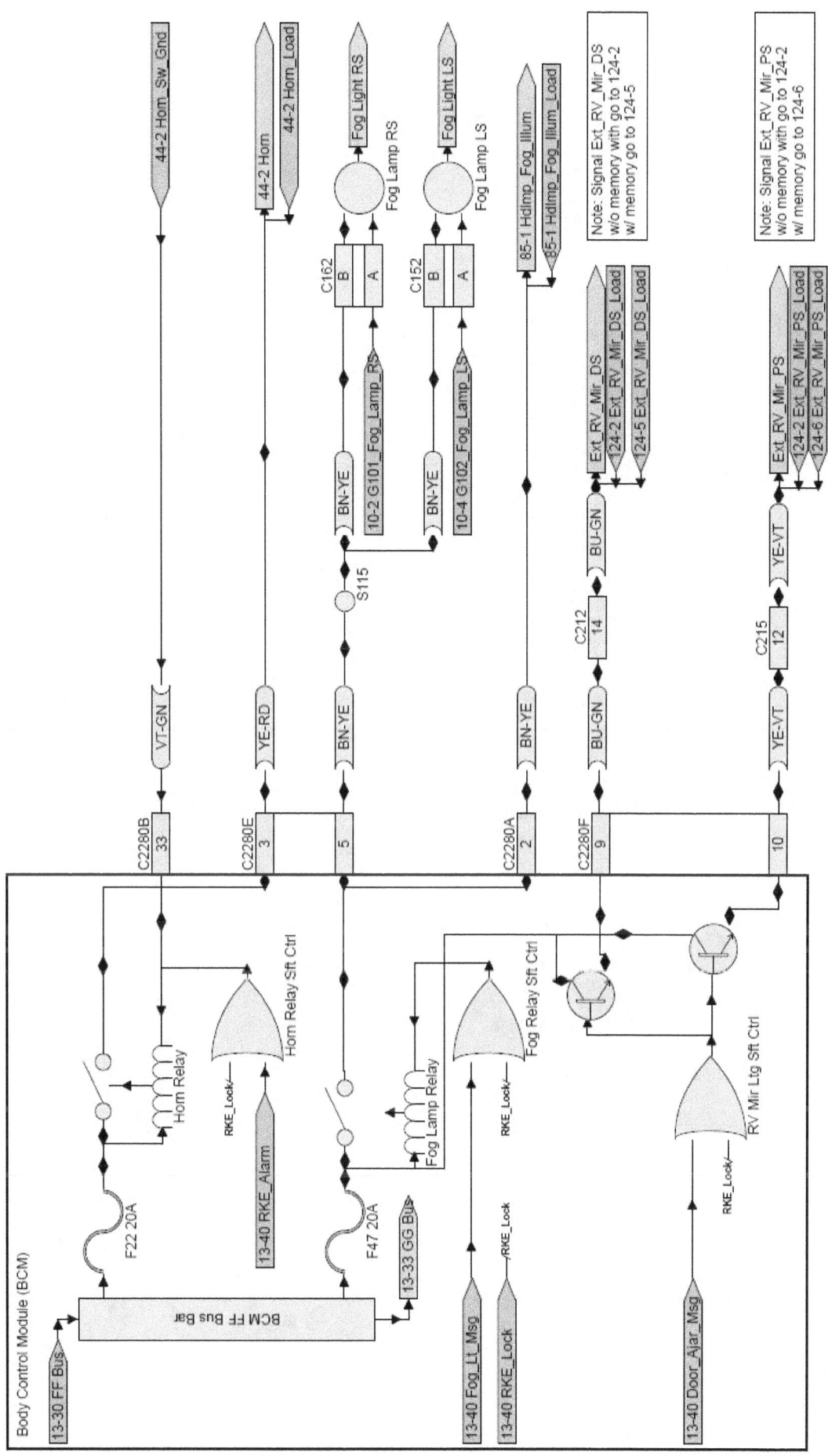

13-33 Power Distribution BCM F17, F16, F10

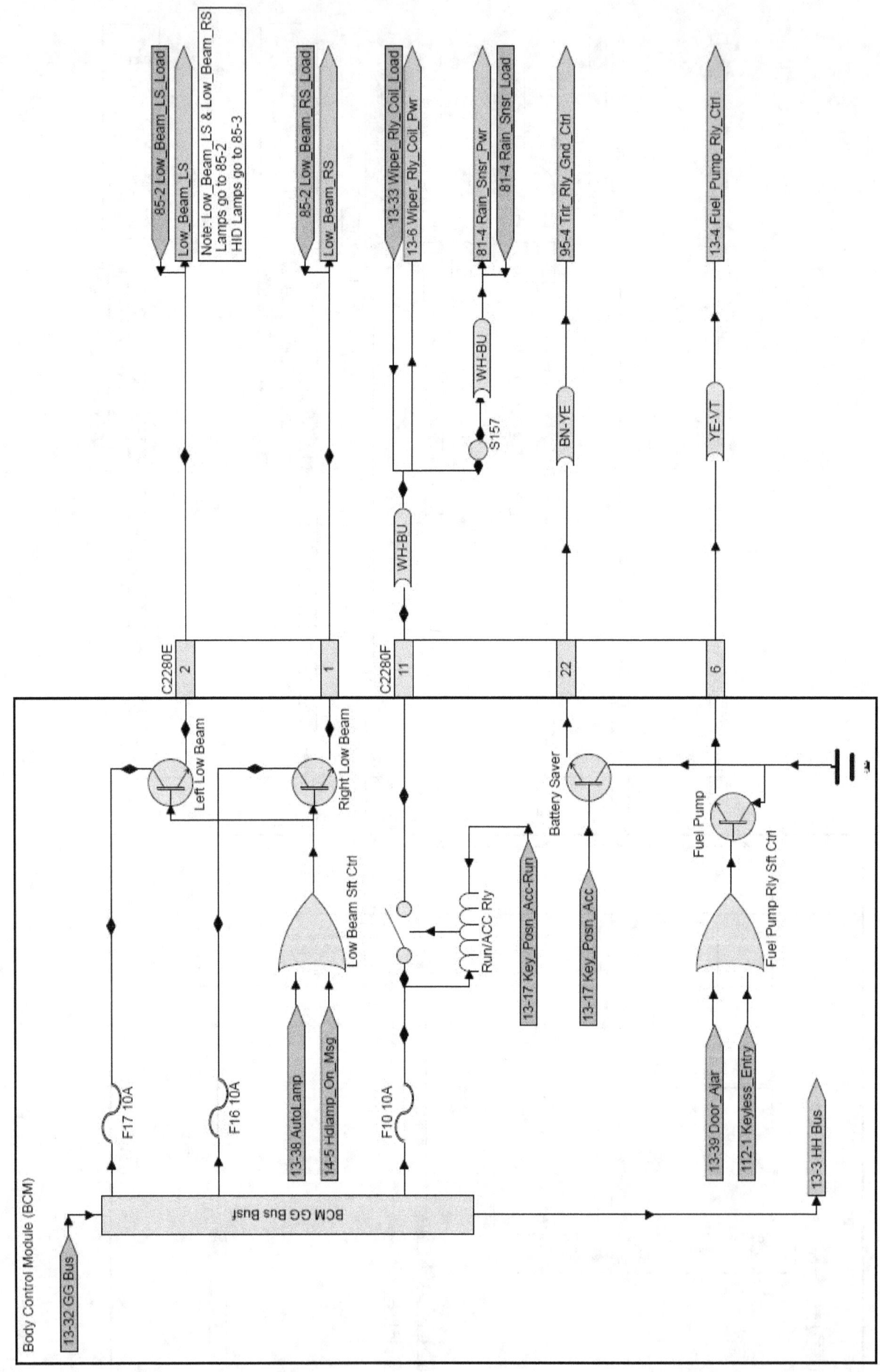

Power Distribution BCM F13 **13-34**

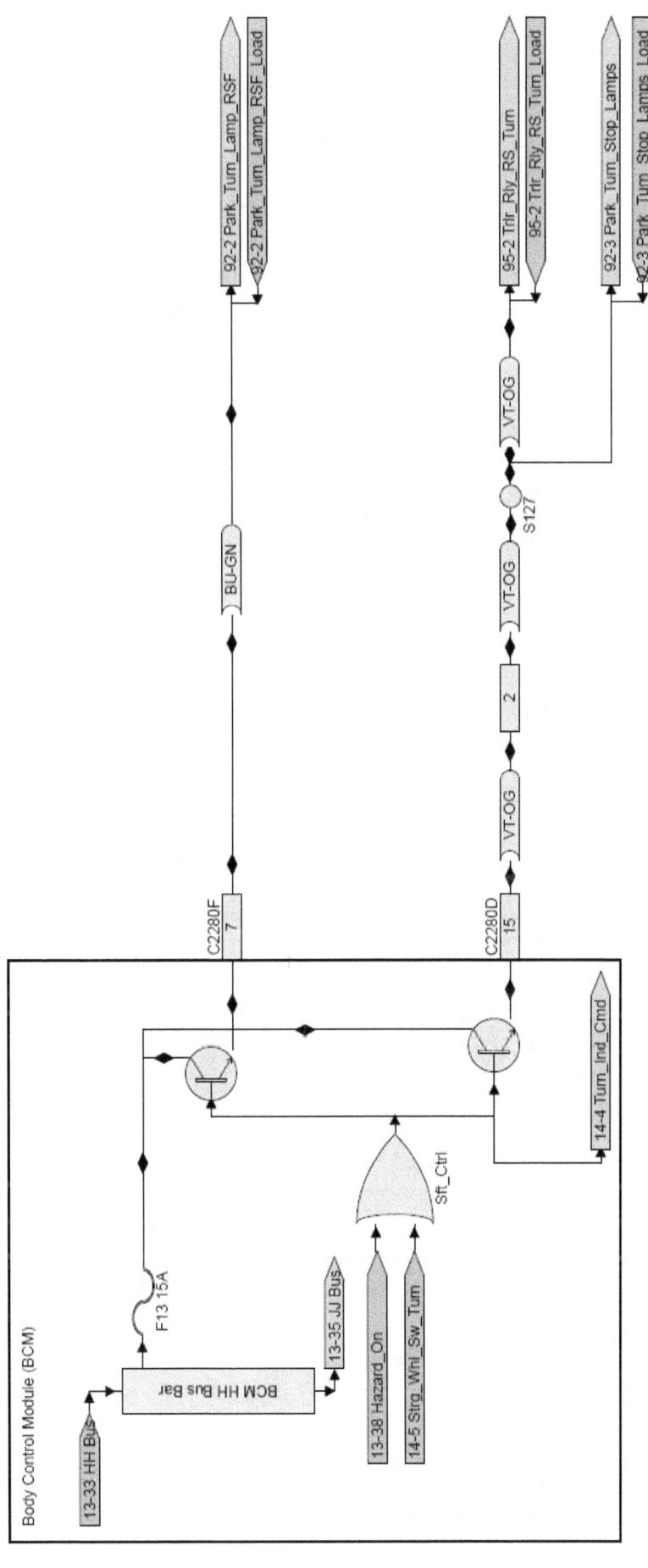

55

13-35 Power Distribution BCM F14

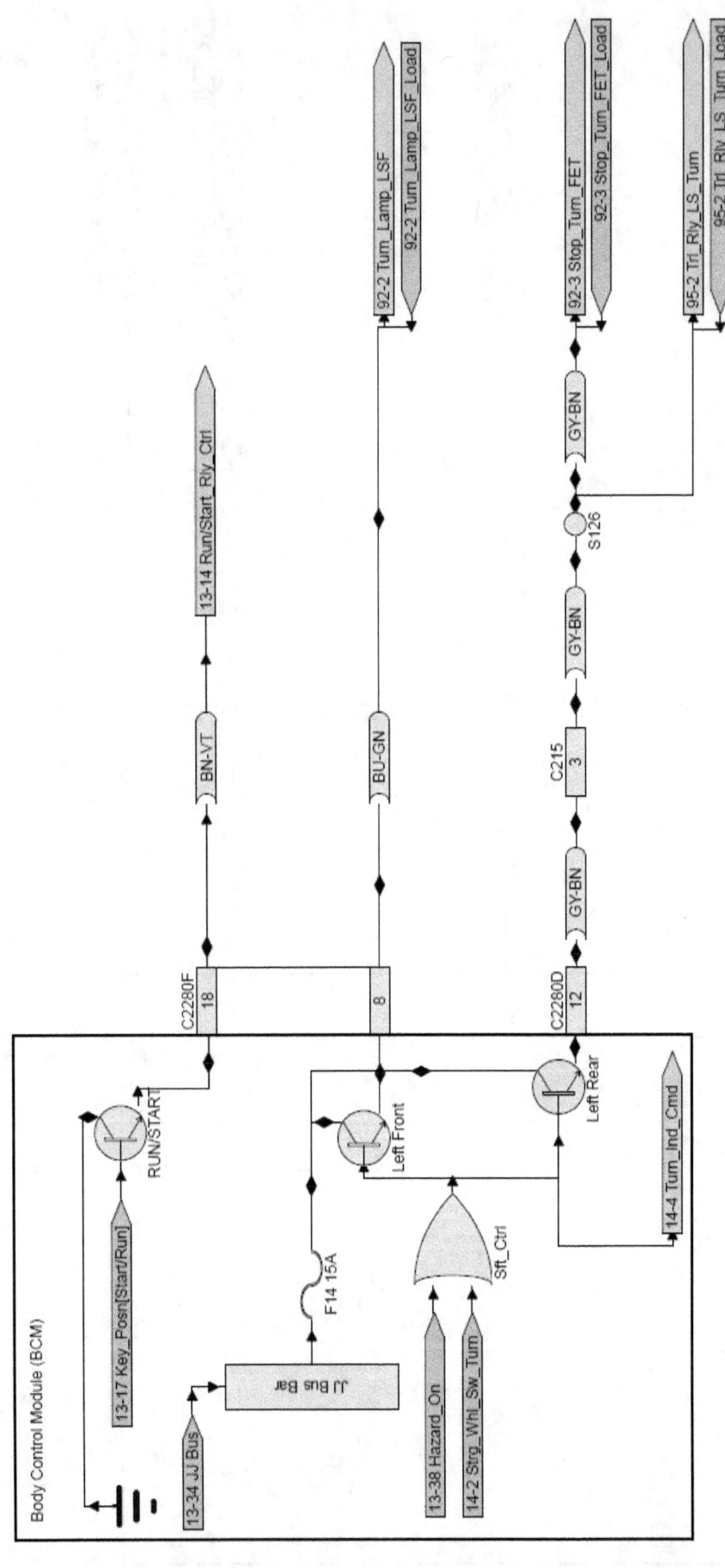

Power Distribution BCM F33, F34, F35 **13-36**

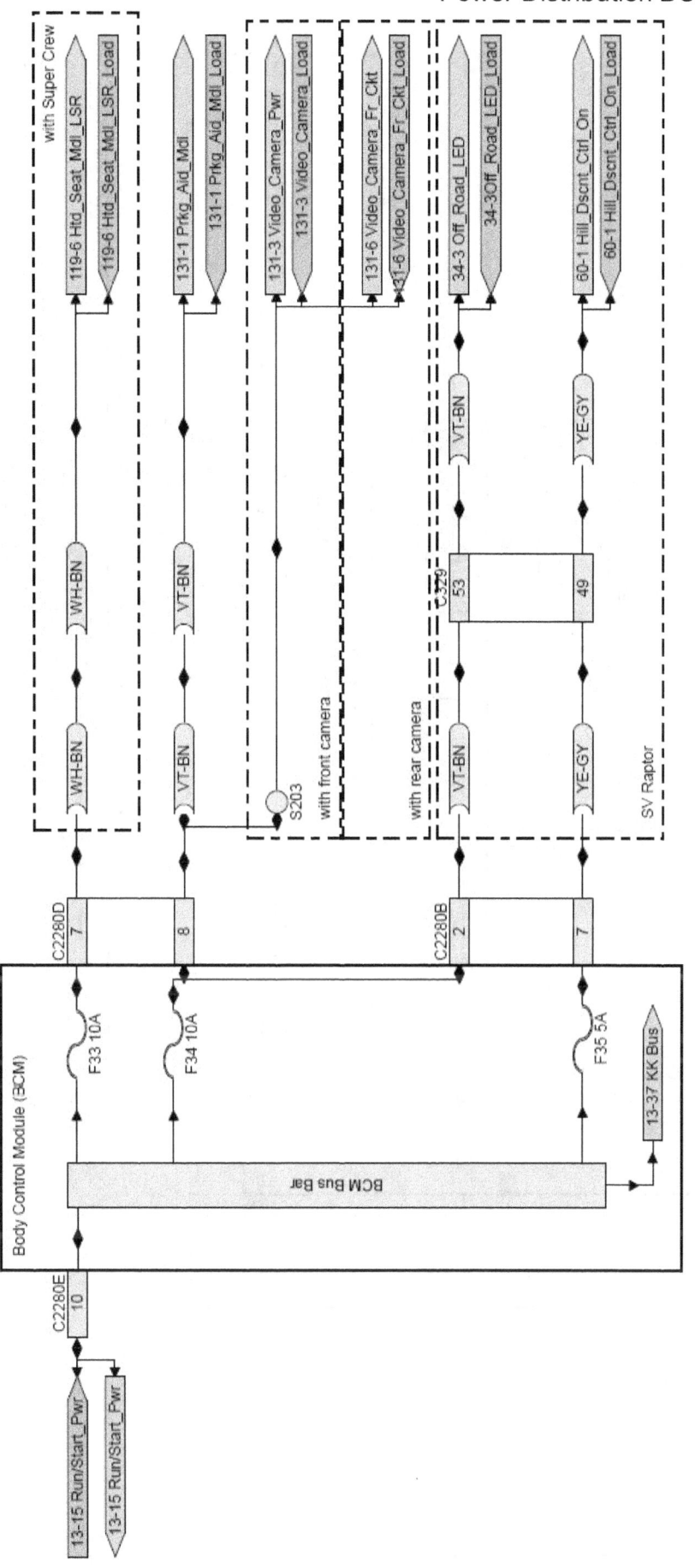

57

13-37 Power Distribution BCM F36, F37, F41, F35

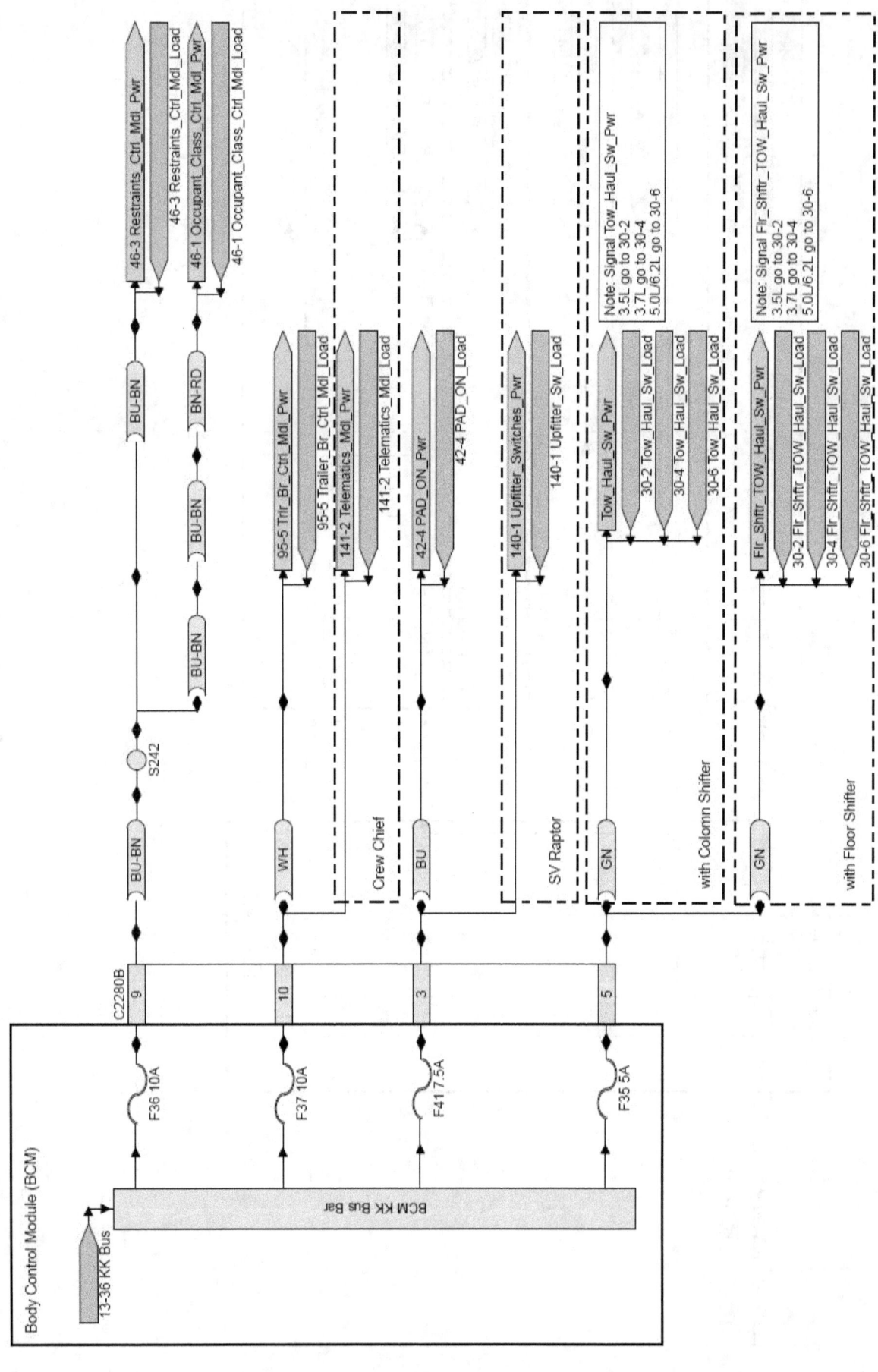

Power Distribution BCM Hazard, AutoLamp & Door Lock 13-38

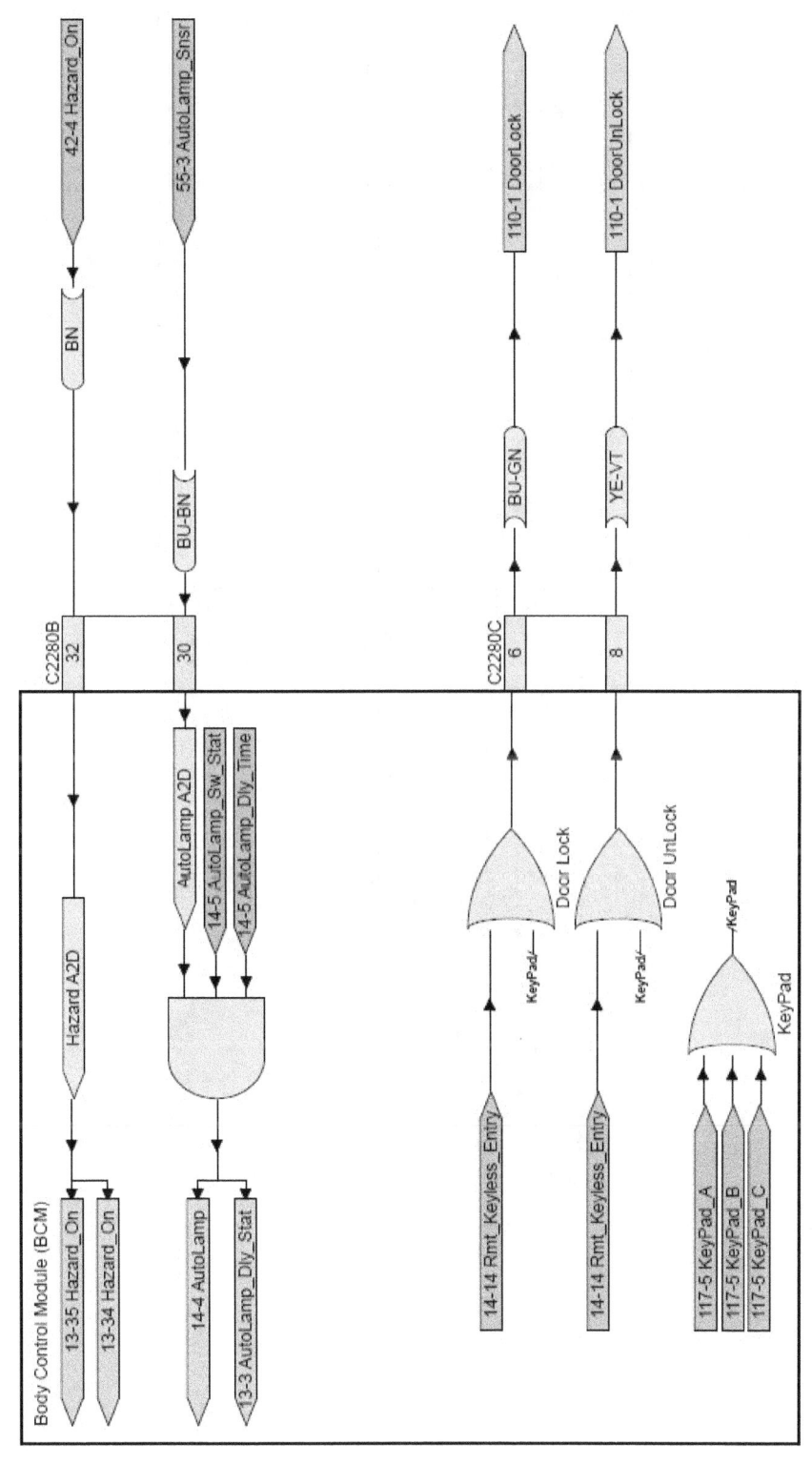

13-39 Power Distribution BCM Ajar Ctrl

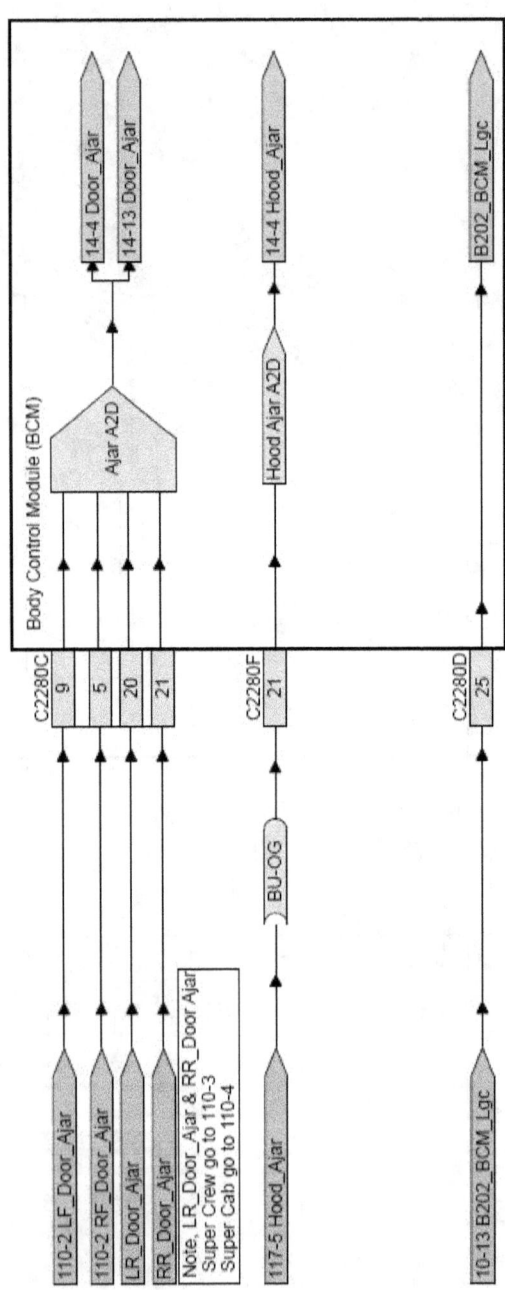

Power Distribution BCM EPATs 13-40

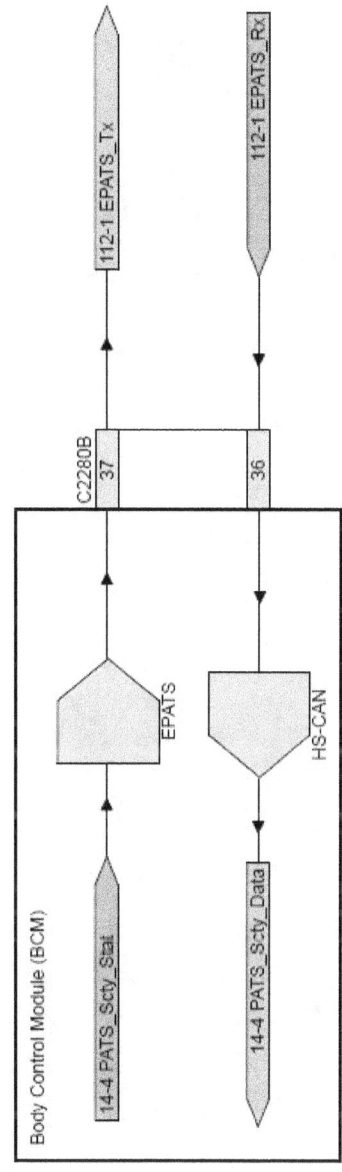

13-41 Power Distribution BCM LIN 01 and LIN 03

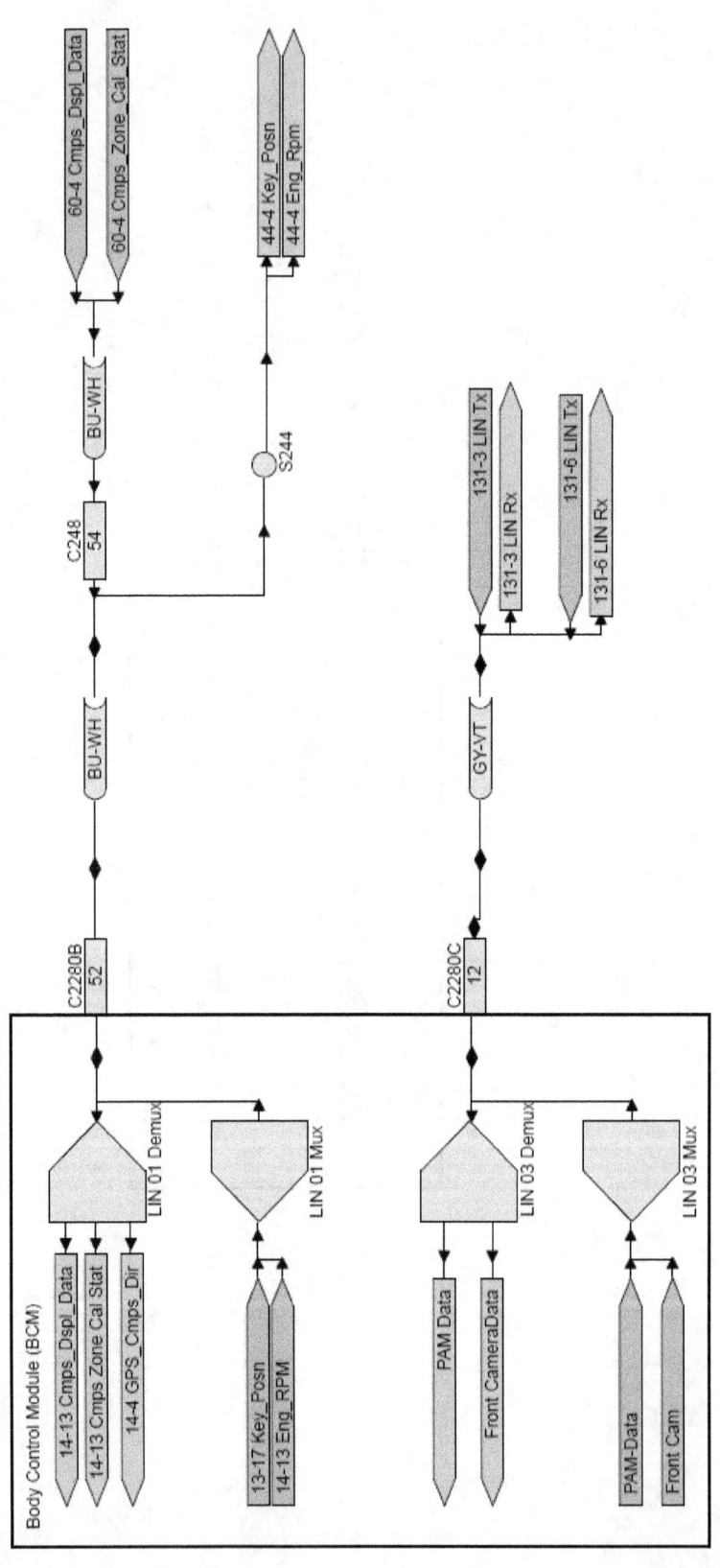

14 Module Communications
Data Link Connector 14-1

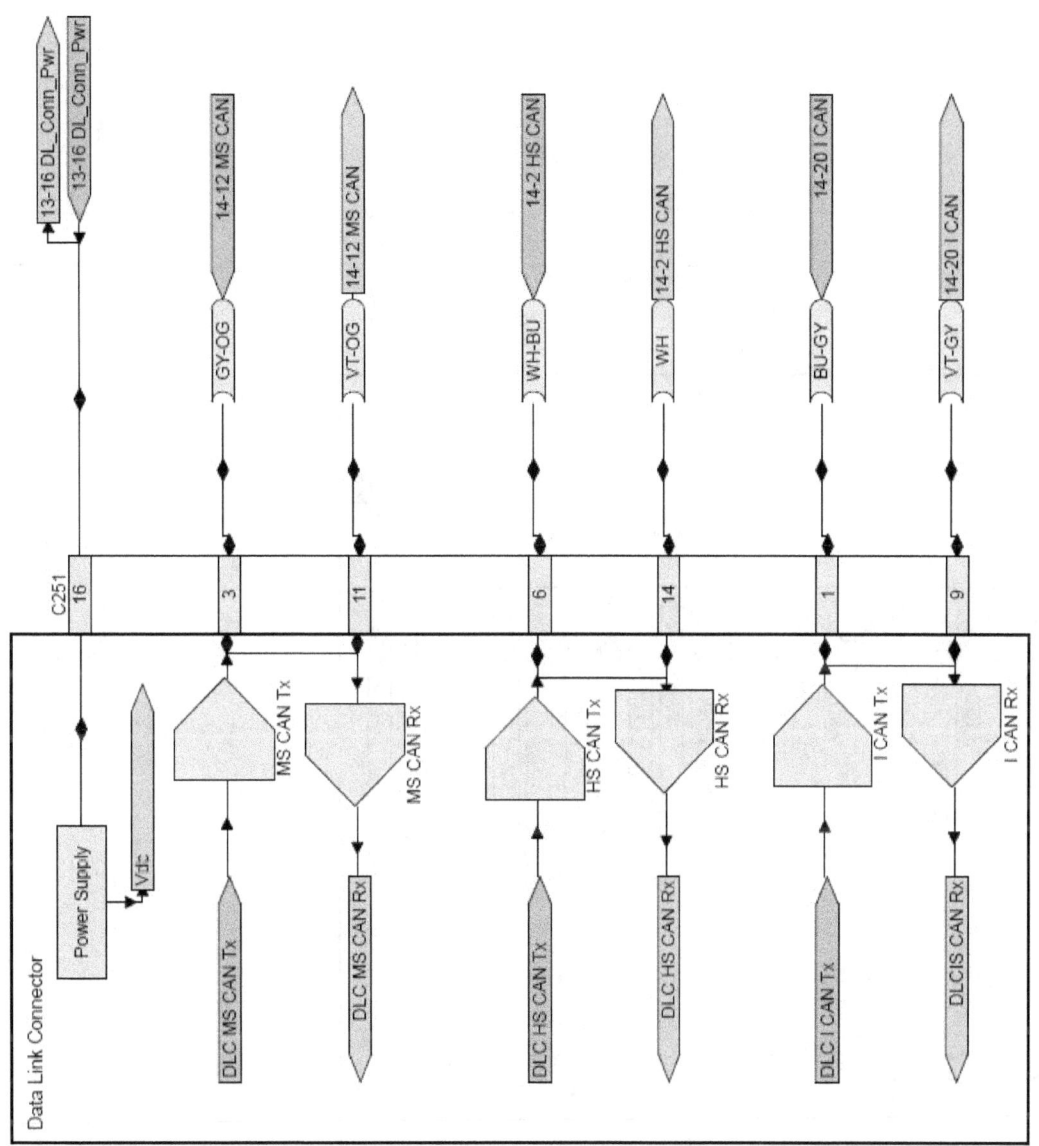

14-2 Steering Column Control Module (SCCM) HS-CAN

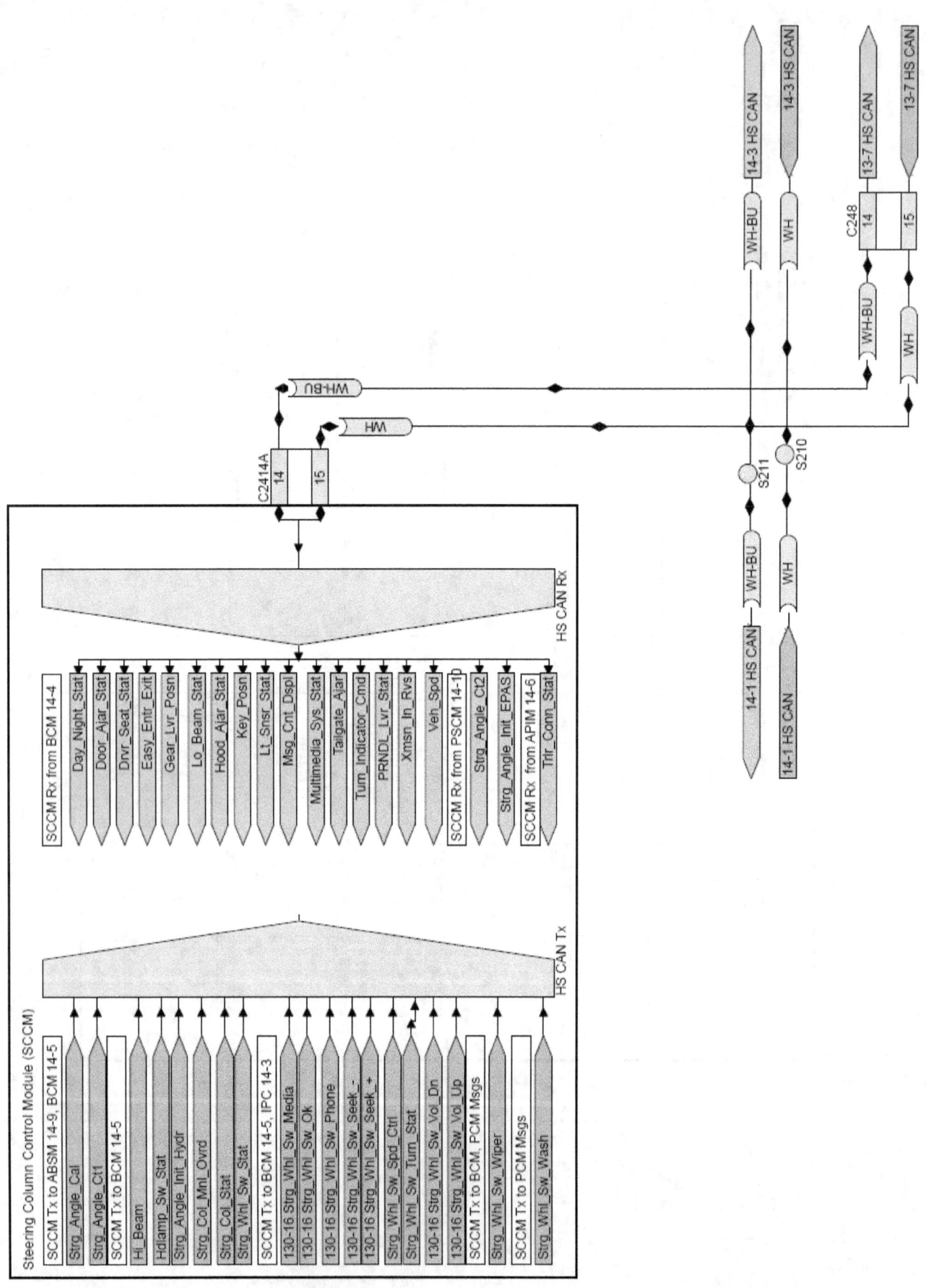

Instrument Panel Cluster (IPC) HS-CAN 14-3

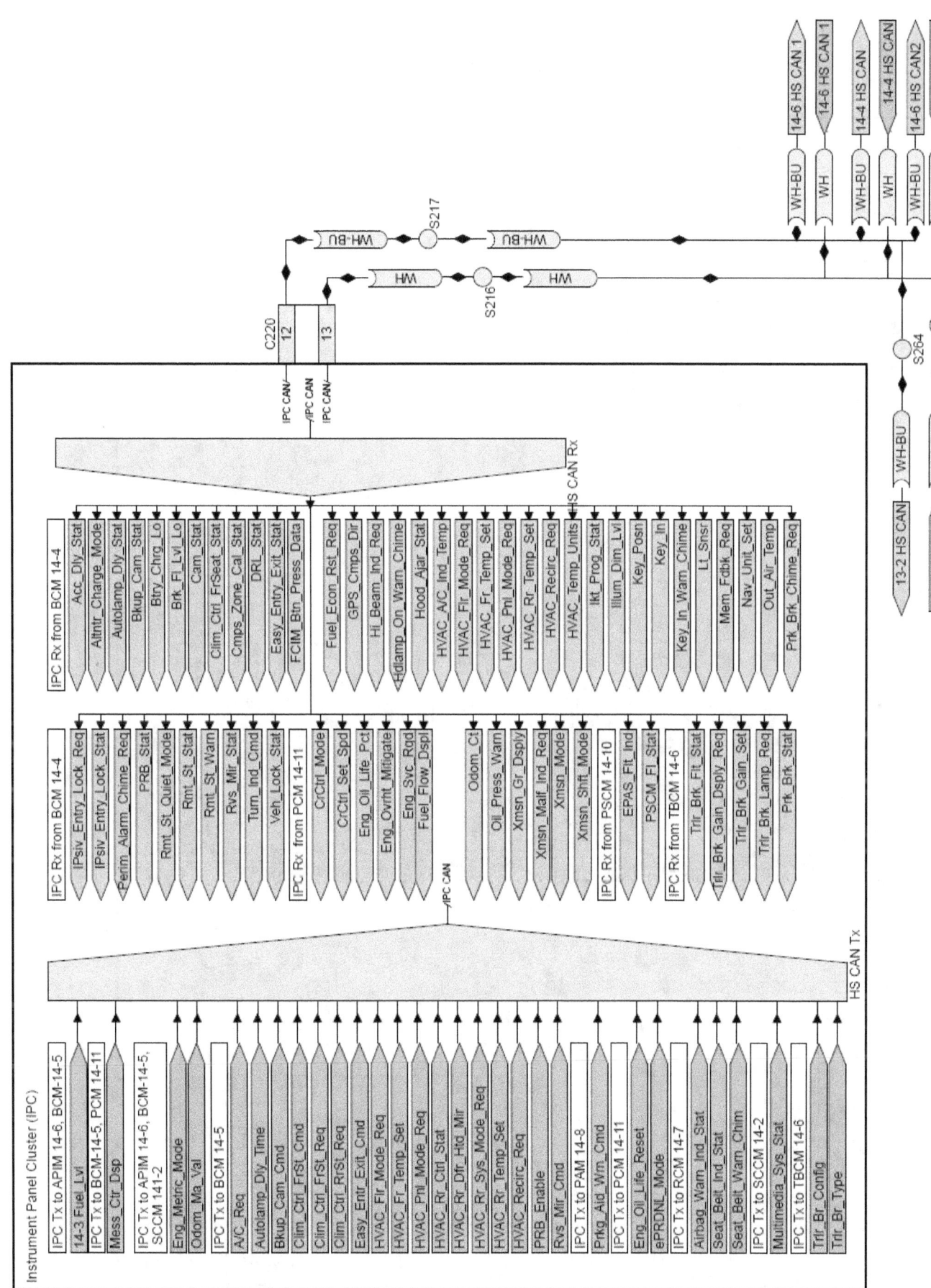

14-4 Body Control Module (BCM) HS-CAN Tx

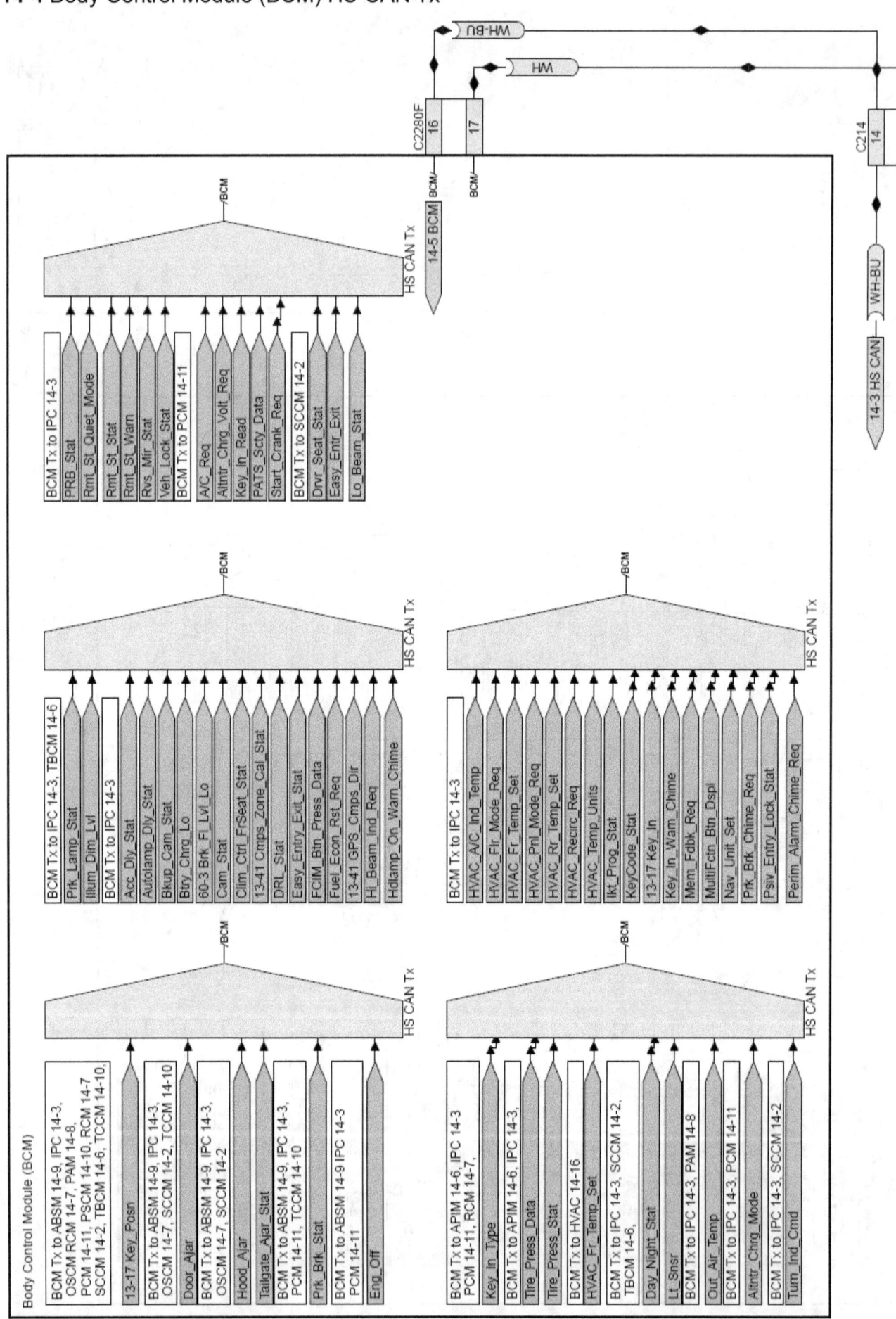

Body Control Module (BCM) HS-CAN Rx **14-5**

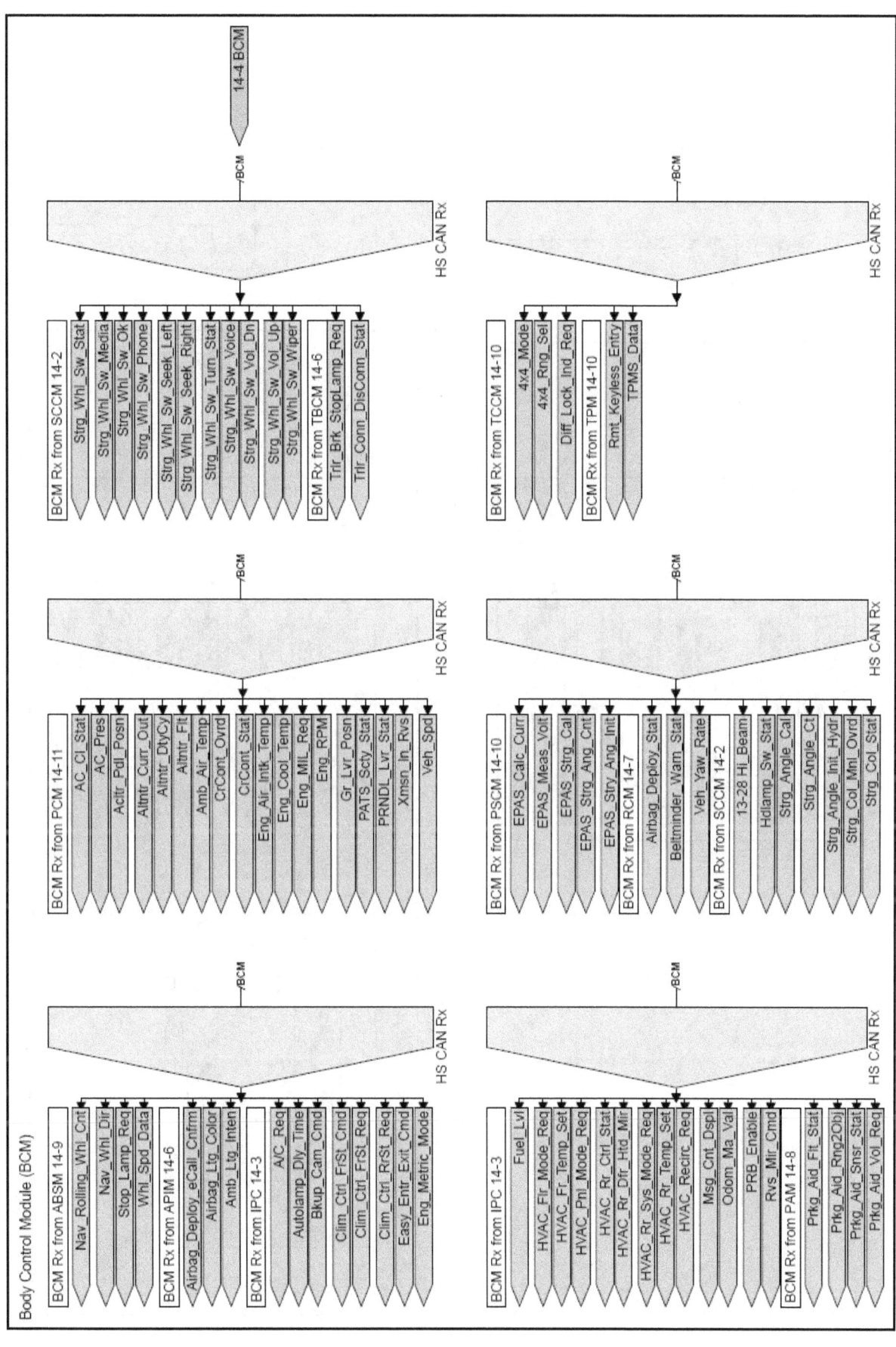

14-6 Accessory Protocol Interface Module (APIM) and Trailer Brake Control Module (TBCM) HS-CAN

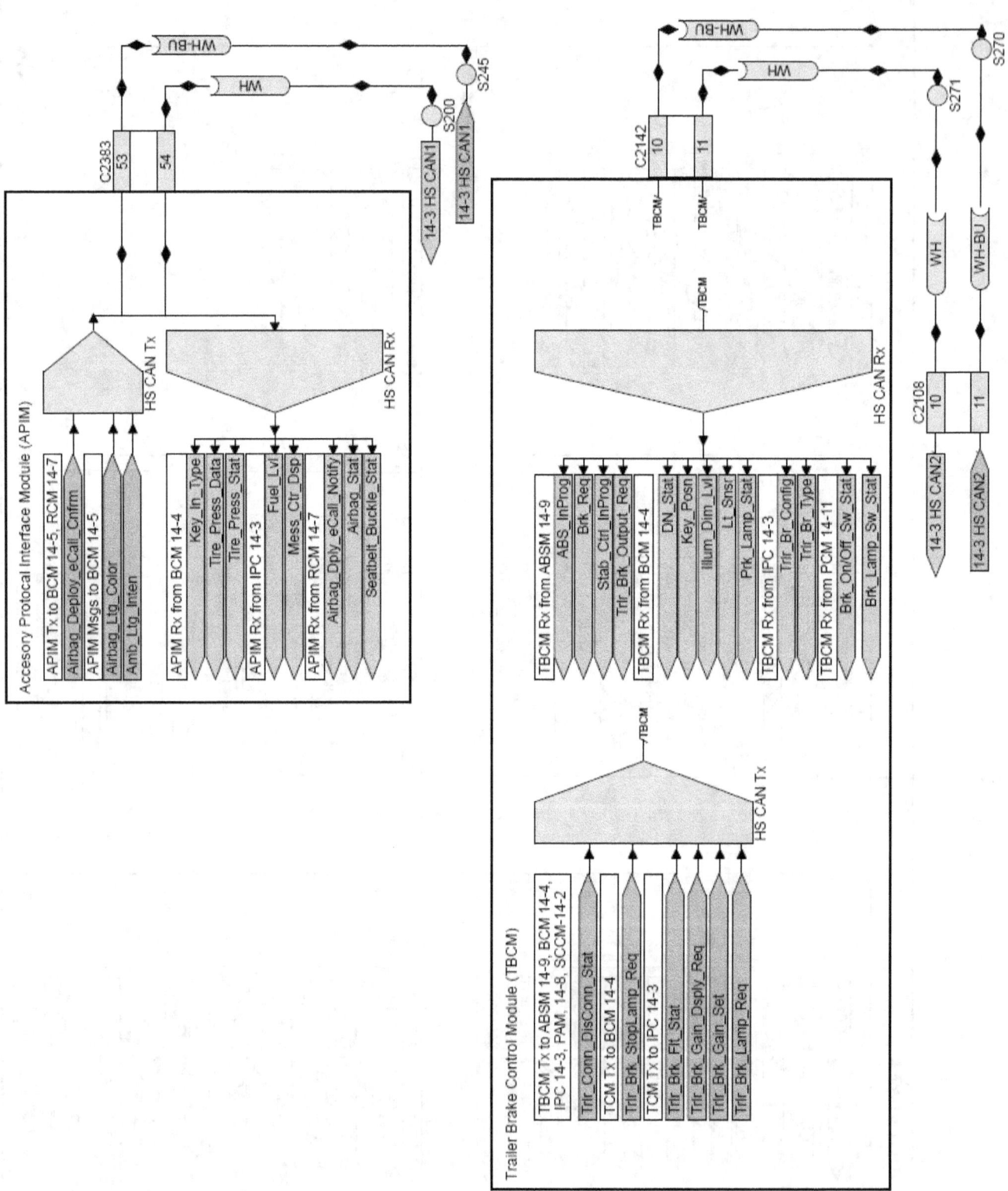

Restraint Control Module (RCM) HS-CAN 14-7

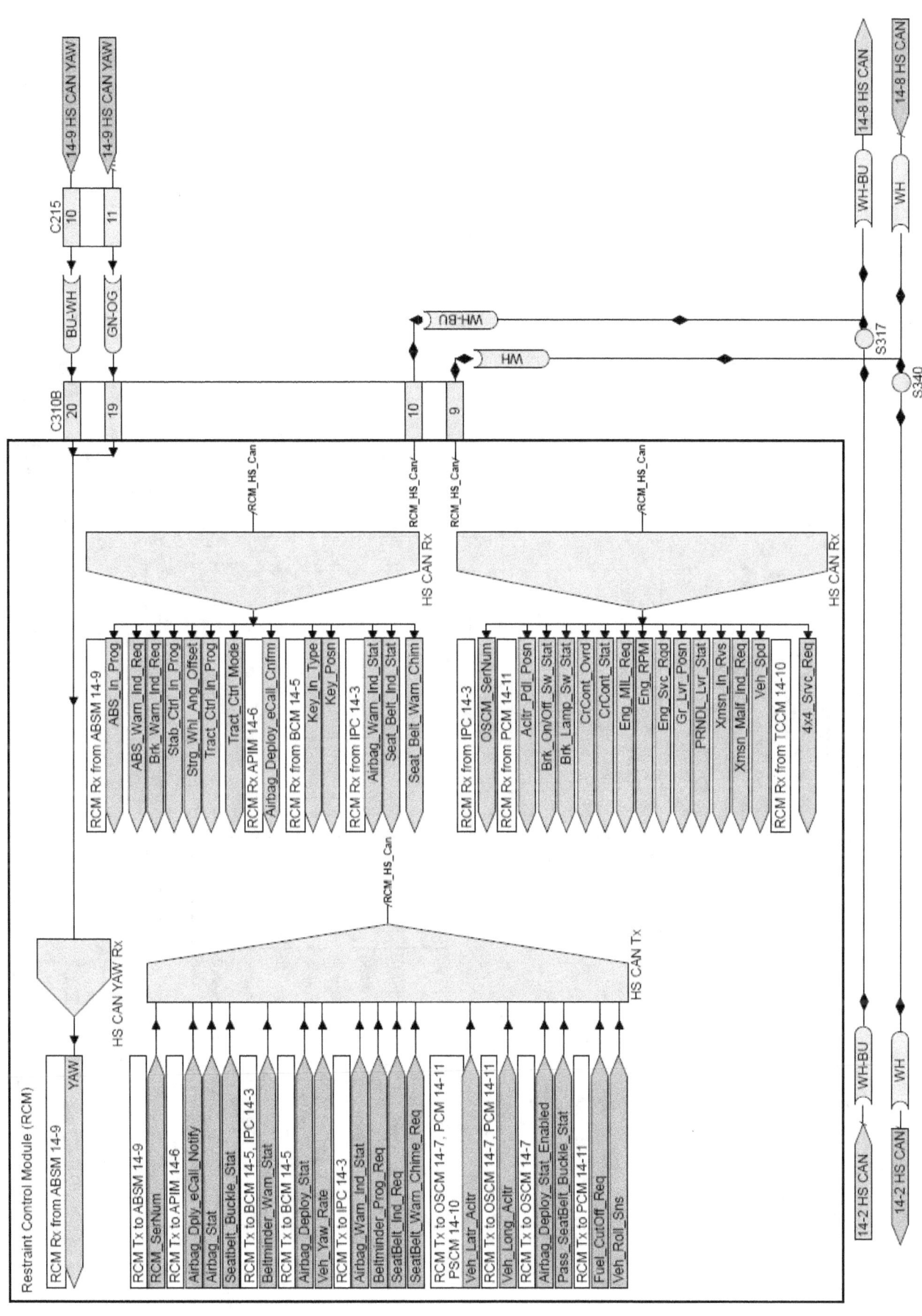

14-8 Parking Aid Module (PAM) and Occupant Classification System Module (OCSM) HS-CAN

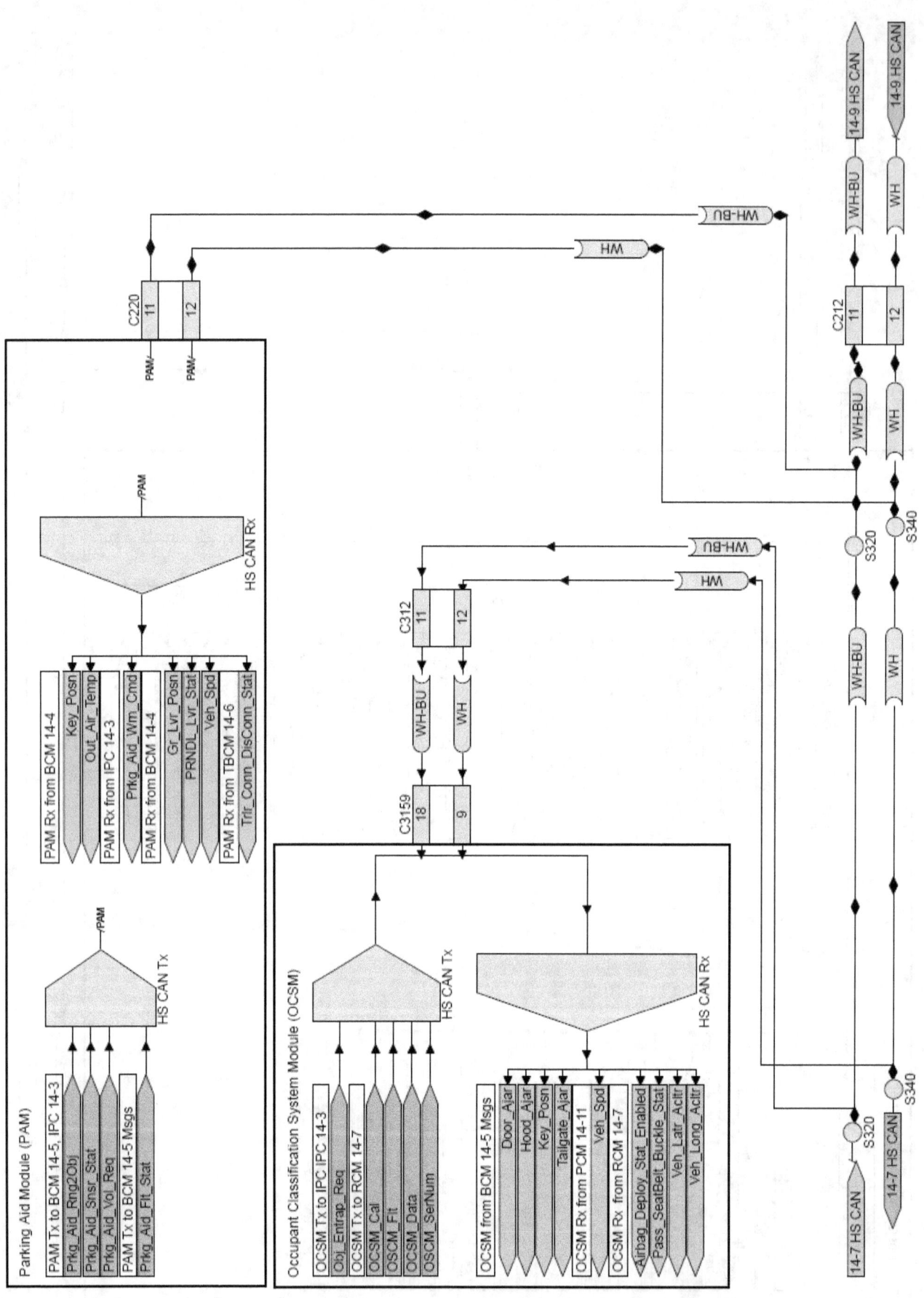

Anti-Lock Brake System Module (ABSM) HS-CAN 14-9

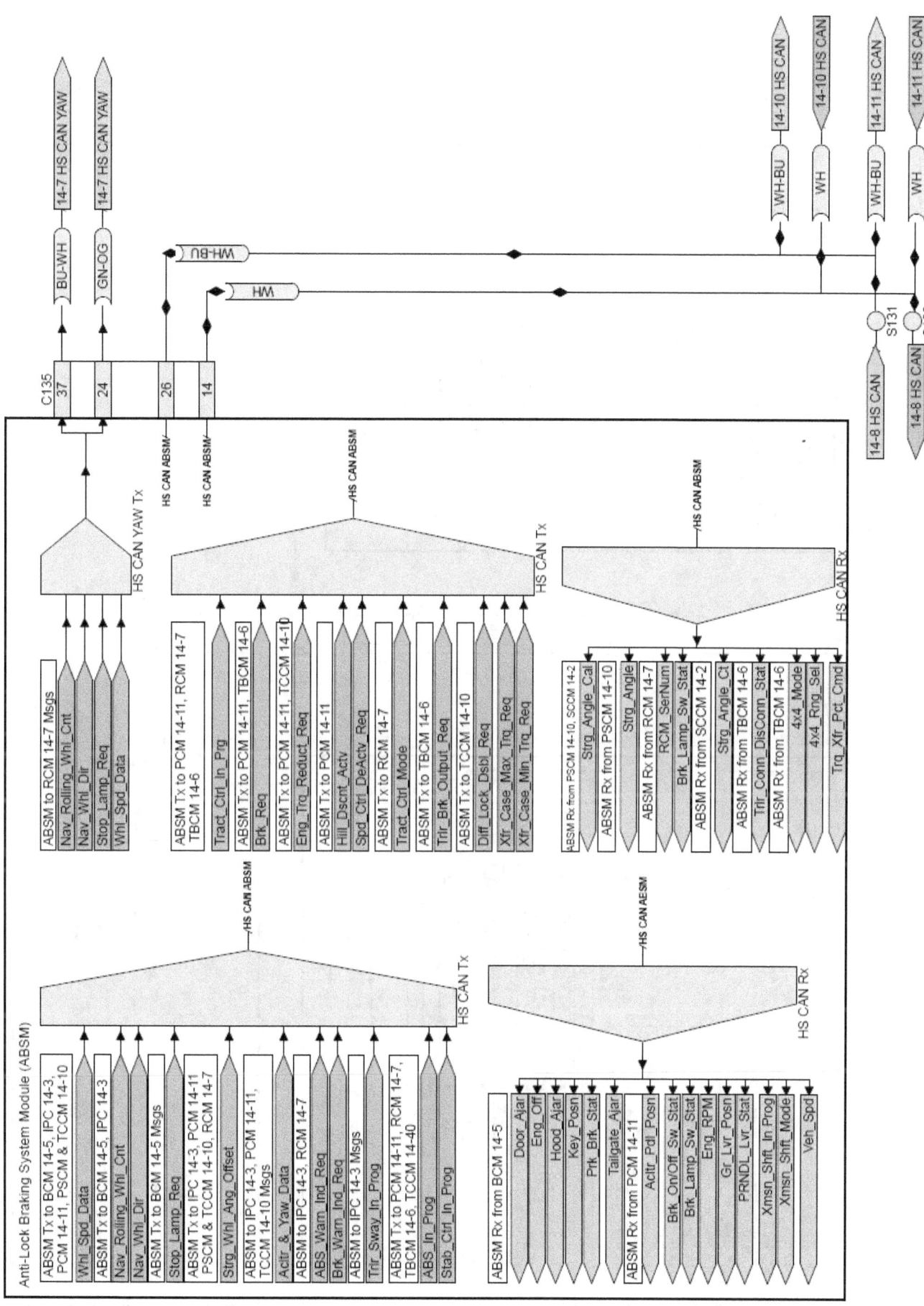

14-10 Transfer Case Ctrl Module (TCCM) & Power Steering Control Module (PSCM) HS-CAN

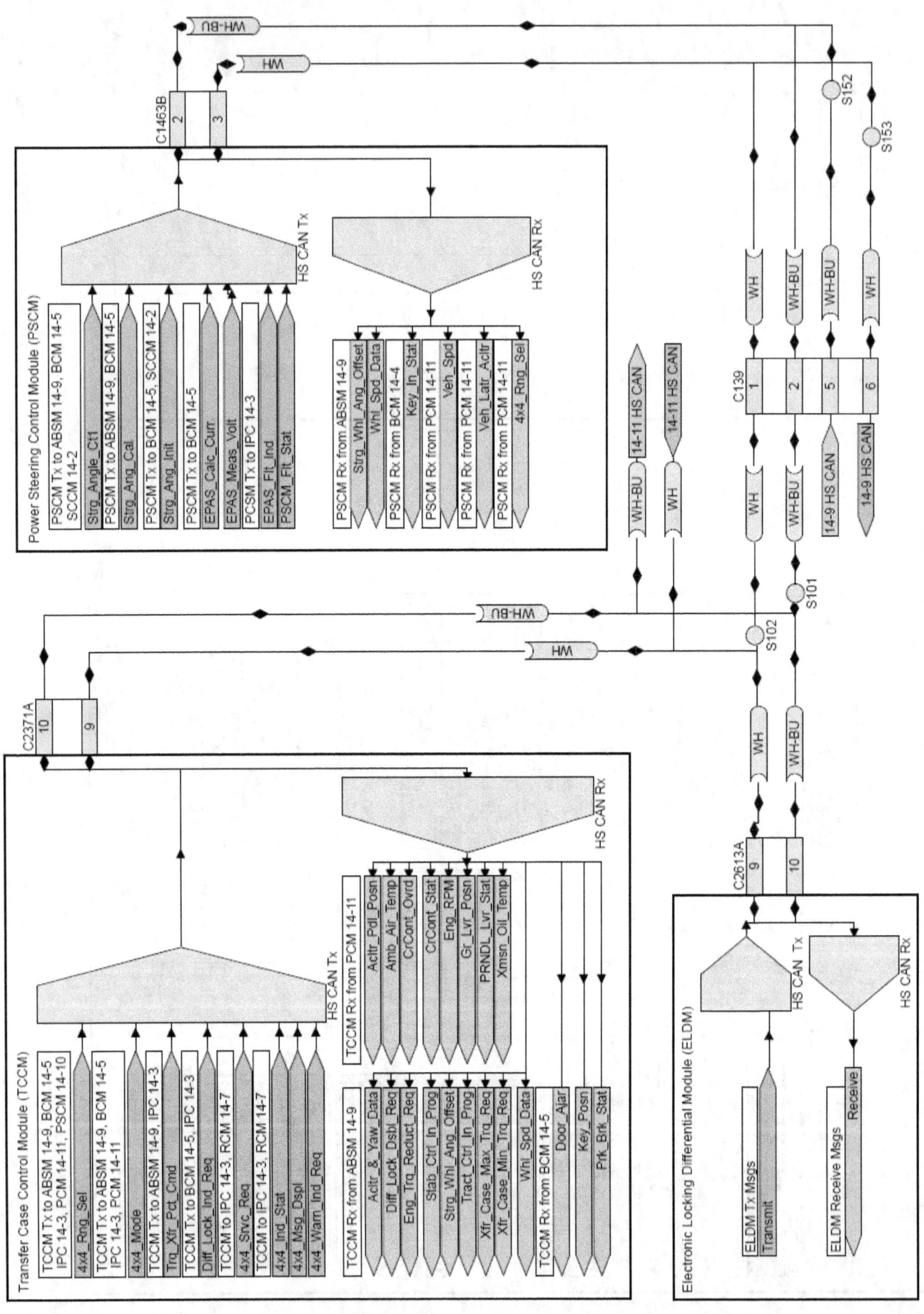

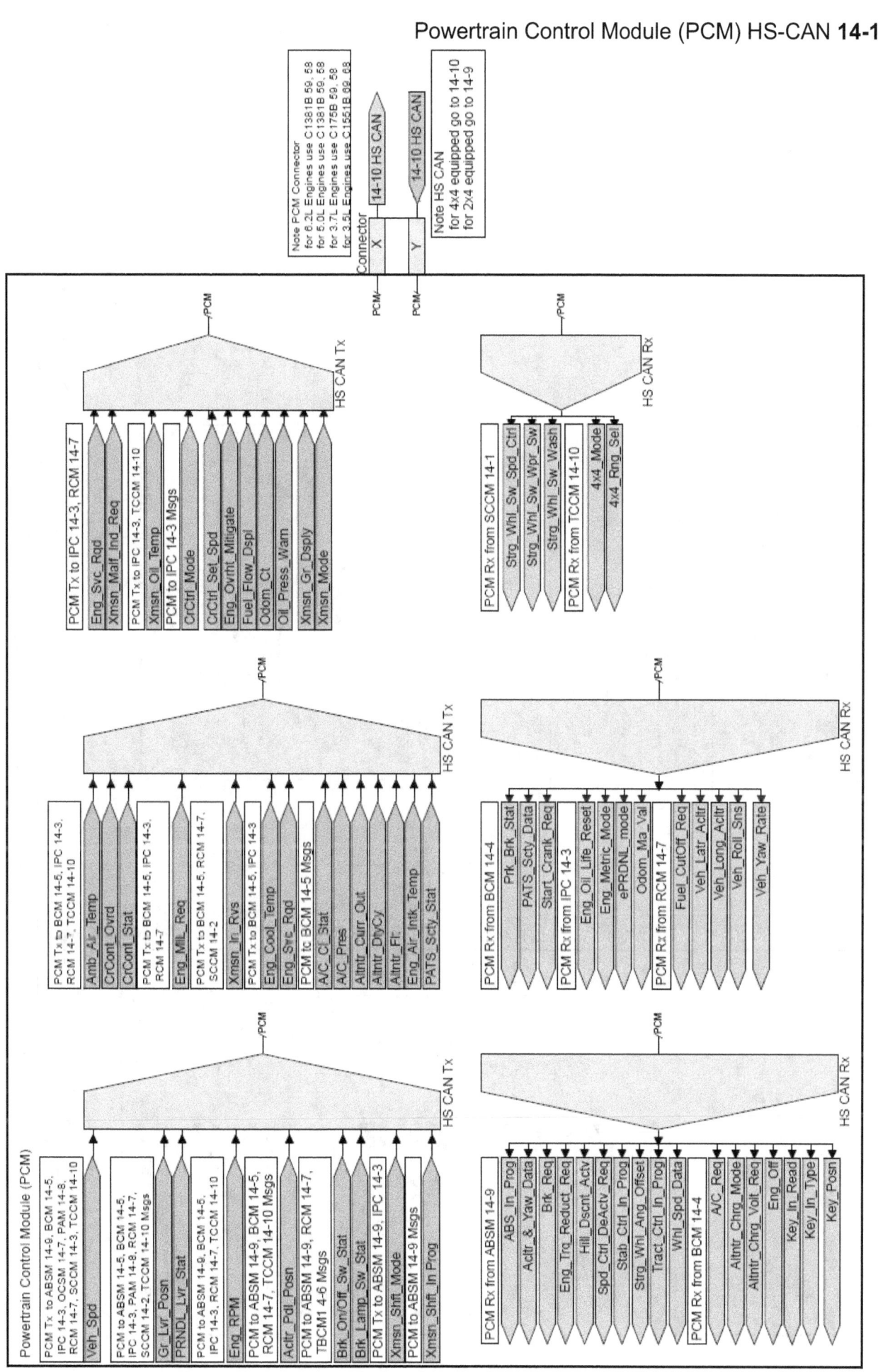

14-12 Aud Ctrl Mdl (ACM), GPS Mdl (GPSM) & Access Protocol Intfc Mdl (APIM) MS-CAN

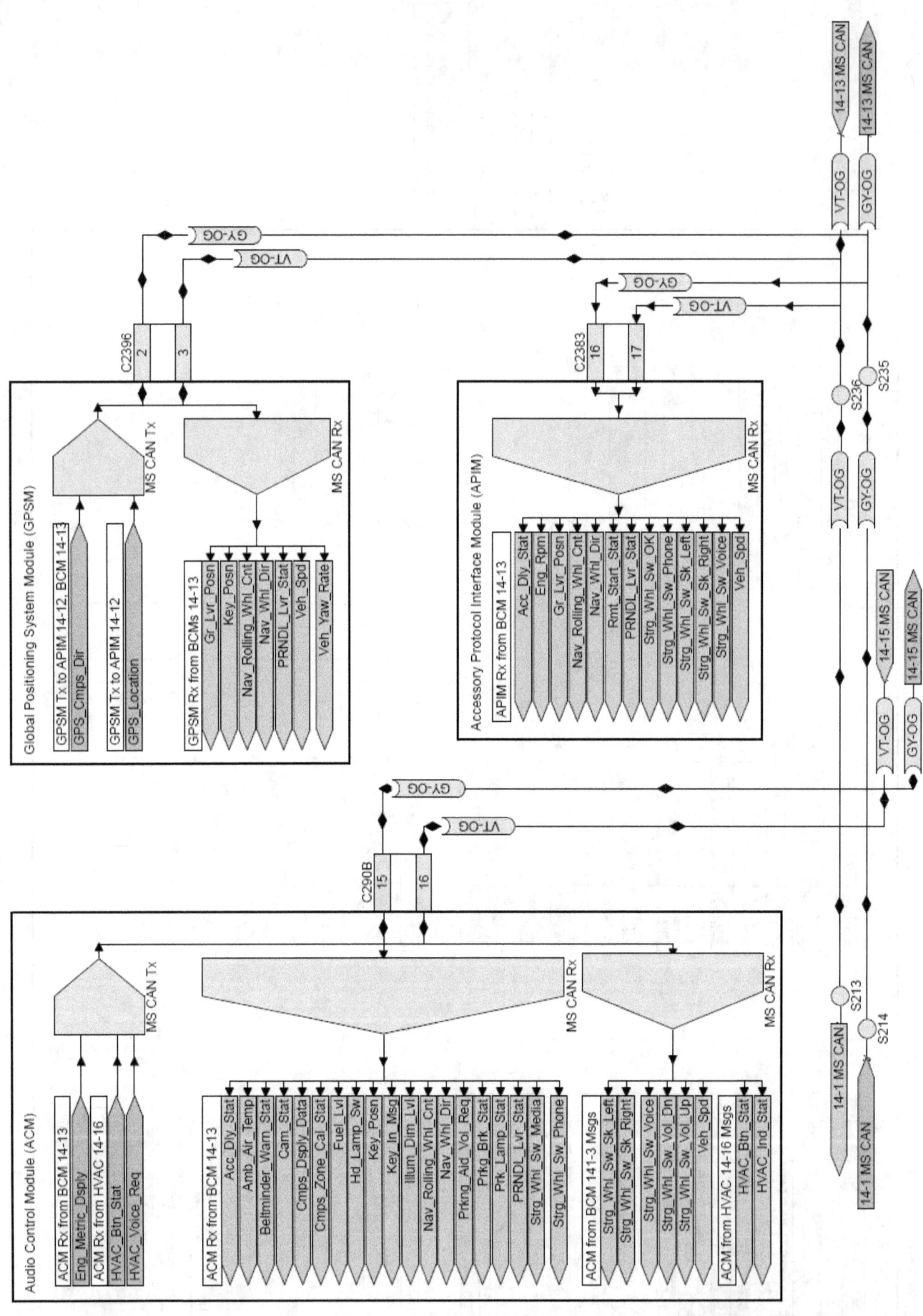

Body Control Module (BCM) MS-CAN 14-13

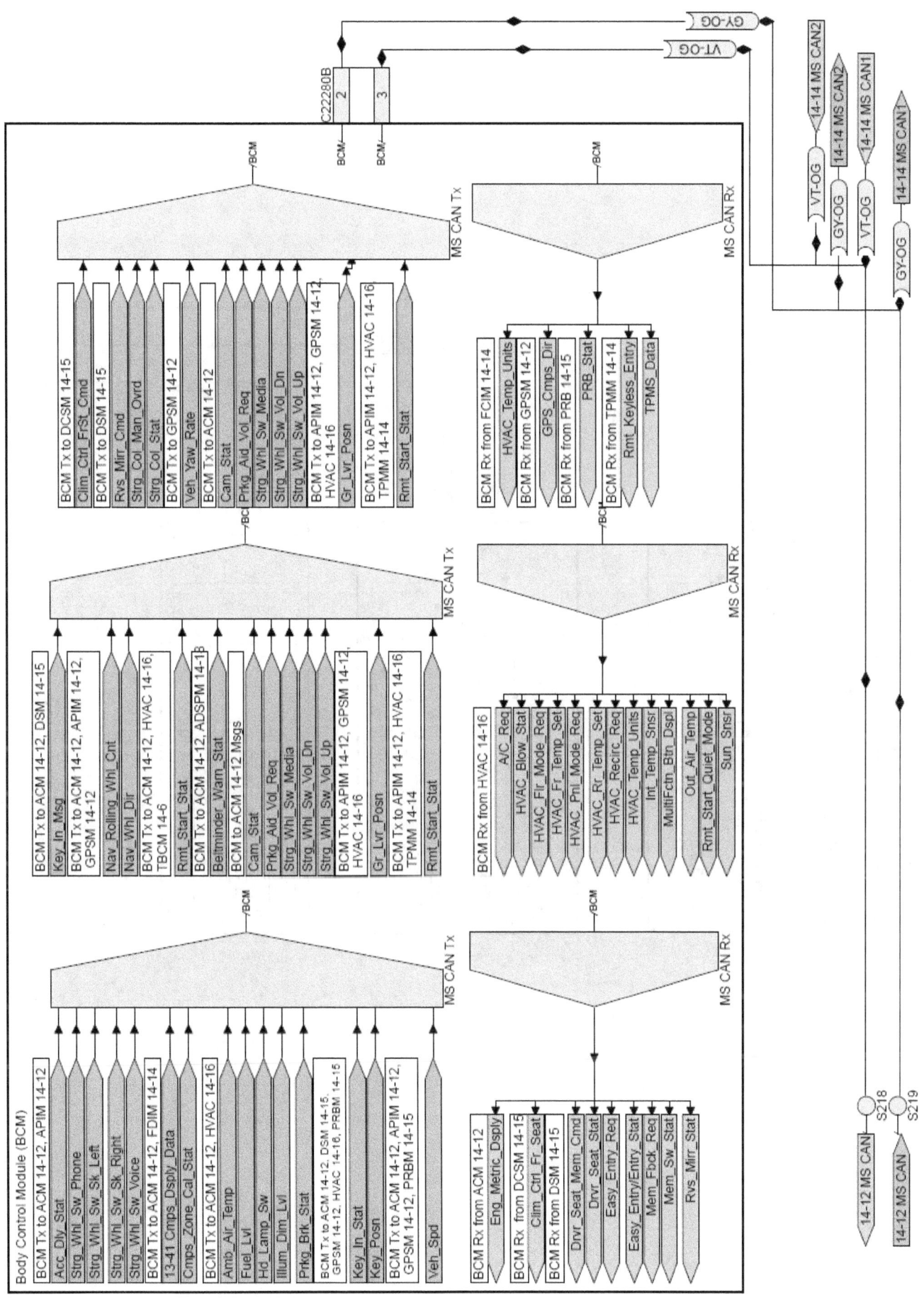

14-14 Tire Press Mon Mdl (TPMM), Fr Ctrl Intfc Mdl (FCIM) & Fr Dspl Intfc Mdl (FDIM) MS-CAN

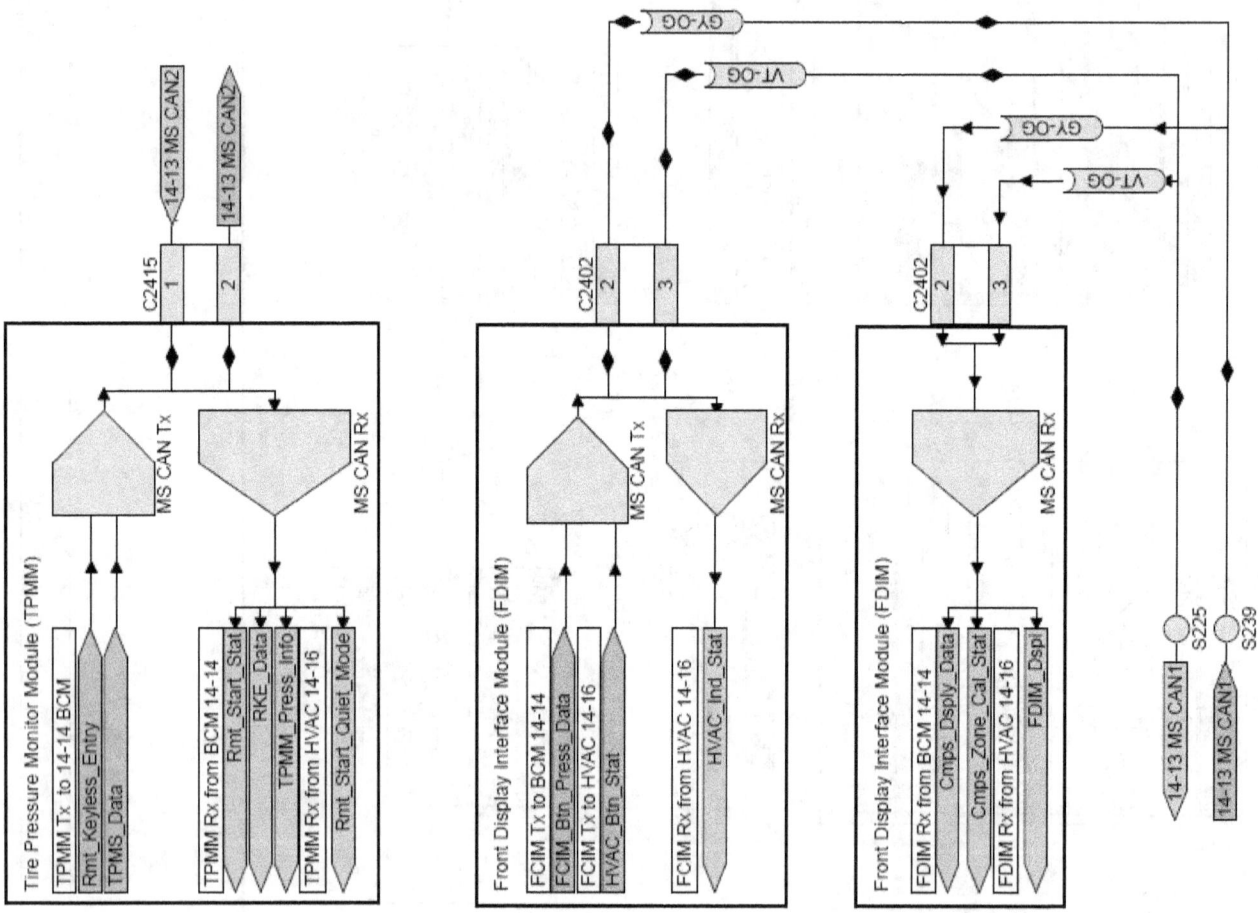

Dual Clim Seat Mdl (DCSM), Pwr Running Brd Mdl (PRBM), & Drvr Sear Mdl (DSM) MS-CAN 14-15

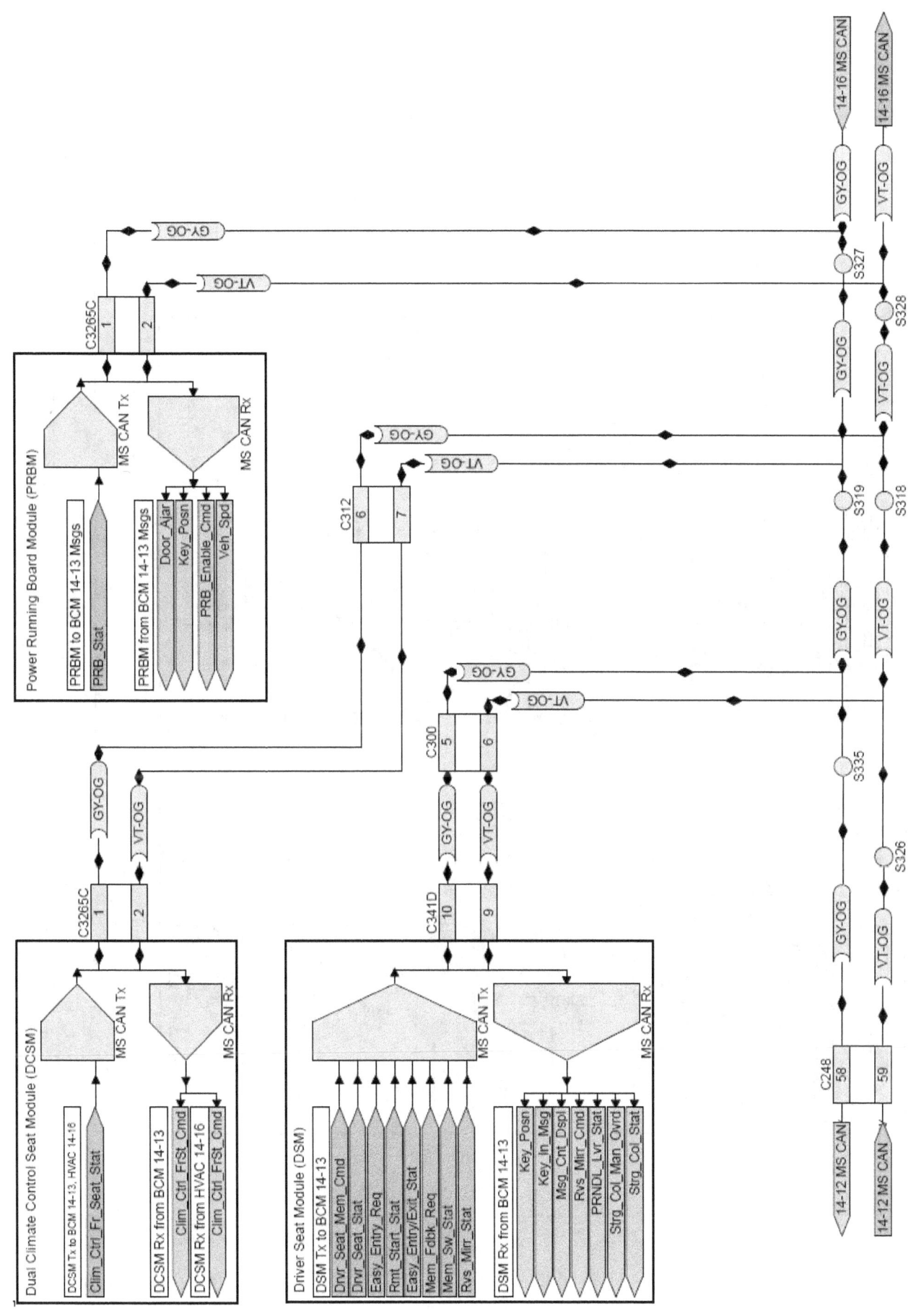

14-16 Heating Ventilation Air Conditioning (HVAC) Module MS-CAN

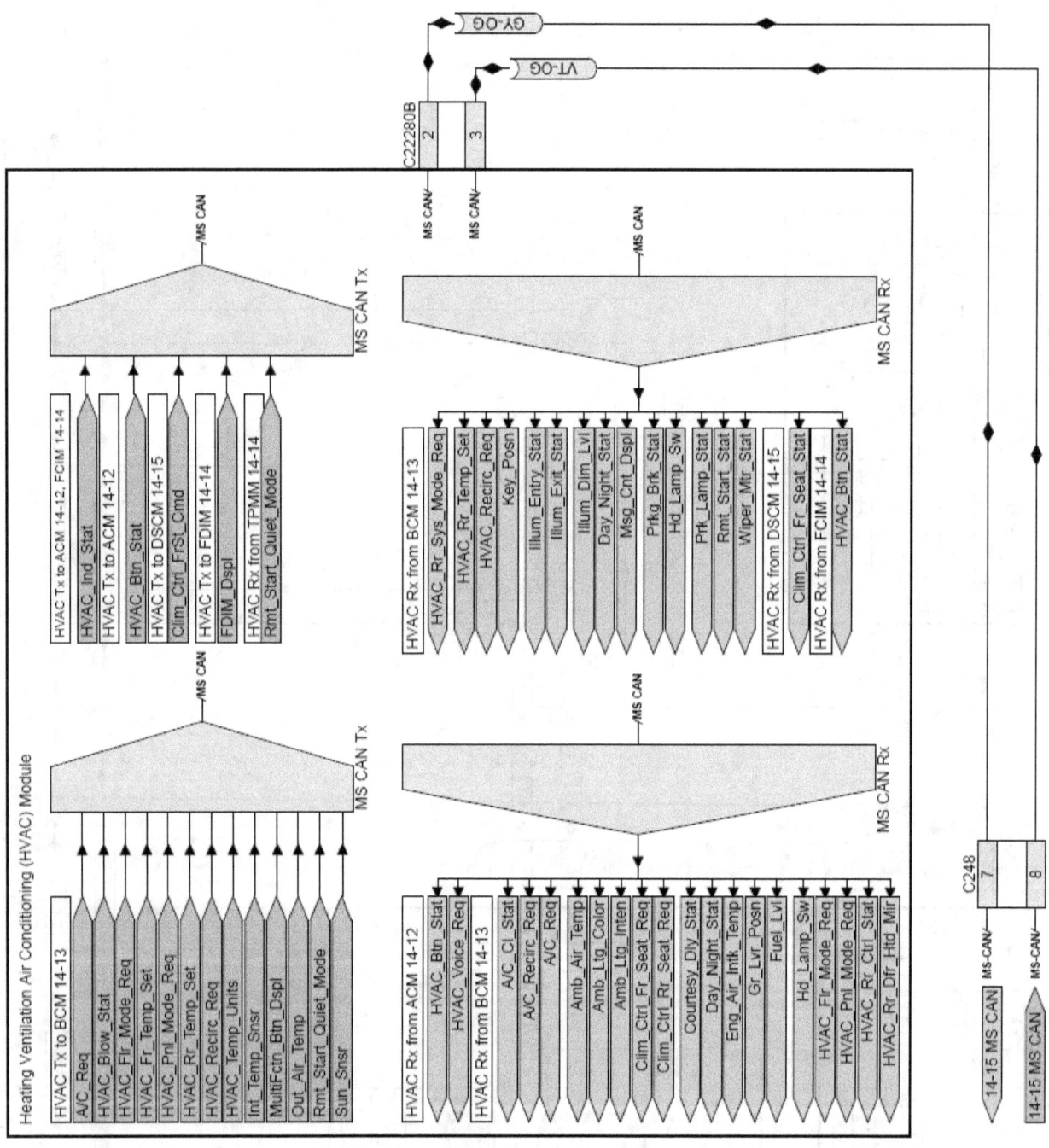

Instrument Panel Cluster (IPC) I-CAN 14-17

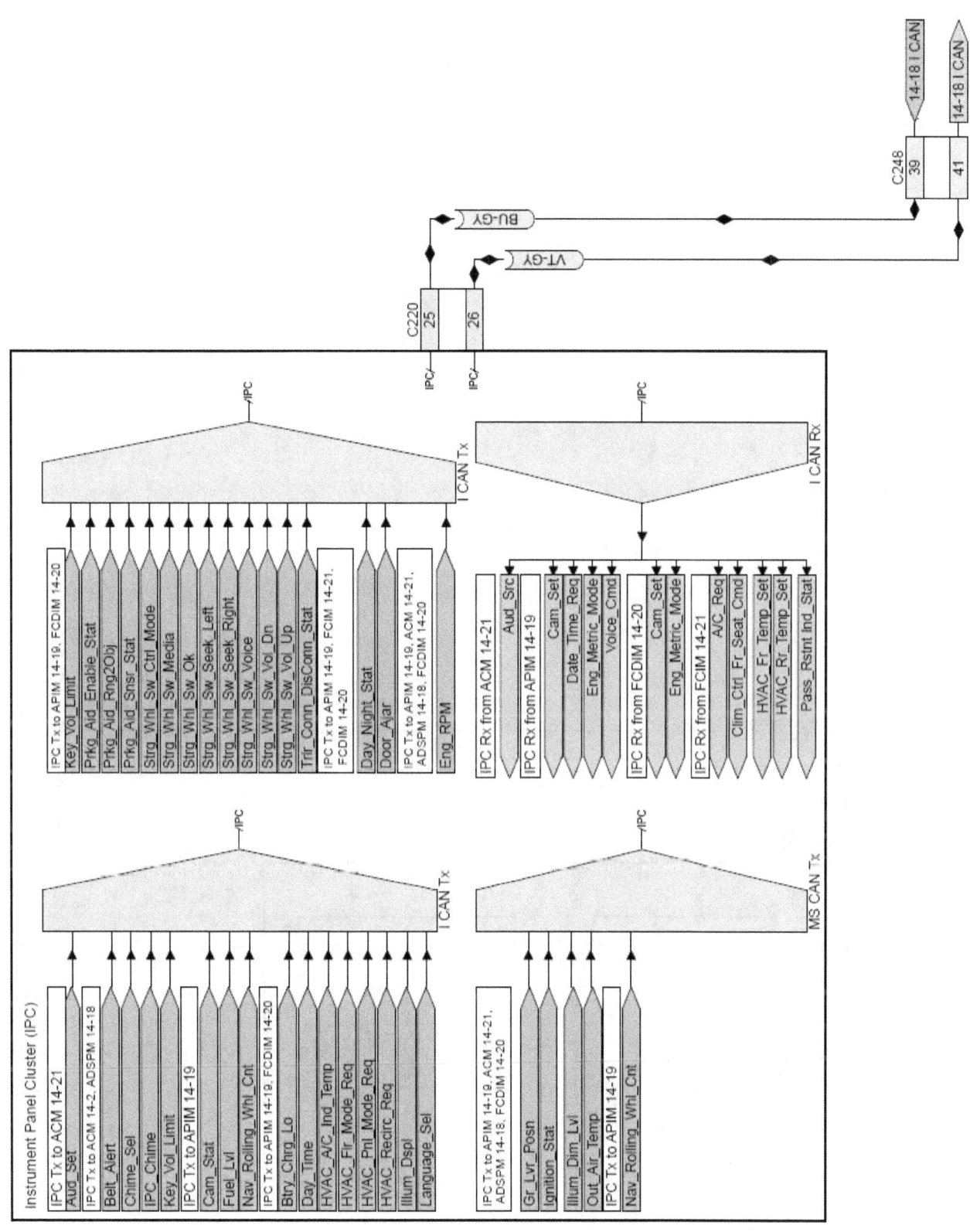

14-18 Audio Digital Signal Processing Module (ADSPM) I CAN

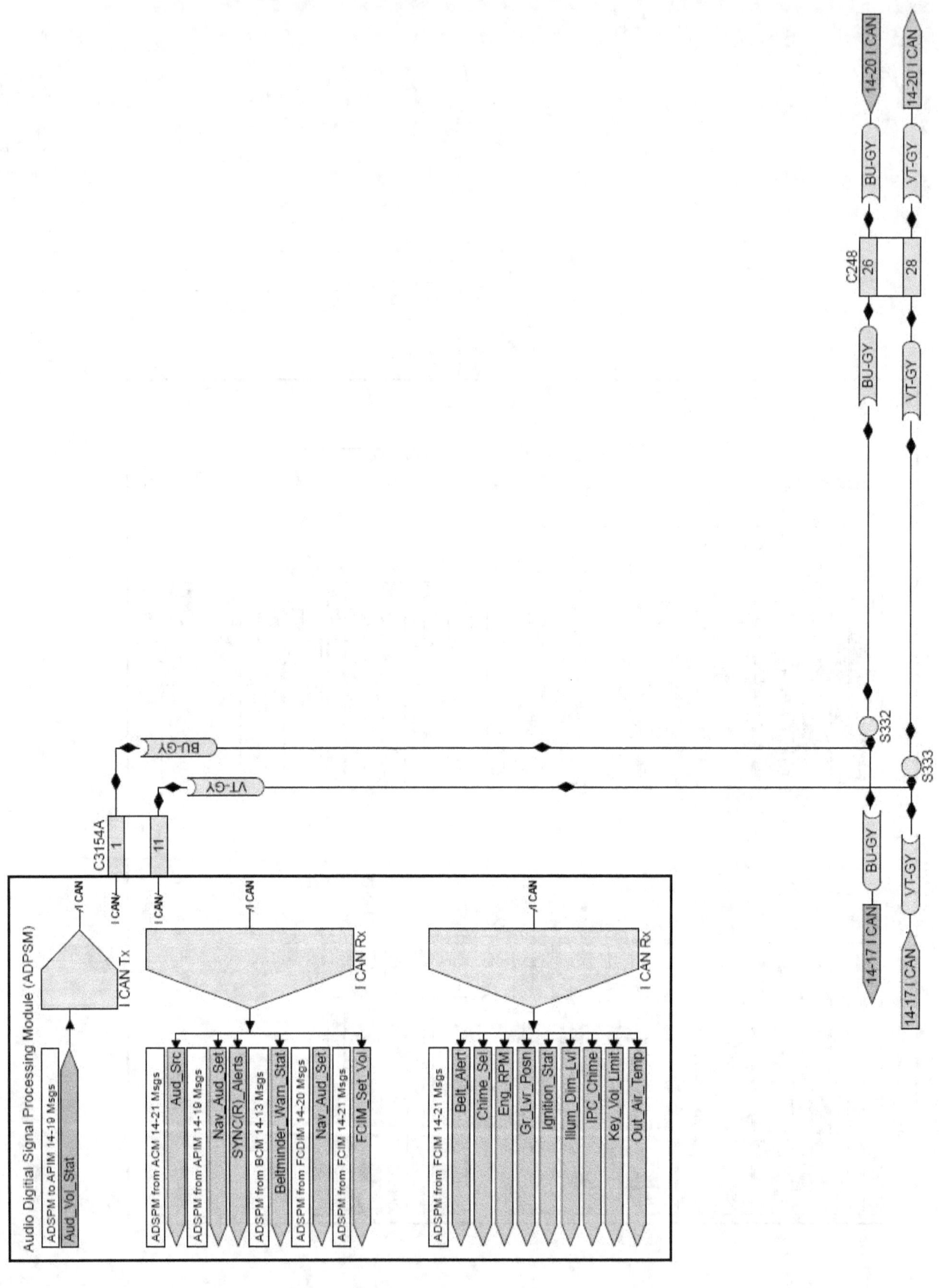

Accessory Protocol Interface Module (APIM) I-CAN 14-19

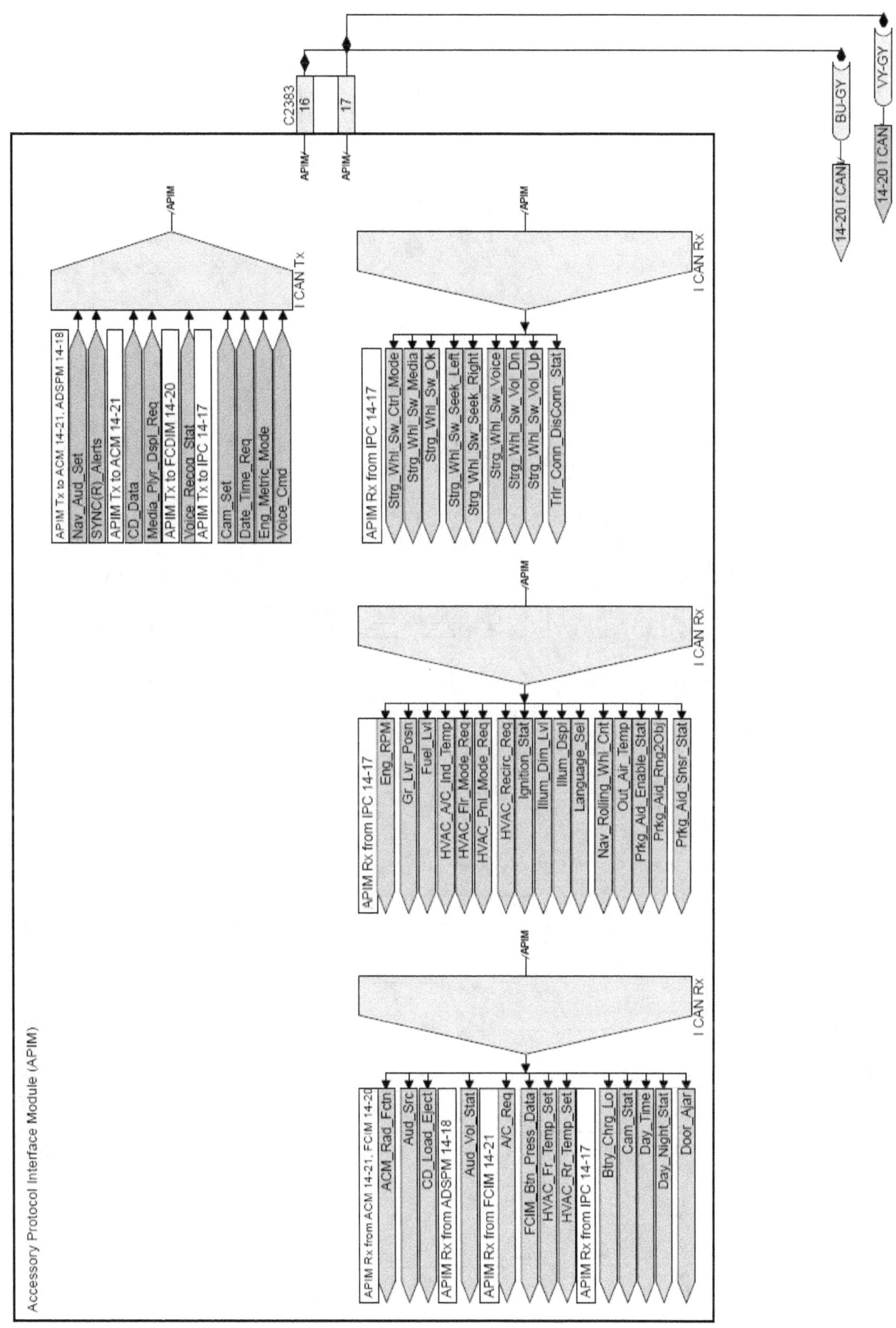

14-20 Front Controls Display Interface Module (FCDIM)

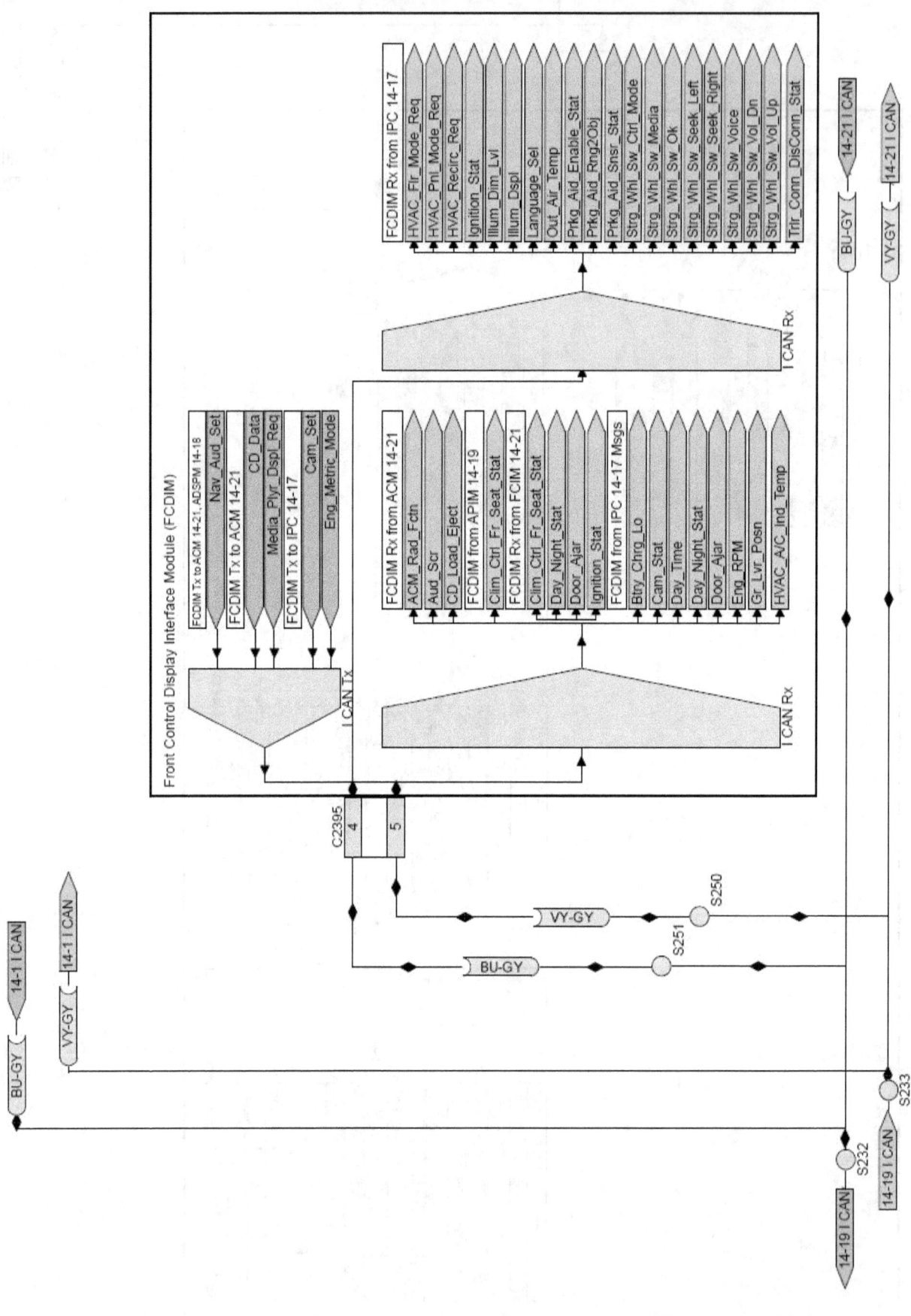

Audio Control Module (ACM) & Front Controls Interface Module (FCIM) 14-21

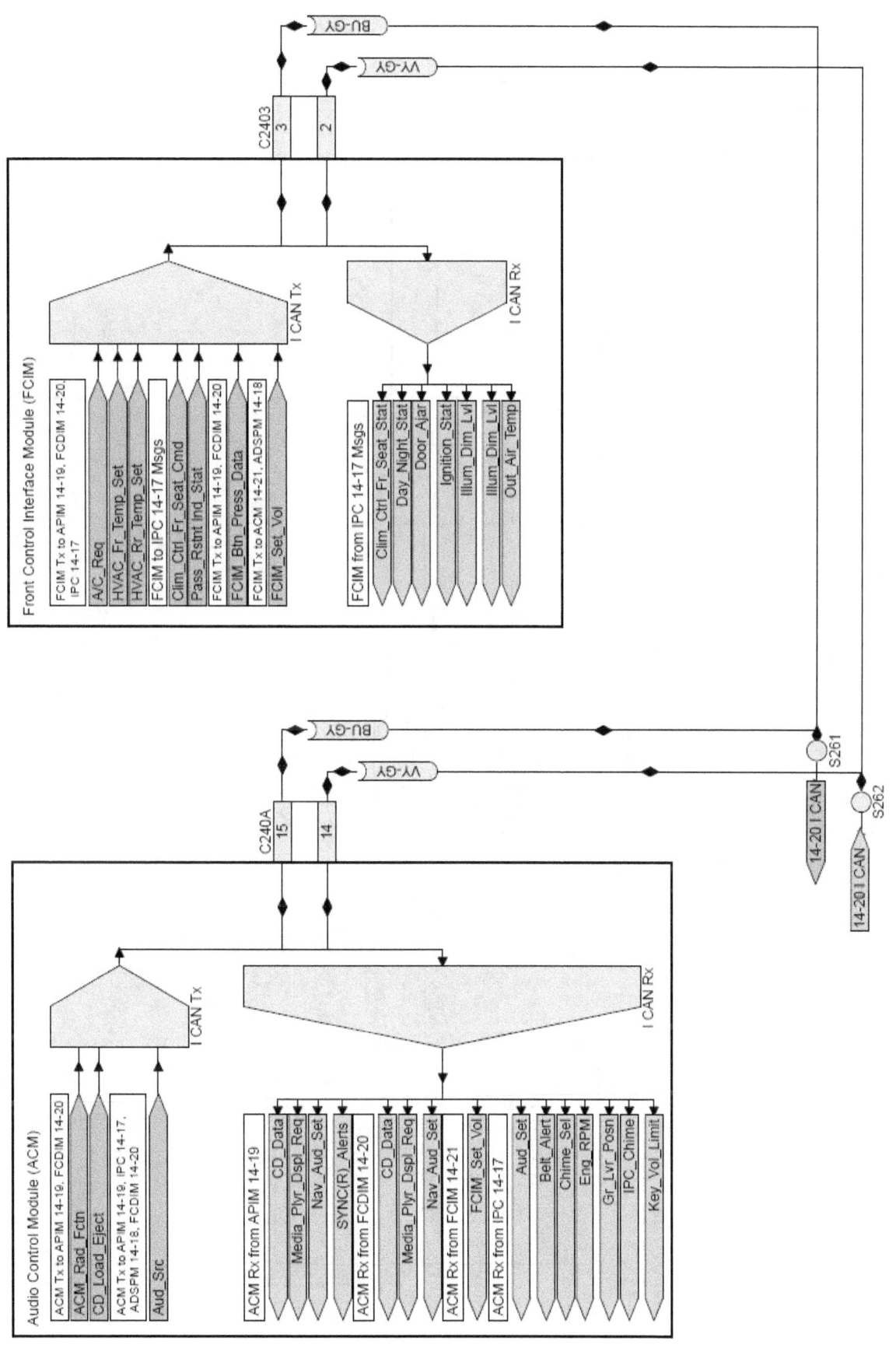

20-1 Starting System

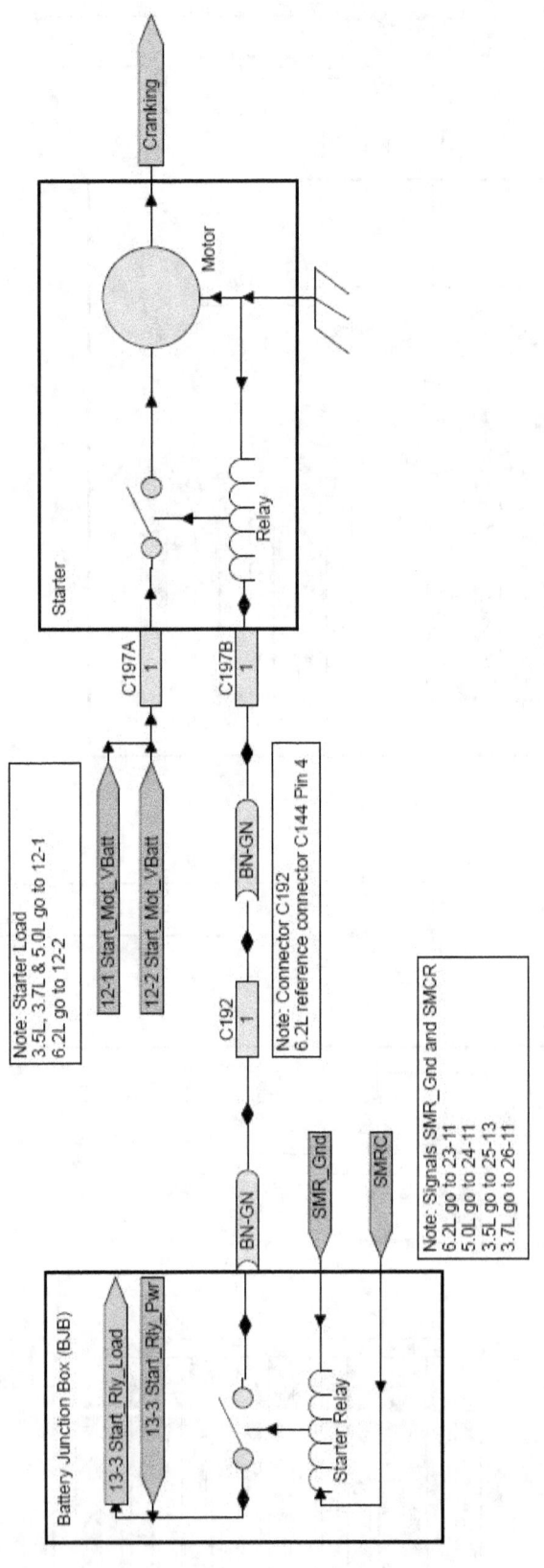

23 Powertrain Control Module (PCM) for 6.2L Engines
PCM for 6.2L Engines – Ignition 23-1

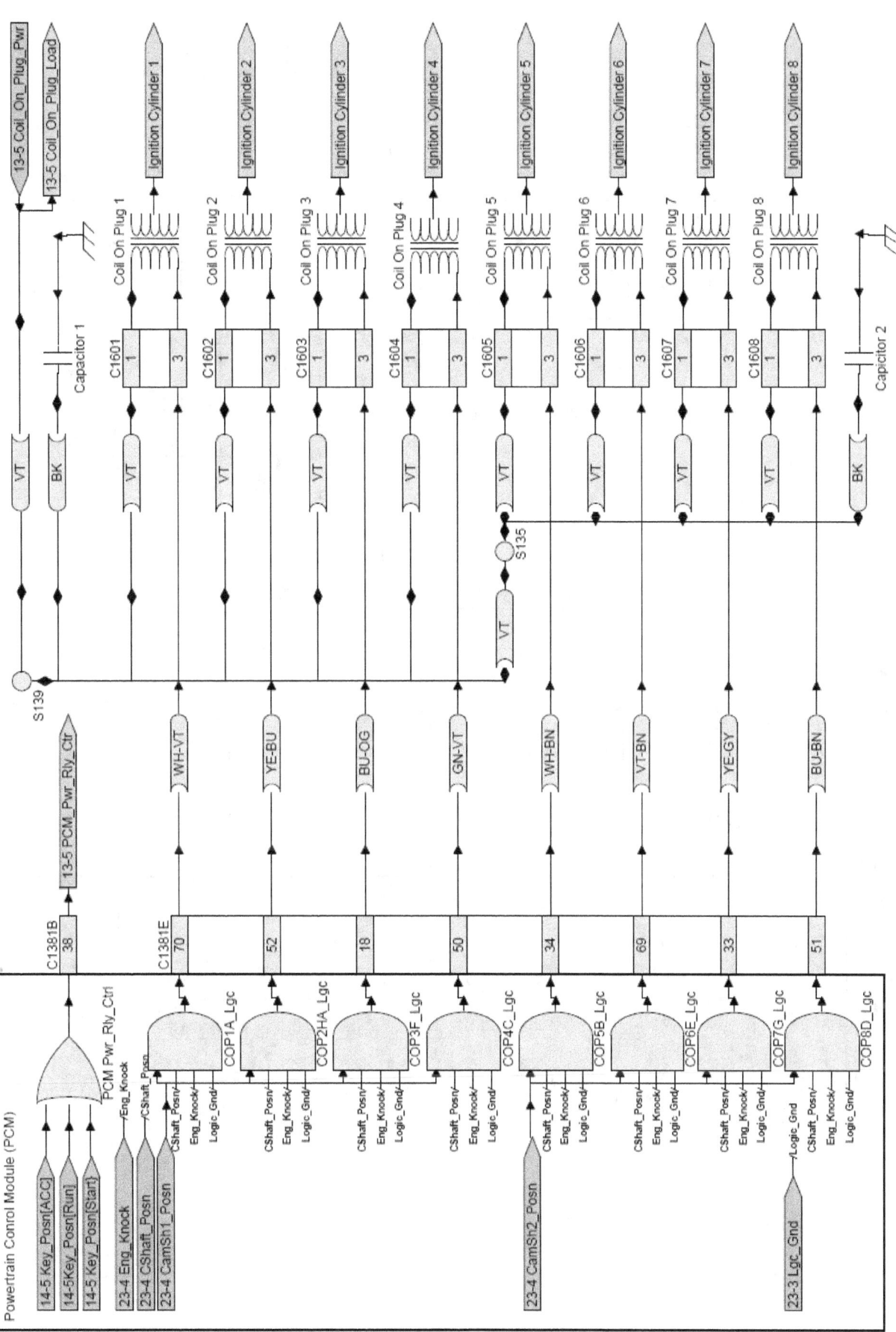

23-2 PCM for 6.2L Engines - Fuel Injection

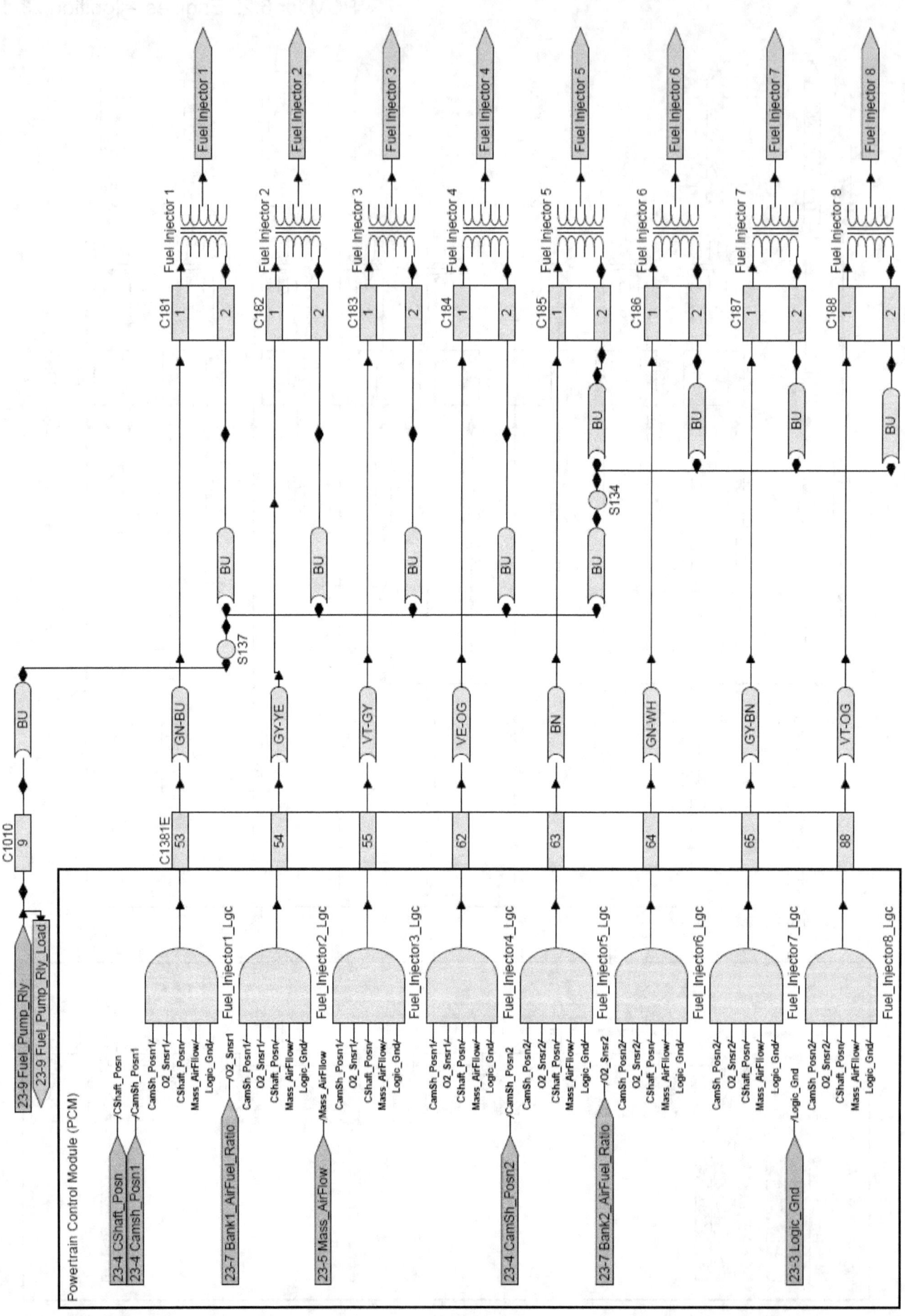

86

PCM for 6.2L Engines – Power & Gnd Inputs with EVAP Solenoid 23-3

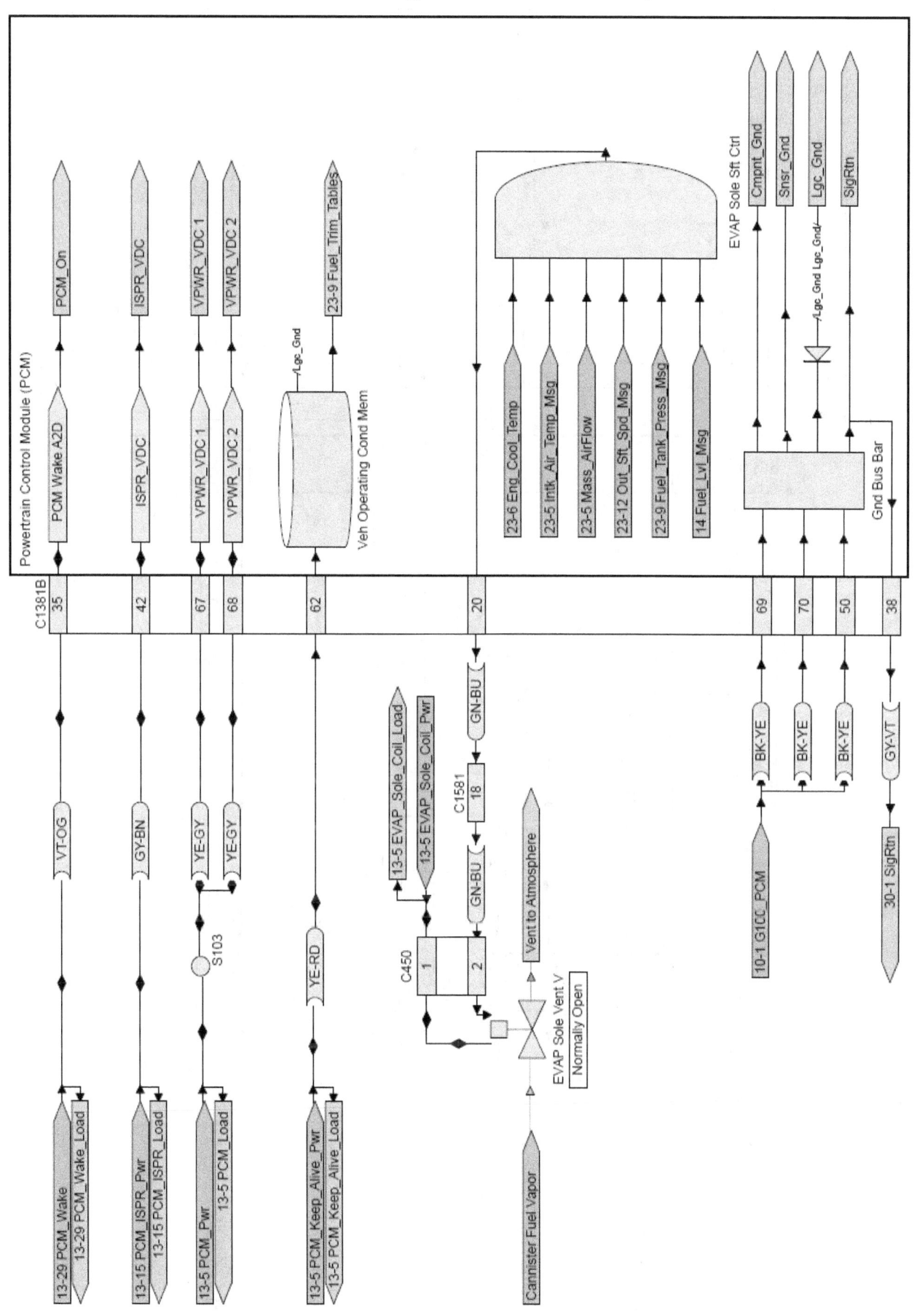

23-4 PCM for 6.2L Engines – Knock, Cam Shaft & Crank Shaft Sensors

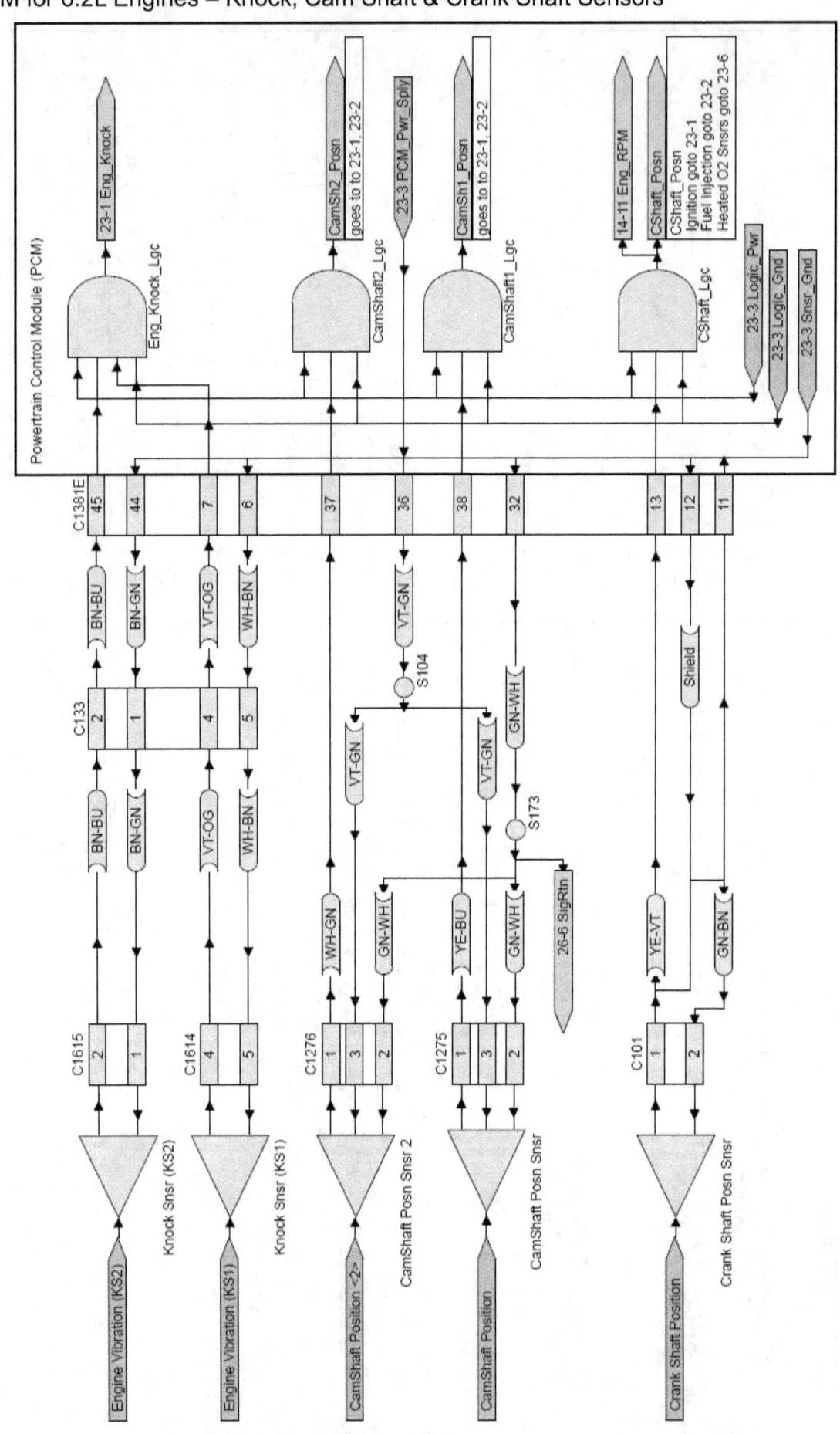

PCM for 6.2L Engines – Air Sensors 23-5

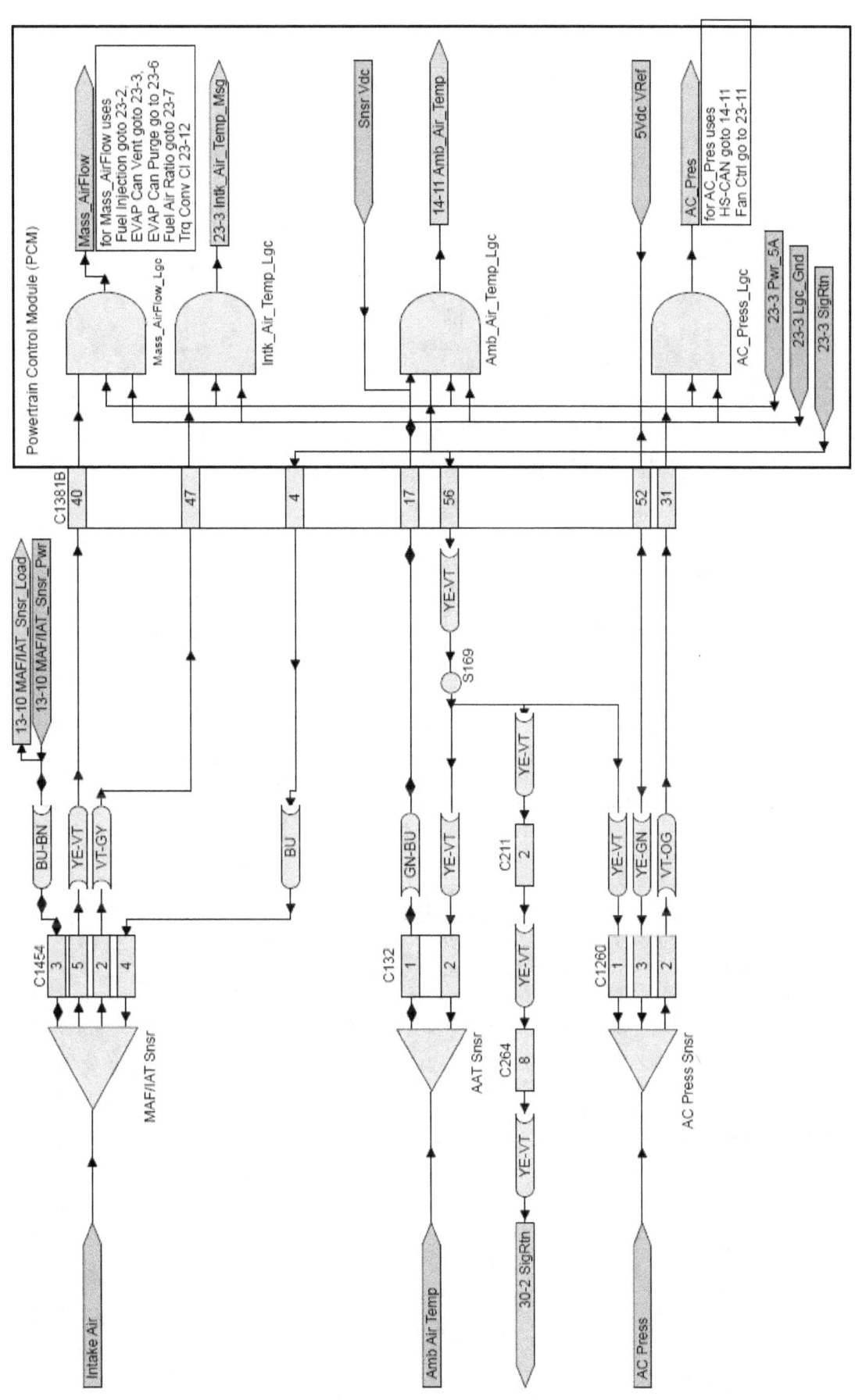

23-6 PCM for 6.2L Engines – Evap Can Prg V, VCT1, VCT2, & Cyl Head Temp Snsr

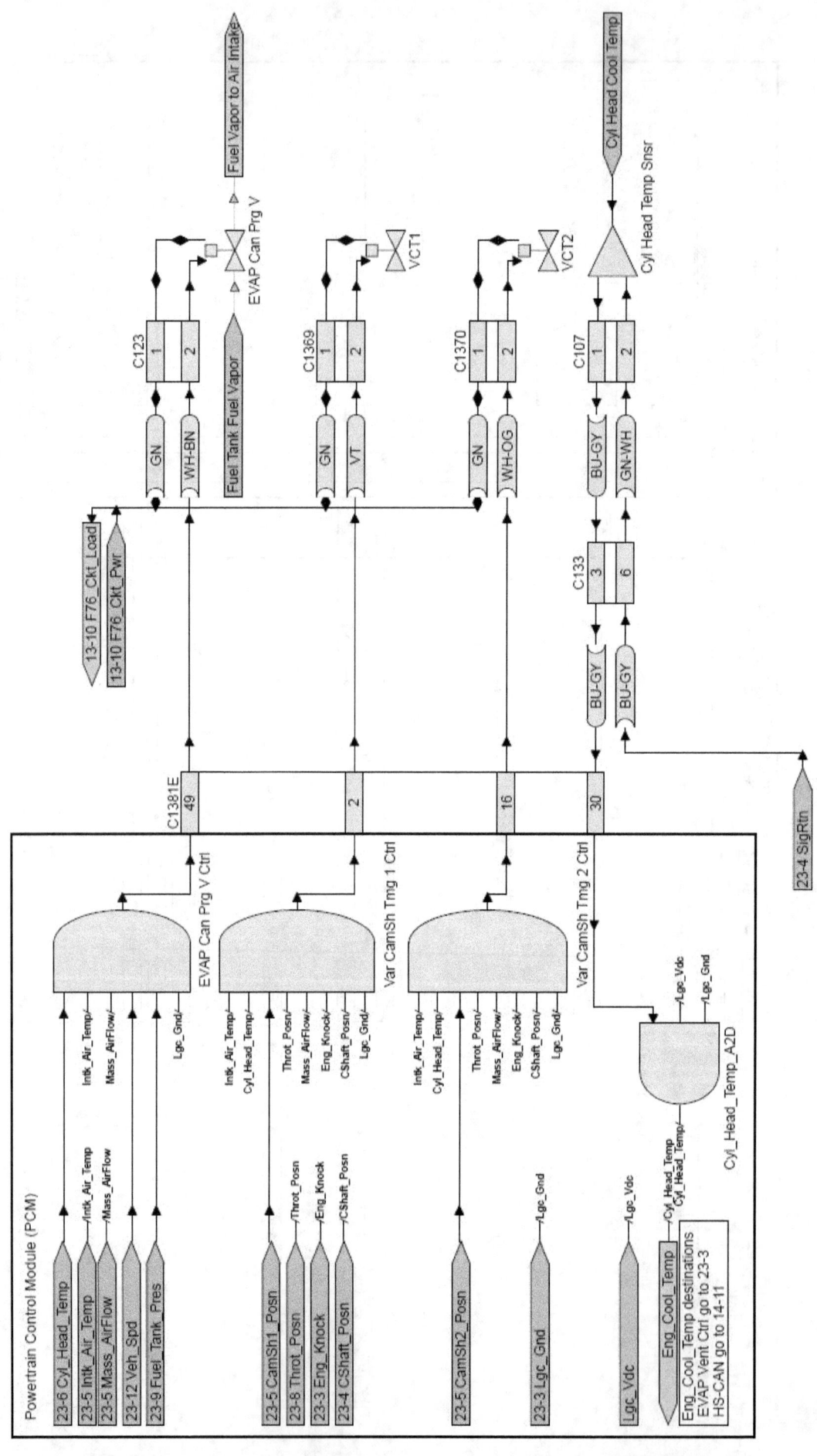

PCM for 6.2L Engines – O2 Sensors **23-7**

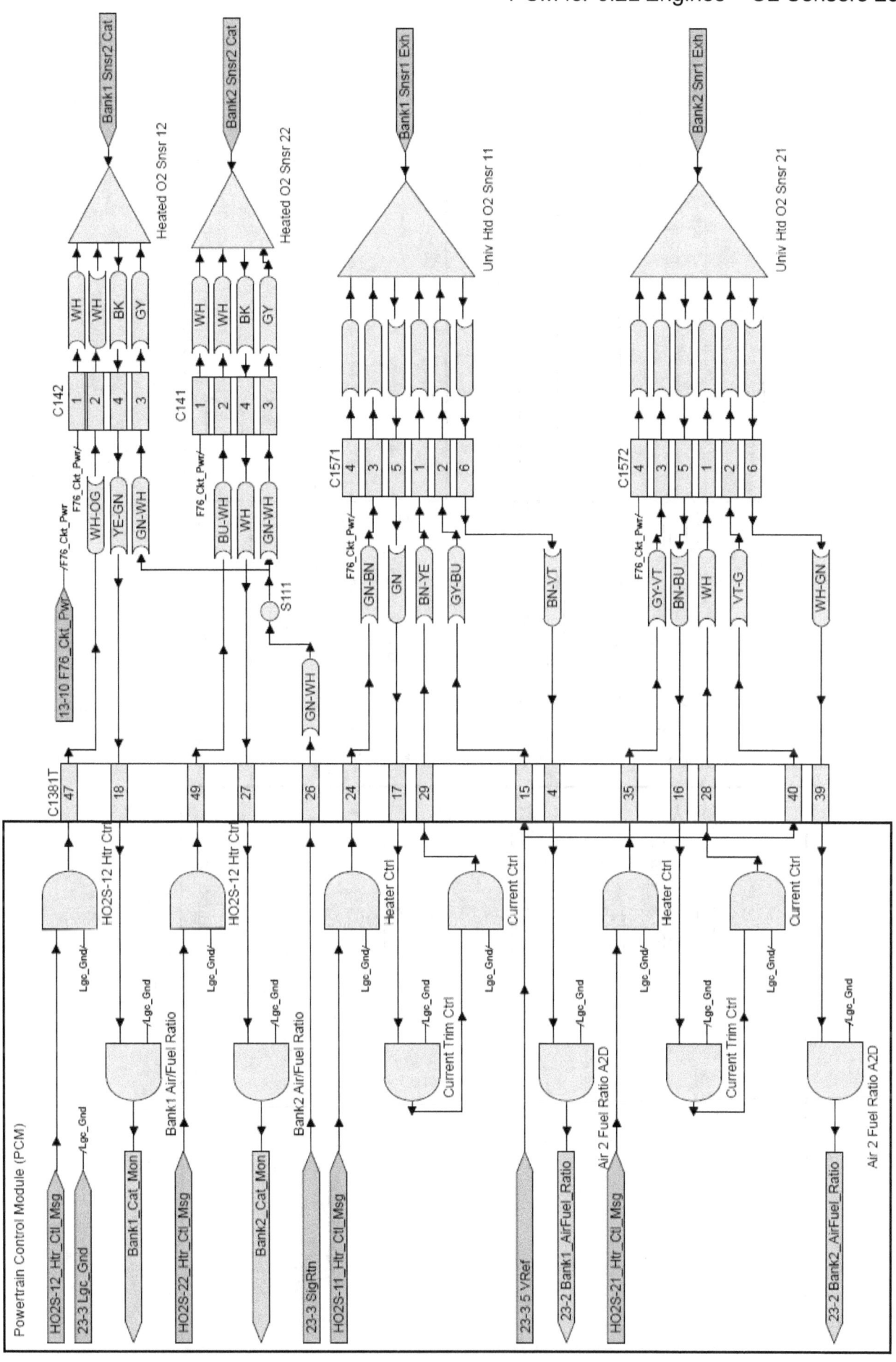

23-8 PCM for 6.2L Engines – Electronic Throttle & Accelerator Pedal Position Sensor

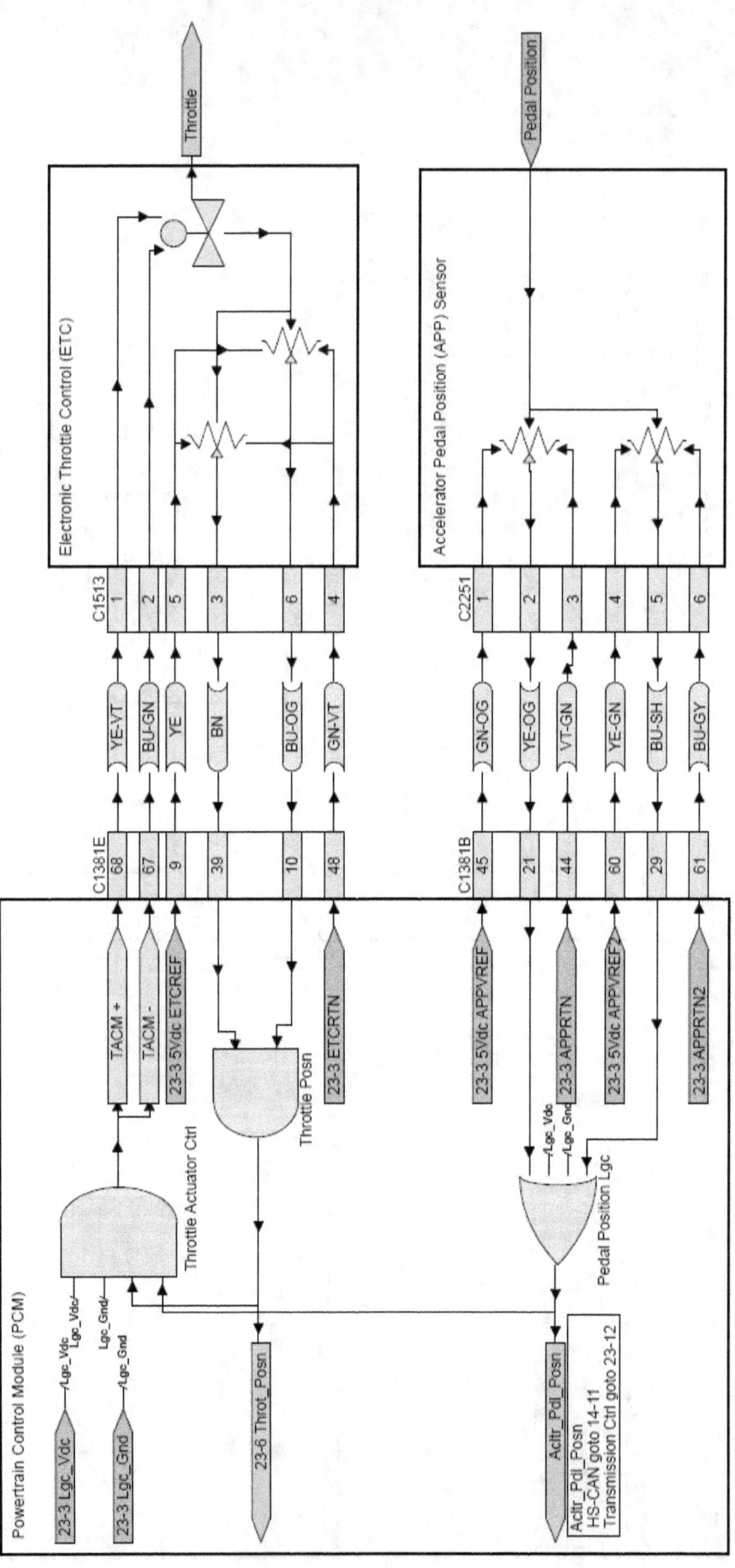

PCM for 6.2L Engines – Fuel Control 23-9

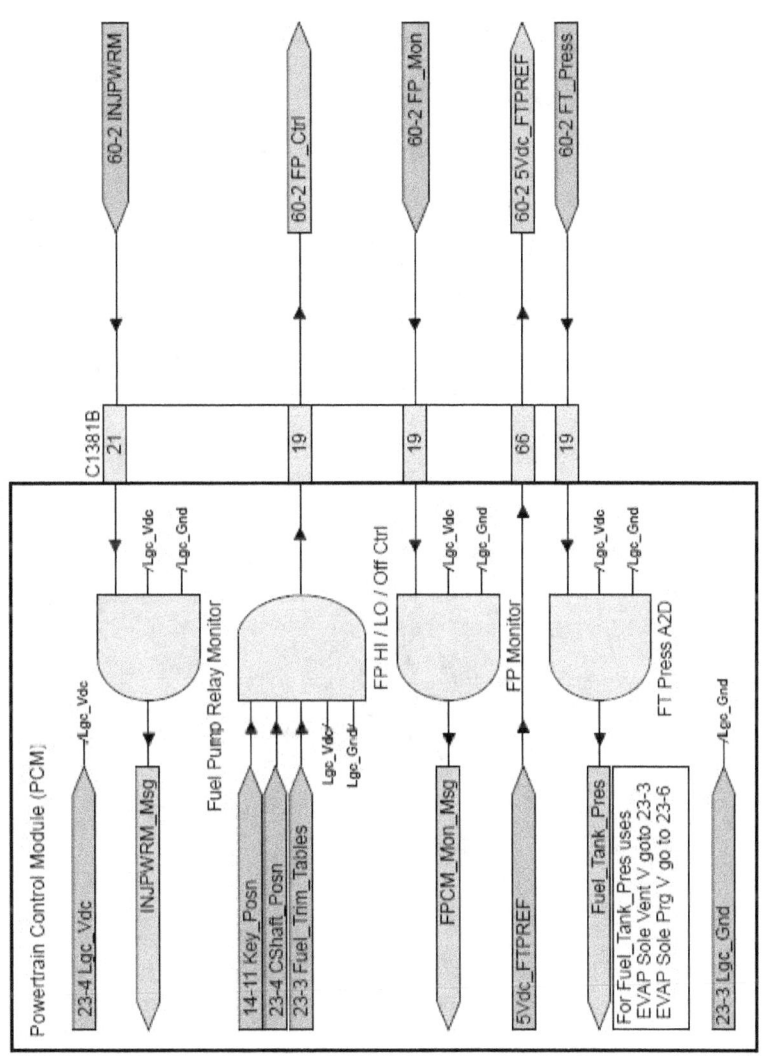

23-10 PCM for 6.2L Engines – Brake Control

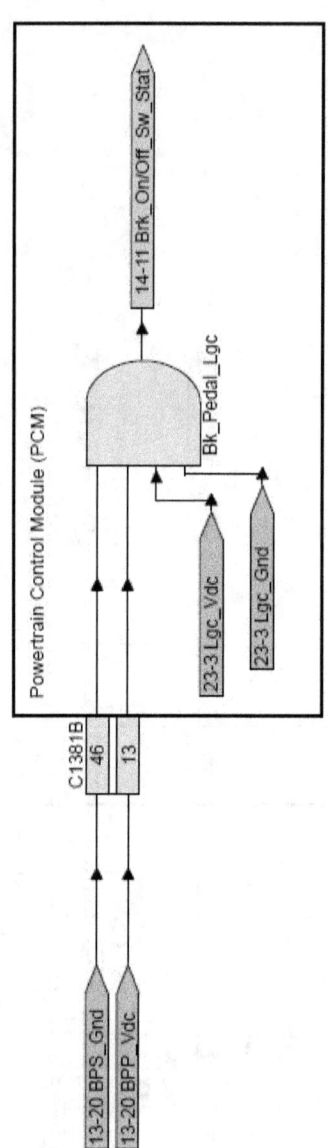

PCM for 6.2L Engines – CAN BUS, I/O & Lo Oil Press Sw 23-11

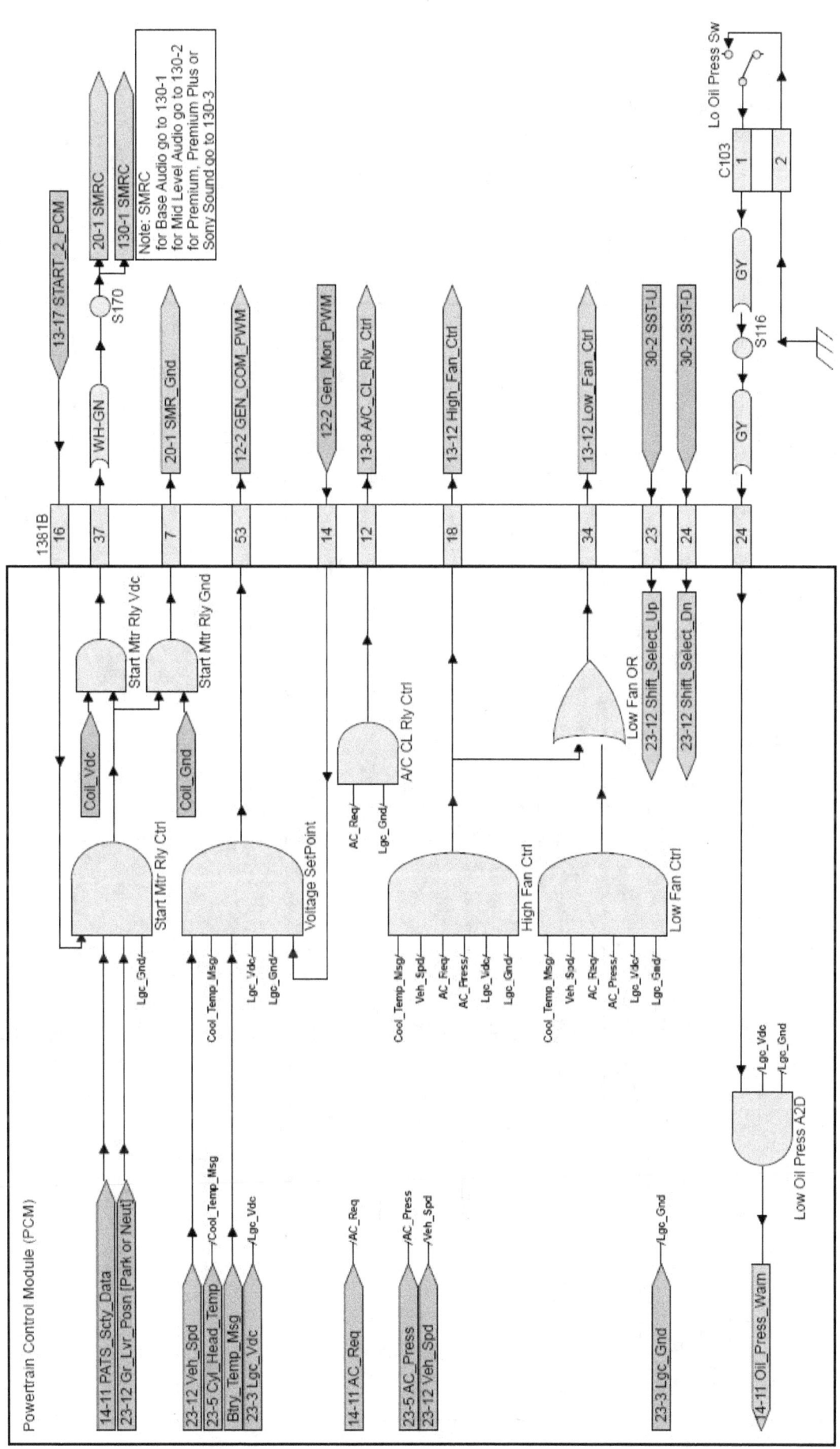

23-12 PCM for 6.2L Engines – Transmission Control

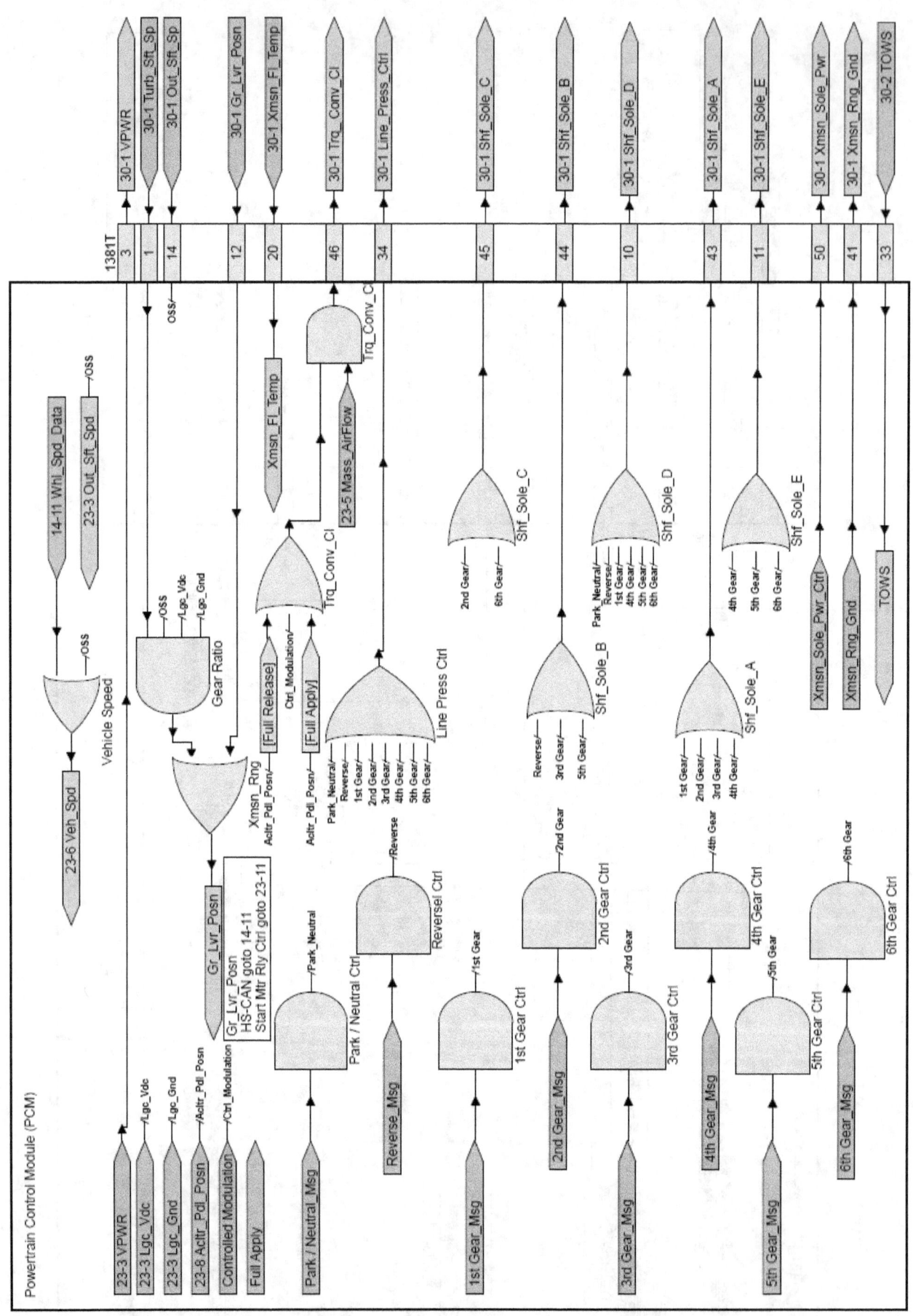

24 Powertrain Control Module (PCM) for 5.0L Engines
Powertrain Control Module for 5.0L Engines – Ignition 24-1

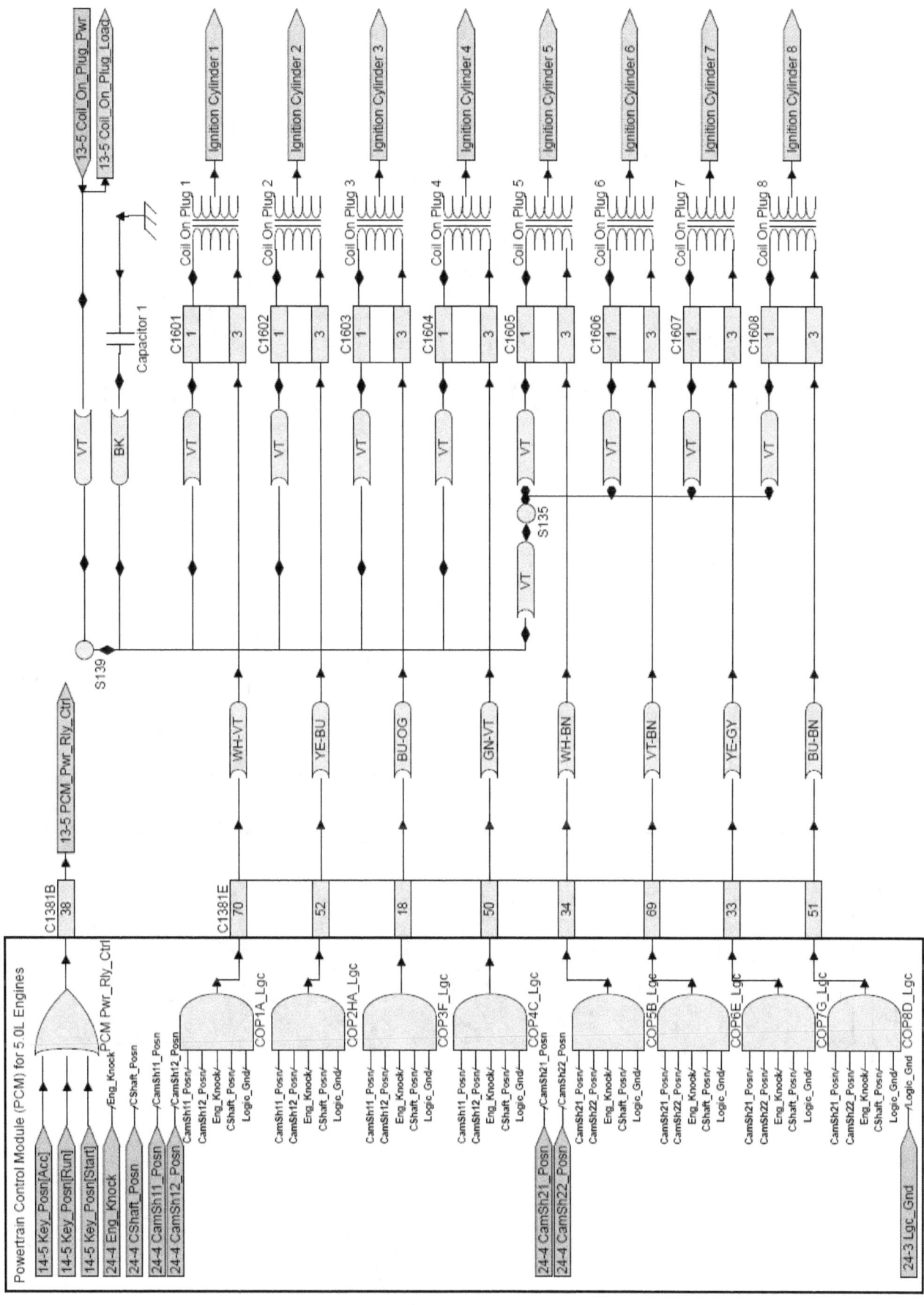

24-2 Powertrain Control Module for 5.0L Engines – Fuel Injection

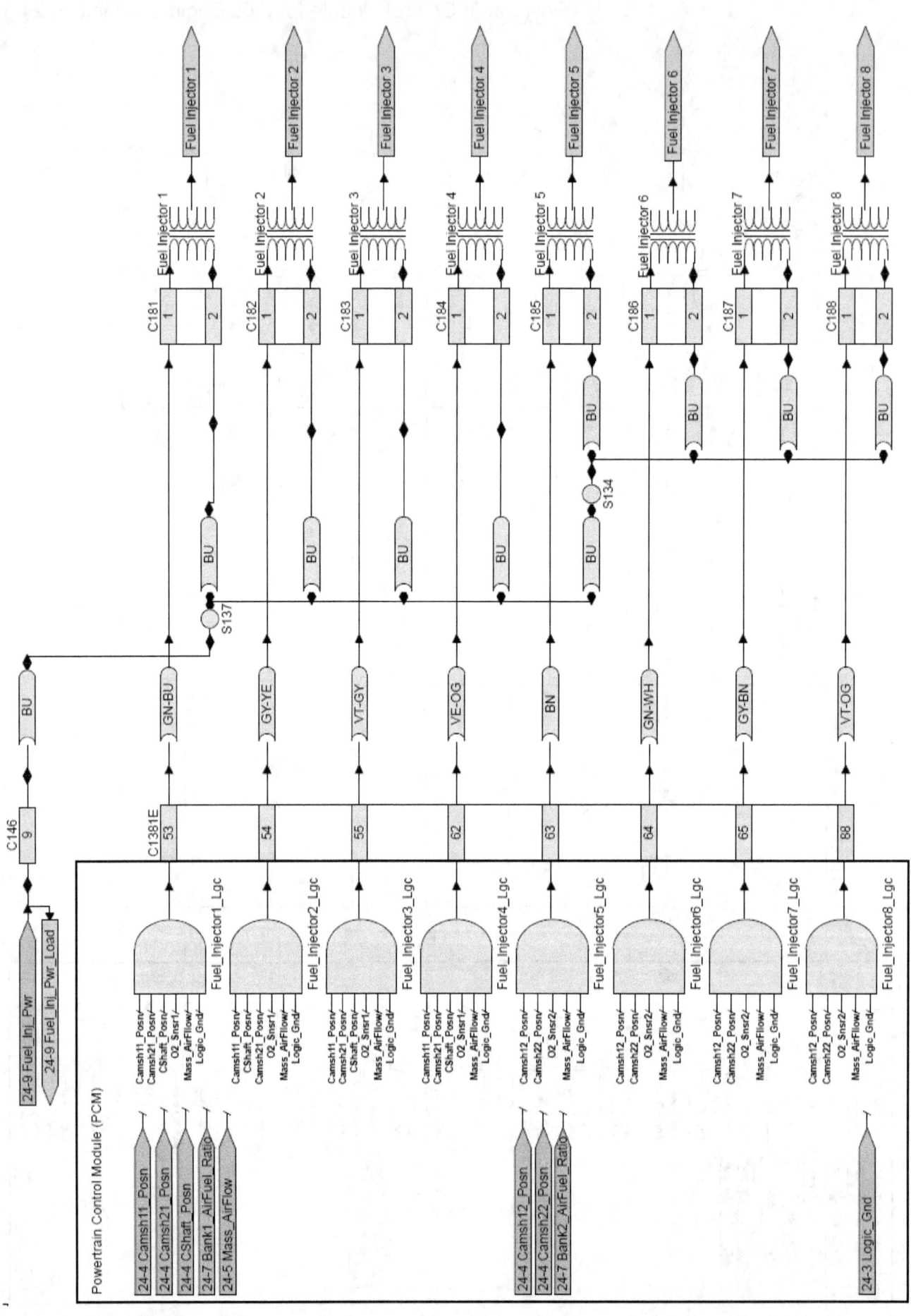

PCM for 5.0L Engines – PCM Power, Gnd & EVAP Sole 24-3

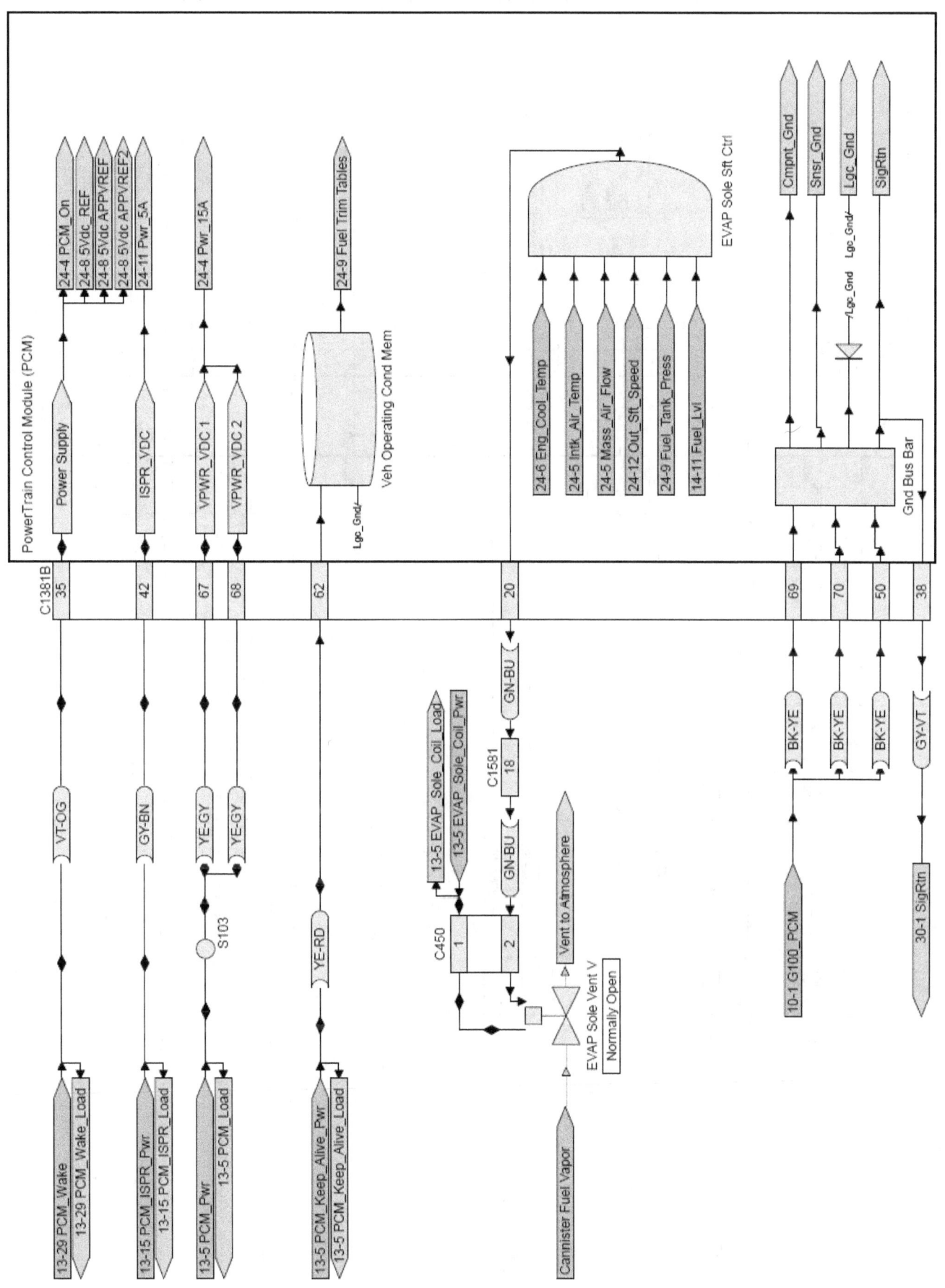

24-4 PCM for 5.0L Engines – Knock, Cam Shaft, & Cam Shaft Sensors

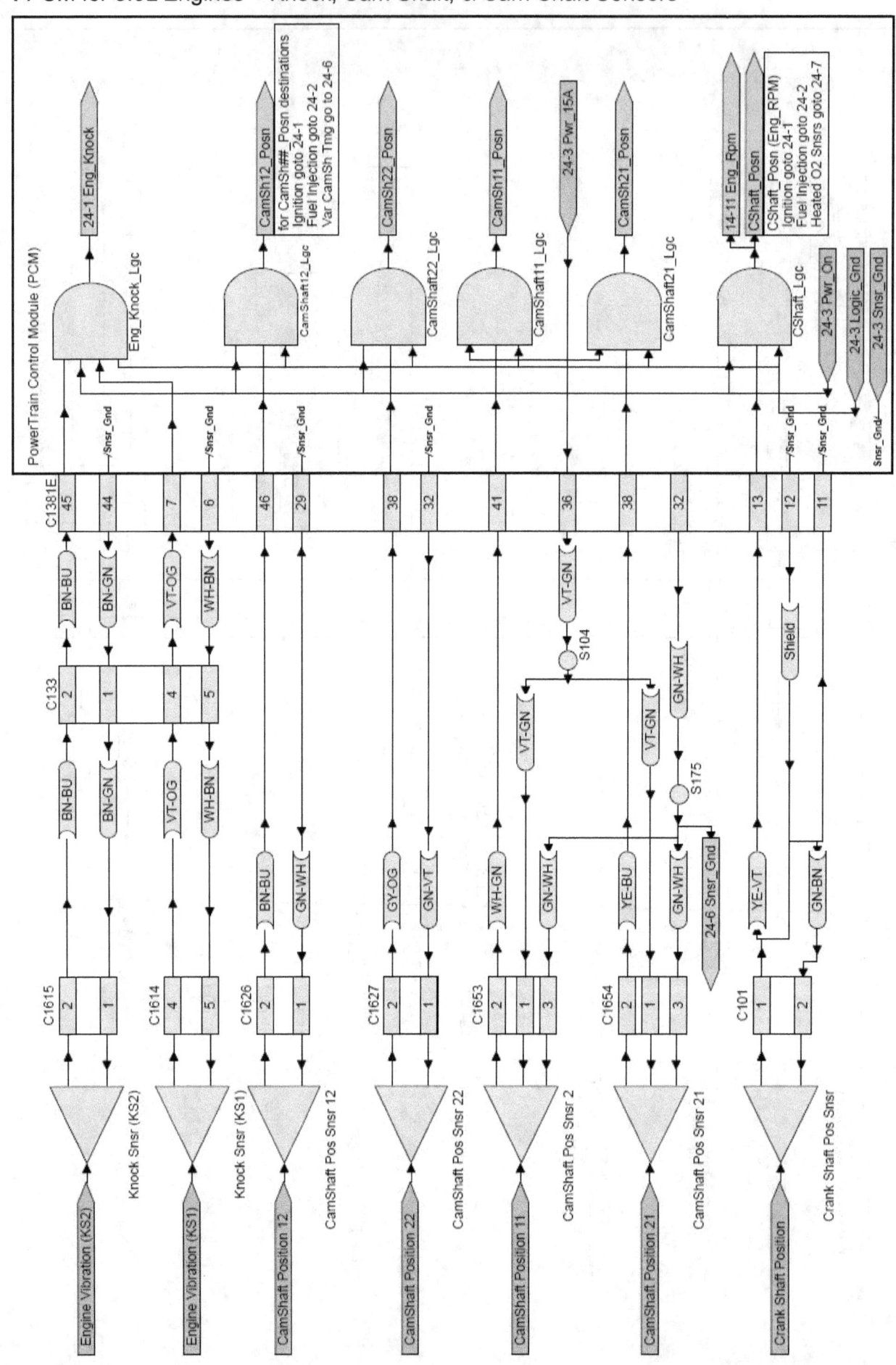

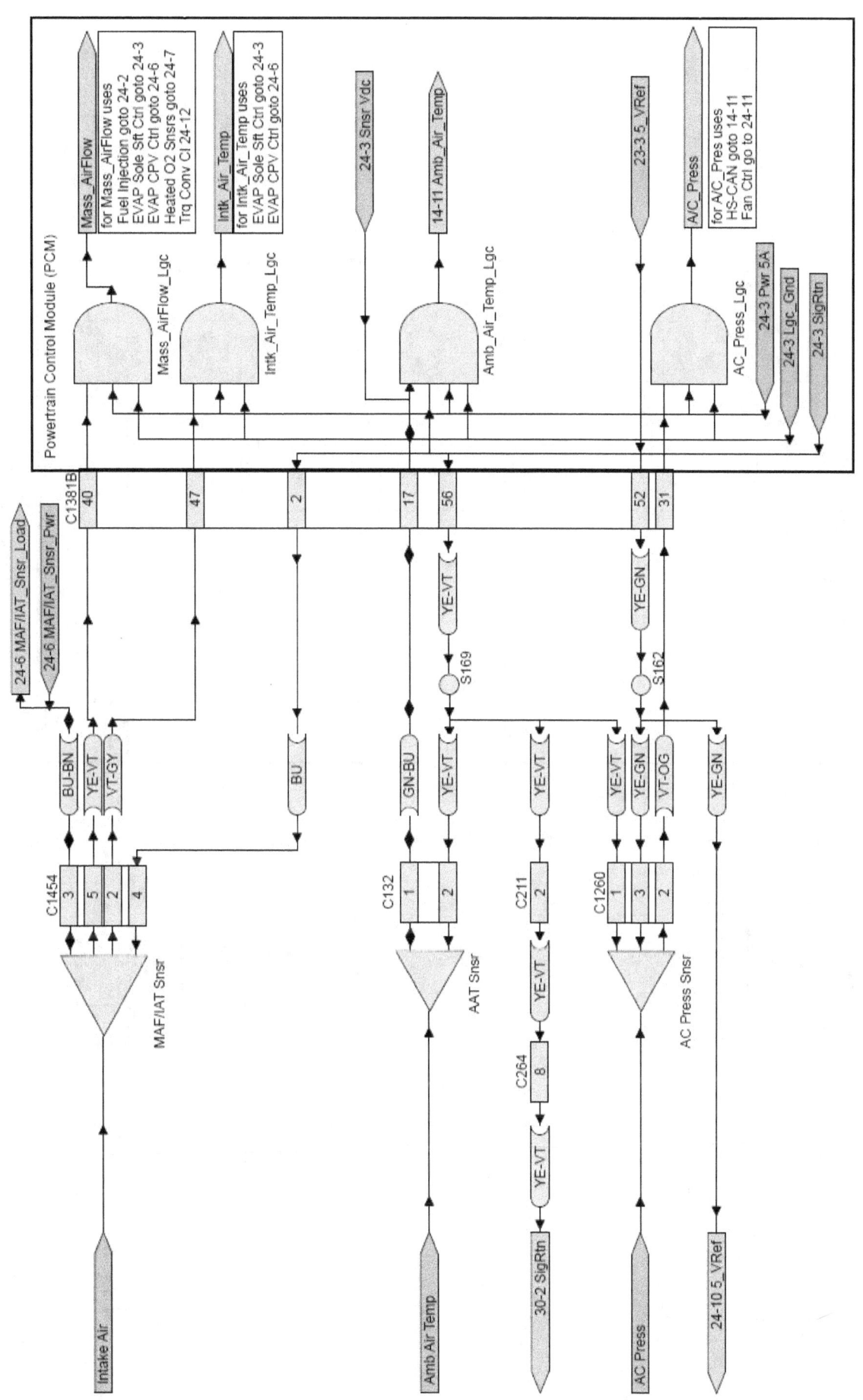

24-6 PCM for 5.0L Engines – EVAP & VCT Sole, Cyl Head Temp and Lo Oil Level Snsrs

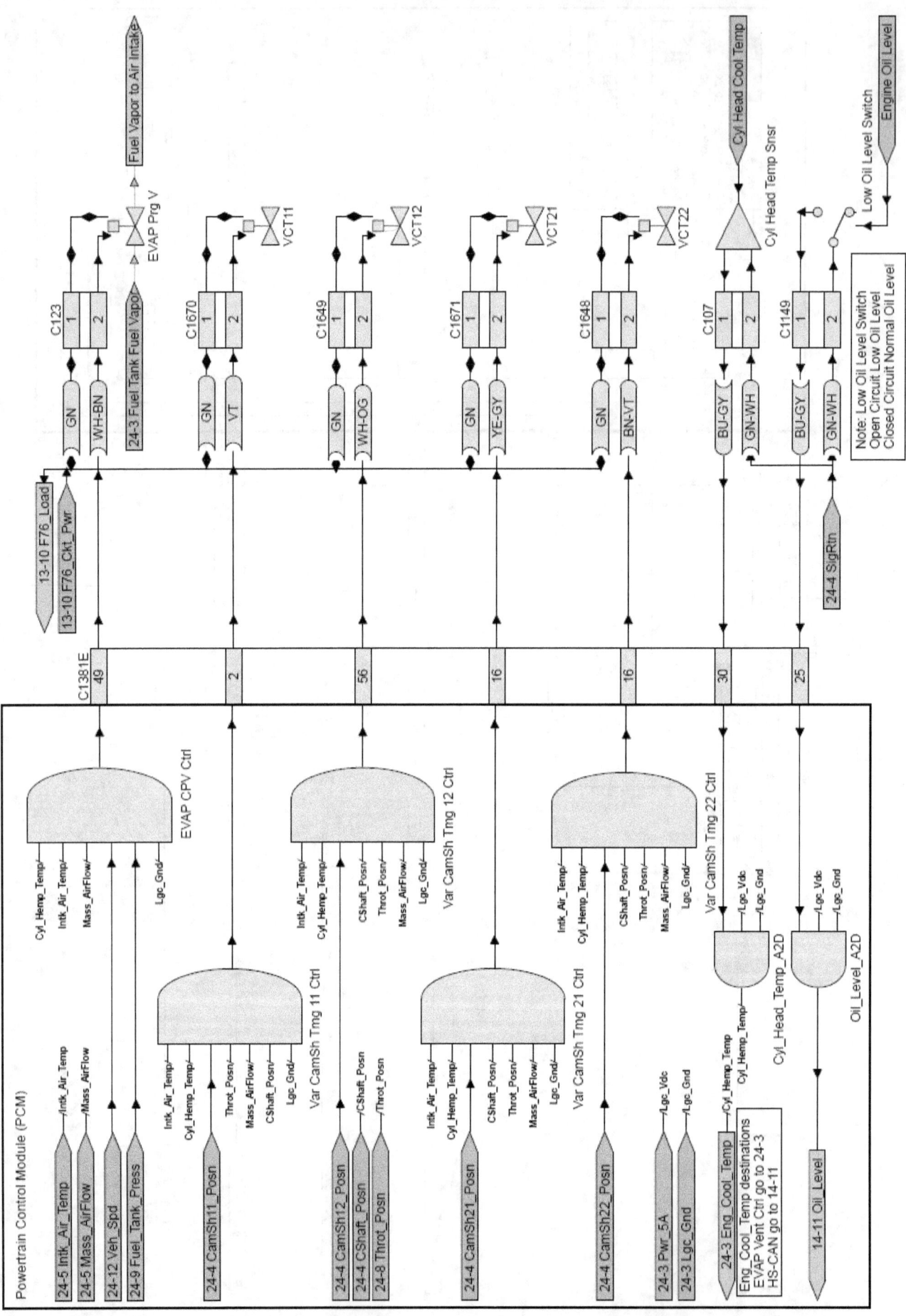

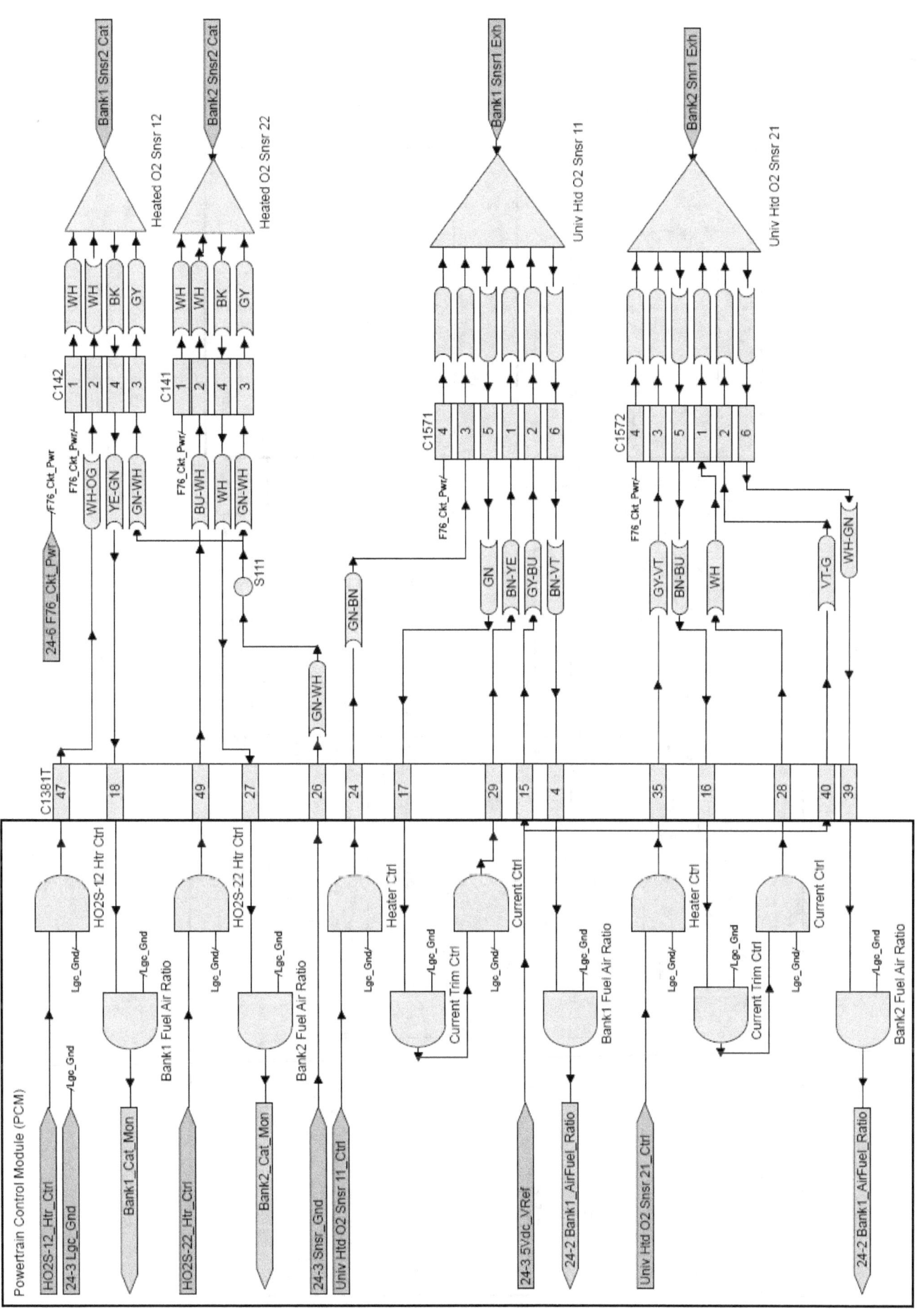

24-8 PCM for 5.0L Engines – Electronic Throttle & Accelerator Pedal Position Sensor

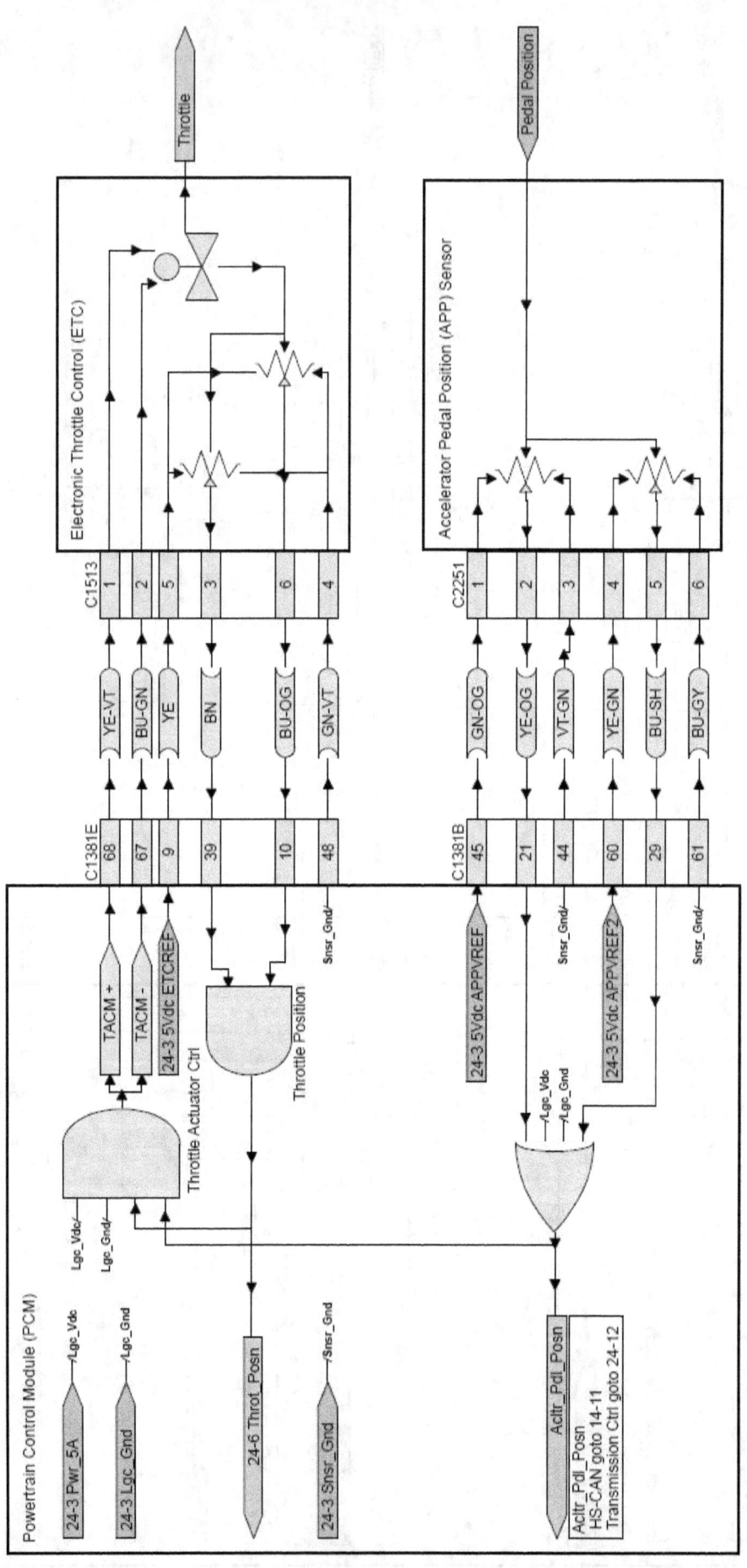

PCM for 5.0L Engines – Fuel Control 24-9

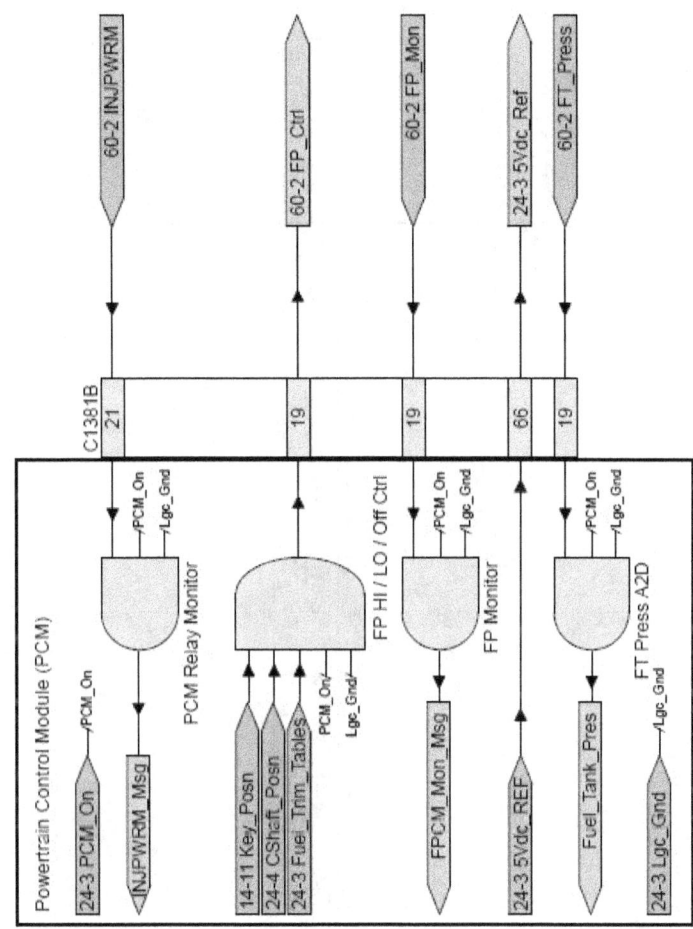

24-10 PCM for 5.0L Engines – Generator Current Snsr

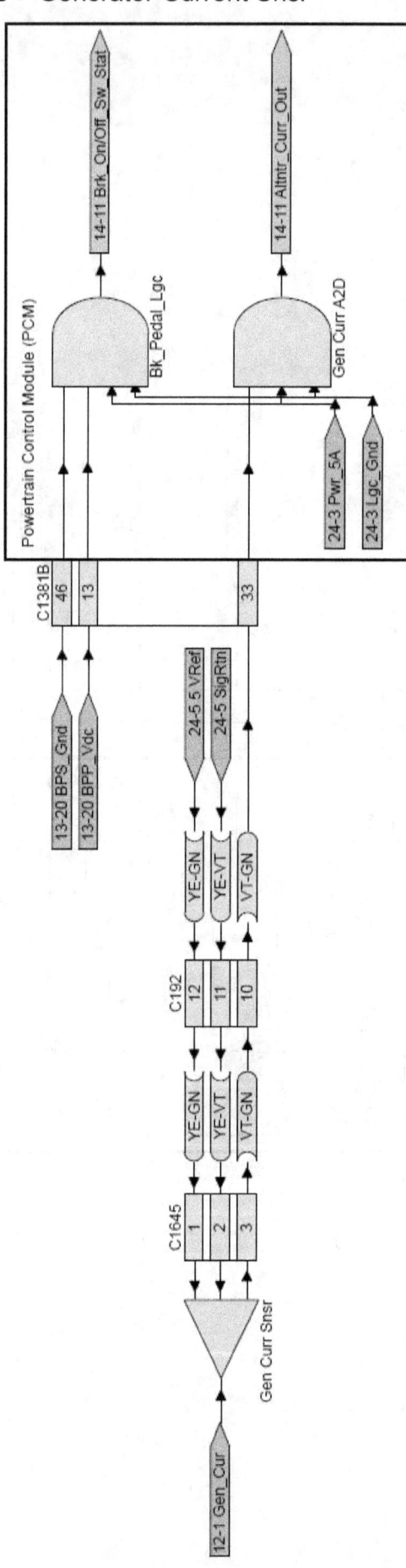

PCM for 5.0L Engines – CAN BUS, I/O & Lo Oil Press Sw 24-11

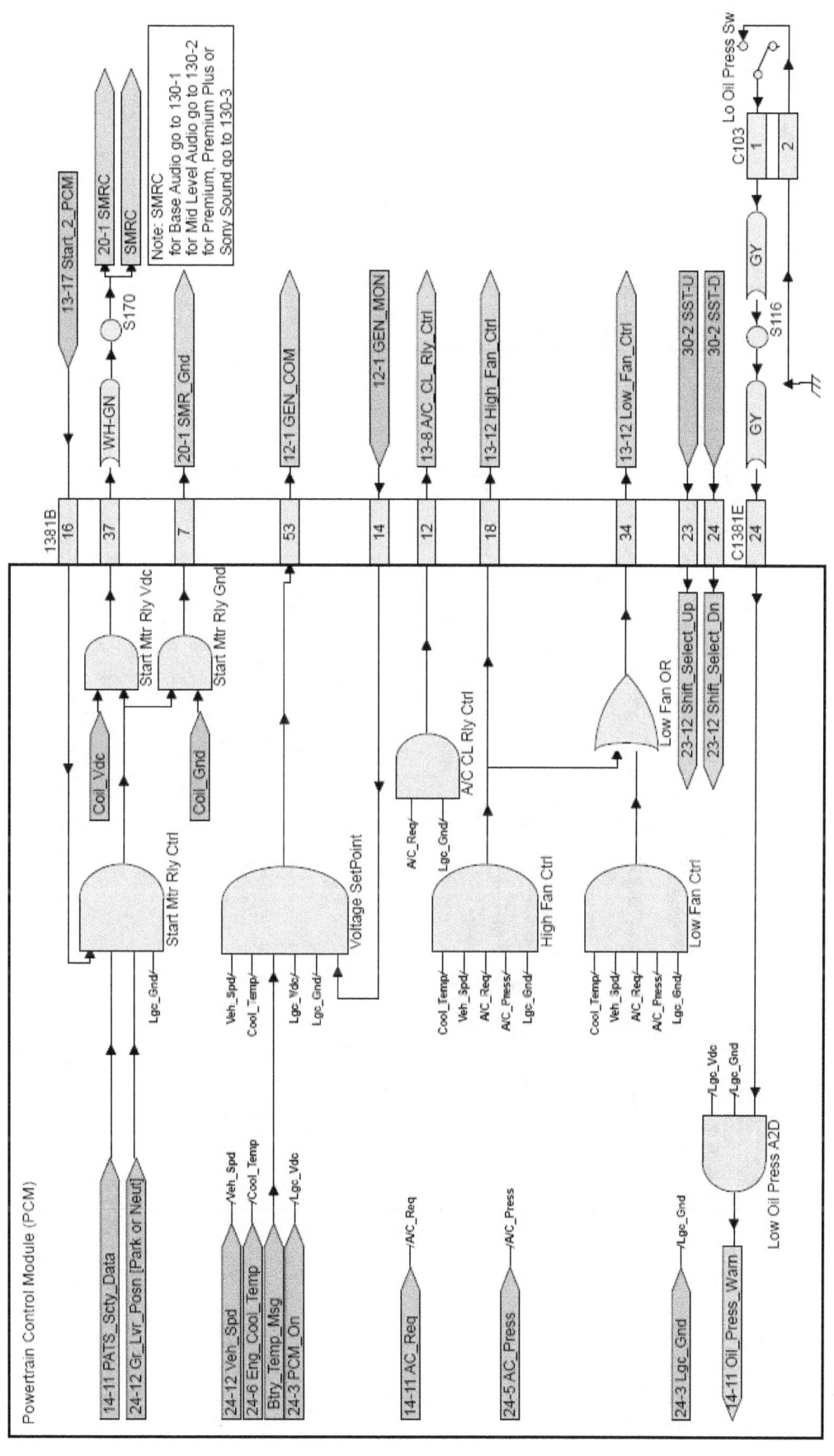

107

24-12 Powertrain Control Module for 5.0L Engines – Transmission Control

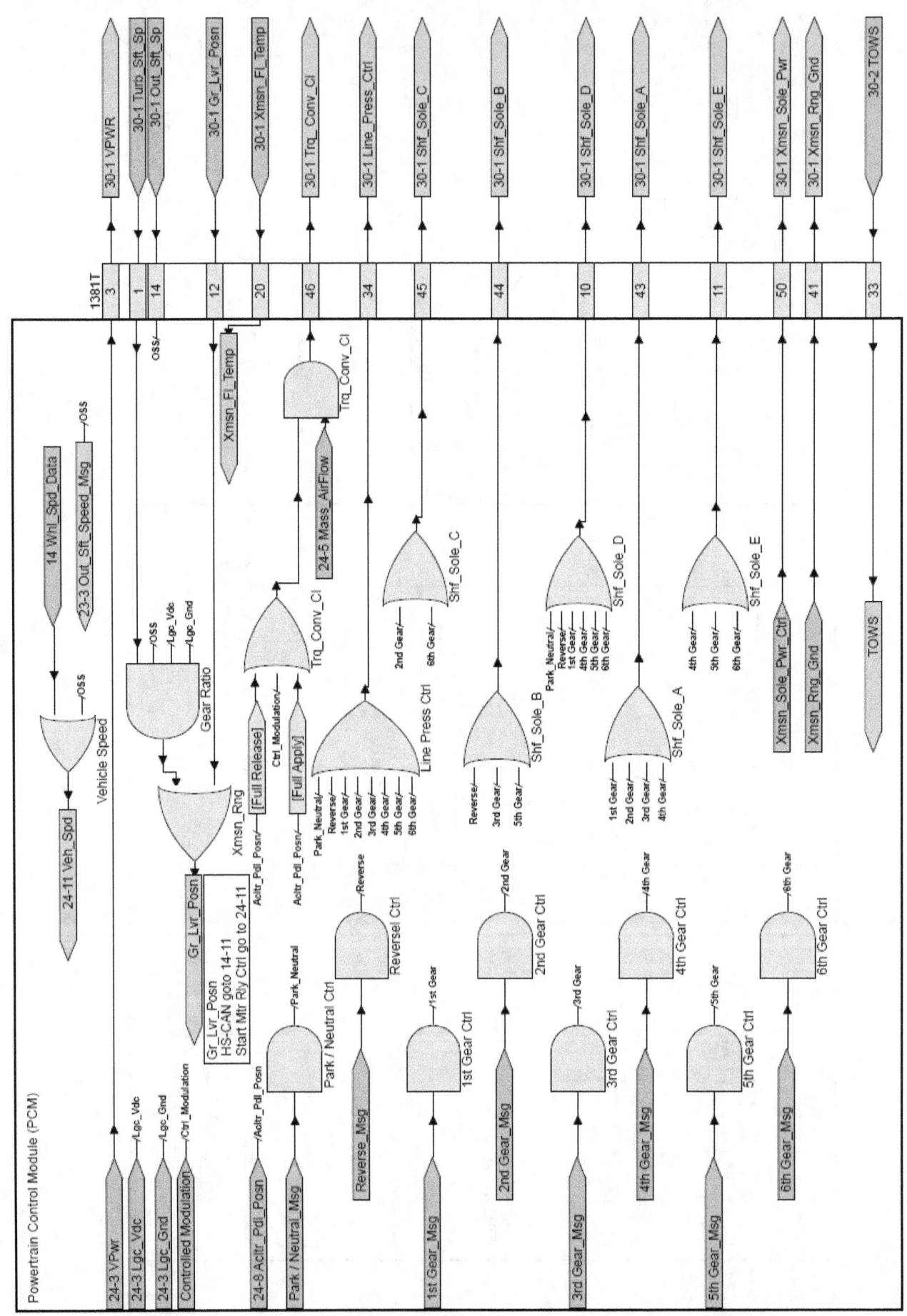

108

25 Powertrain Control Module (PCM) for 3.5L Engines
PCM for 3.5L Engines – Ignition 25-1

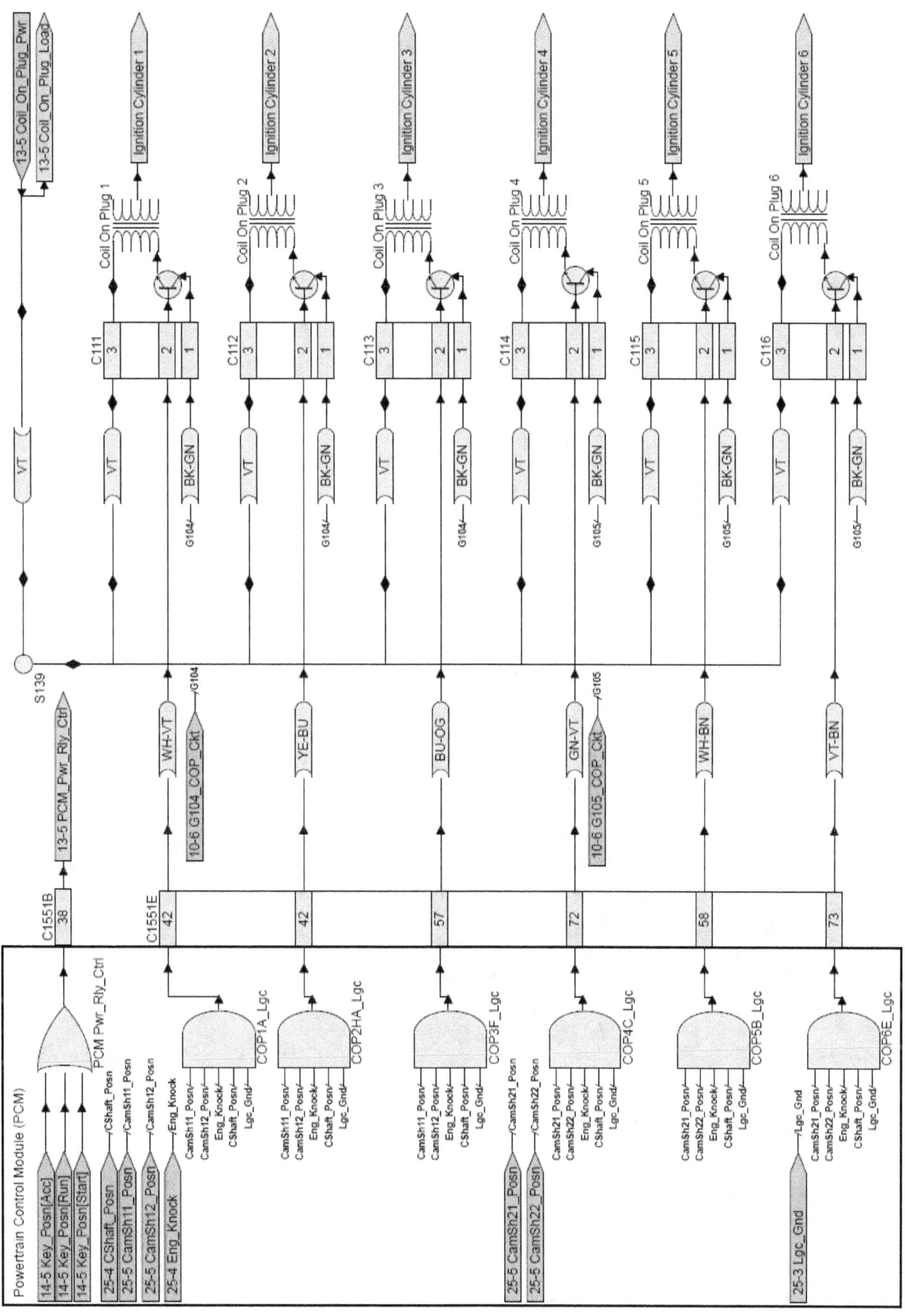

25-2 PCM for 3.5L Engines – Fuel Injection

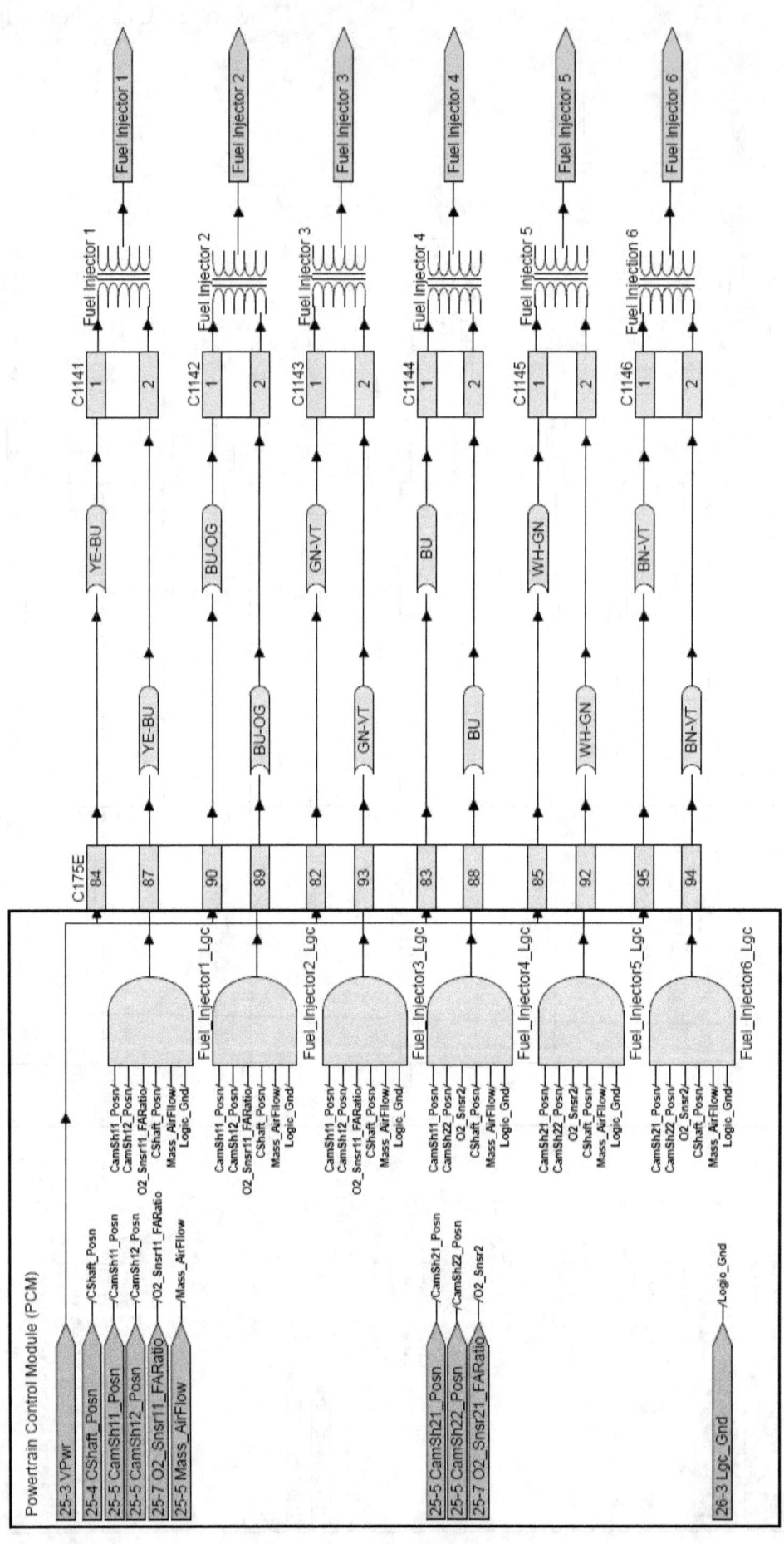

PCM for 3.5L Engines – PCM Power, Gnds & EVAP Solenoid 25-3

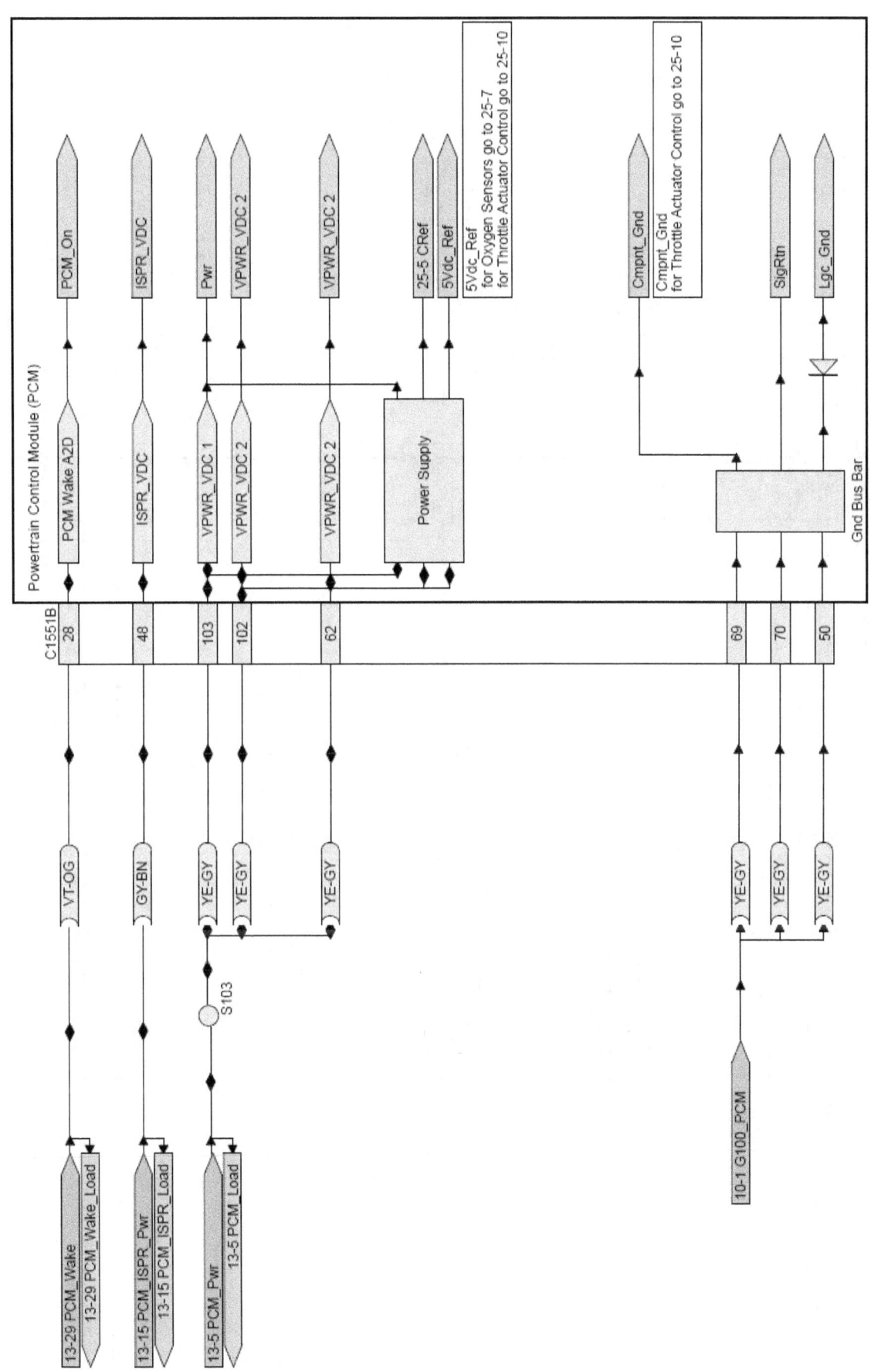

25-4 PCM for 3.5L Engines – Knock, Cam Shaft & Crank Shaft Sensors

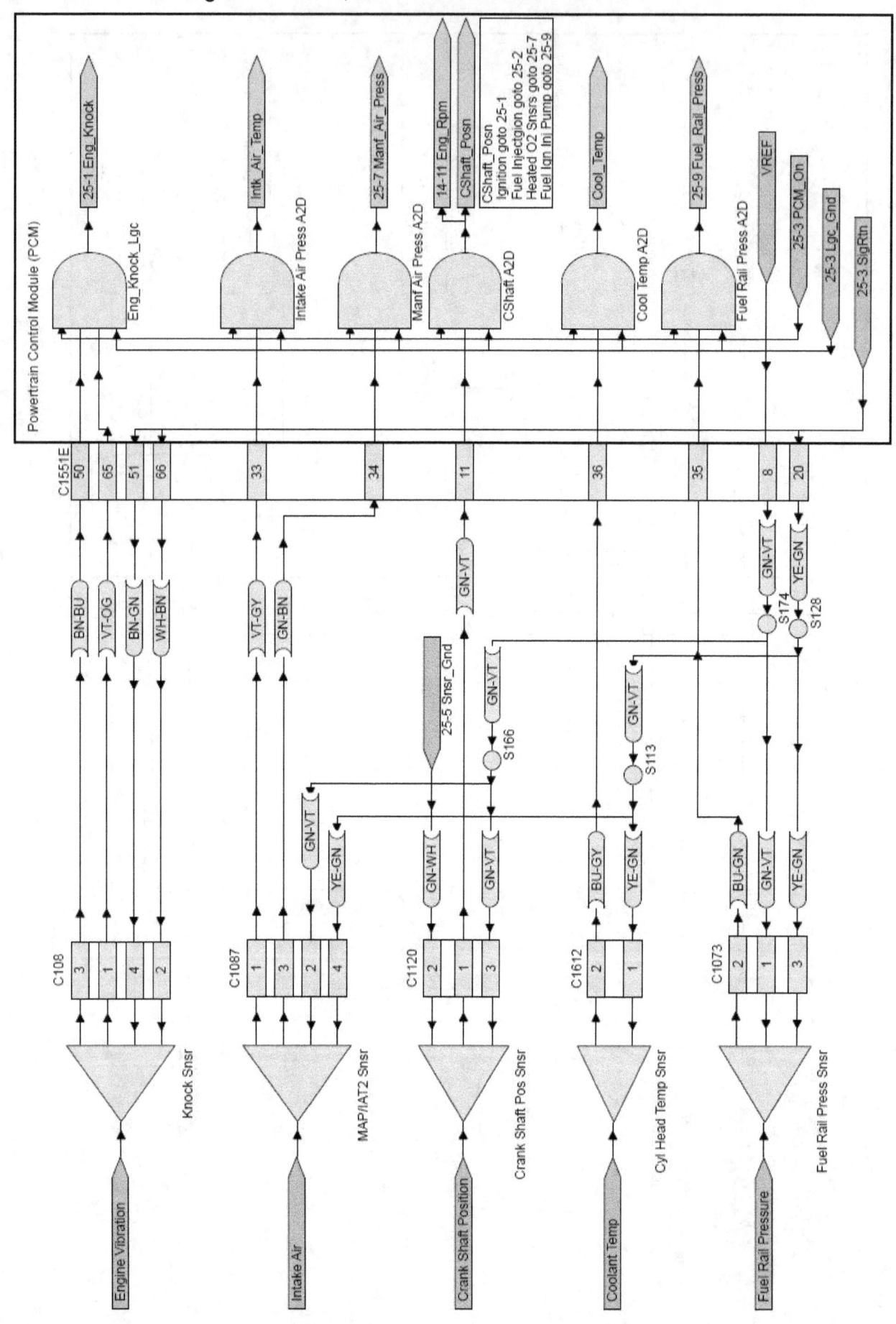

PCM for 3.5L Engines – Cam Shaft Sensors 25-5

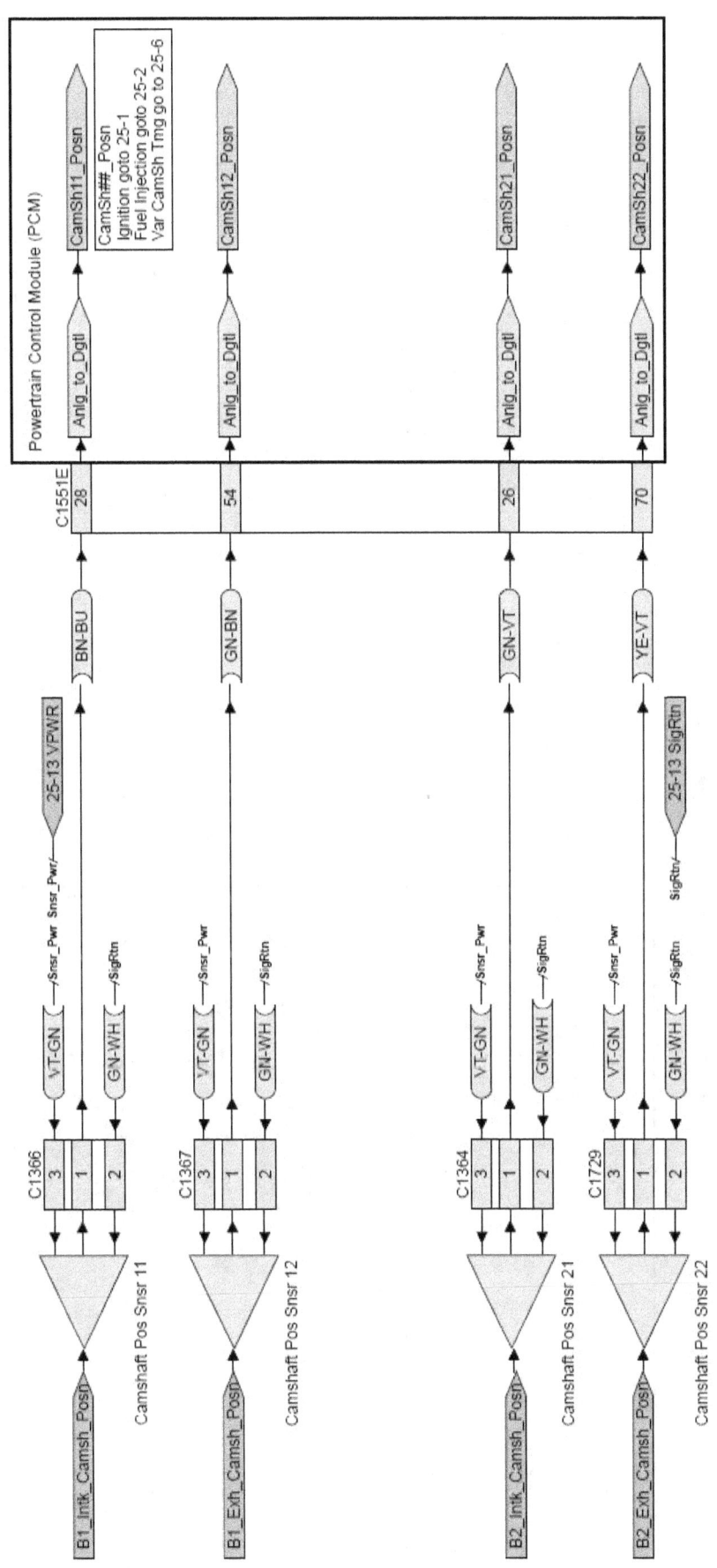

25-6 PCM for 3.5L Engines – Evap, VCT Solenoids

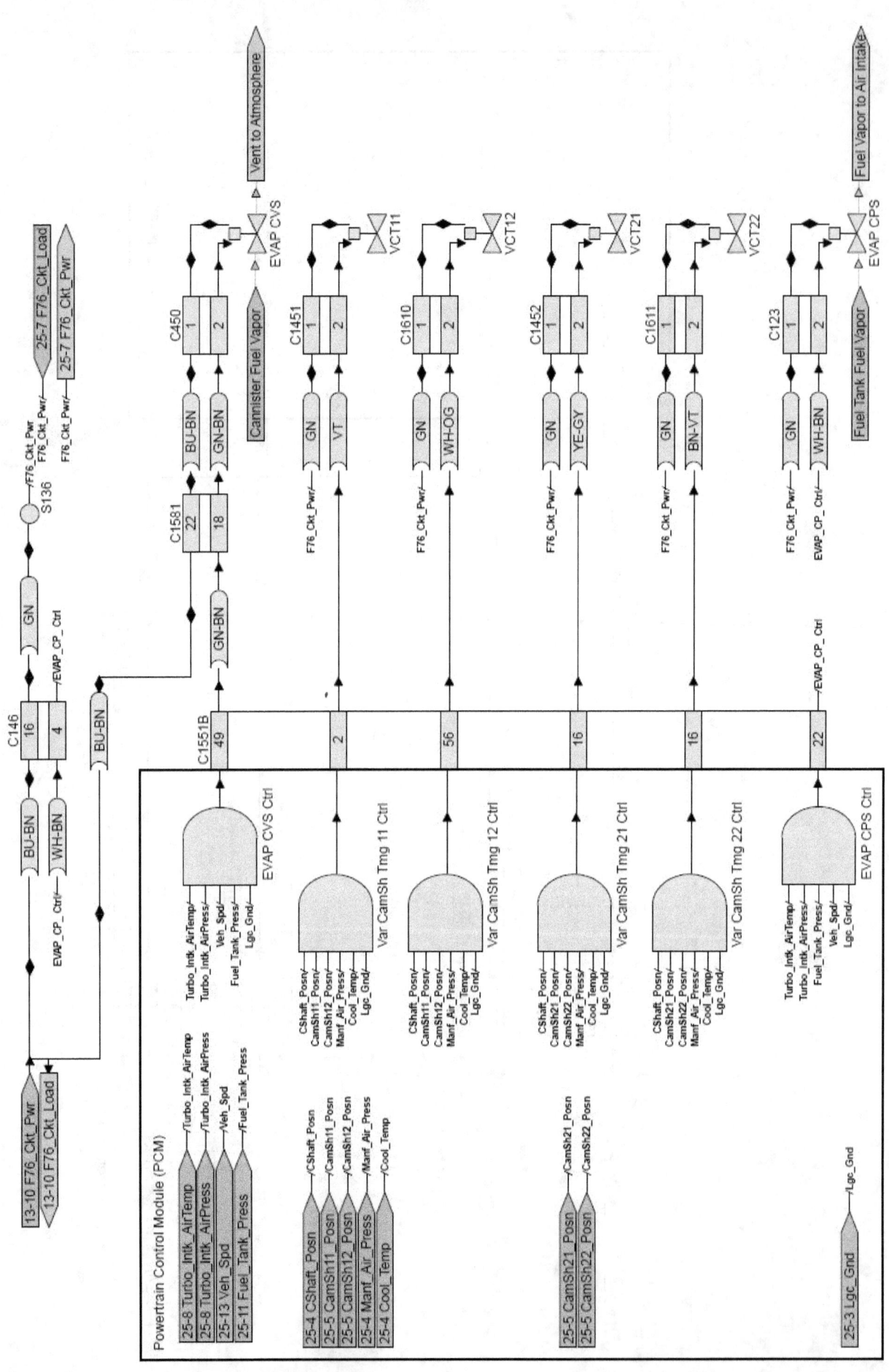

PCM for 3.5L Engines – Oxygen Sensors 25-7

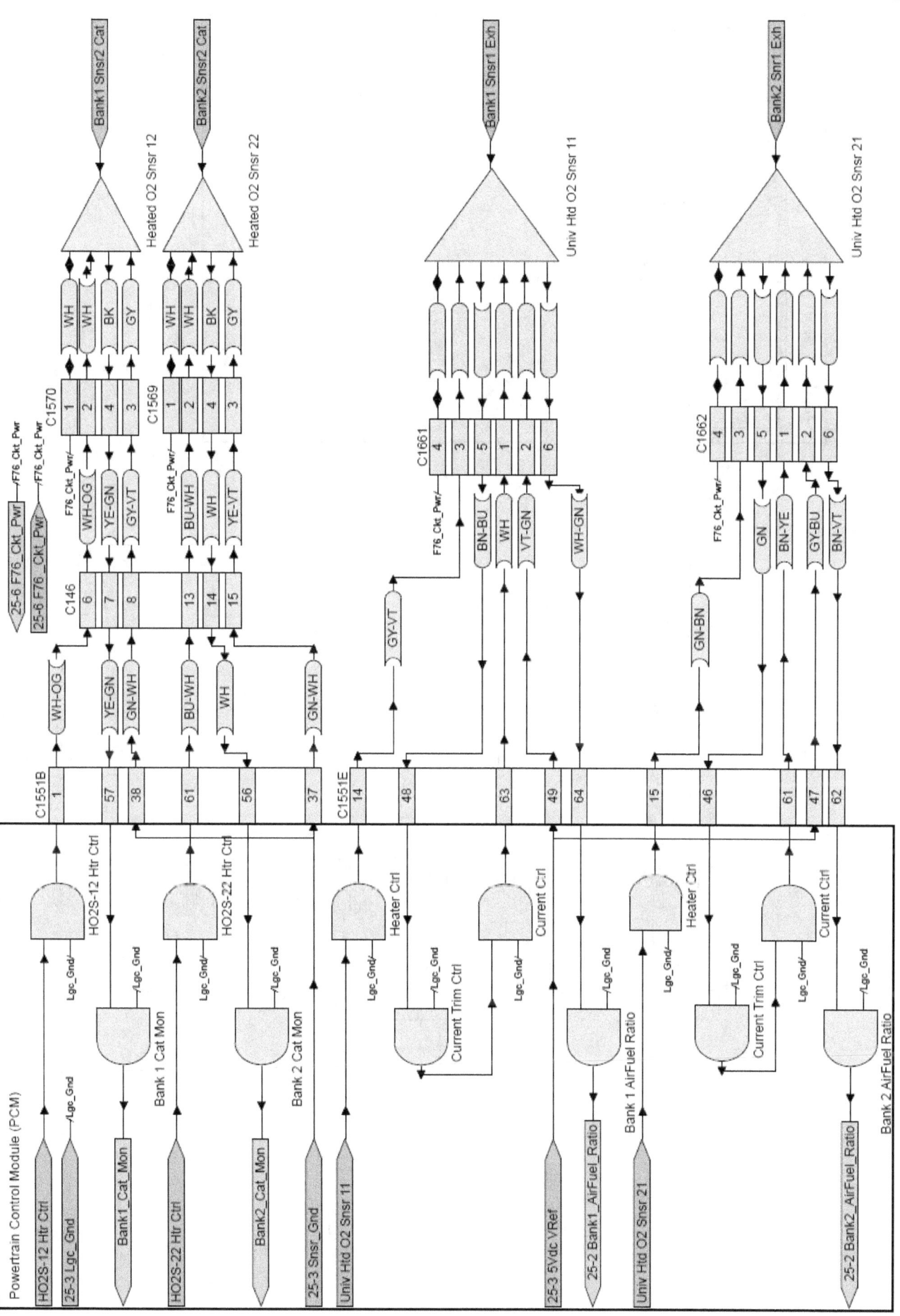

25-8 PCM for 3.5L Engines – Turbo, Gen Curr, AC Press & Air Intake Sensors

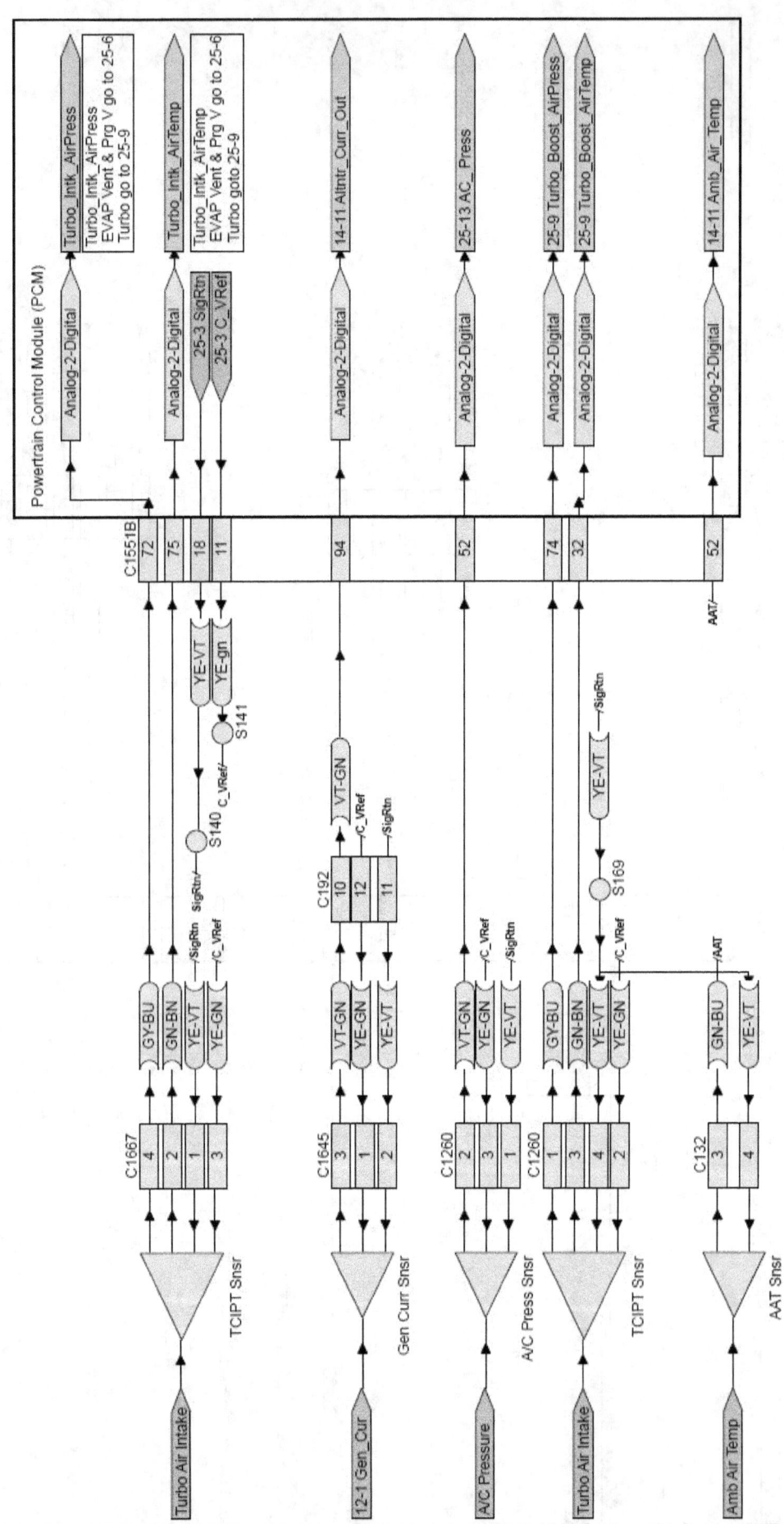

PCM for 3.5L Engines – Turbo, Gen Curr, AC Press & Air Intake Sensors **25-9**

117

25-10 PCM for 3.5L Engines – Elek Throttle Control & Accelerator Pedal Posn Snsr

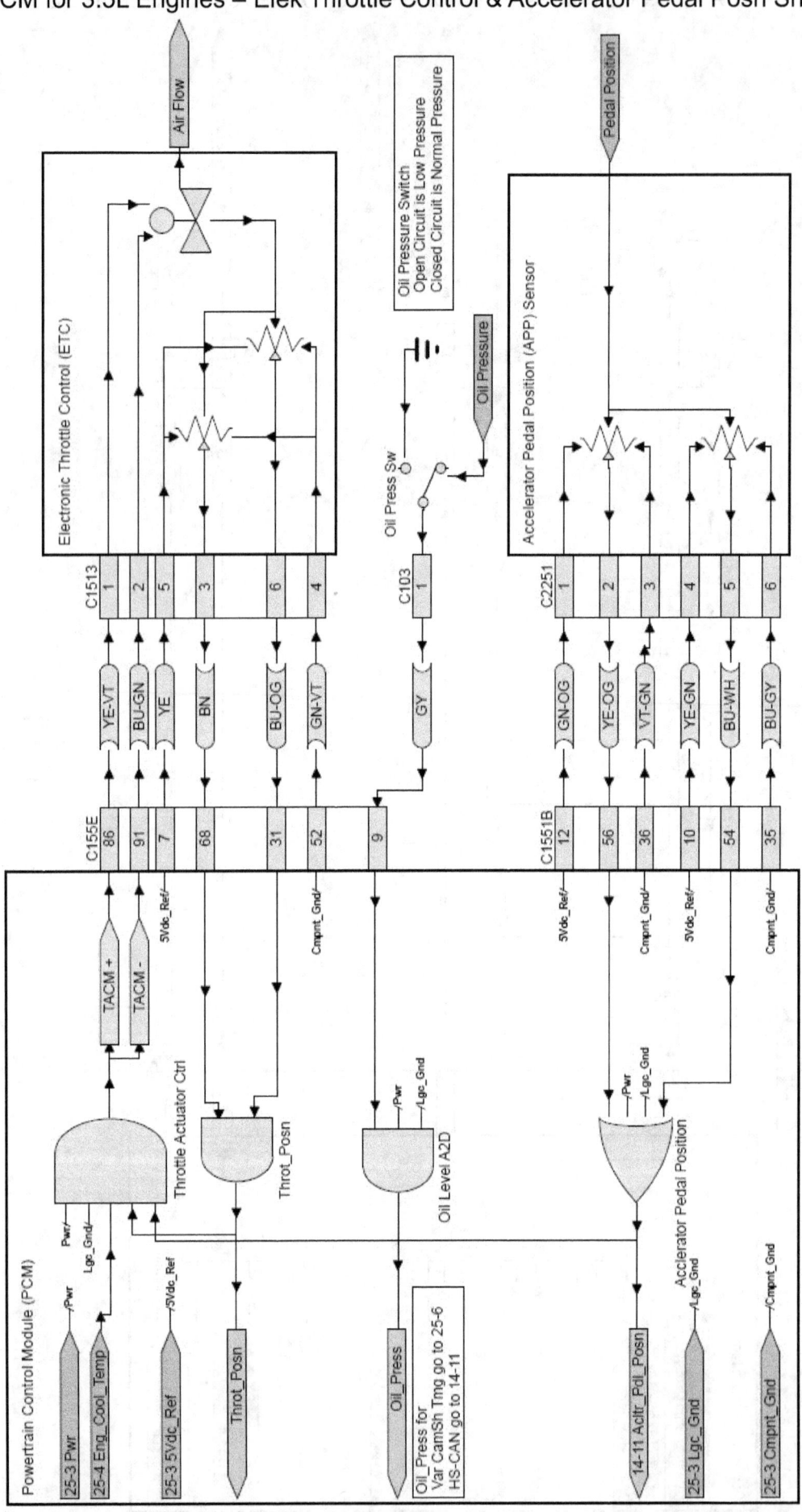

Powertrain Control Module for 3.5L Engines – Fuel Control **25-11**

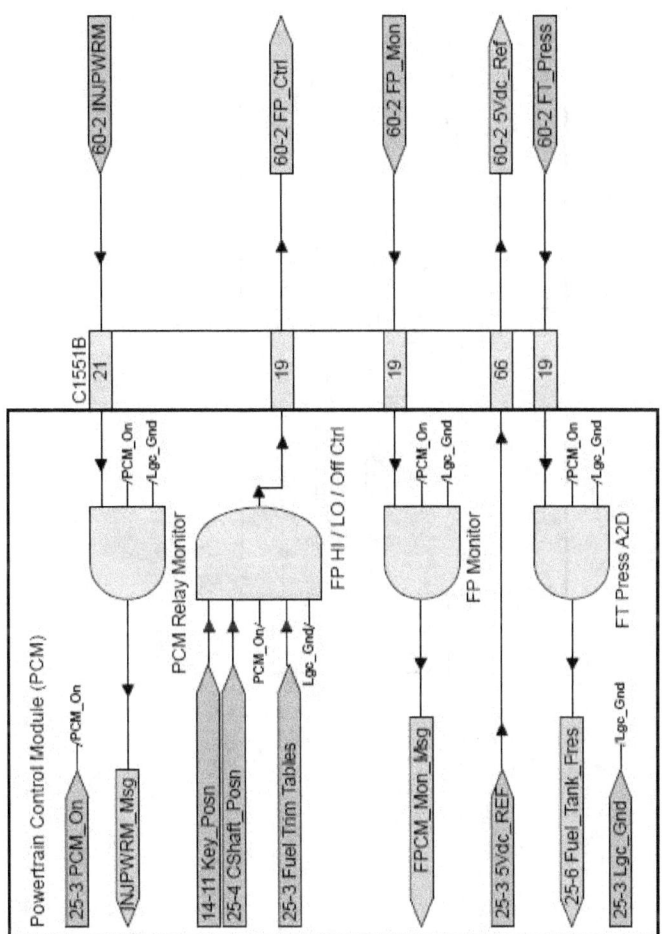

25-12 Powertrain Control Module for 3.5L Engines – Brake Control

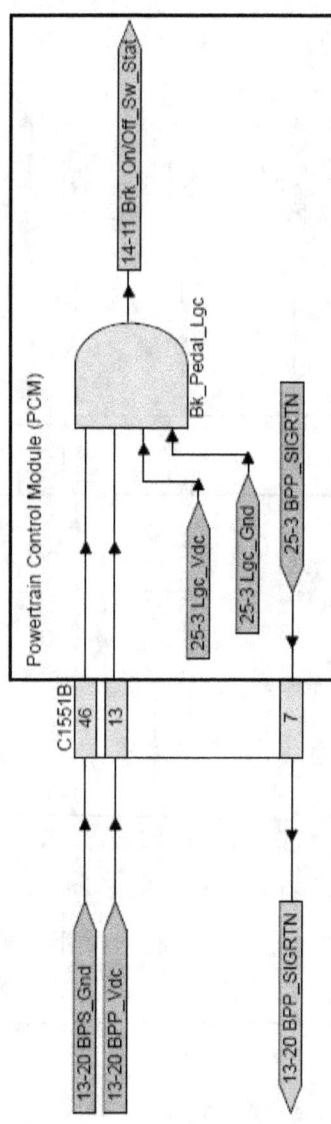

PCM for 3.5L Engines – CAN BUS, and I/O 25-13

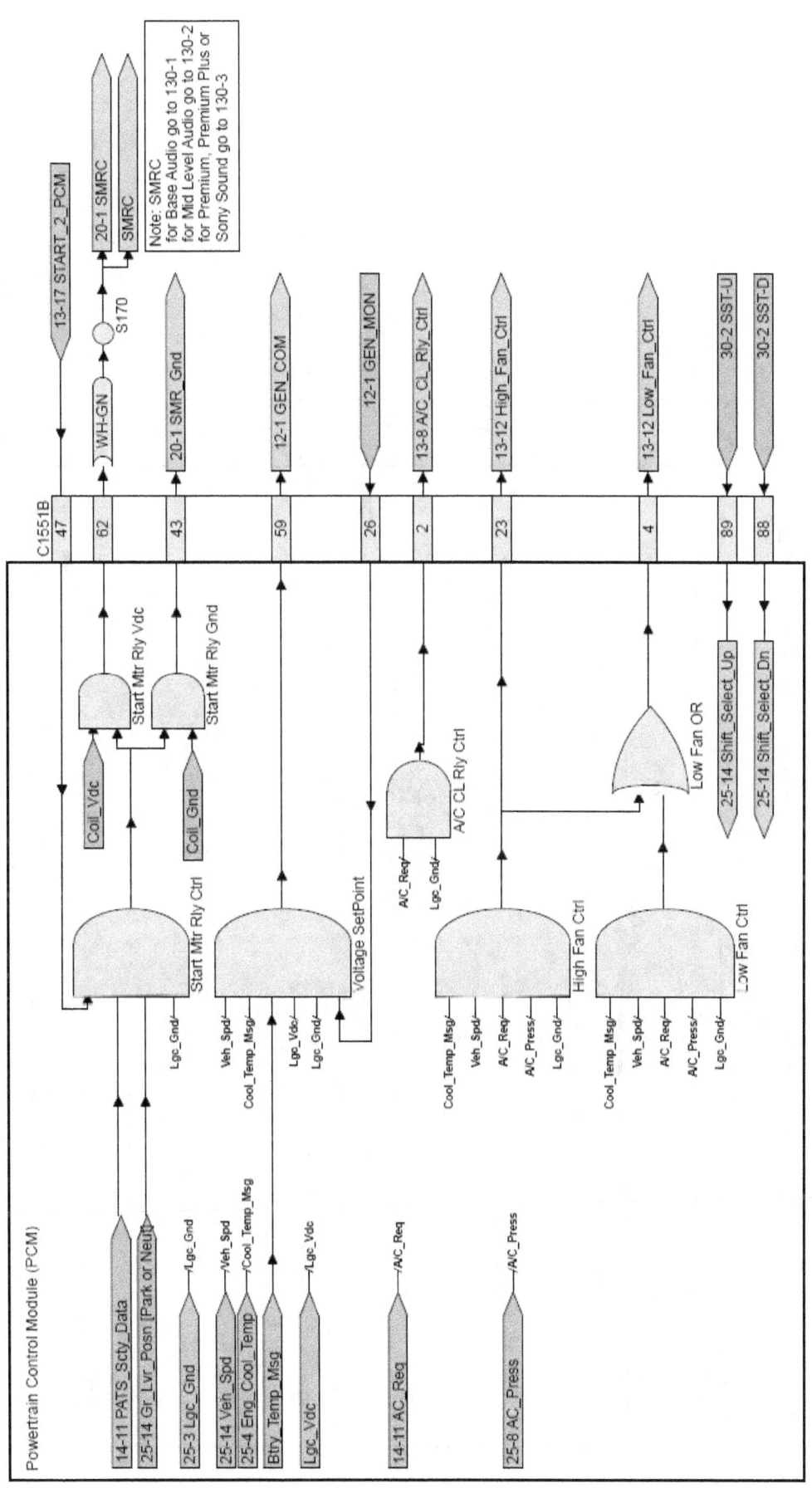

25-14 PCM for 3.5L Engines – Transmission Control

26 Powertrain Control Module (PCM) for 3.7L Engines

PCM for 3.7L Engines – Ignition 26-1

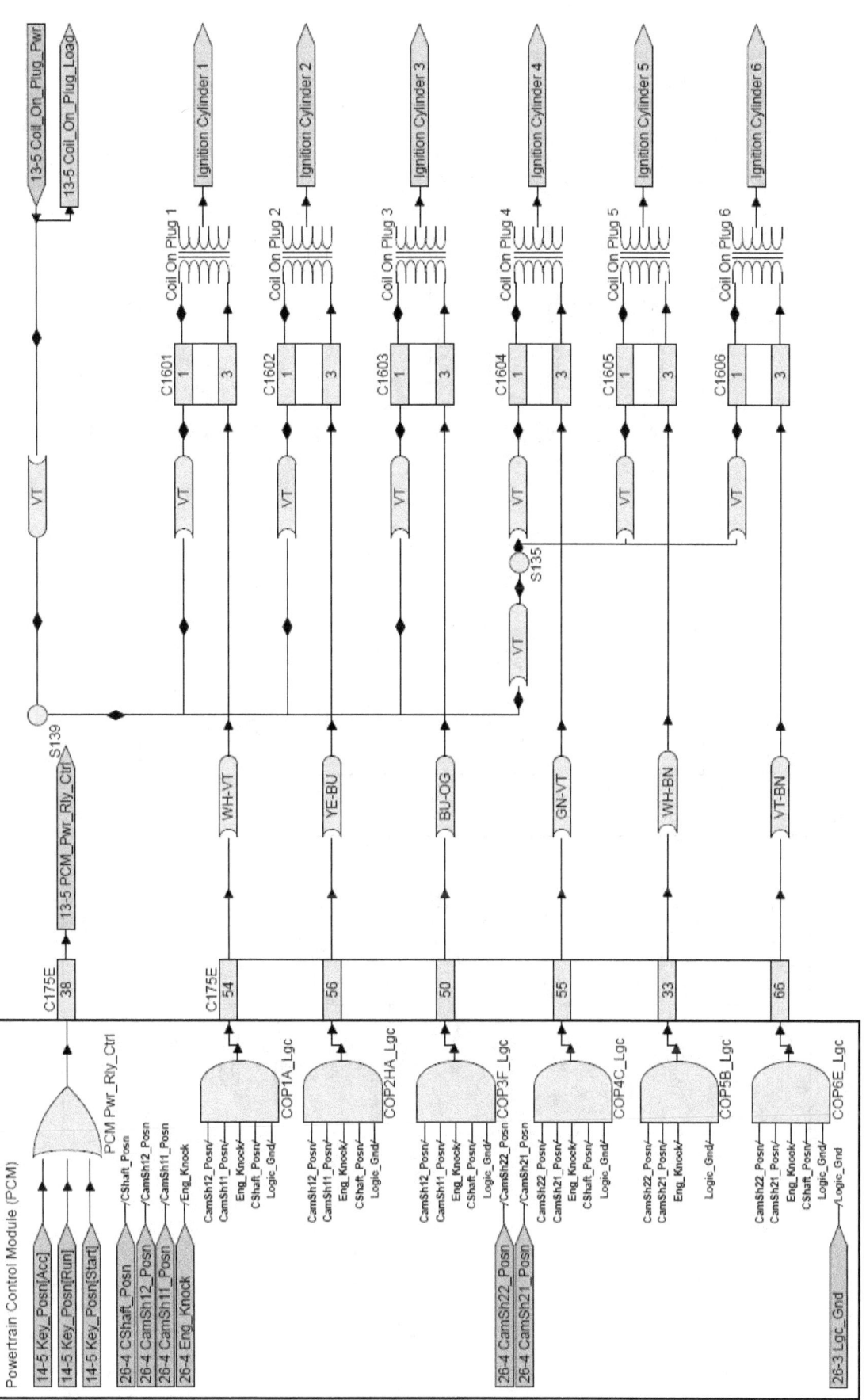

26-2 PCM for 3.7L Engines – Fuel Injection

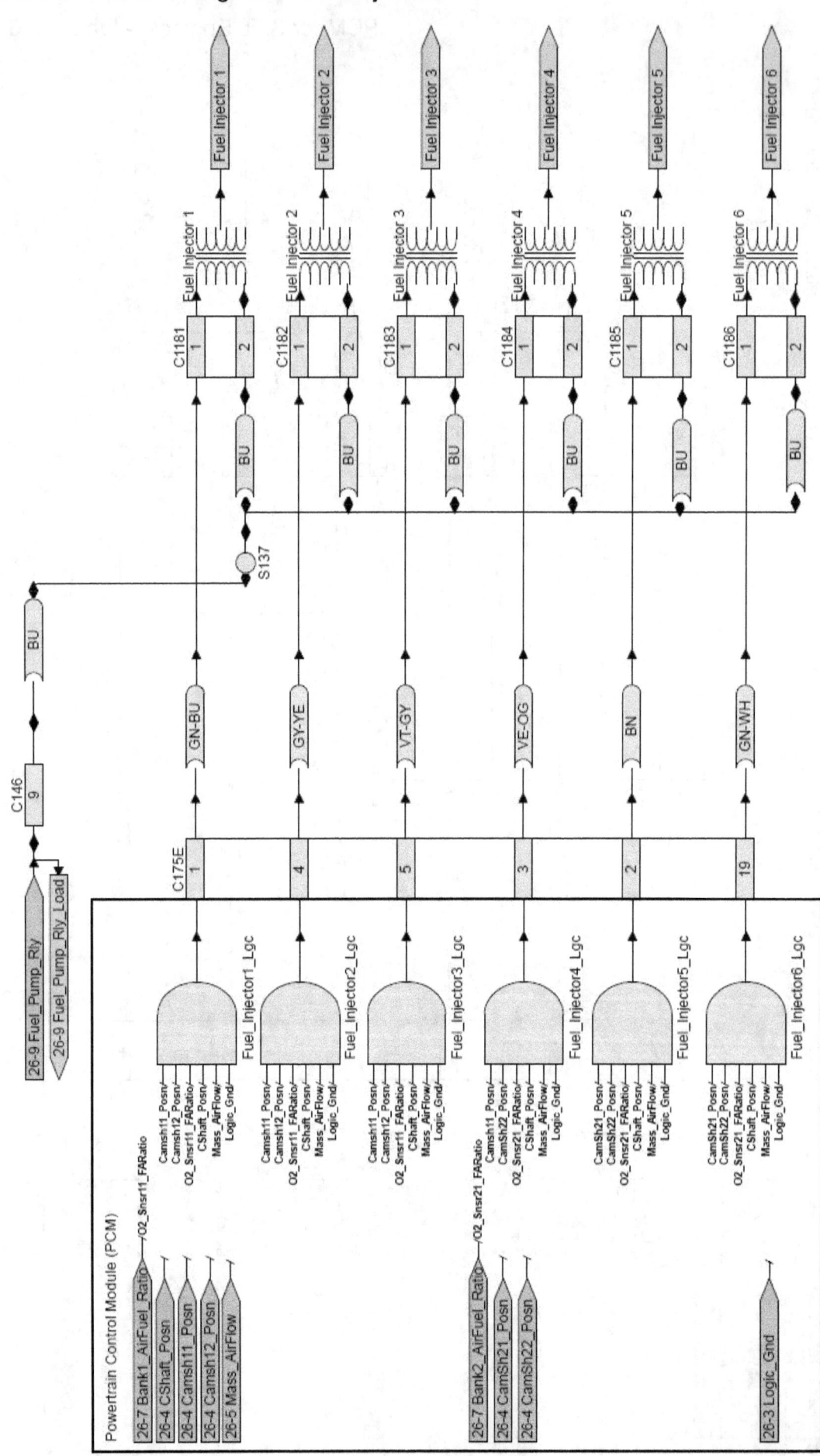

124

PCM for 3.7L Engines – Power, Gnds and EVAP Solenoid 26-3

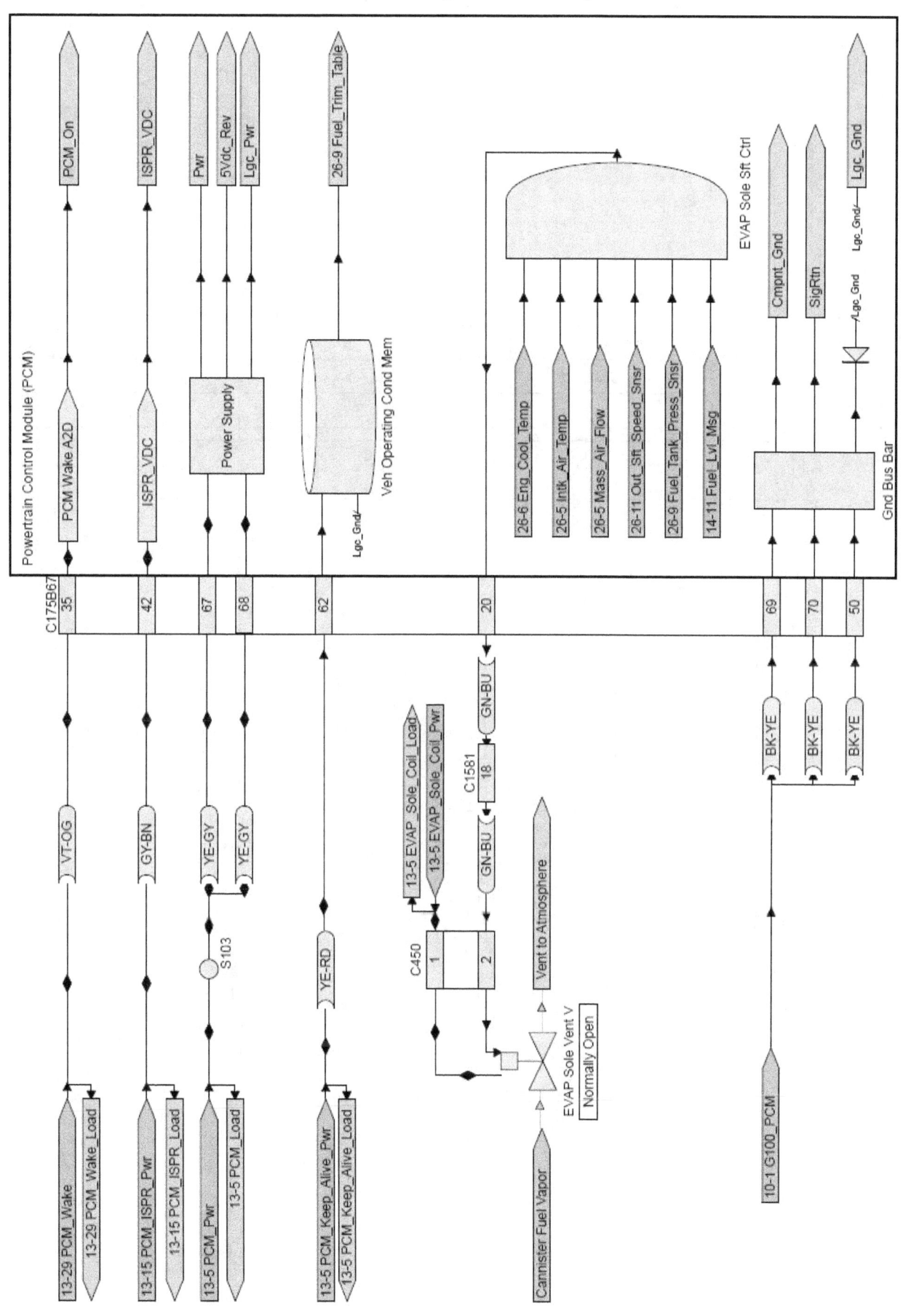

26-4 PCM for 3.7L Engines – Knock, Cam Shaft and Crank Shaft Sensors

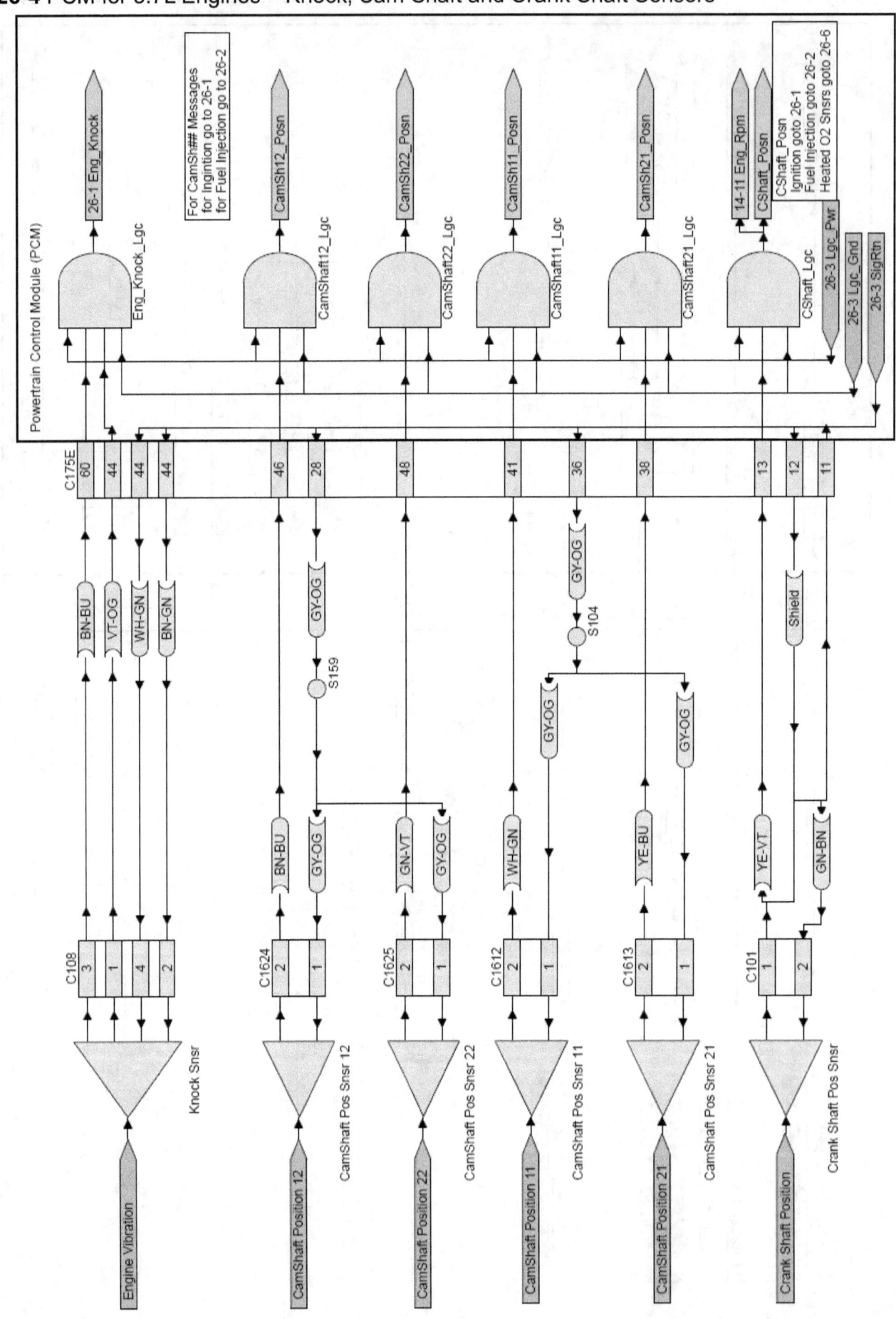

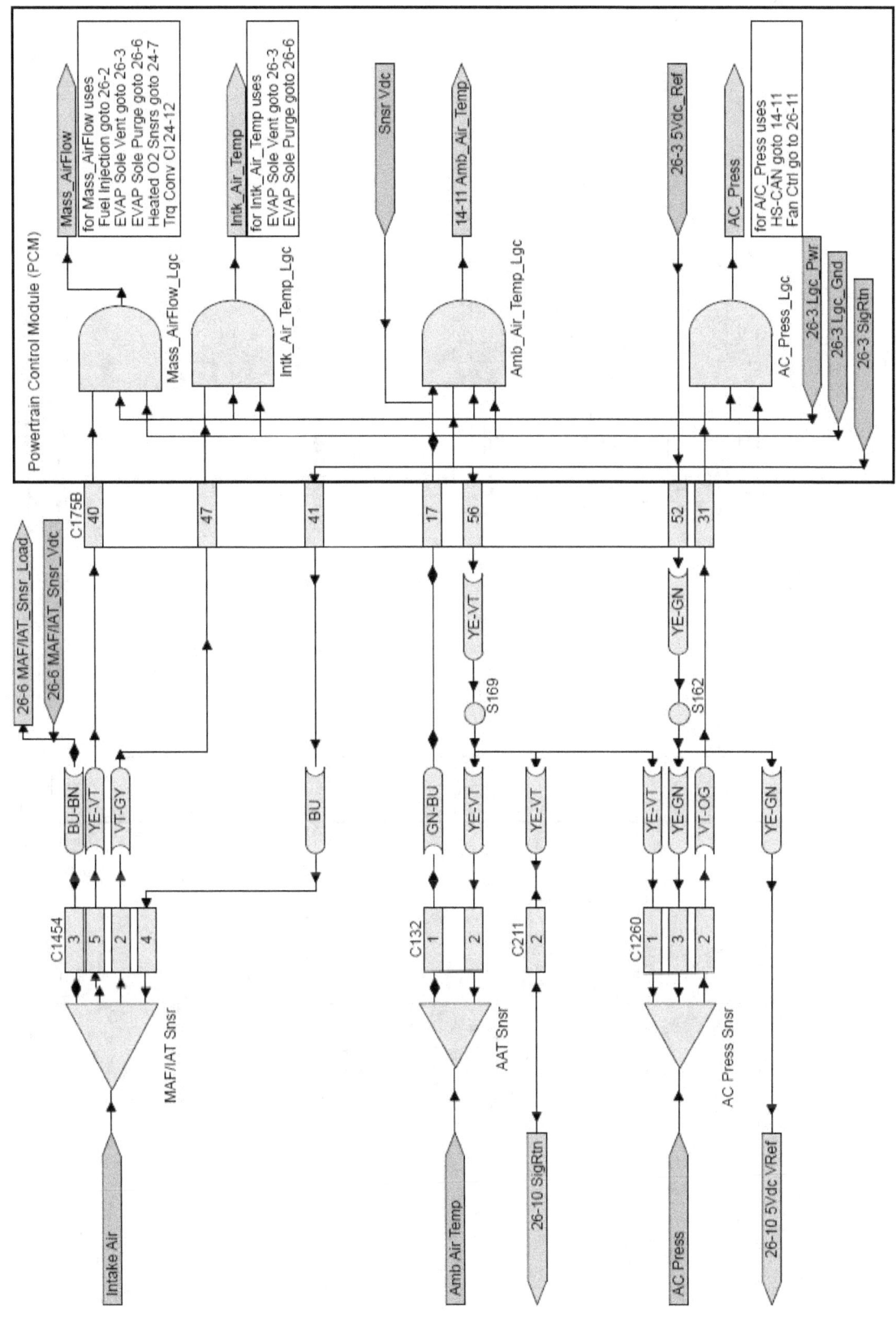

26-6 PCM for 3.7L Engines – EVAP, & VCT Solenoids and Cyl Head Temp Sensor

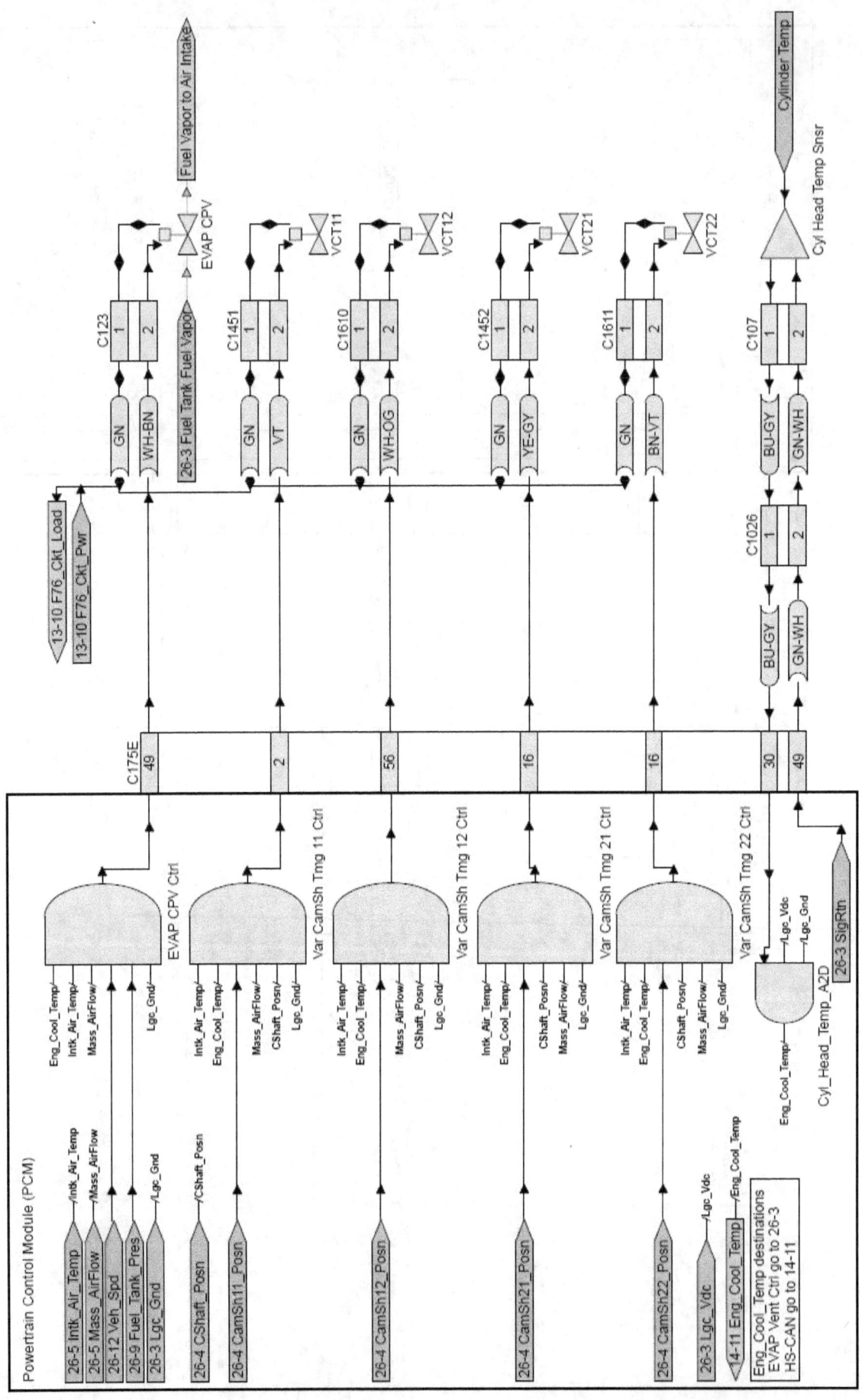

PCM for 3.7L Engines – Oxygen Sensors 26-7

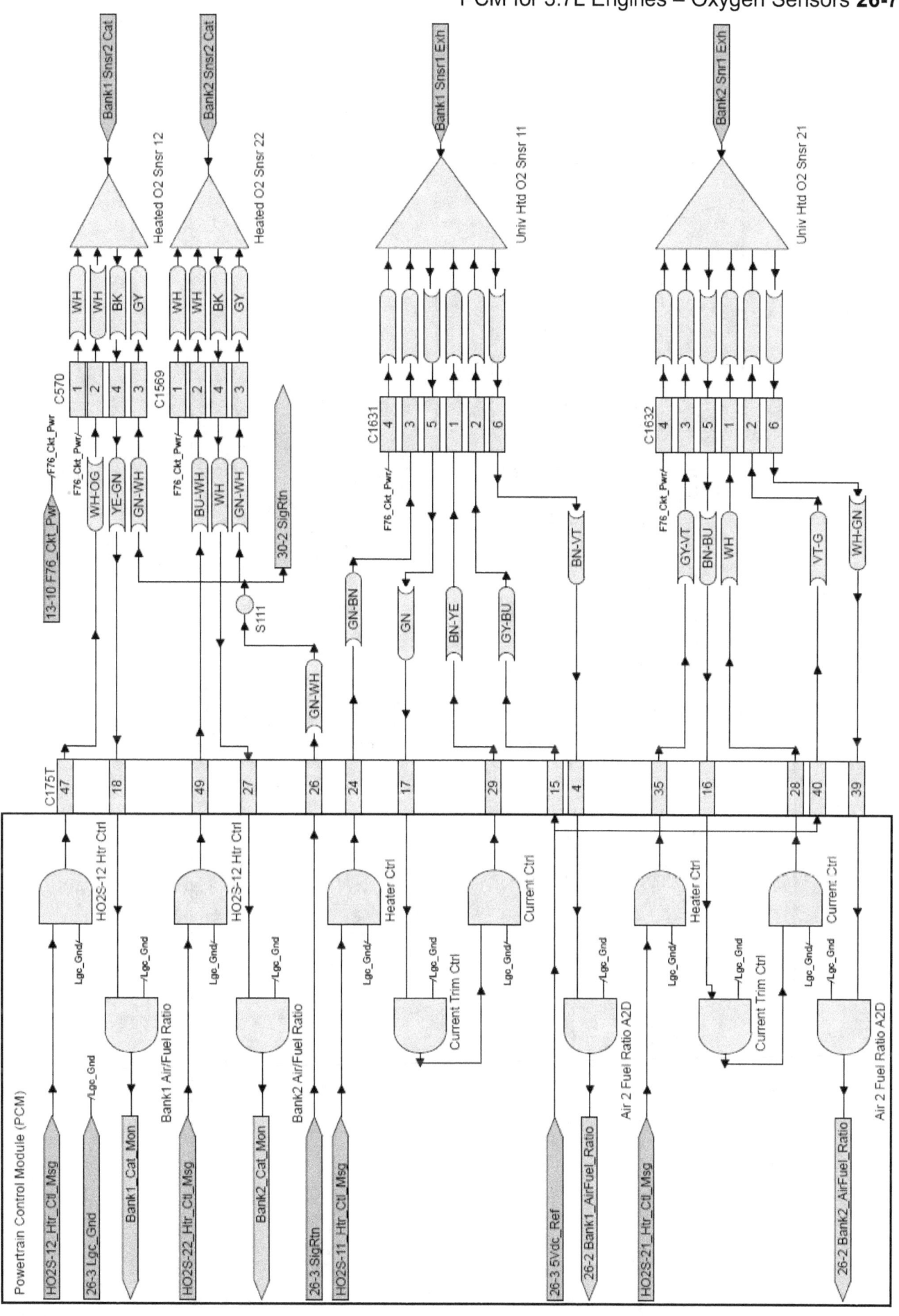

129

26-8 PCM for 3.7L Engines – Elek Throttle Control & Accelerator Pedal Posn Snsr

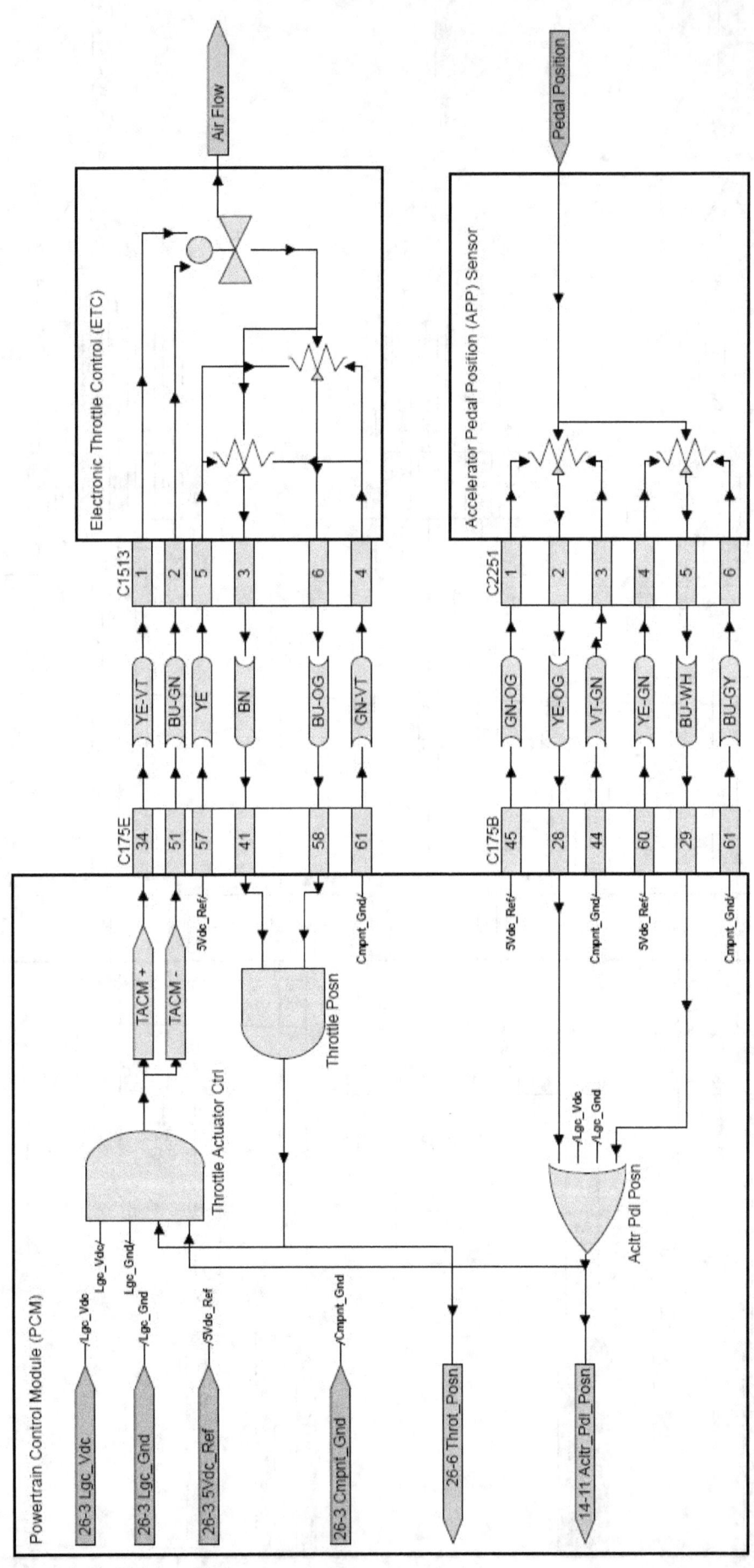

Powertrain Control Module for 3.7L Engines – Fuel Control 26-9

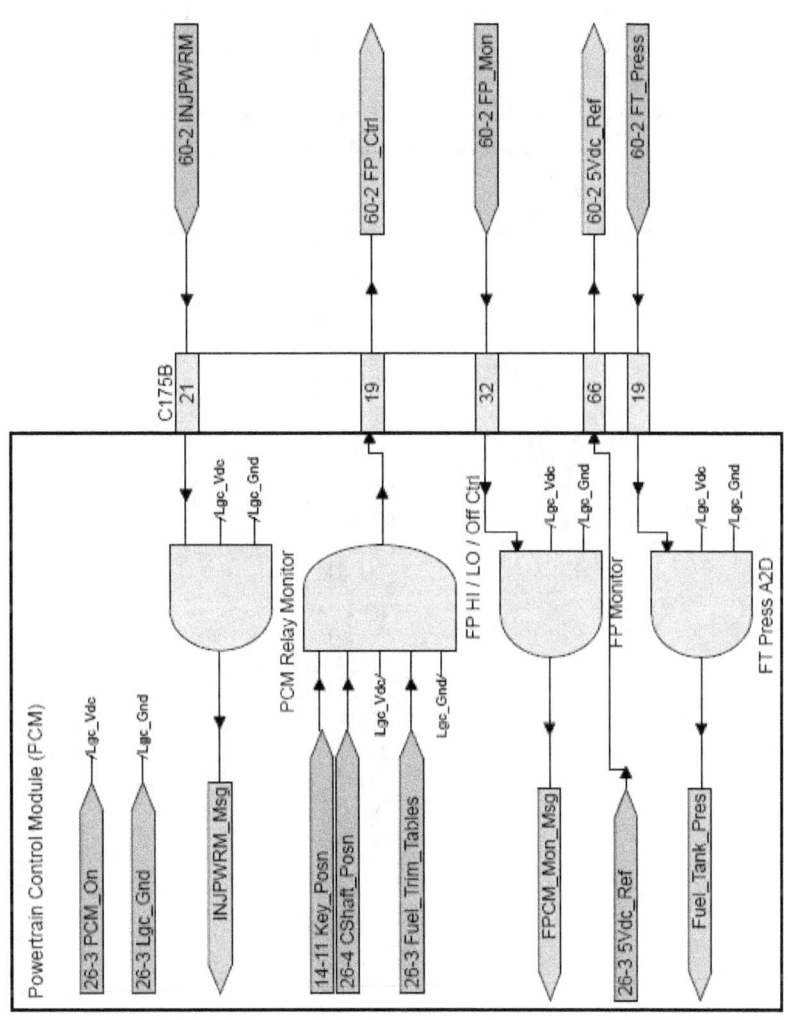

26-10 Powertrain Control Module for 3.7L Engines – Generator Current Sensor

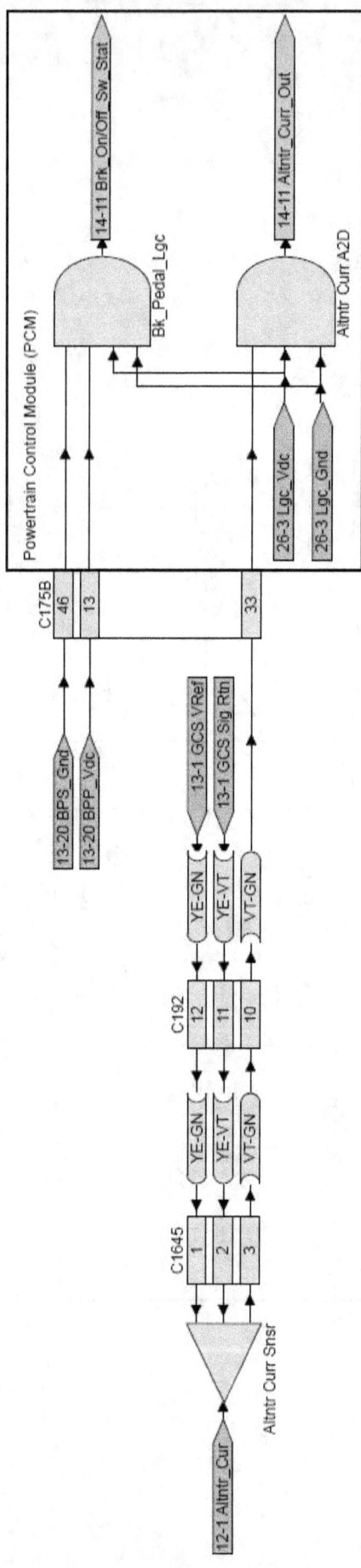

PCM for 3.7L Engines – CAN BUS, I/O, and Lo Oil Press Sw 26-11

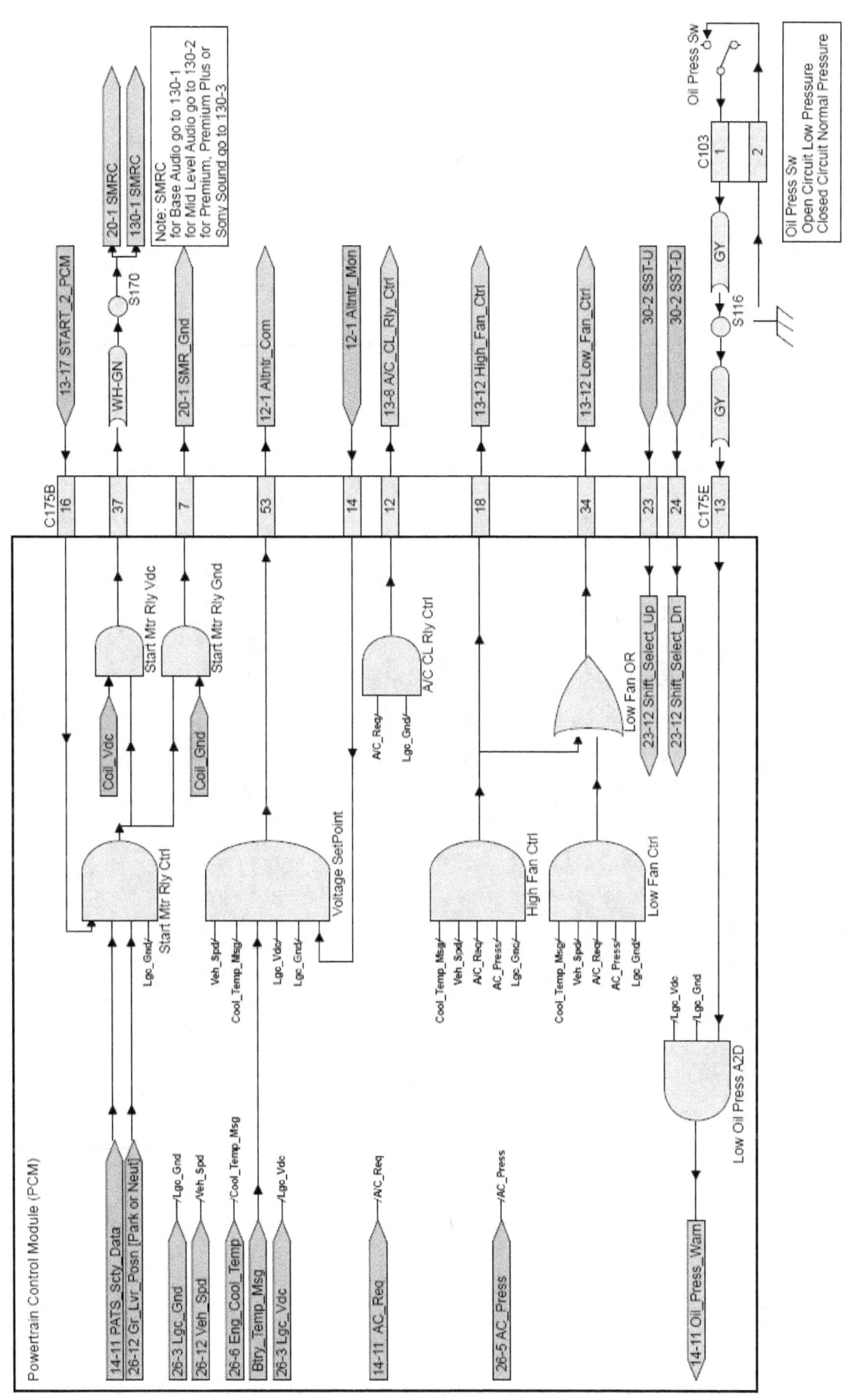

26-12 PCM for 3.7L Engines – Transmission Control

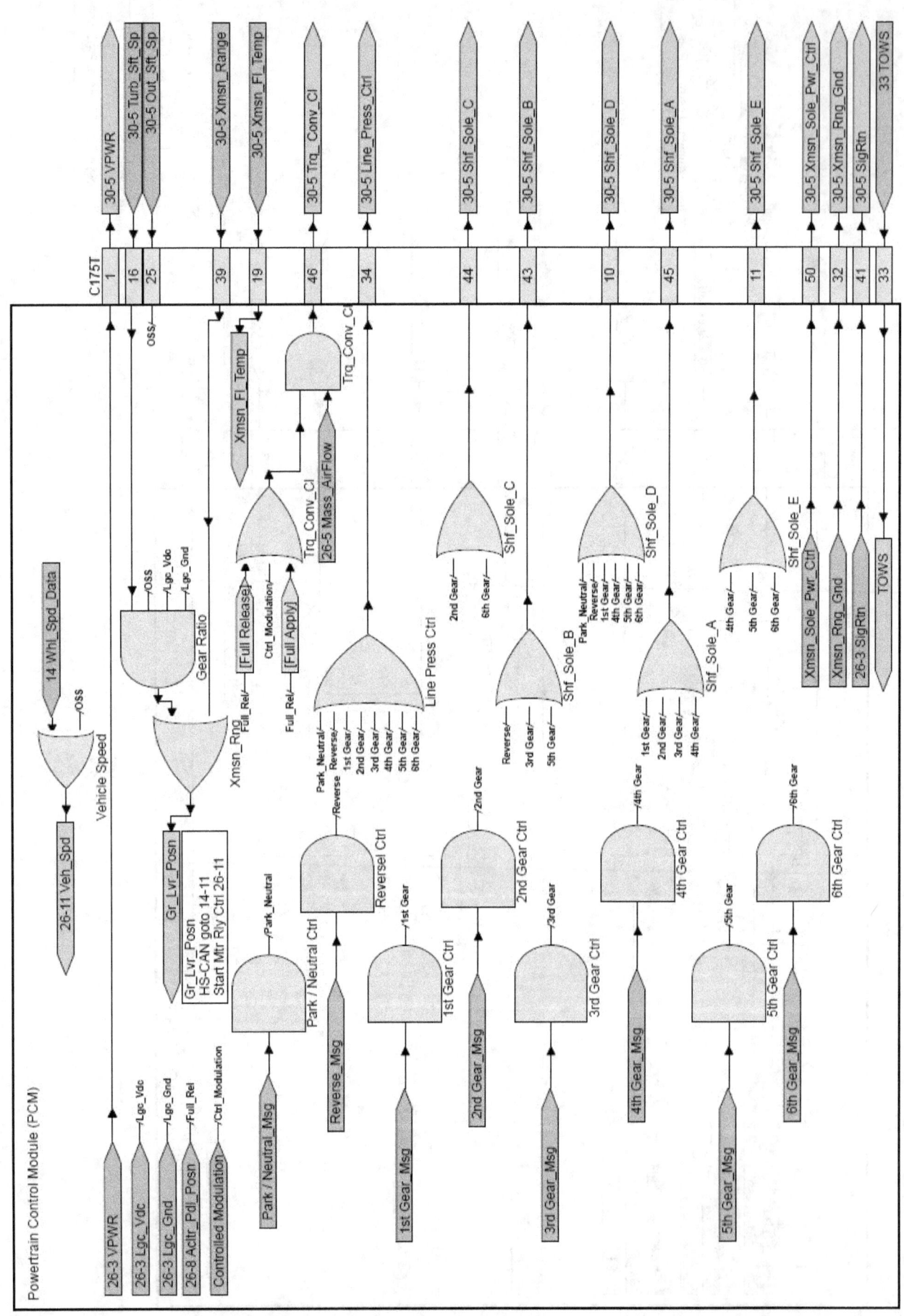

30 Transmission Controls 6R80

Transmission Controls 6R80 **30-1**

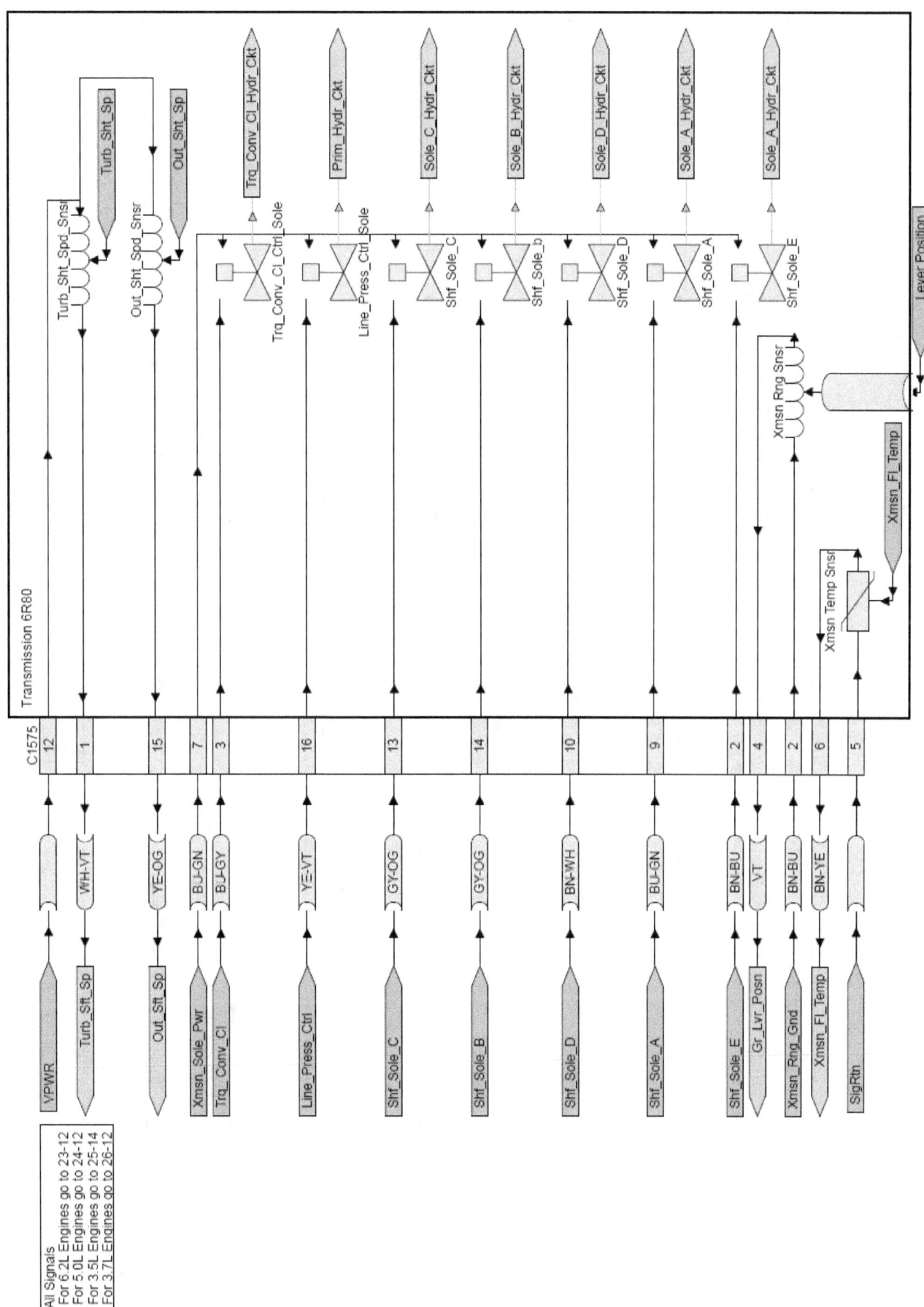

30-2 Transmission Controls Tow Haul Switch

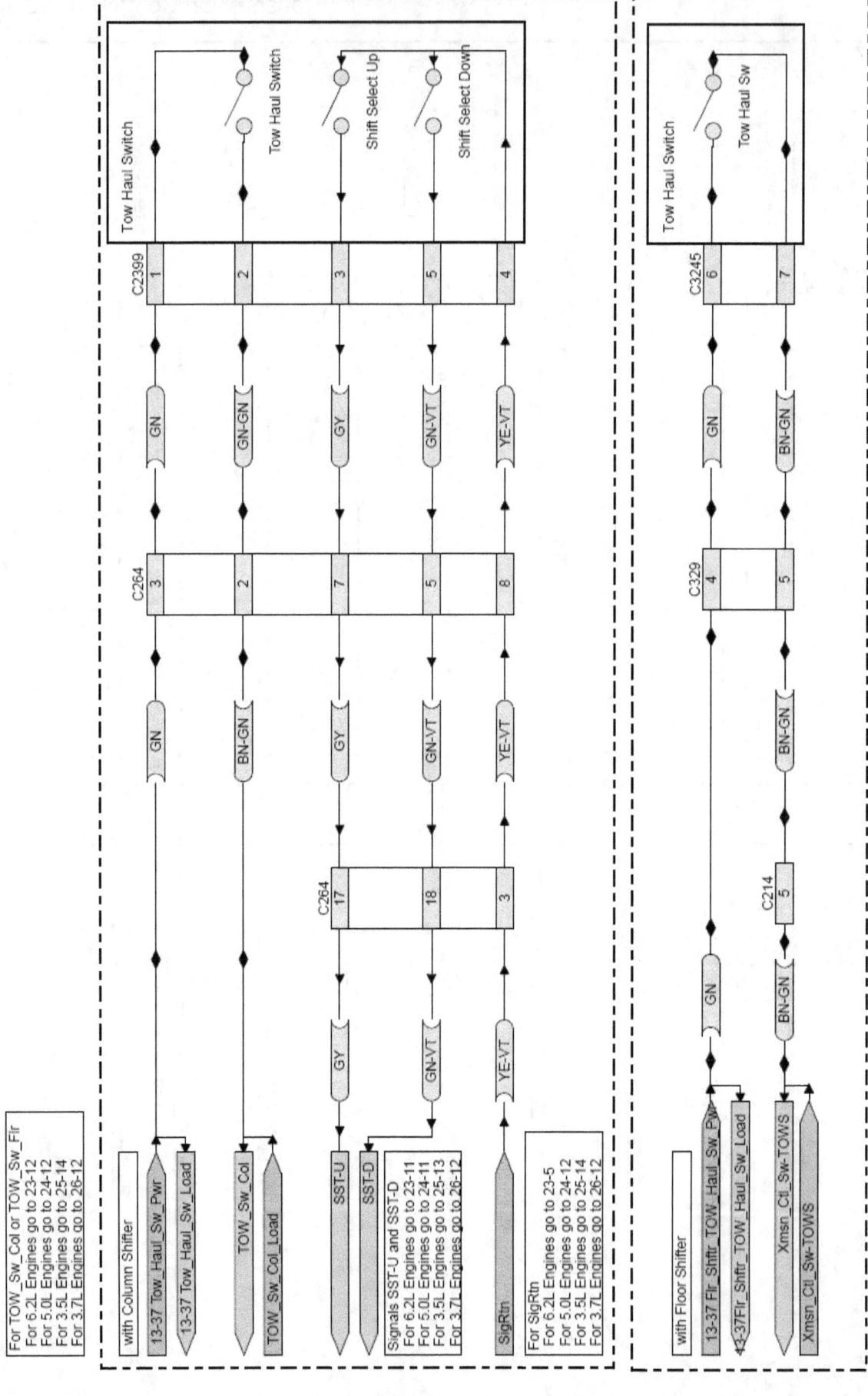

31 Steering Column Control Module (SCCM)
SCCM– Power, Ground, and Multi-Function Switch 31-1

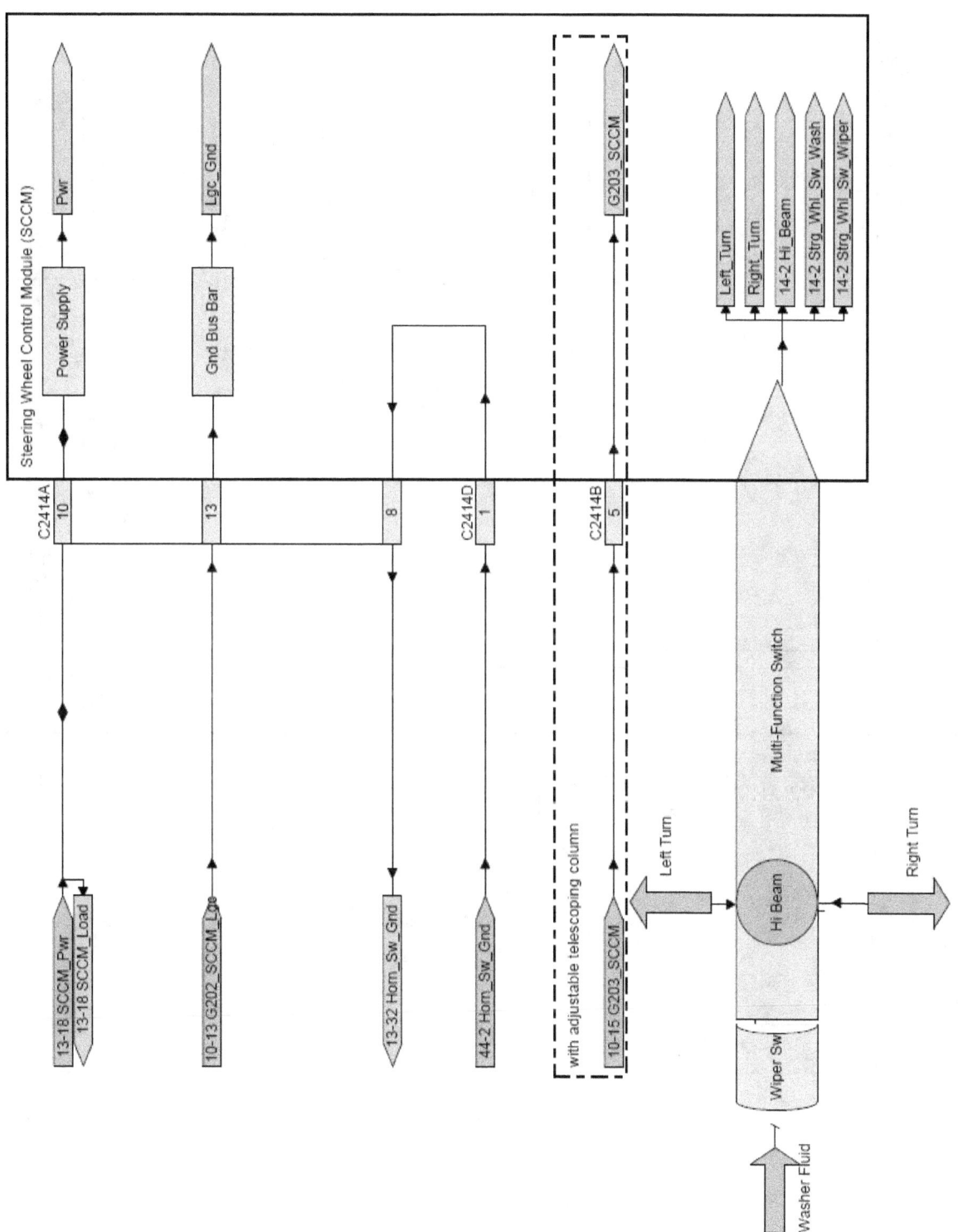

31-2 SCCM – Steering Wheel Left Side Memory Set Switches

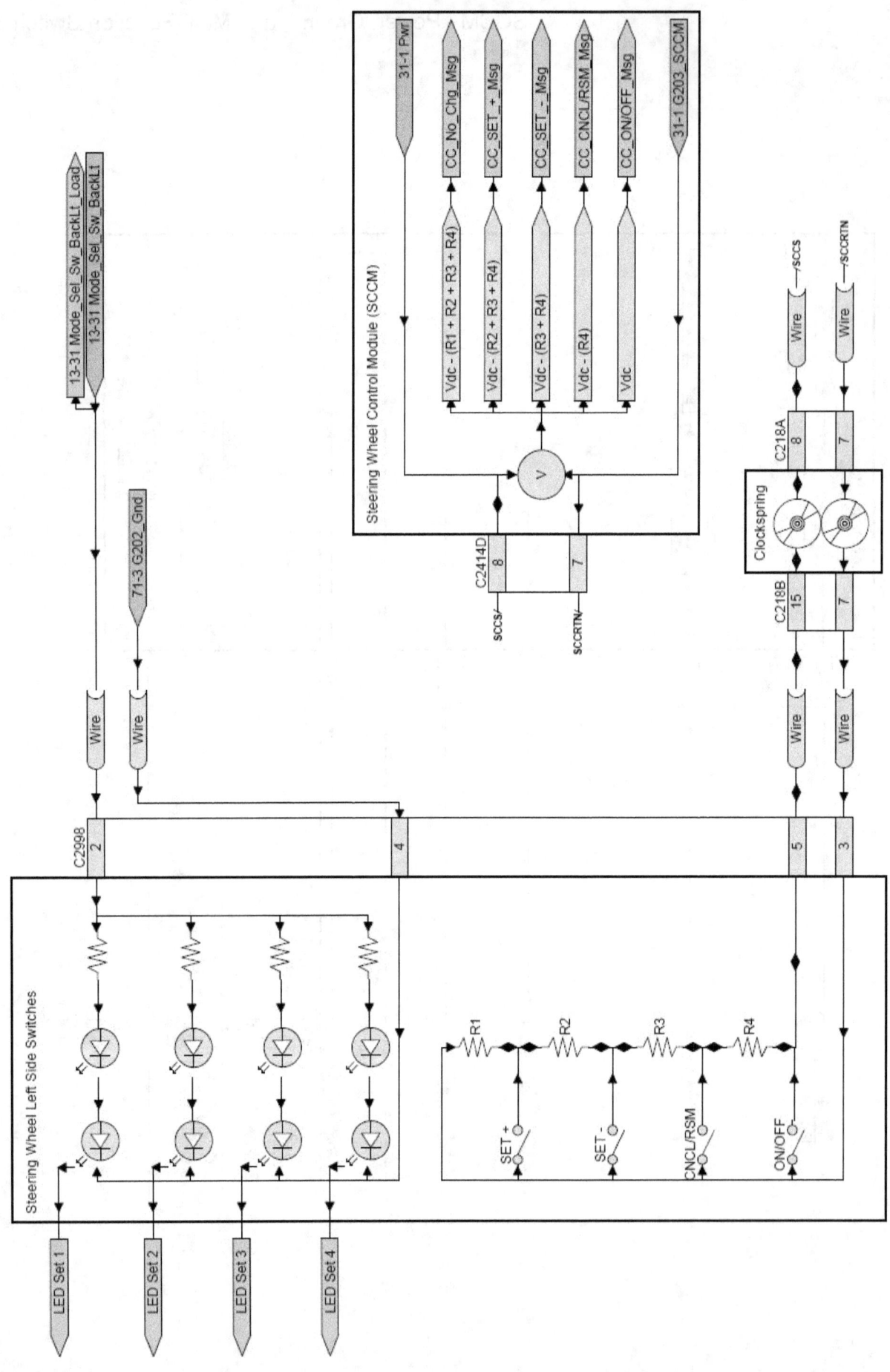

33 Engine Cooling Fans

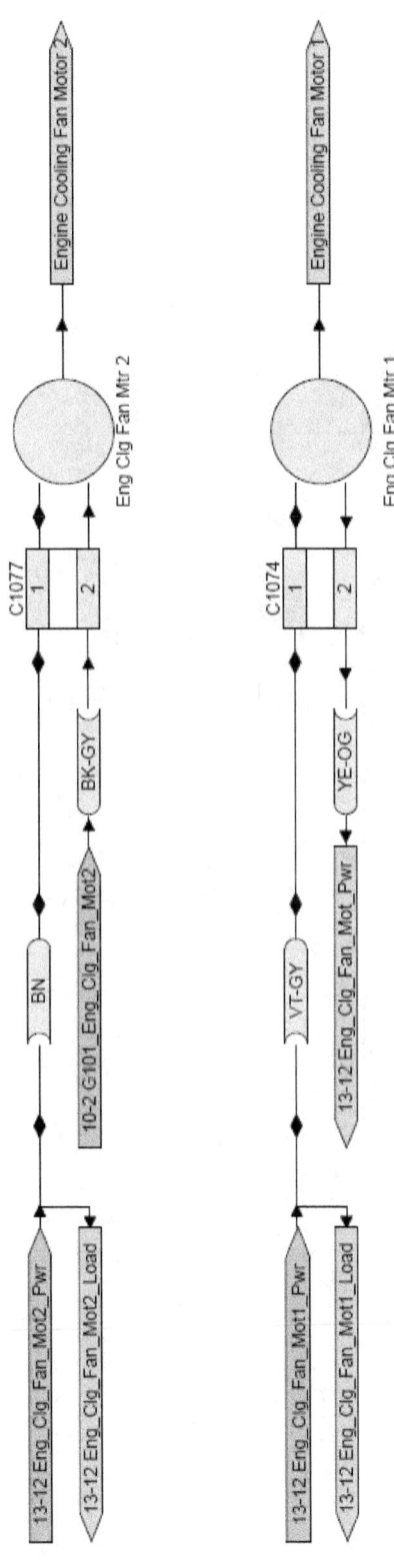

139

34 Transfer Case Control Module (TCCM)
34-1 TCCM, Mode Select Switch

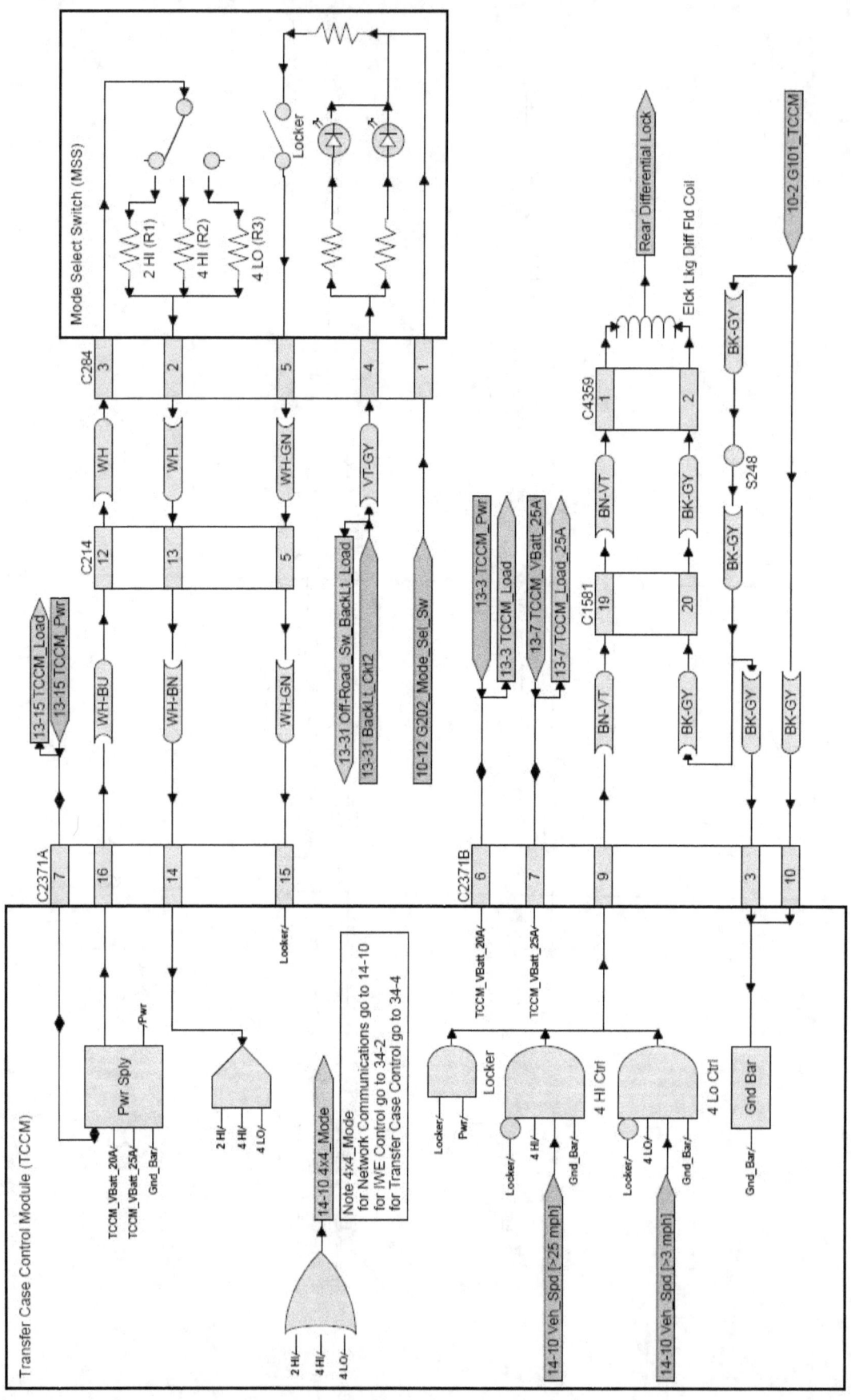

TCCM – Electronic Locking 34-2

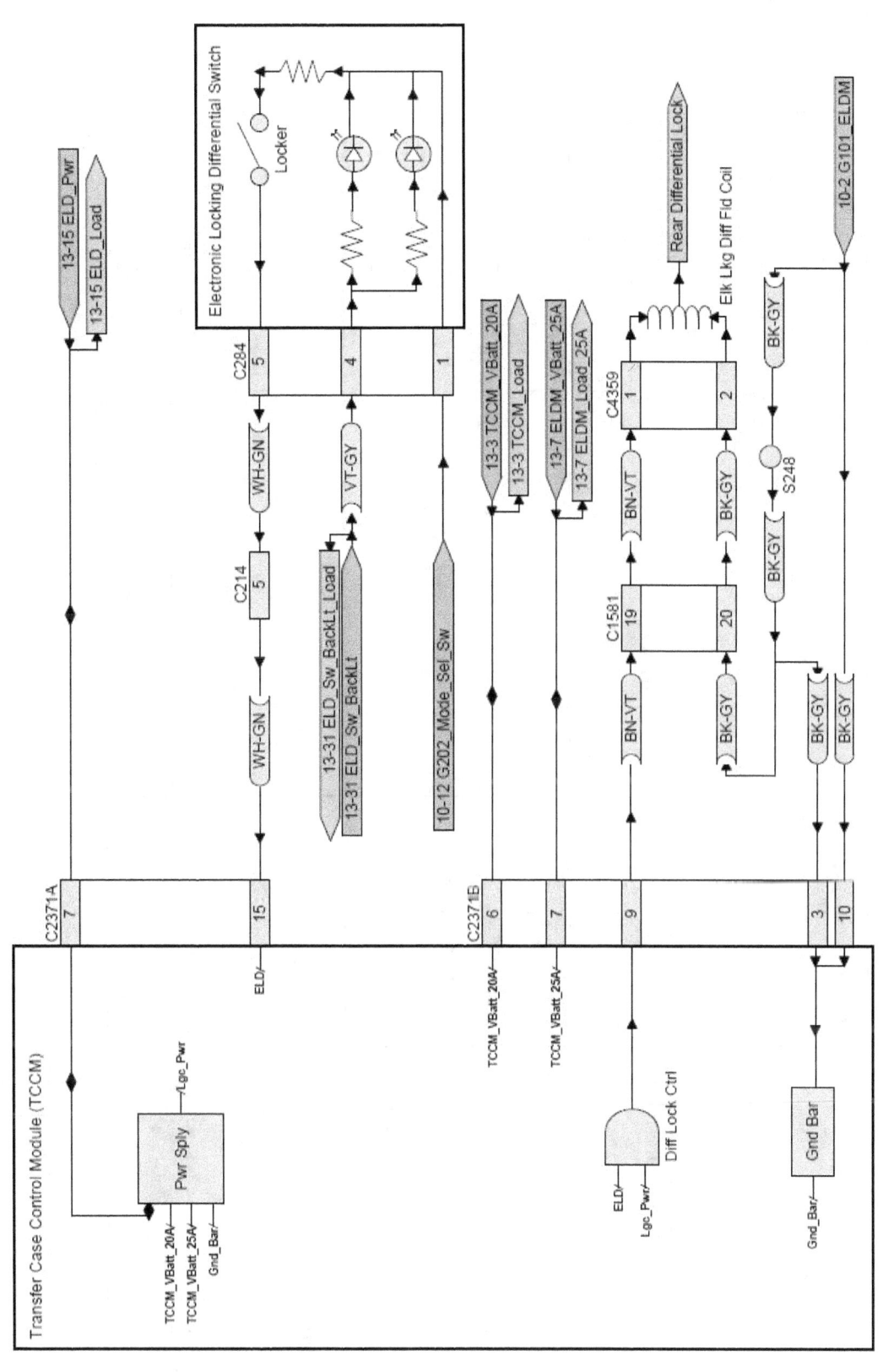

34-3 TCCM – ESOF / Torque On Demand

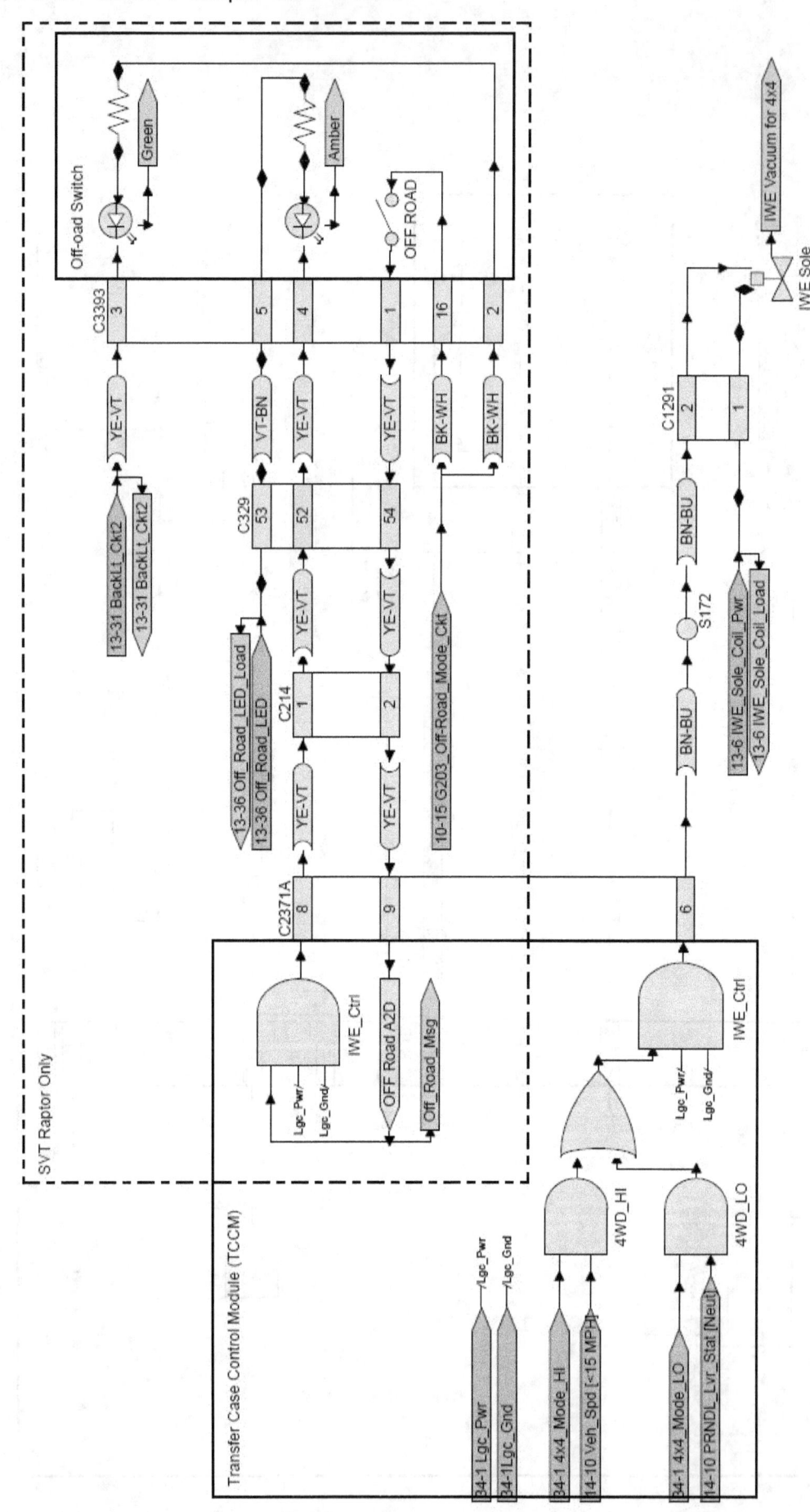

TCCM – ESOF / Torque On Demand **34-4**

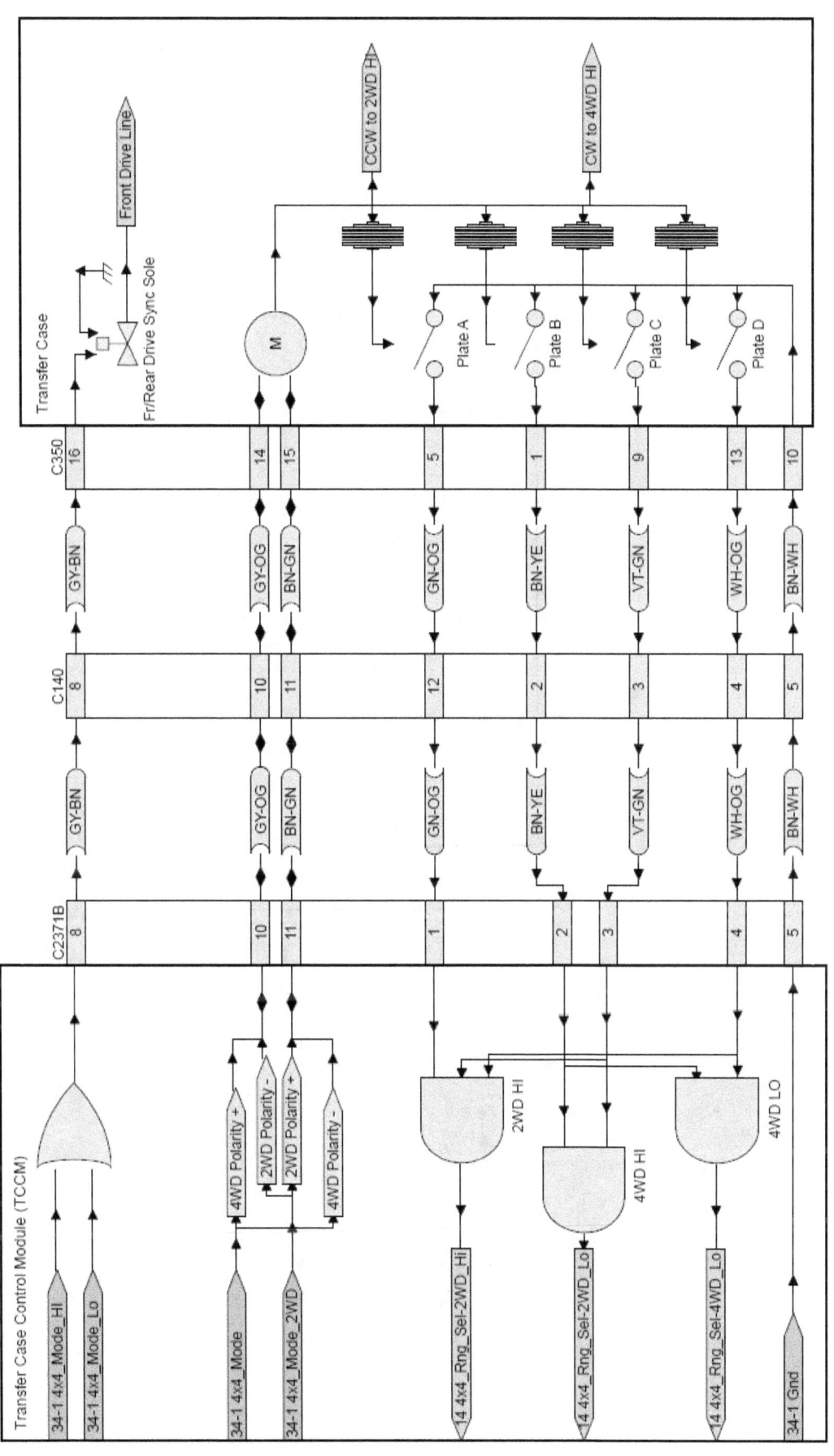

143

37 Brake Shift Interlock
37-1 Brake Shift Interlock – Column Shifter

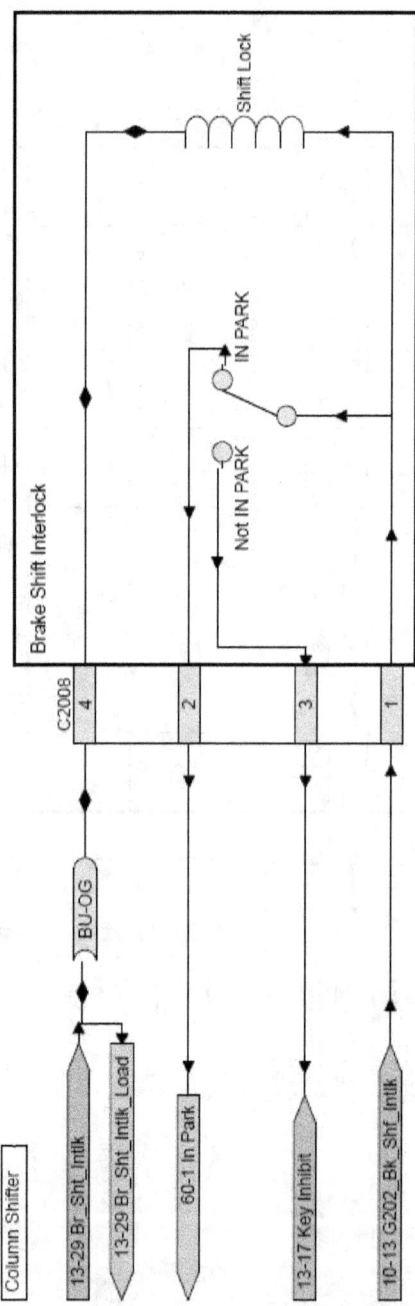

144

Brake Shift Interlock – Floor Shifter 37-2

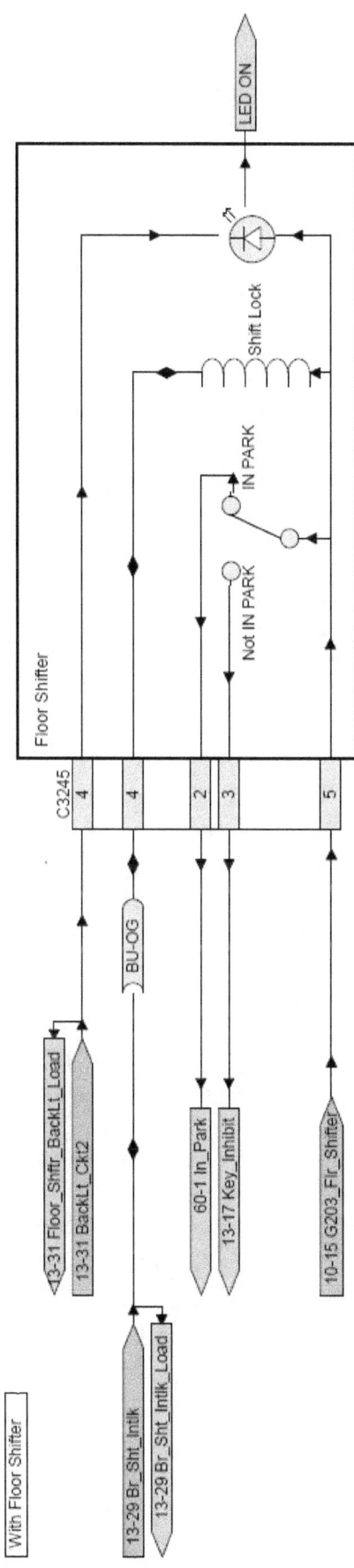

42 Anti-Lock Braking System Module (ABSM)

42-1 ABSM – CAN Bus, Power, Ground and Brake Cylinder Press Snsr

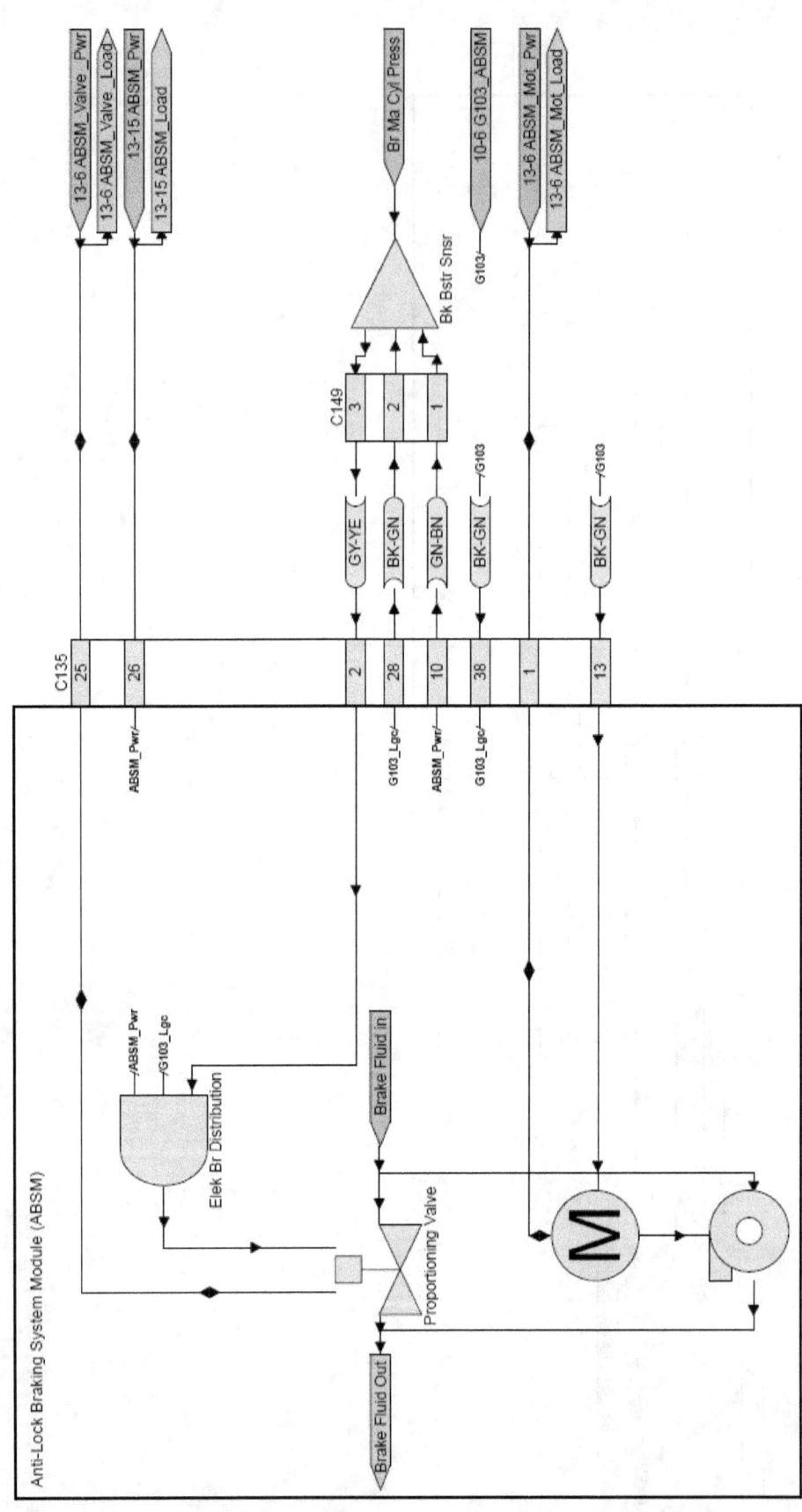

ABSM – Wheel Speed Sensors and Stability Control 42-2

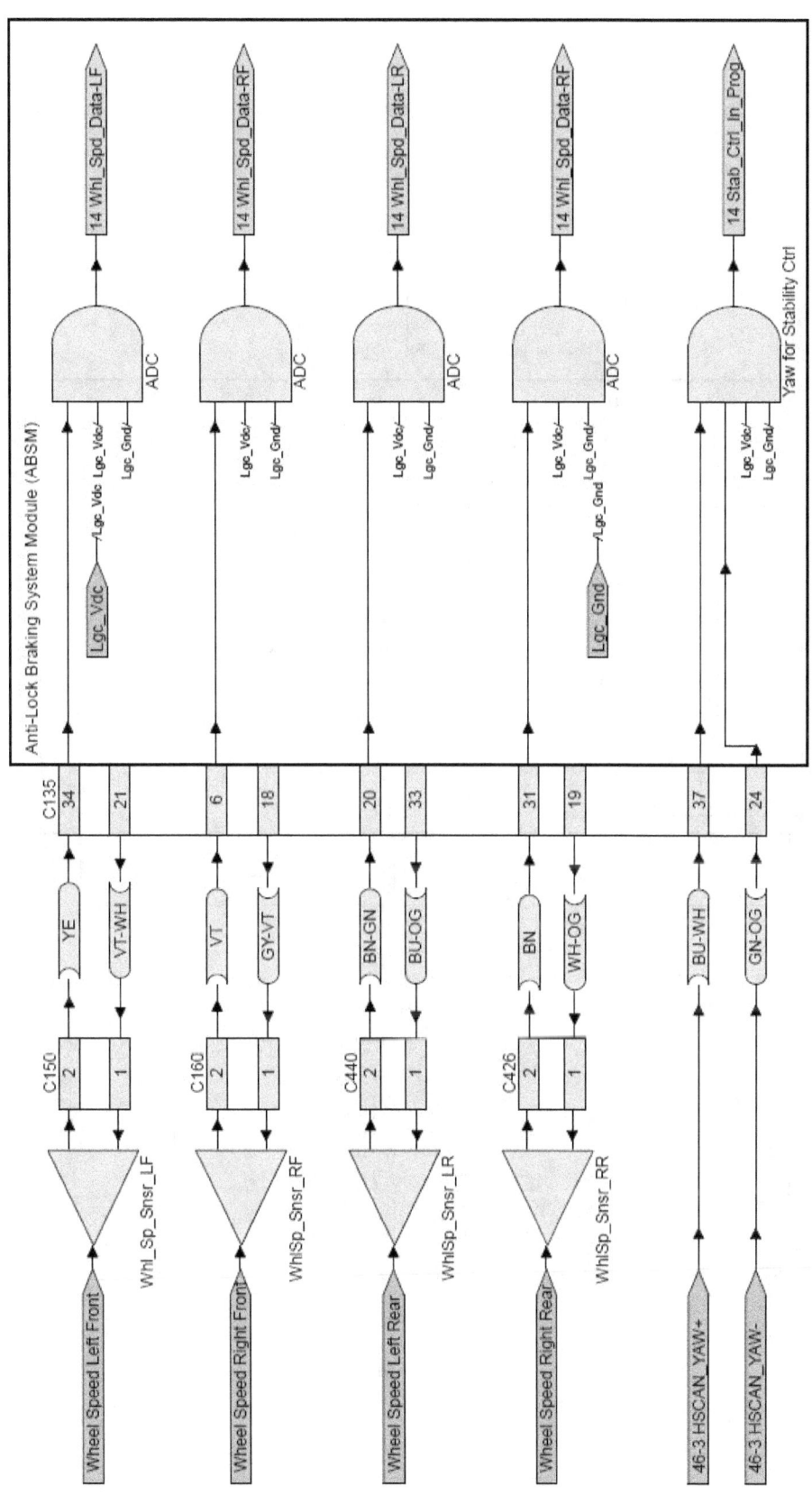

42-4 Hazard / PAD / Traction Switch

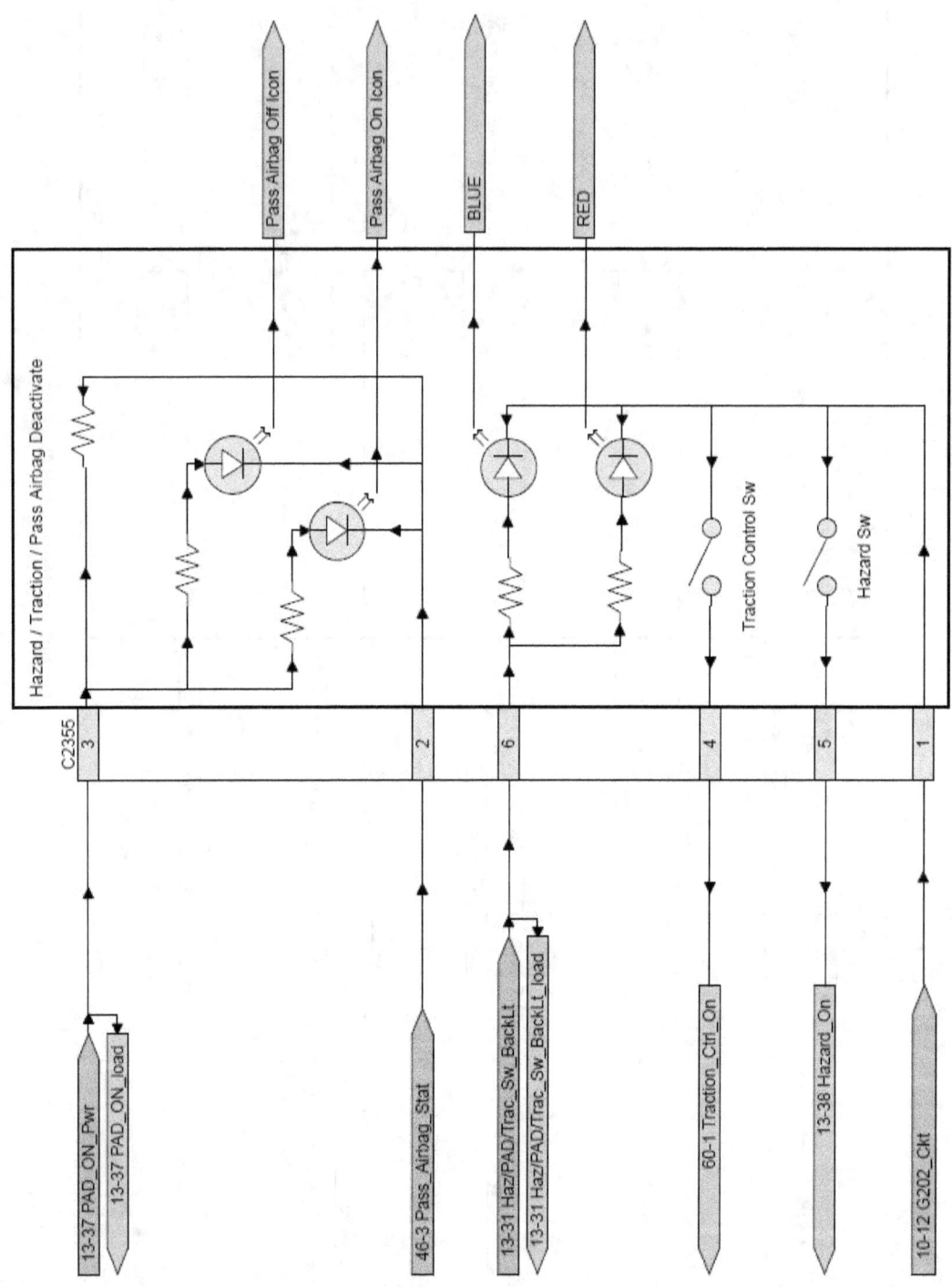

43-1 Power Steering Control Module – Steering Gear

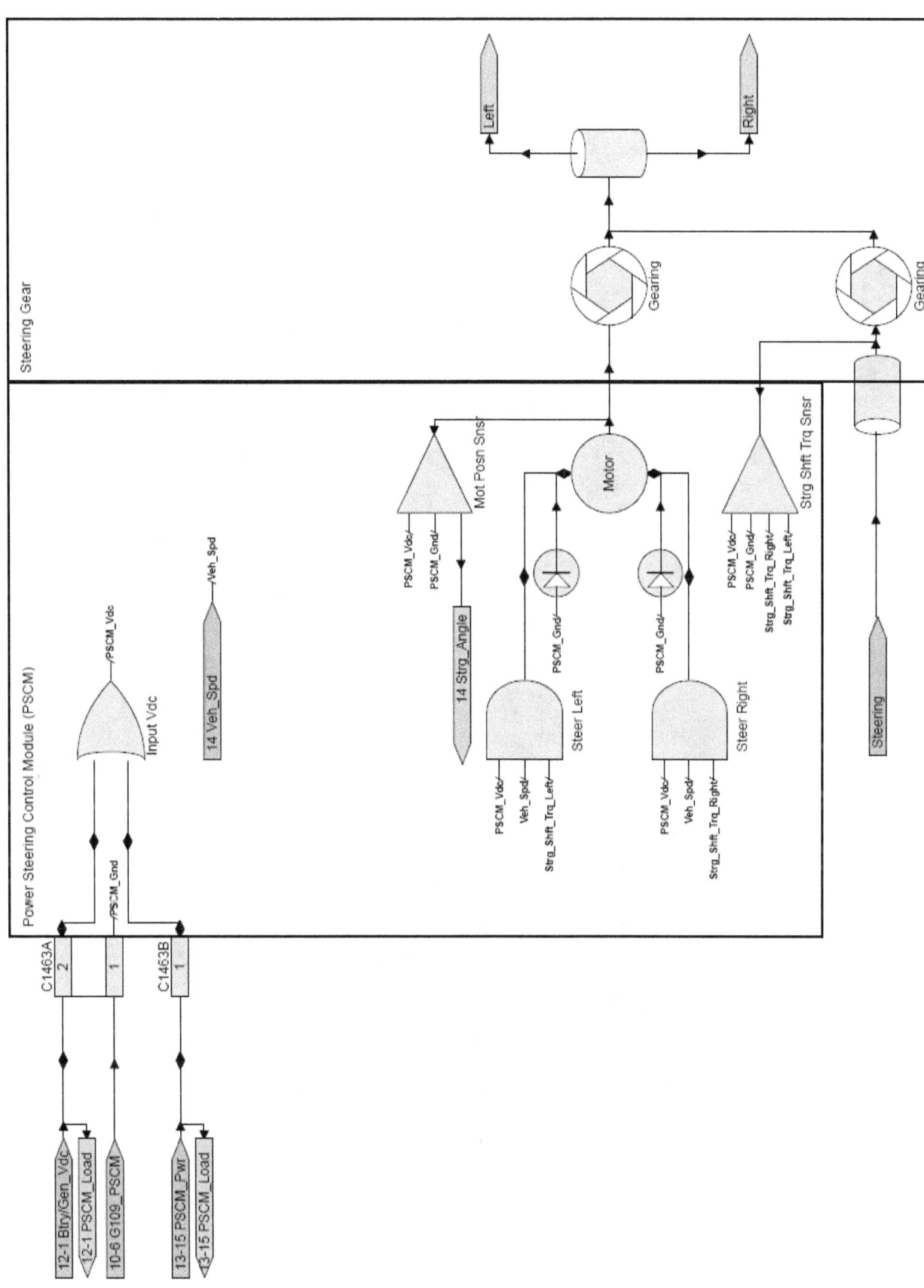

44-2 Horn Circuit

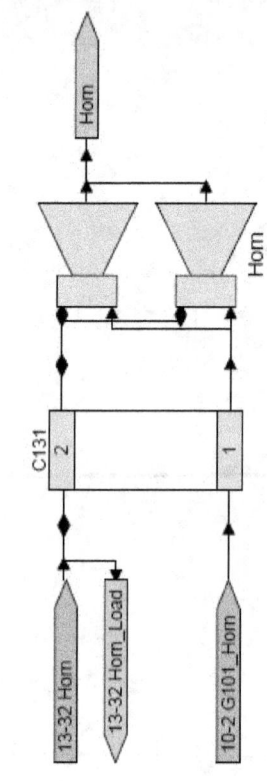
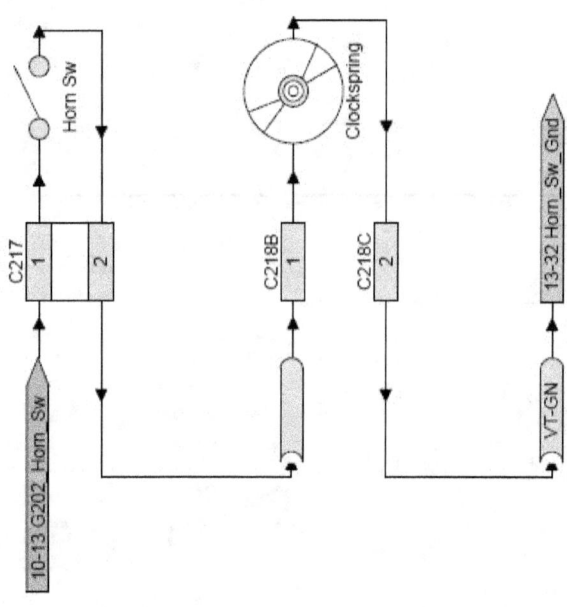

44-4 DC / AC Inverter Module – AC Outlet

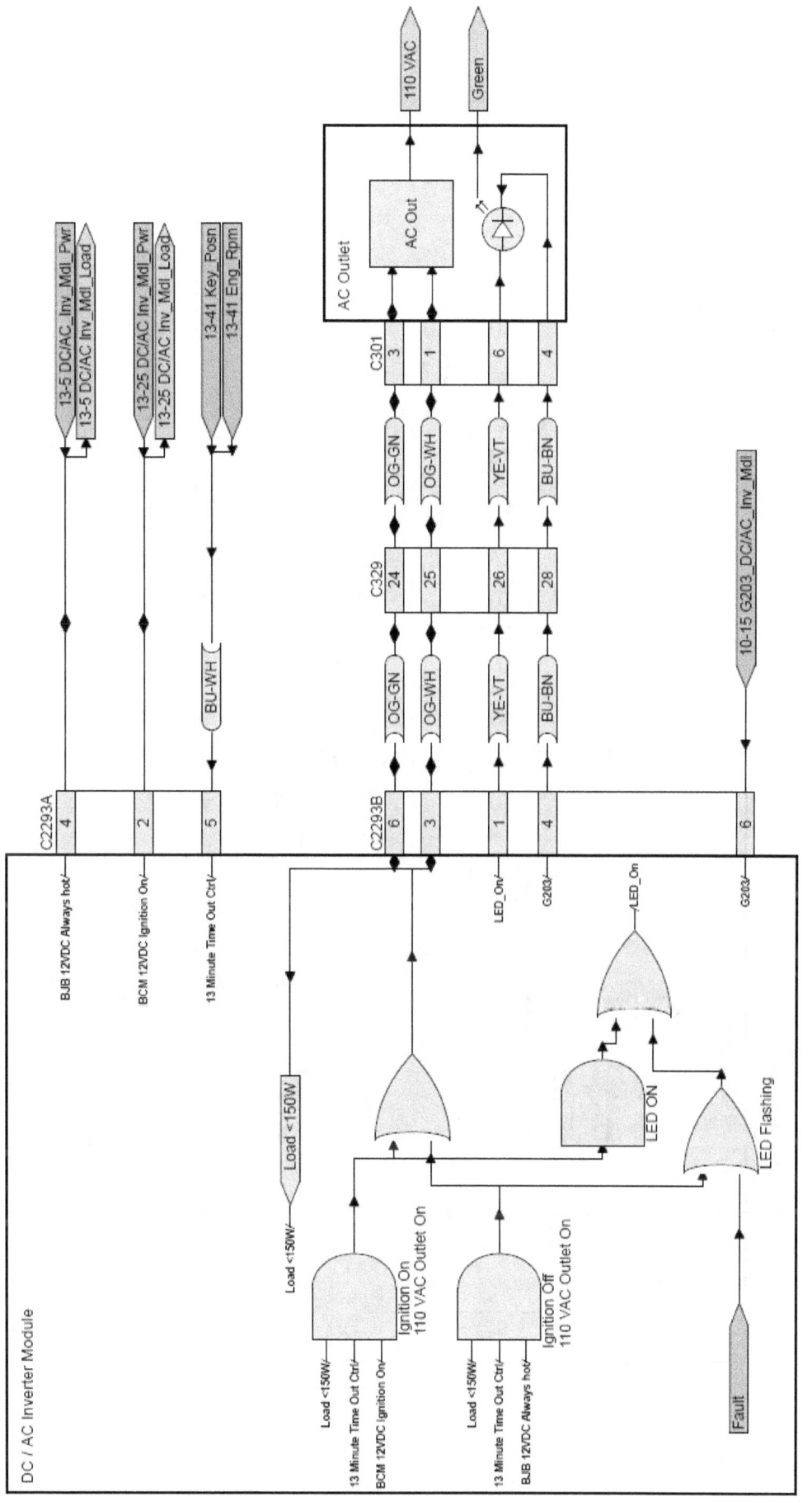

46 Occupant Classification Module (OCM) & Restraint Control Module (RCM)

46-1 OCM – CAN Bus, Power, Grounds and Weight Sensors

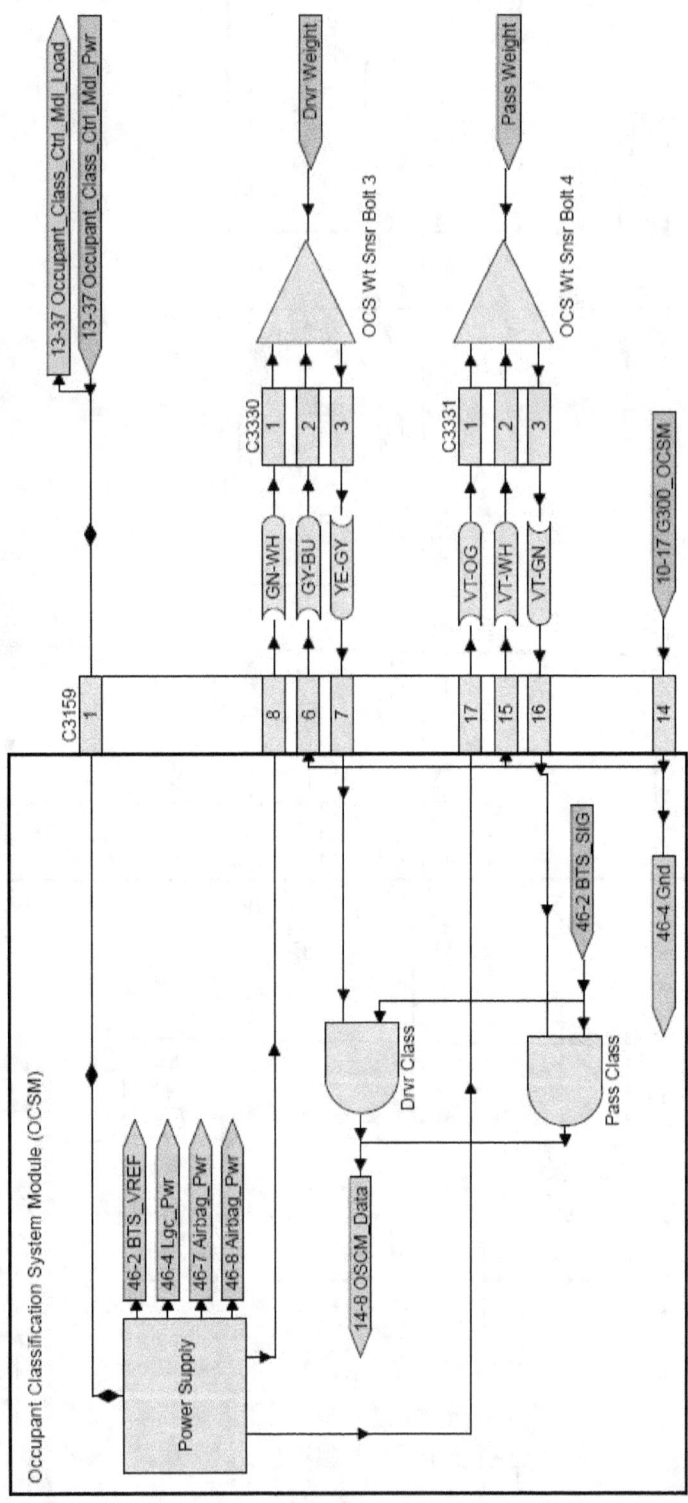

OCM – Belt Tensioners 46-2

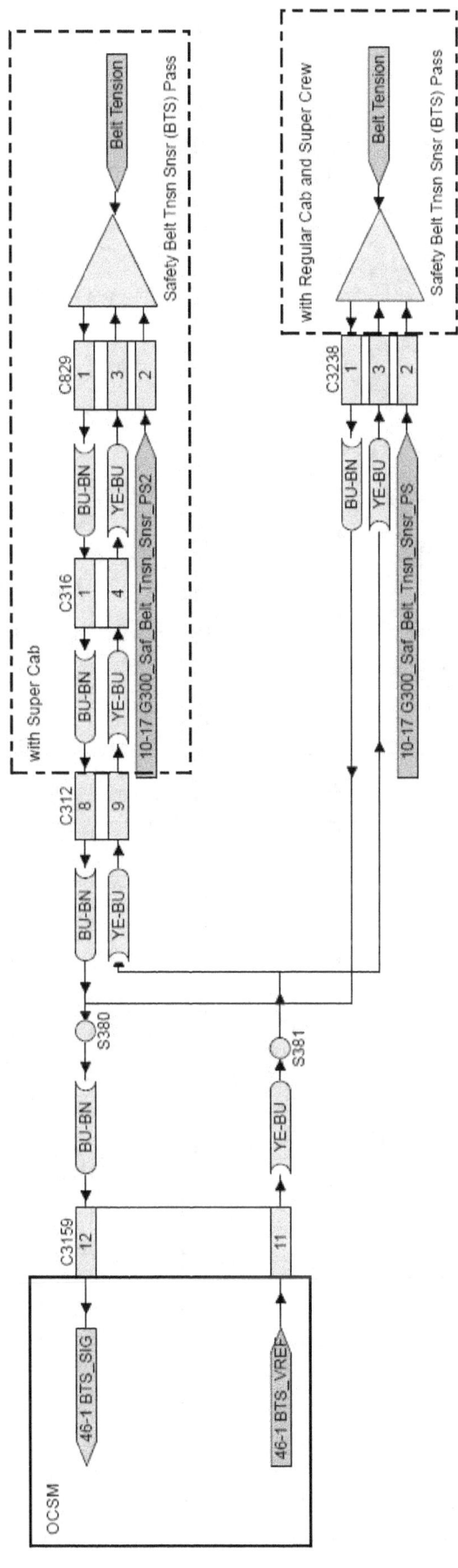

46-3 RCM – CAN Bus, Fuel Pump Enable, Stability Yaw Gyro and PAD

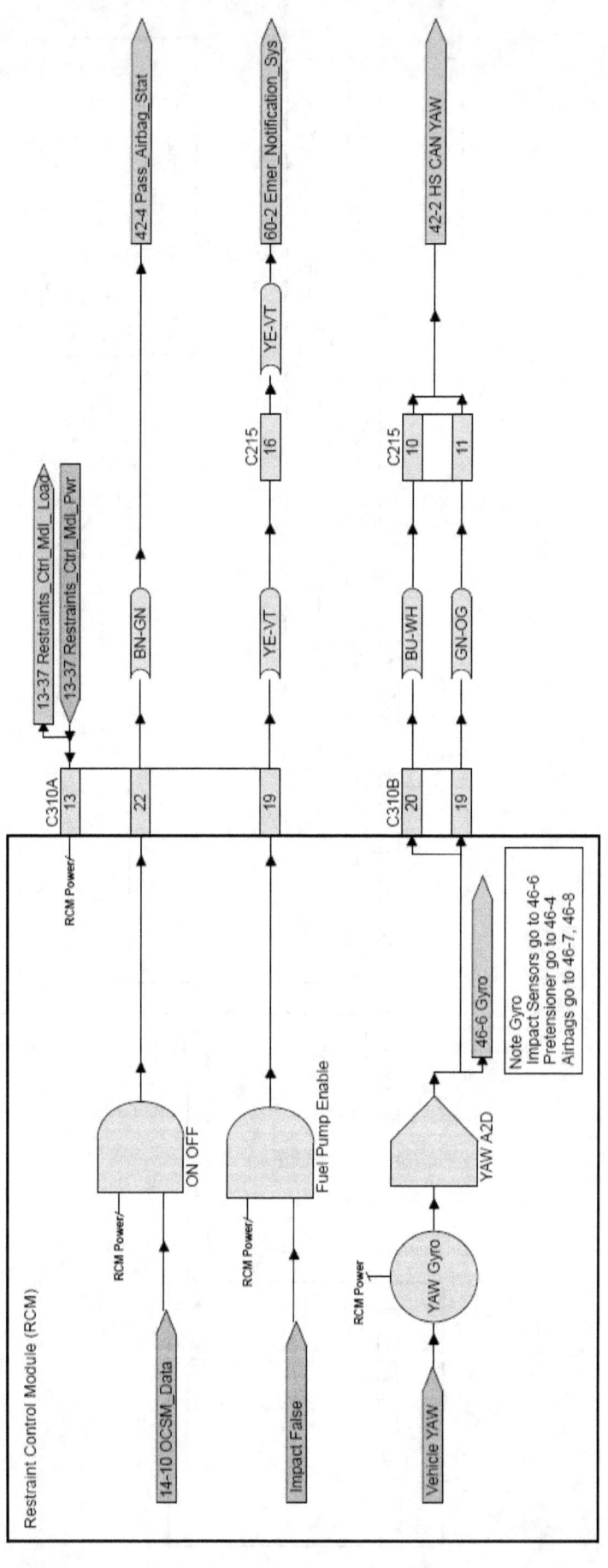

RCM – Driver Seat Belt Pretensioner, Buckle Switch and Seat Position Snsr 46-4

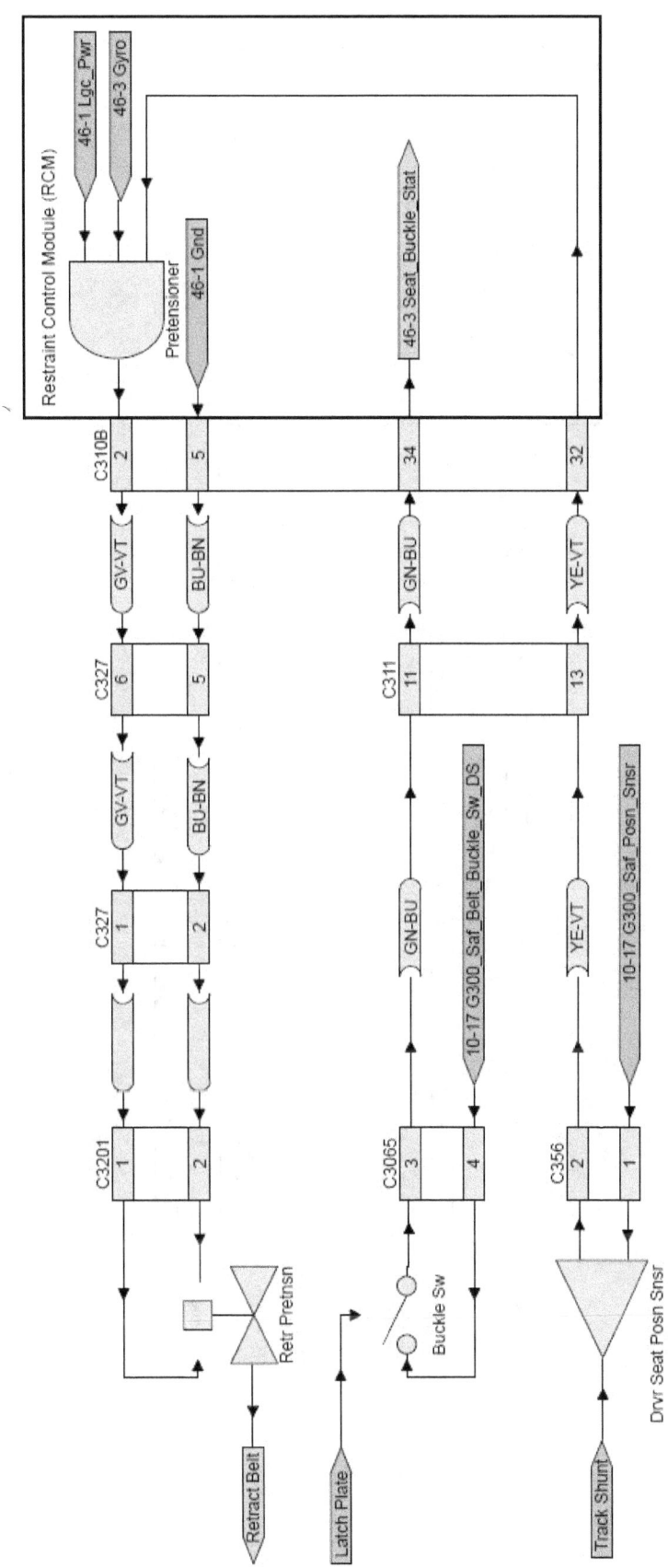

46-5 RCM – Passenger Seat Belt Pretensioner, and Buckle Switch

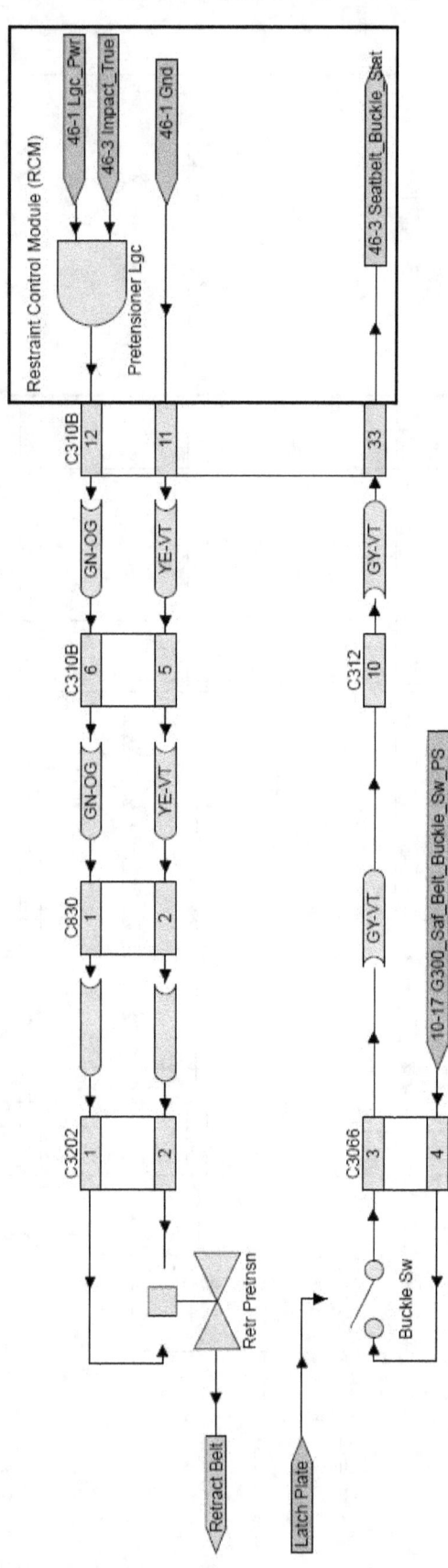

156

RCM – Impact Sensors **46-6**

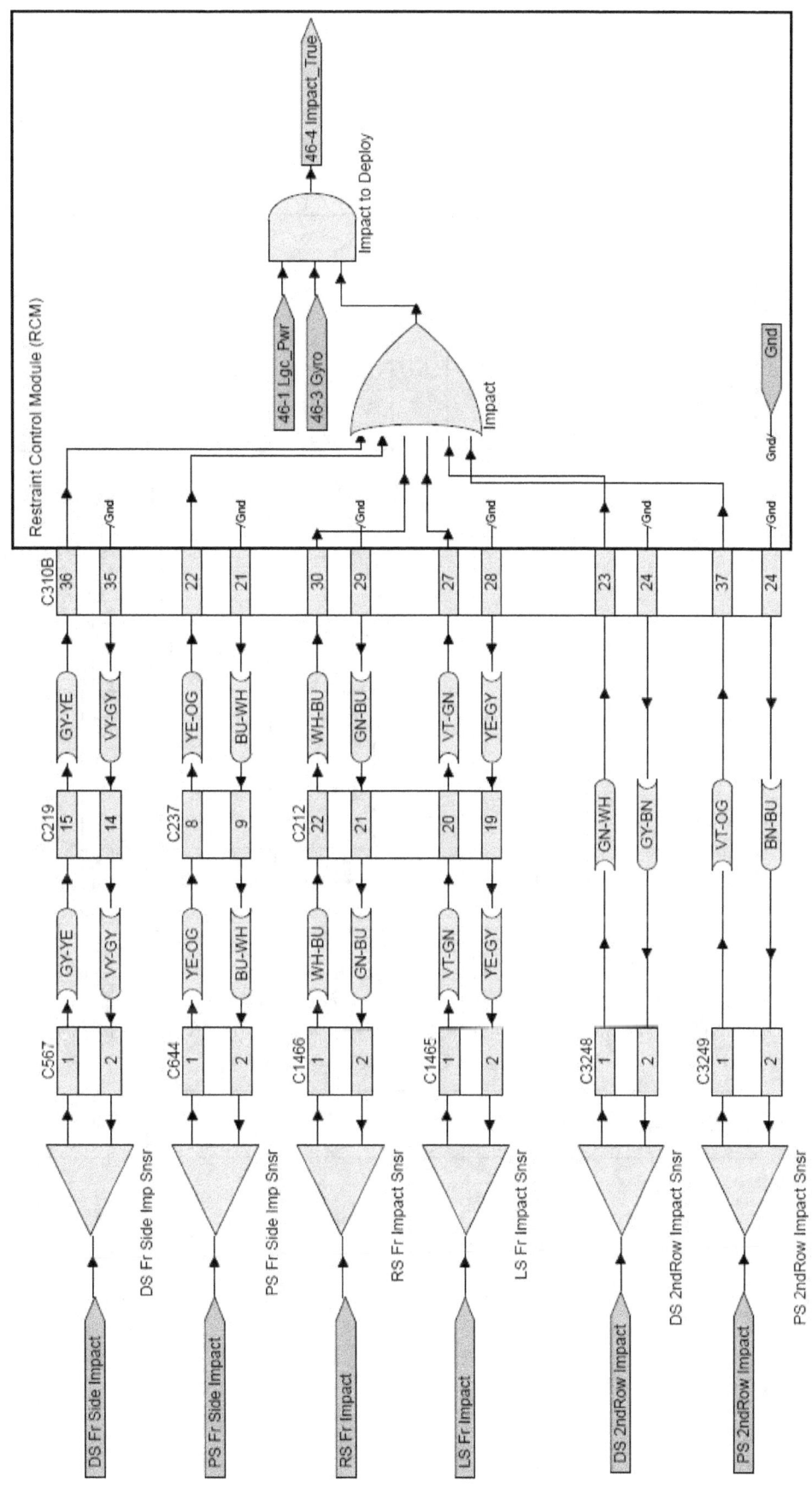

46-7 RCM – Airbags

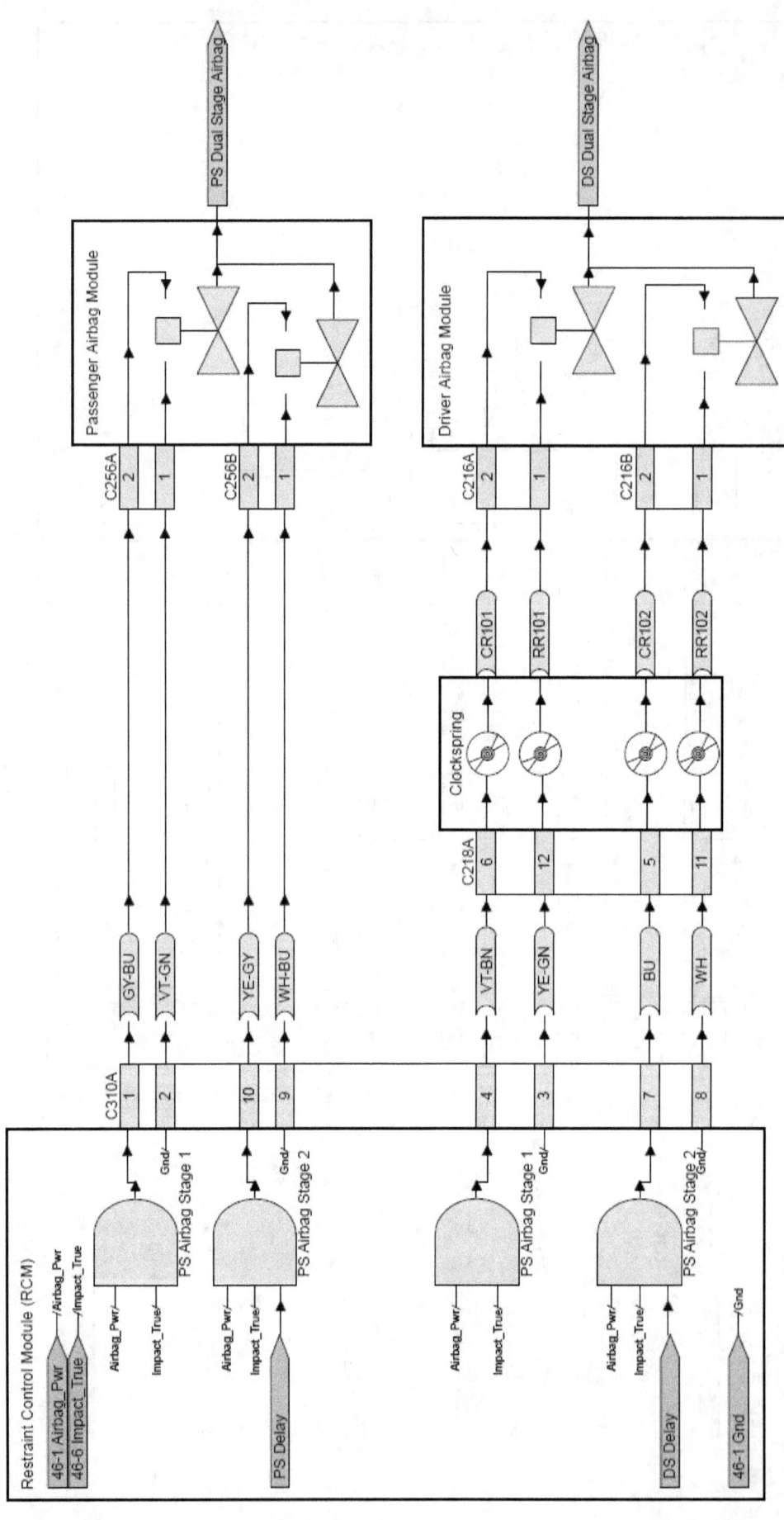

RCM – Side Airbags 46-8

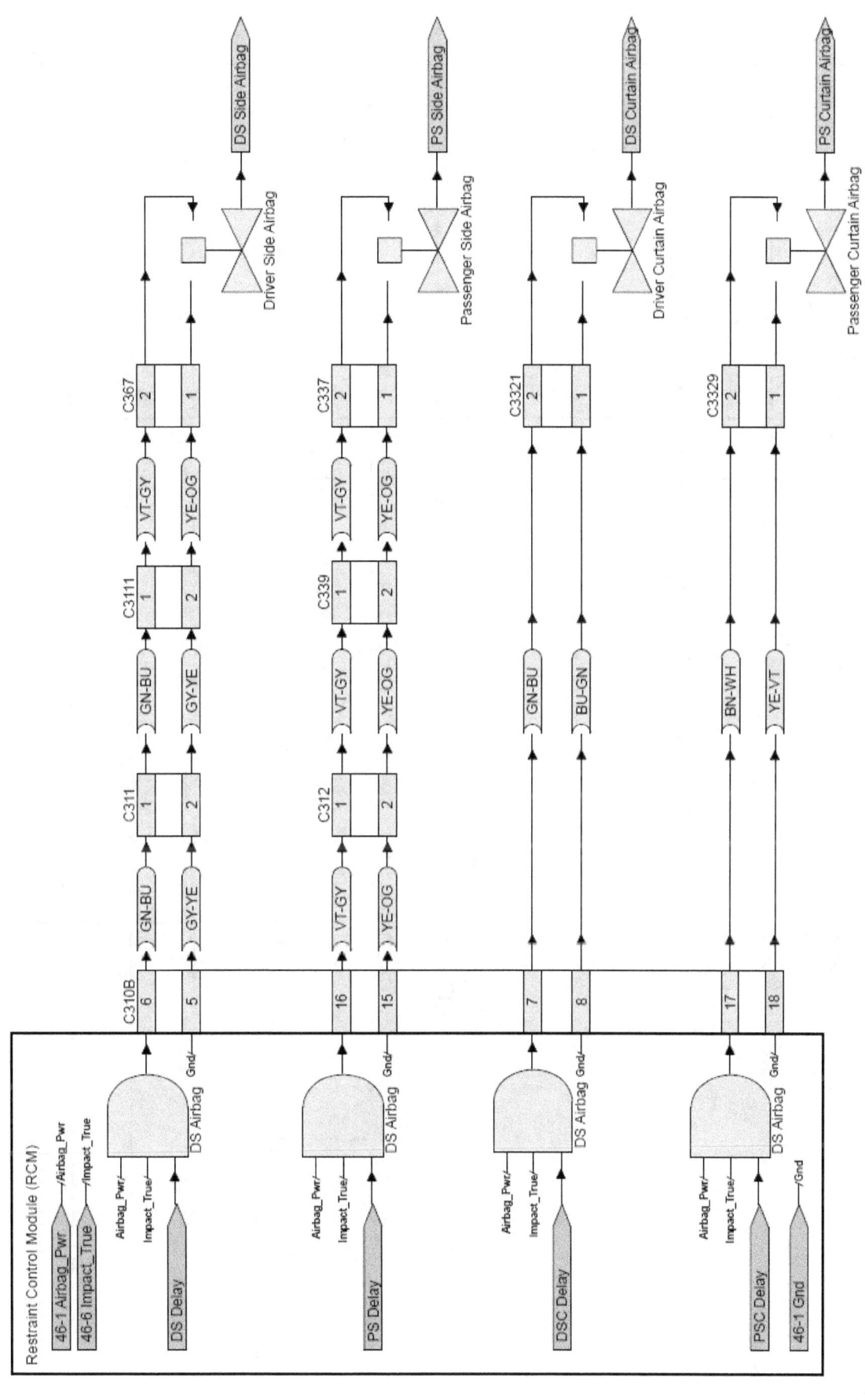

54 Electronic Manual Temperature Control (EMTC) System
54-1 EMTC Controls

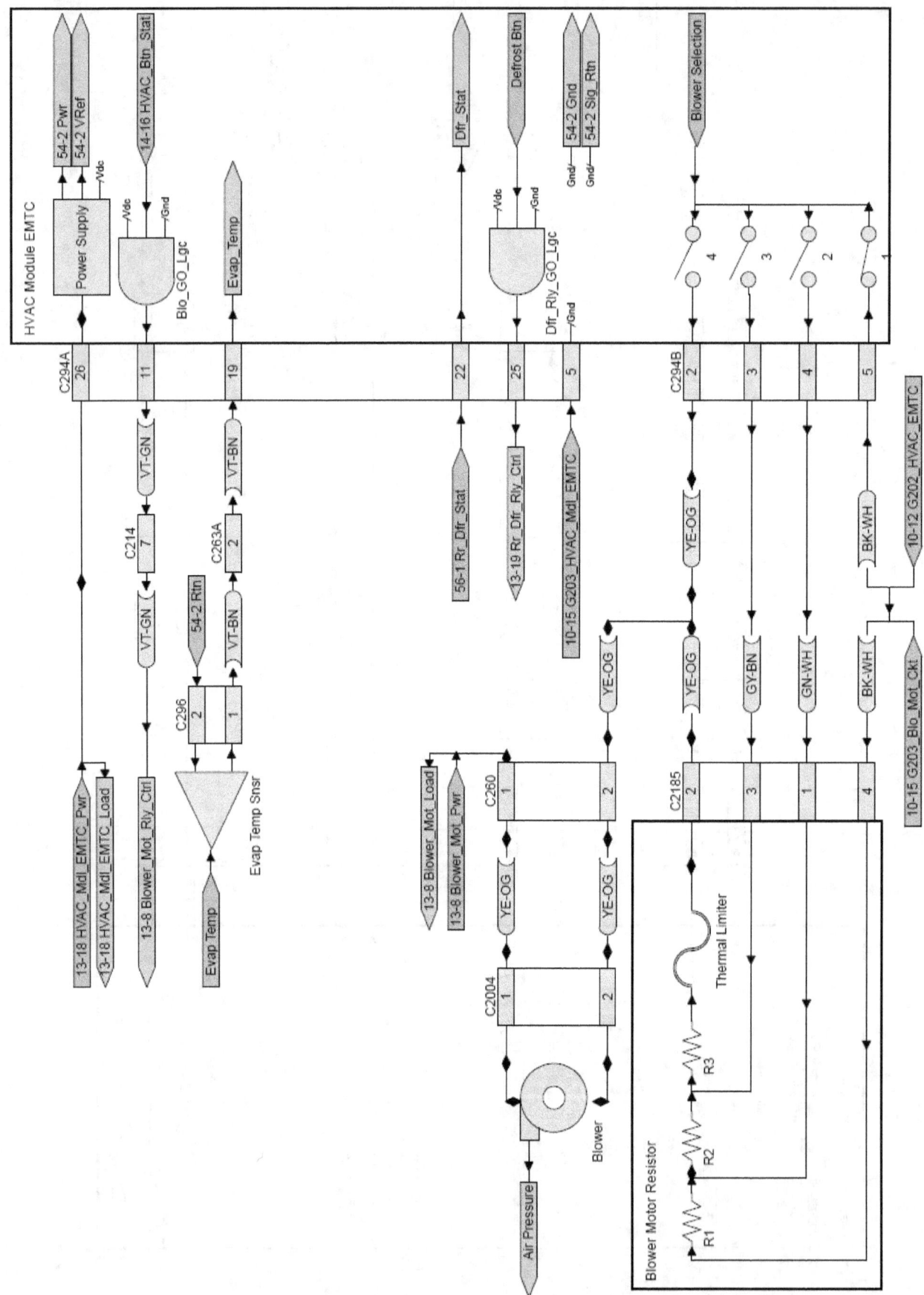

EMTC, Actuators **54-2**

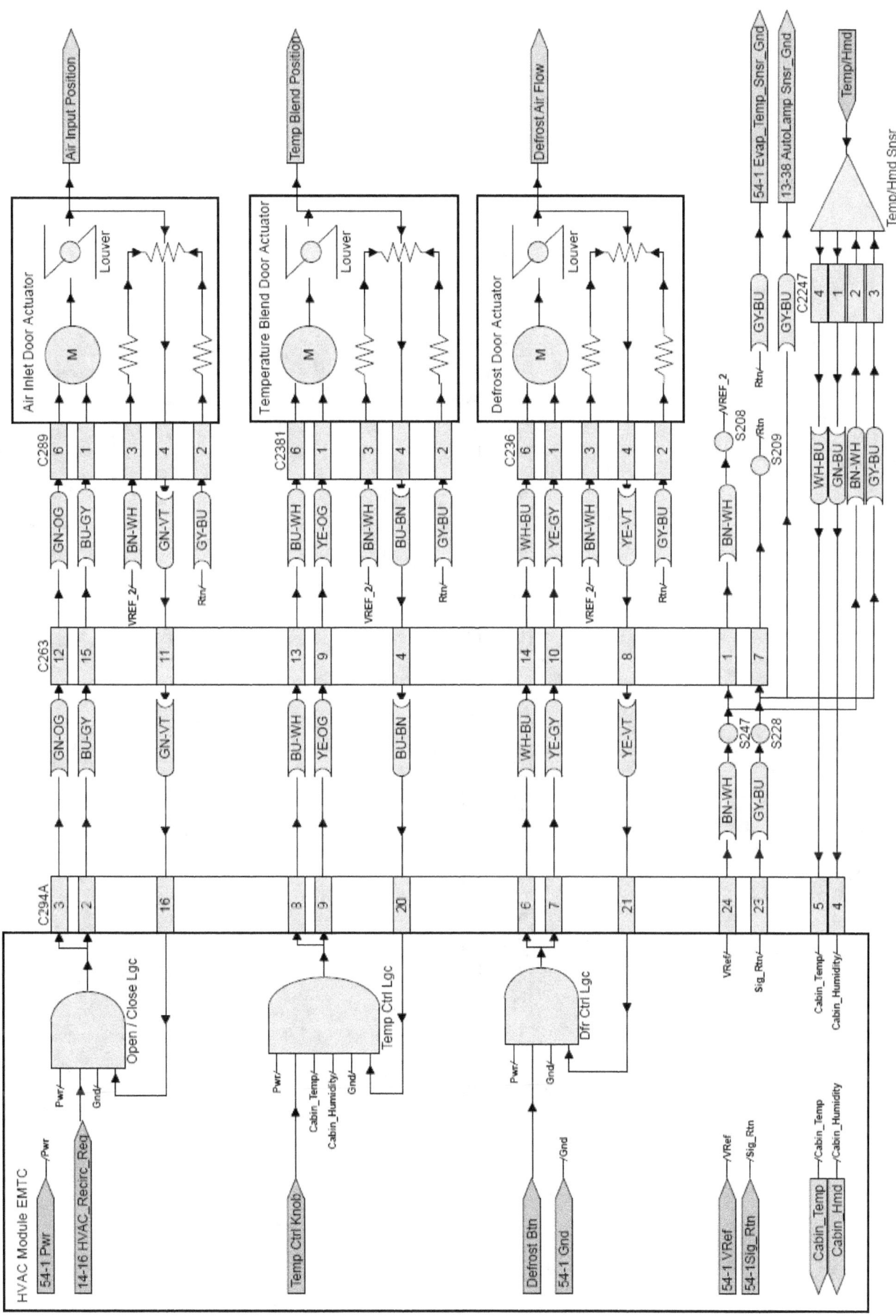

54-3 A/C Compressor Clutch

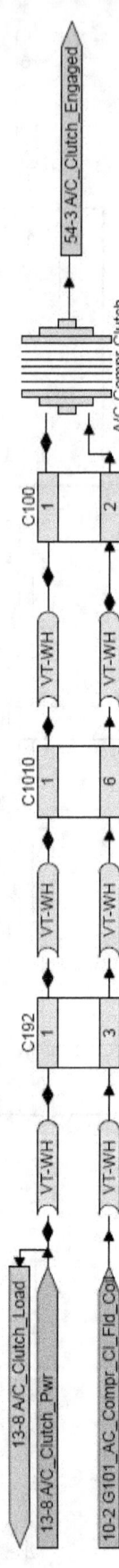

EMTC Remote Mount 54-4

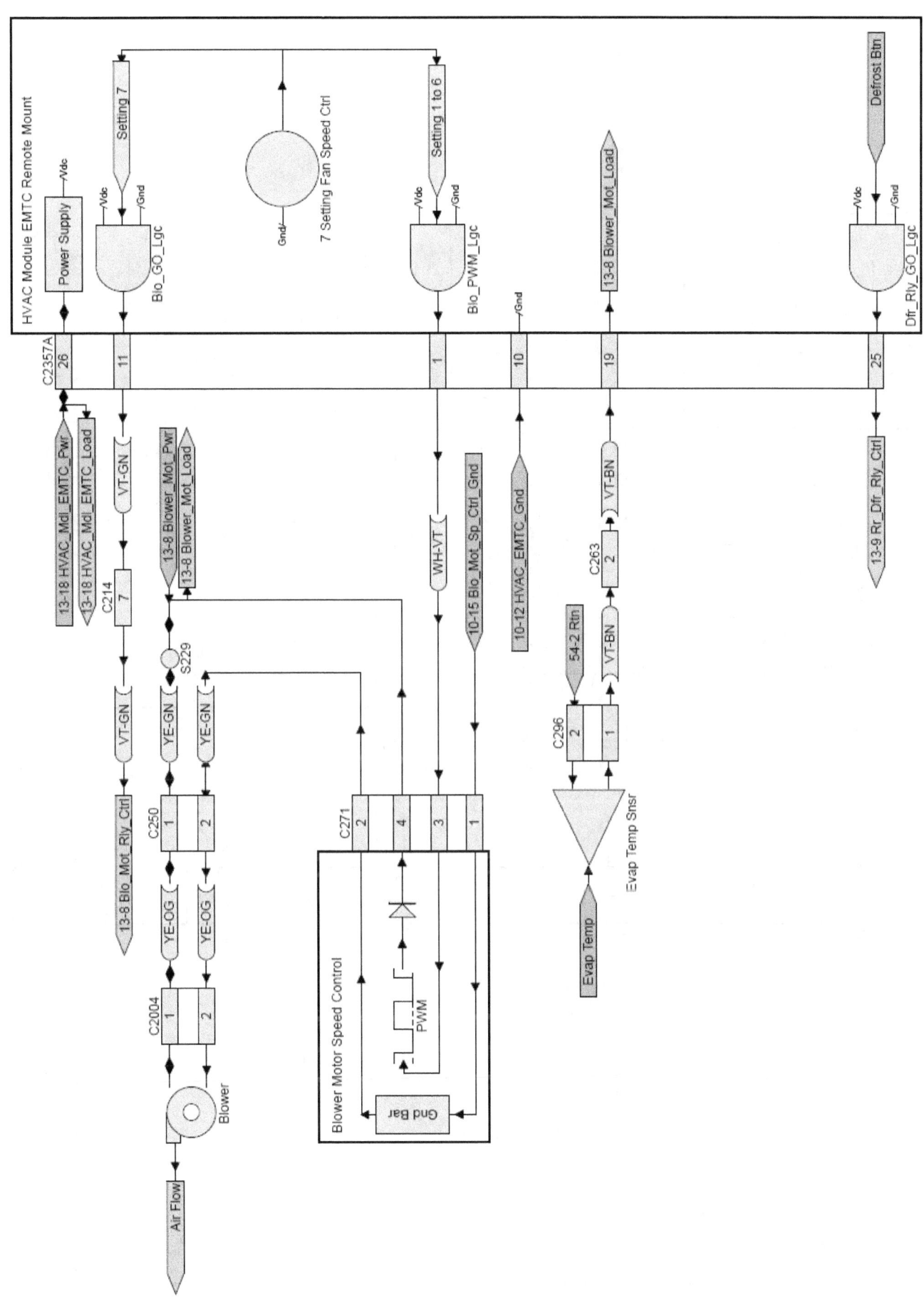

54-5 EMTC Remote Mount Actuators

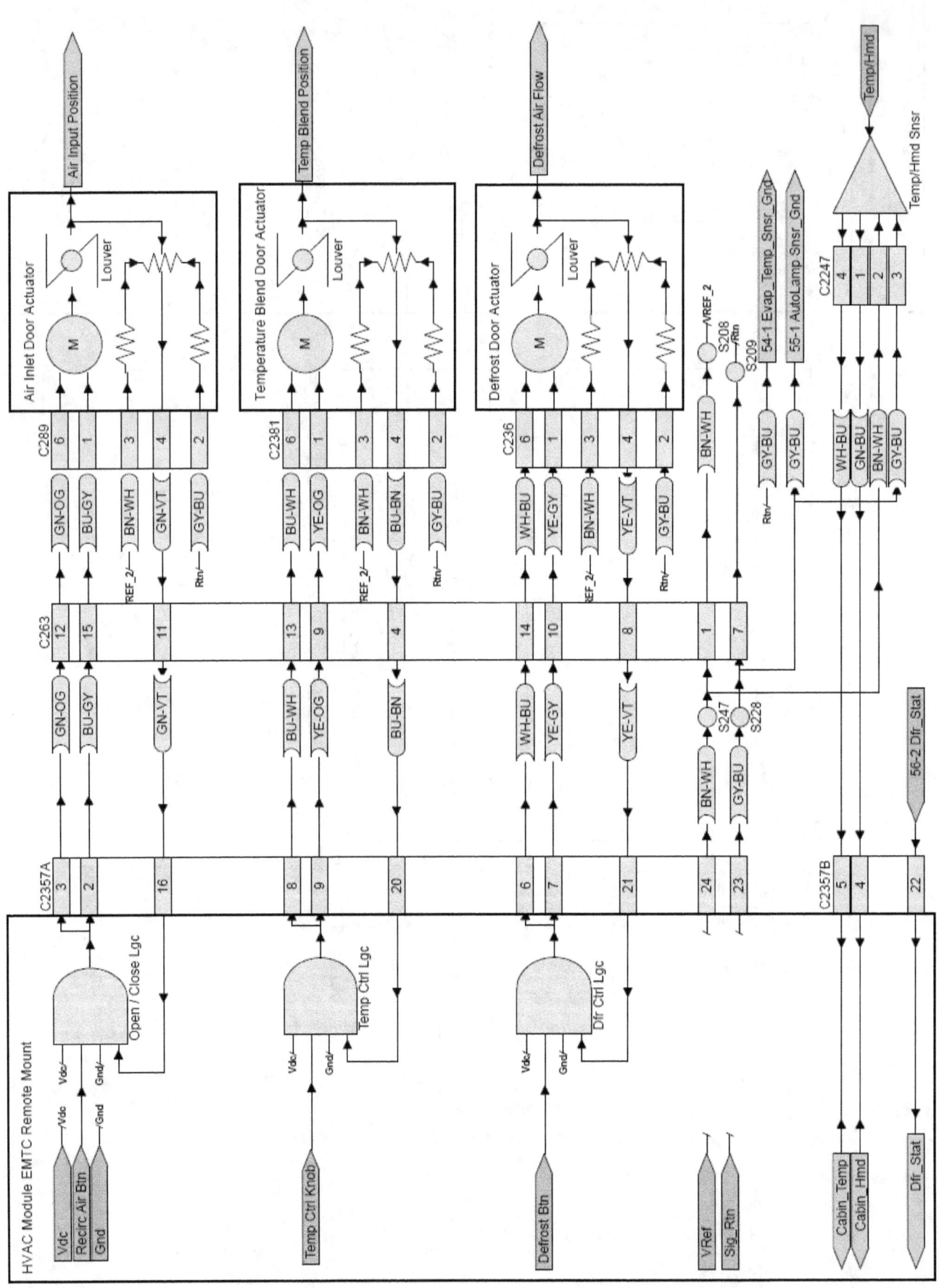

55 Electronic Automatic Temperature Control (EATC) System

EATC Control 55-1

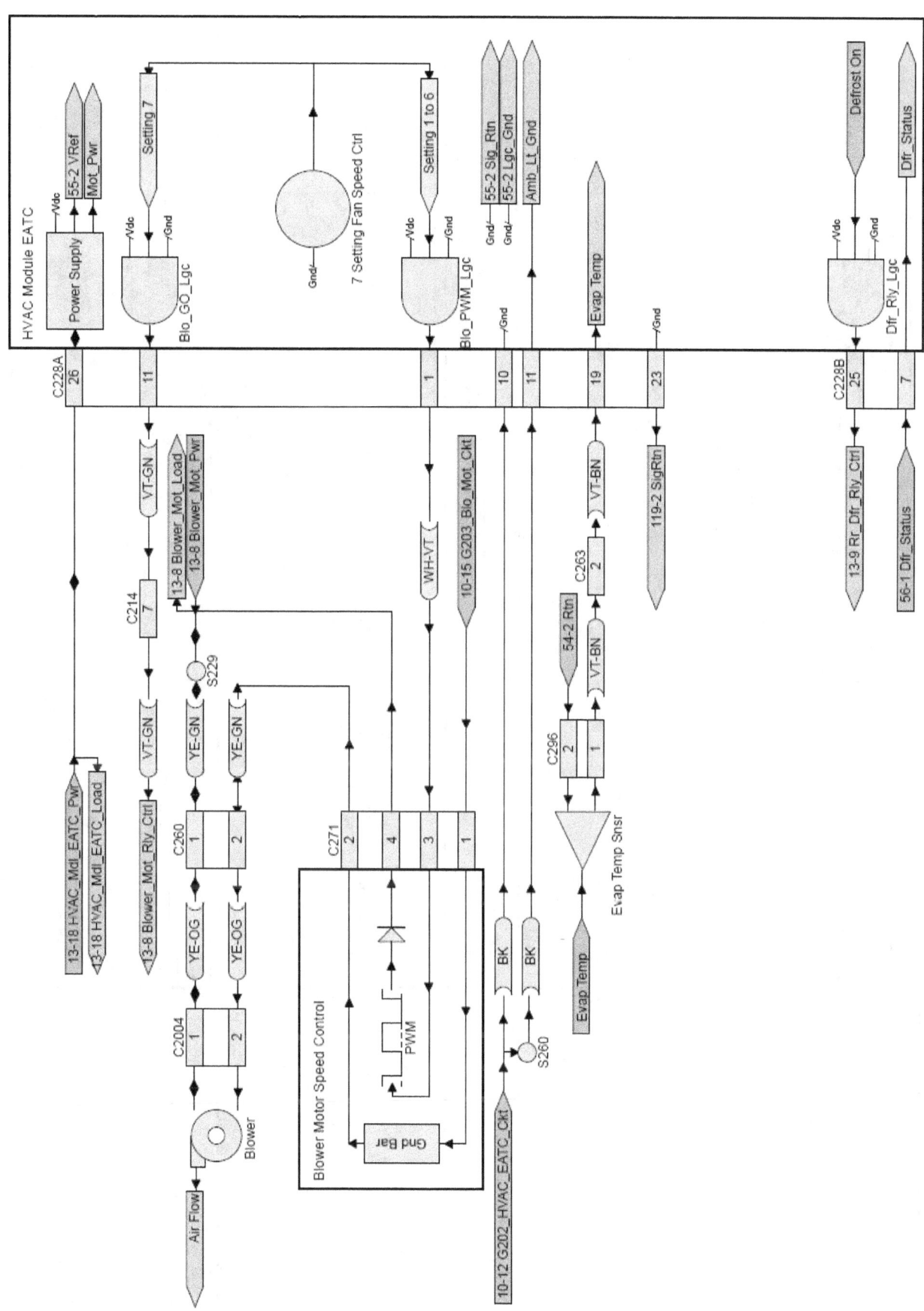

165

55-2 EATC Actuators

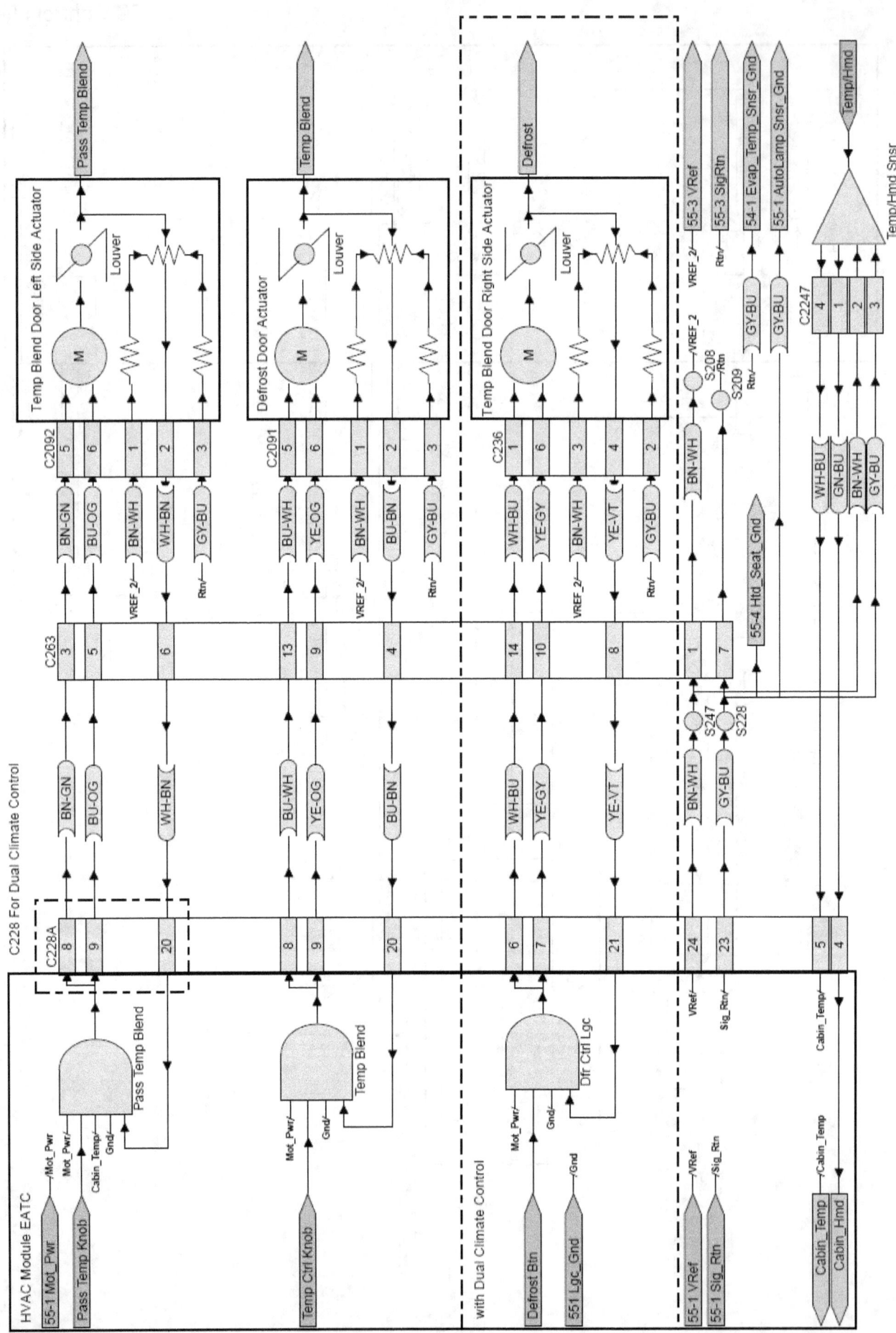

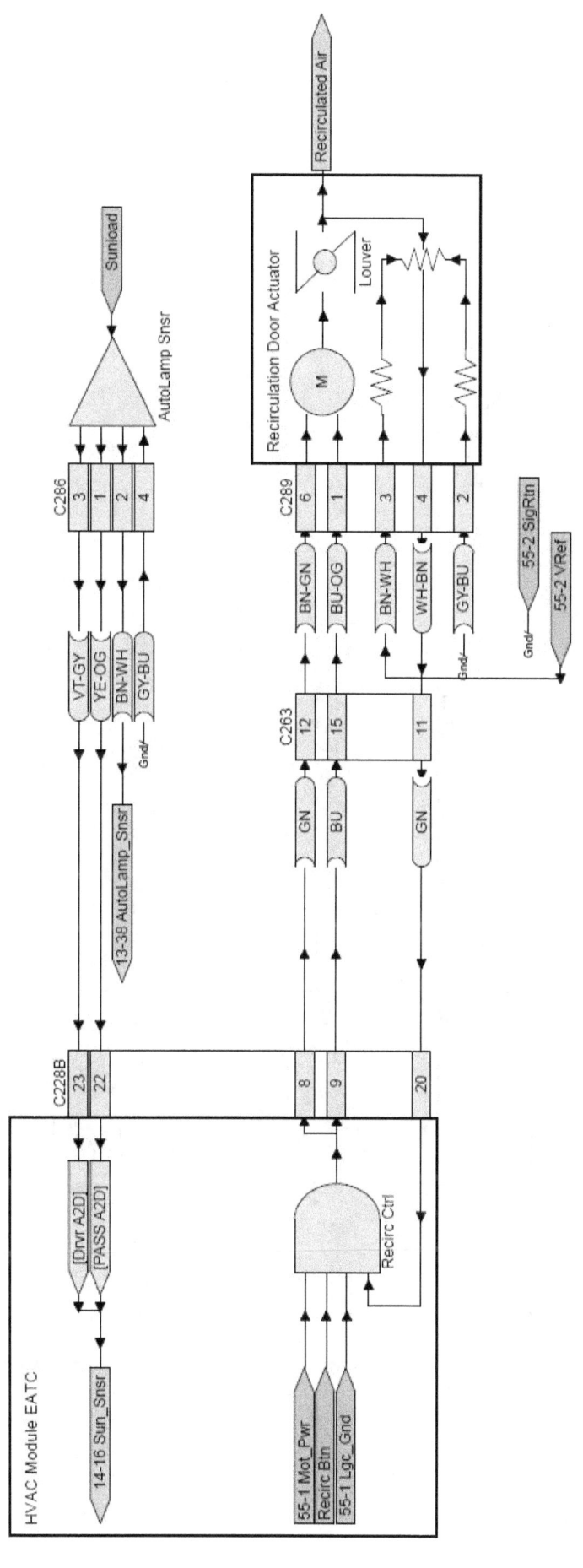

55-4 EATC Heated Seats

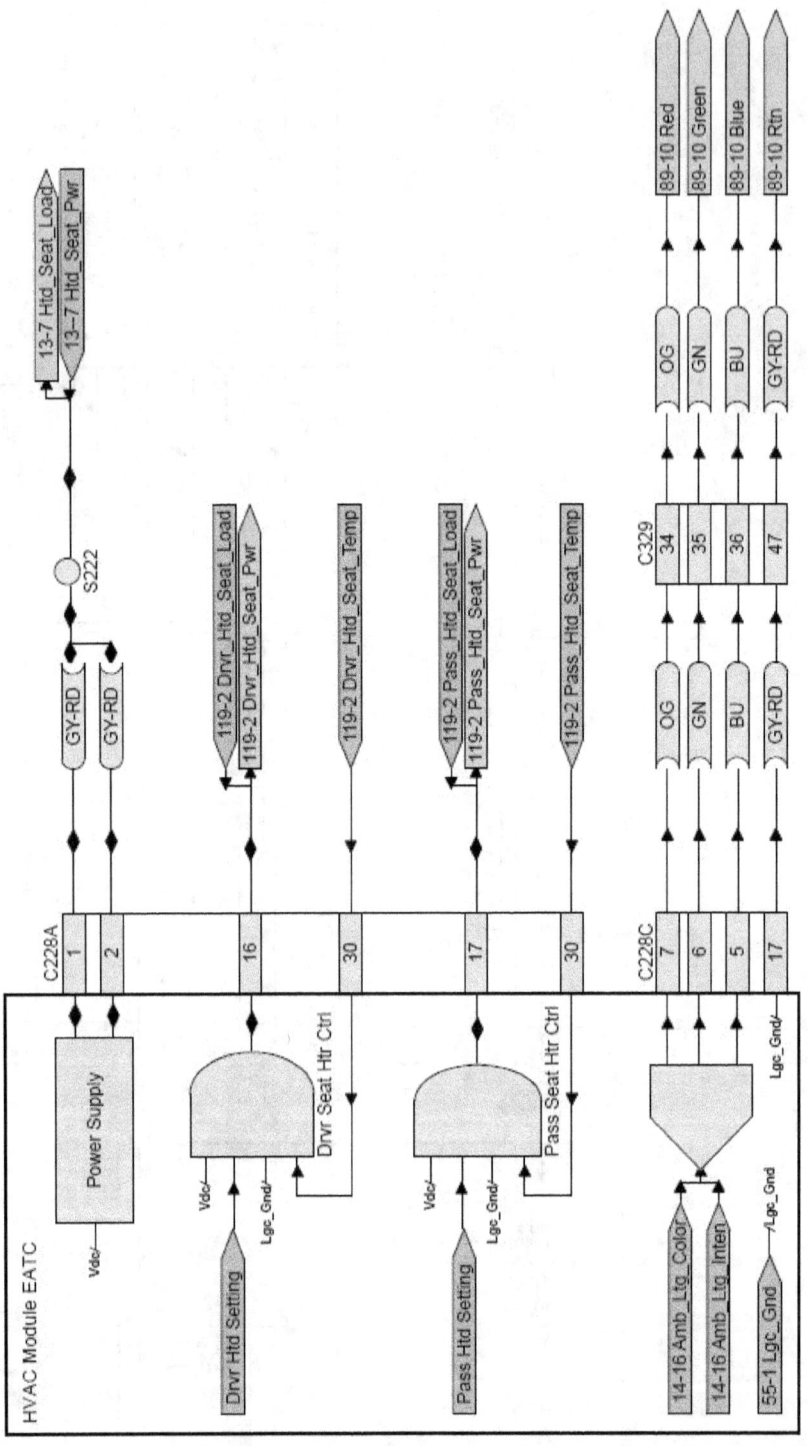

56-1 Heated Windows Rear Defrost Grid

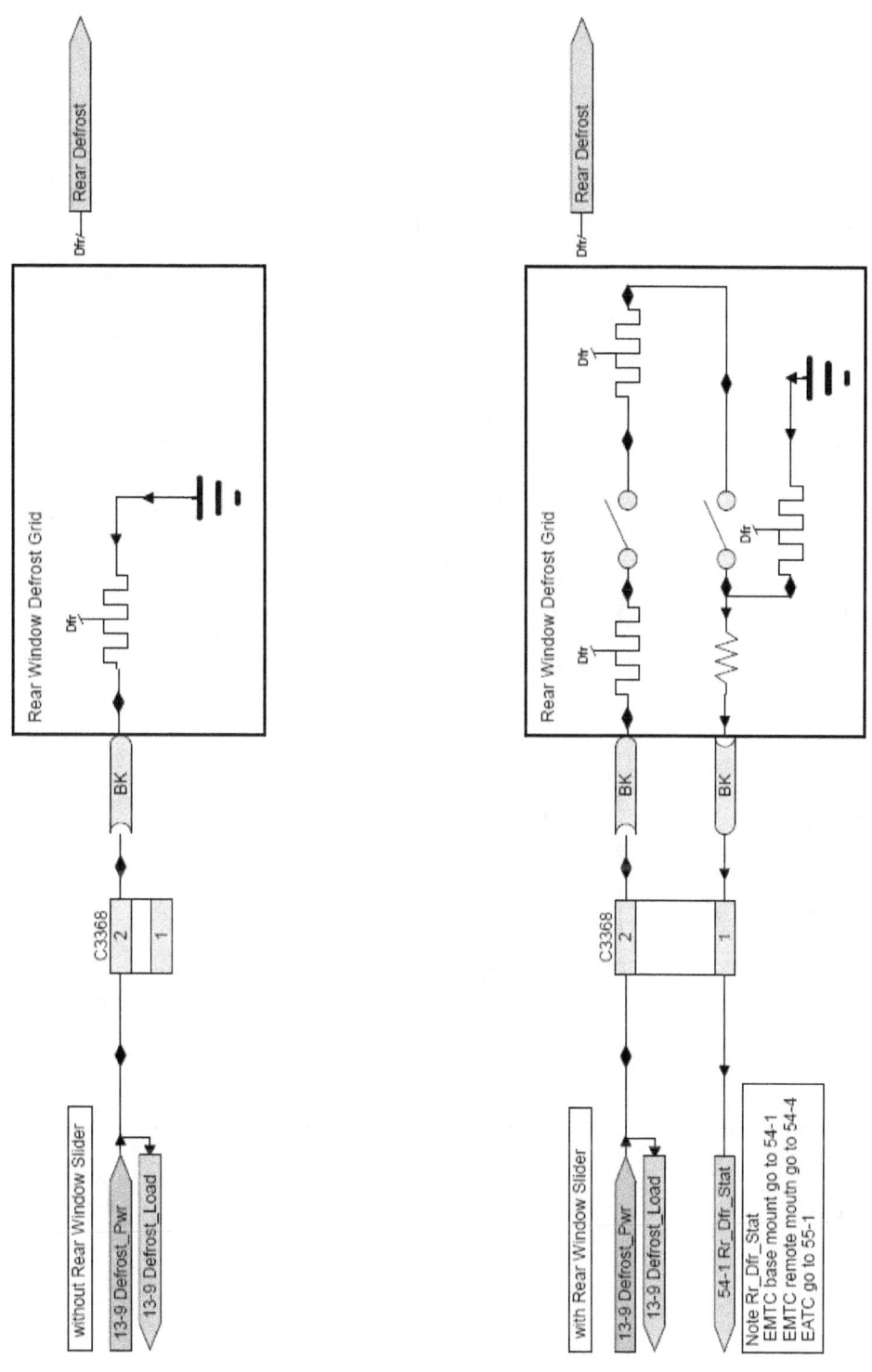

60 Instrument Panel Cluster (IPC)
60-1 IPC – CAN Bus, Power & Grounds

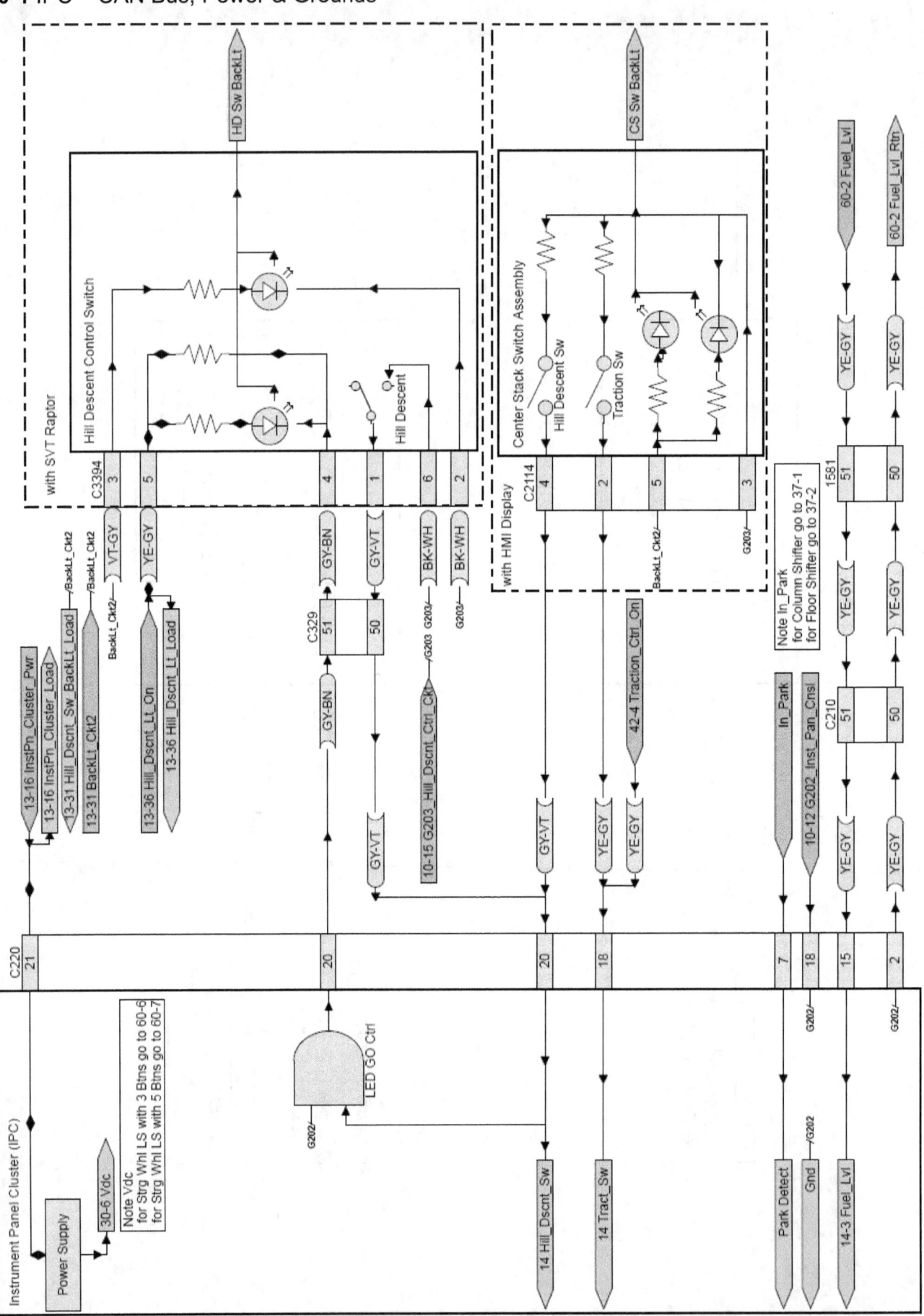

IPC – Hill Descent Control and Fuel Level **60-2**

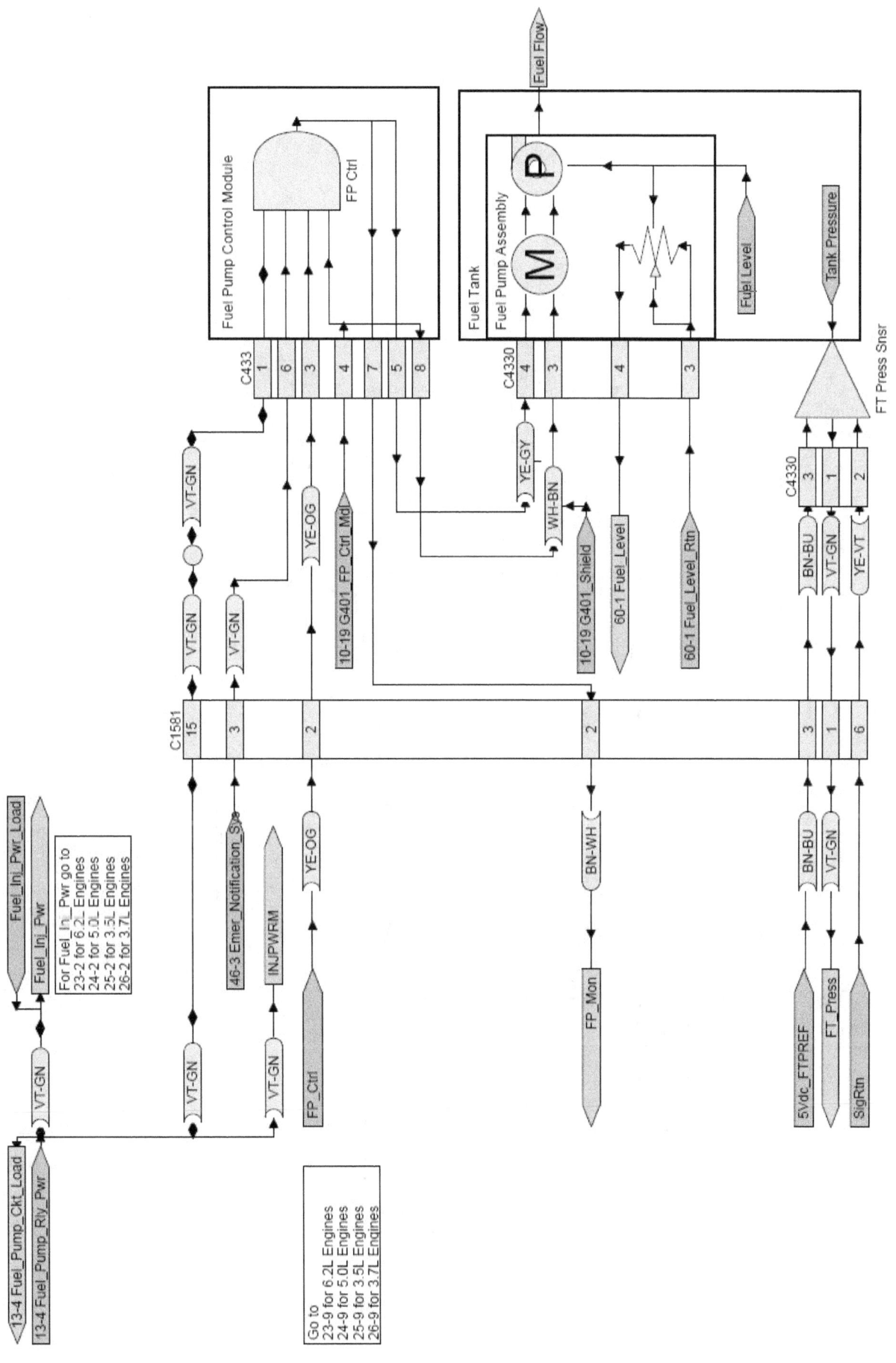

171

60-3 IPC – Brake Fluid Level and Parking Brake

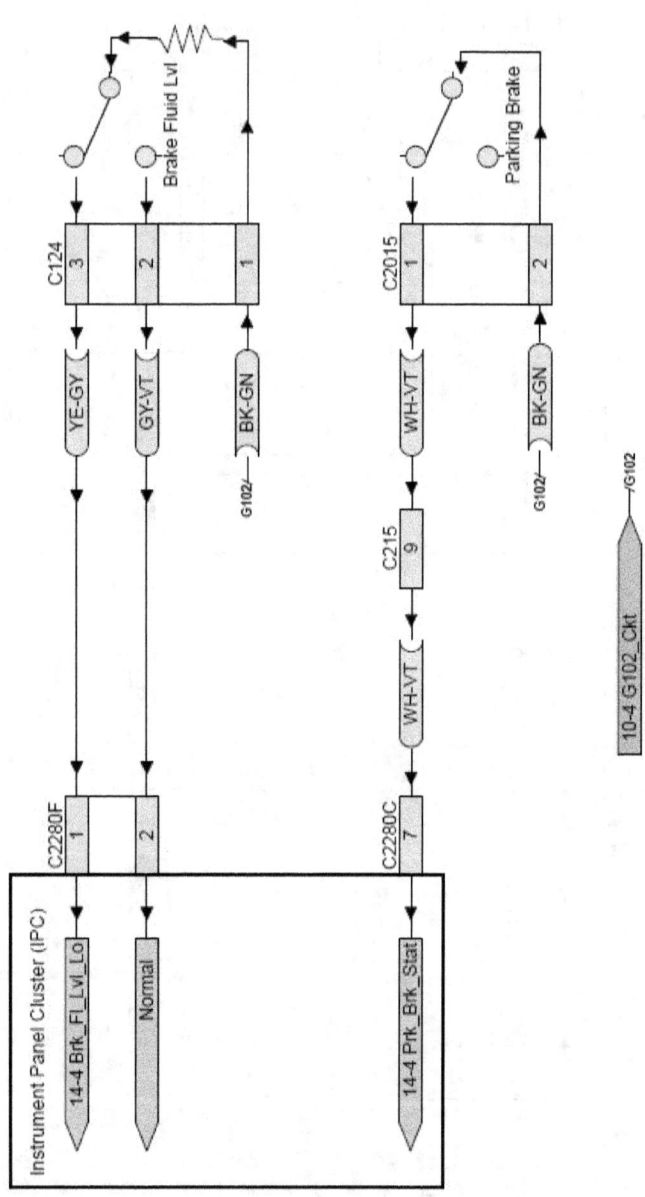

Electronic Compass **60-4**

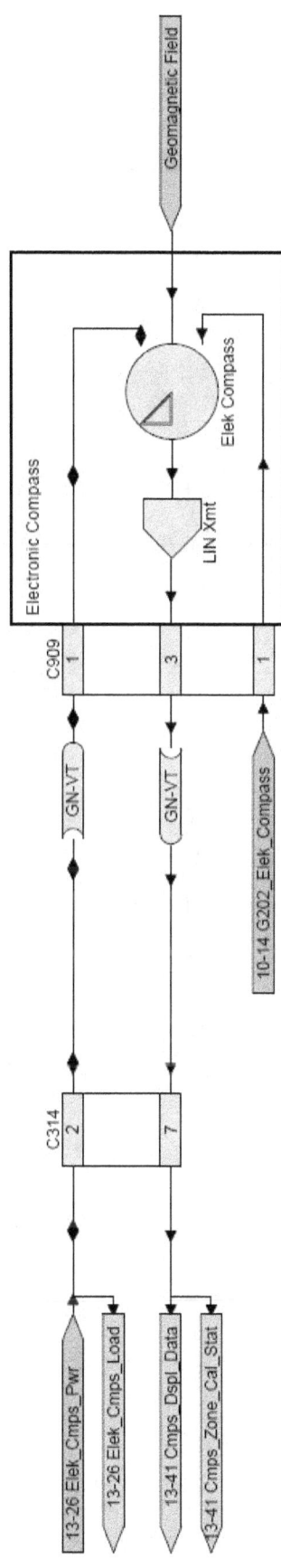

173

60-6 IPC – Steering Wheel Switch Assembly Left Side

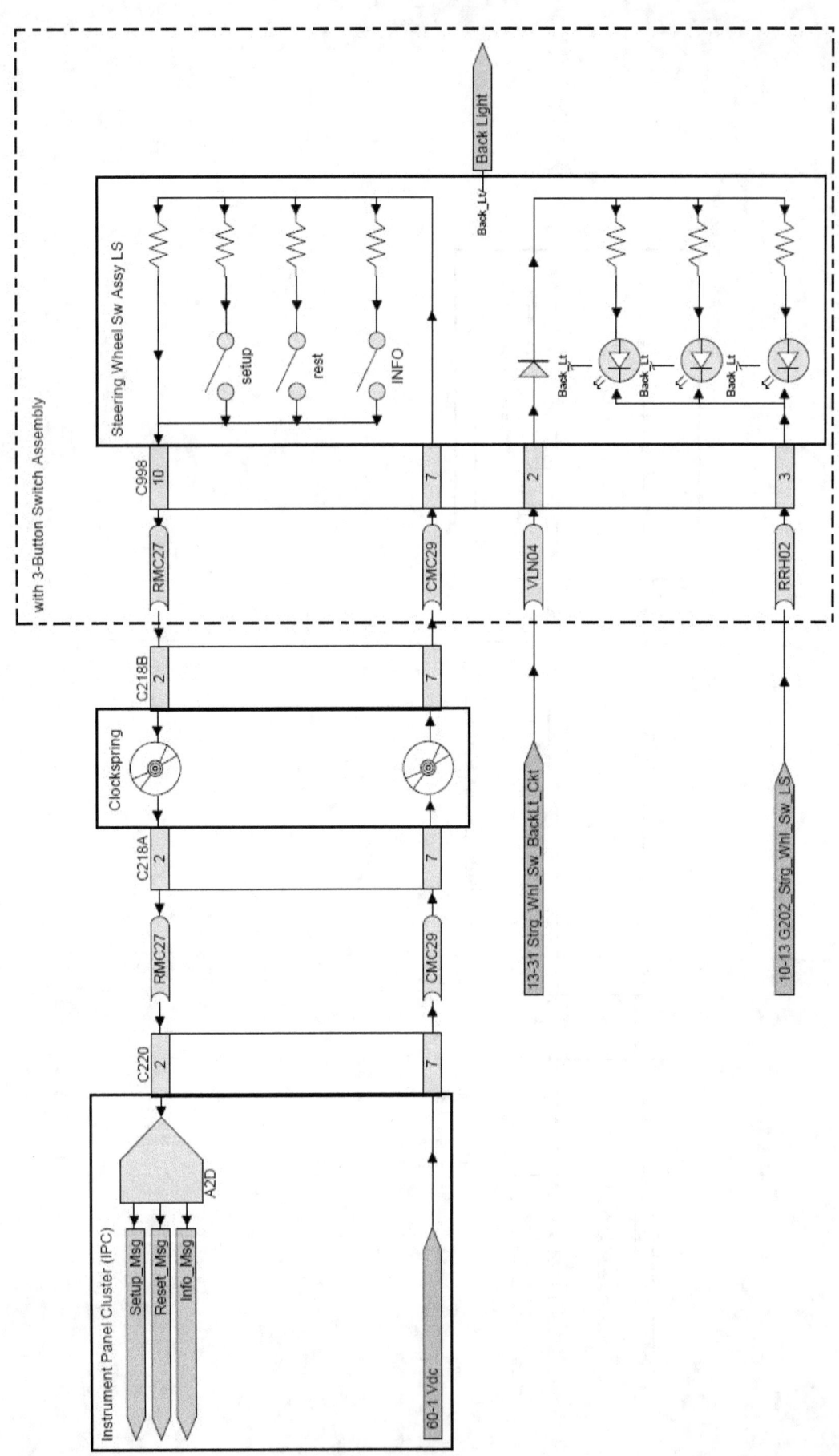

IPC – Steering Wheel Switch Assembly Left Side 60-7

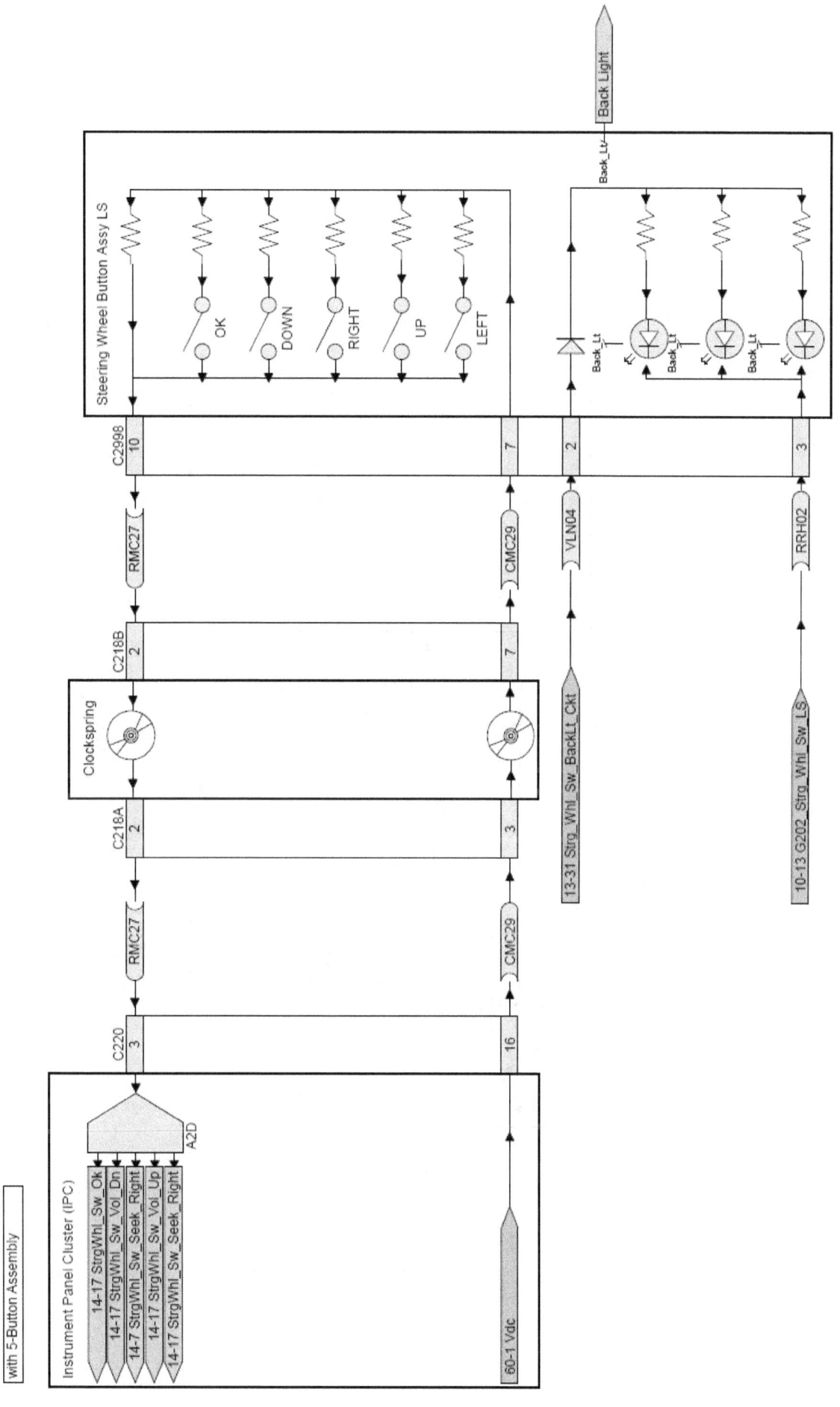

71-7 Steering Column Control Module – Instrument Panel Dimmer Switch

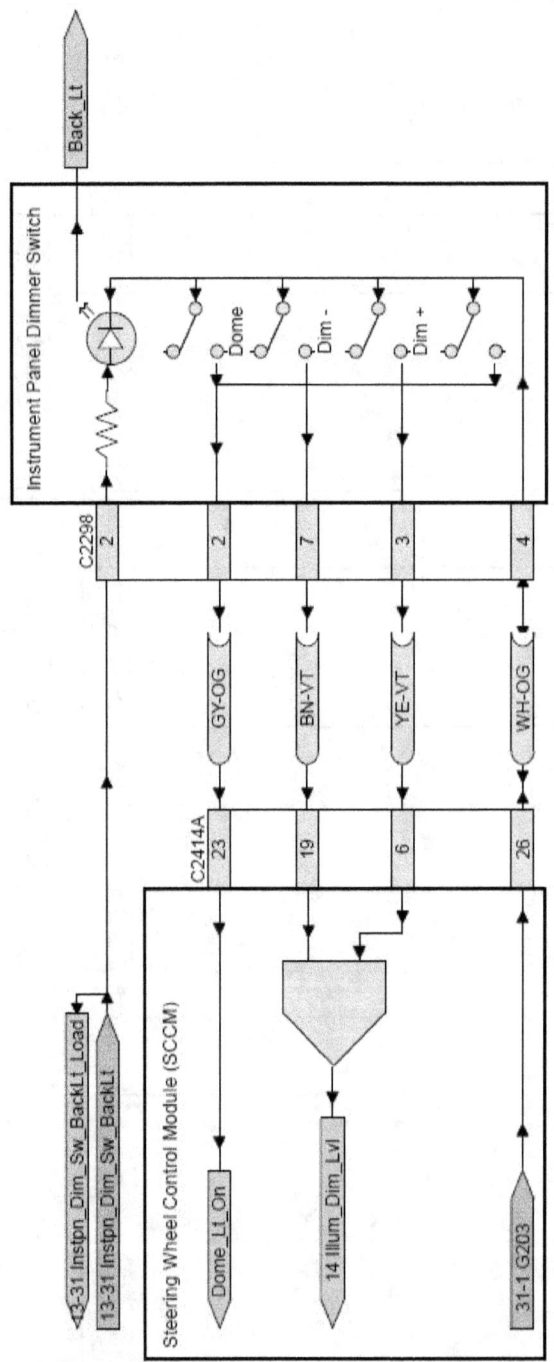

81 Wipers & Washers
Windshield Wiper & Washer Motors 81-3

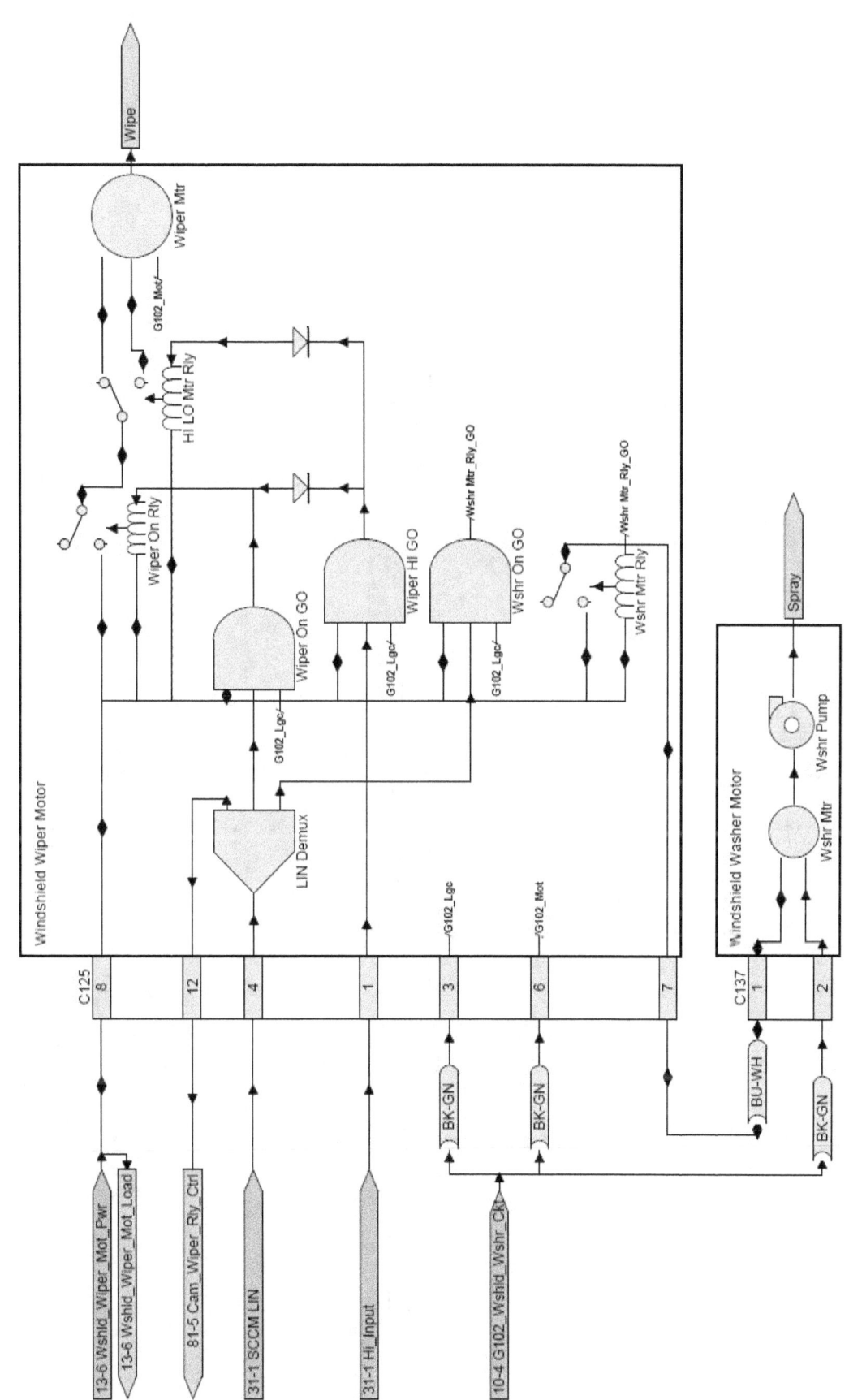

81-4 Rain Sensor

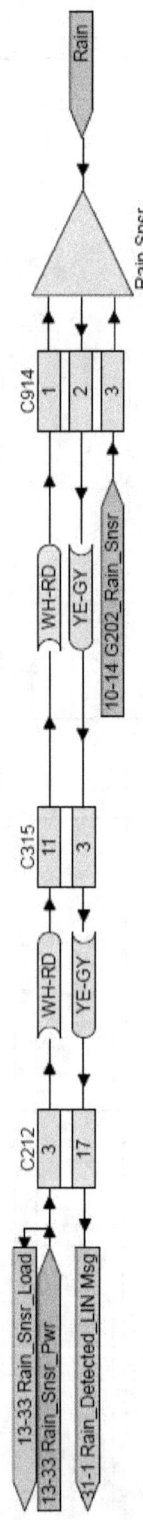

85 Headlamp Assemblies
SCCM and Headlamp Switch 85-1

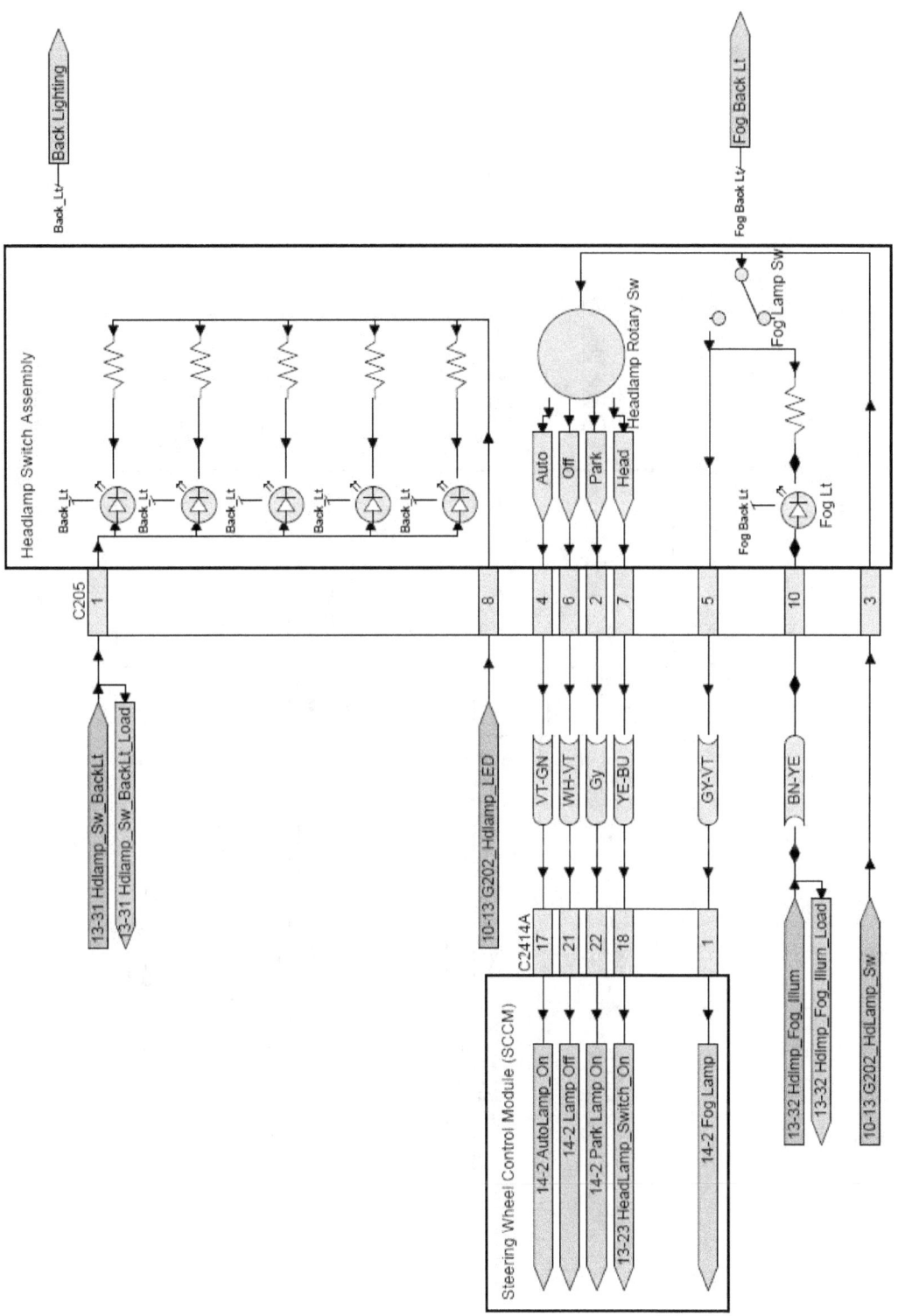

85-2 Headlamp Assemblies

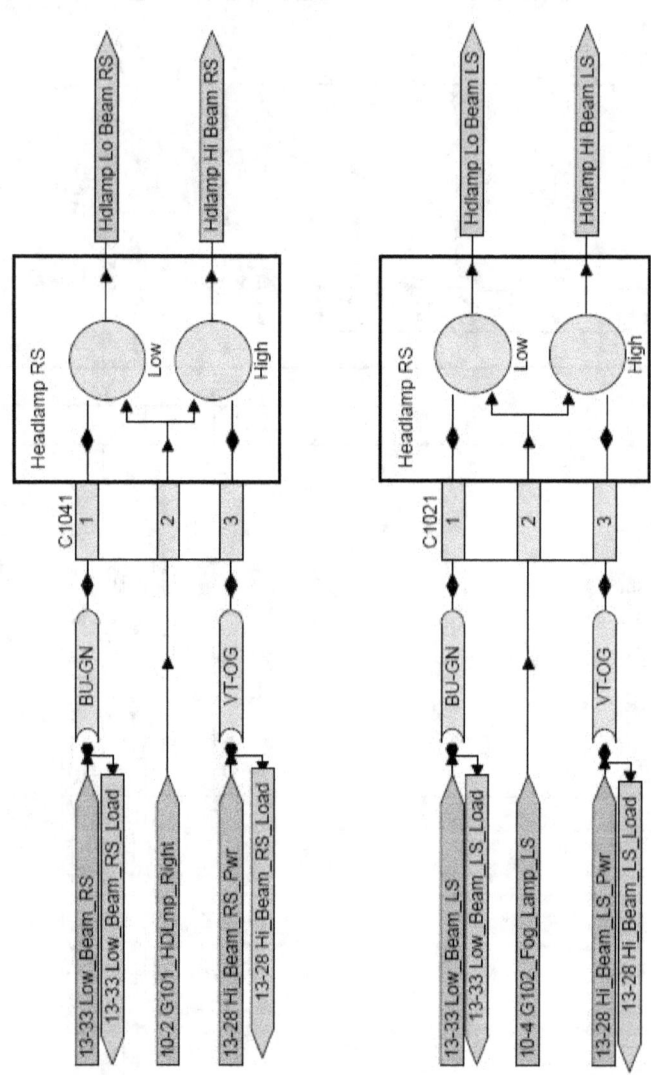

Headlamp Assemblies with HID 85-3

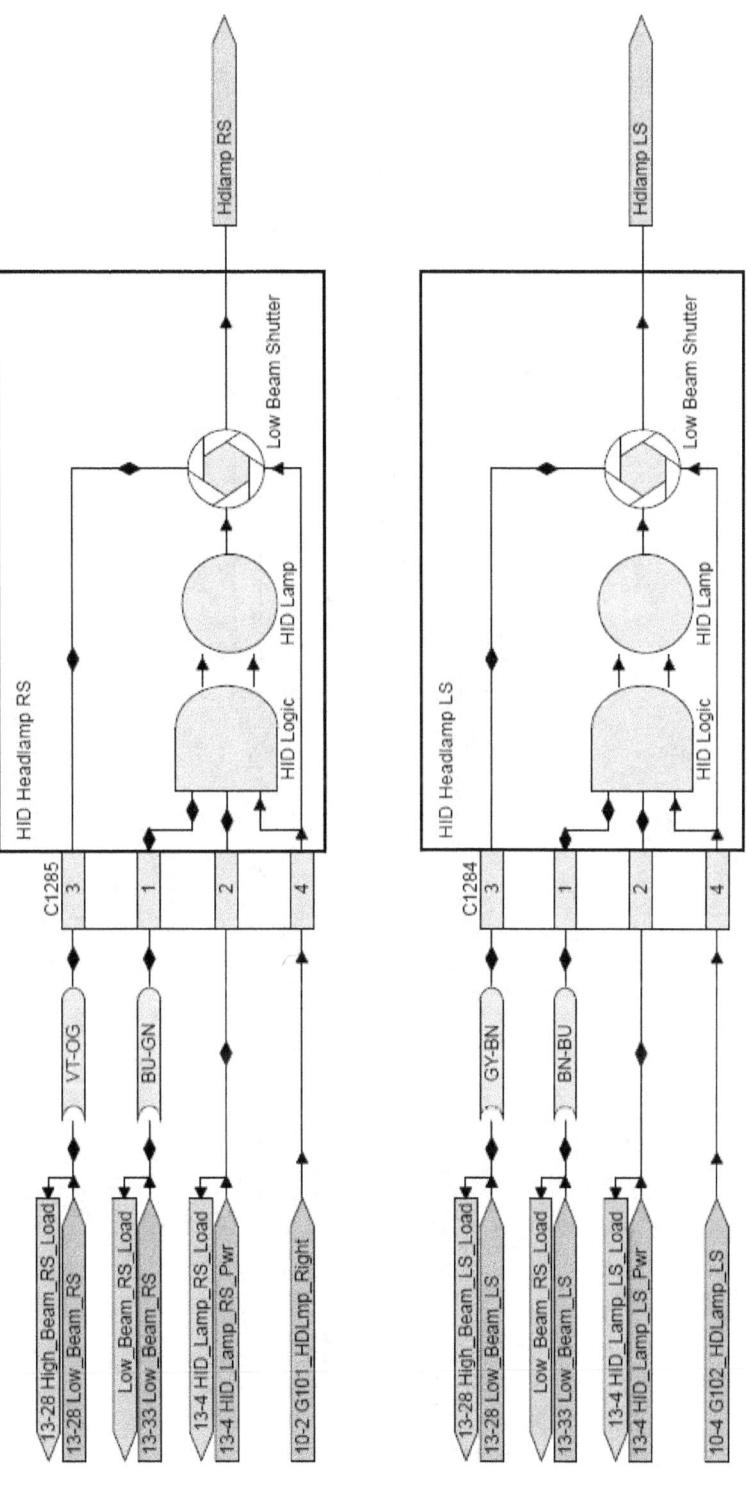

89 Interior Lighting
89-3 Interior Lamps – Dome Lamp Front

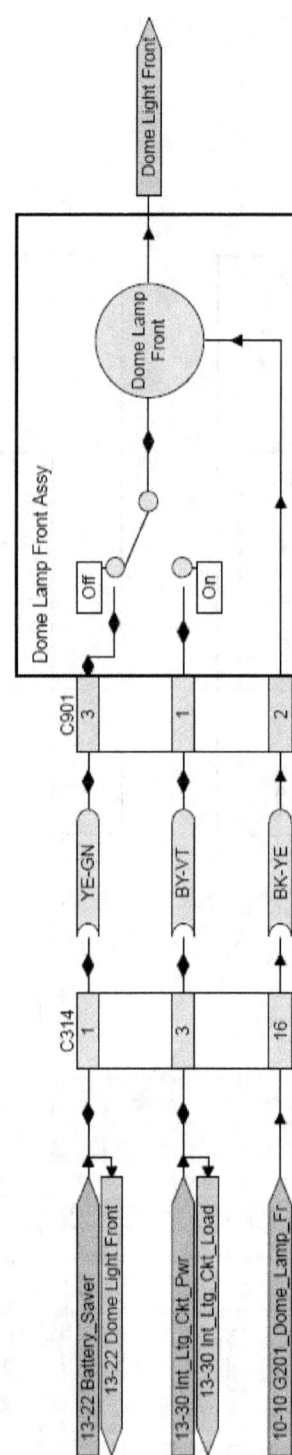

Interior Lamps – Dome Lamps **89-4**

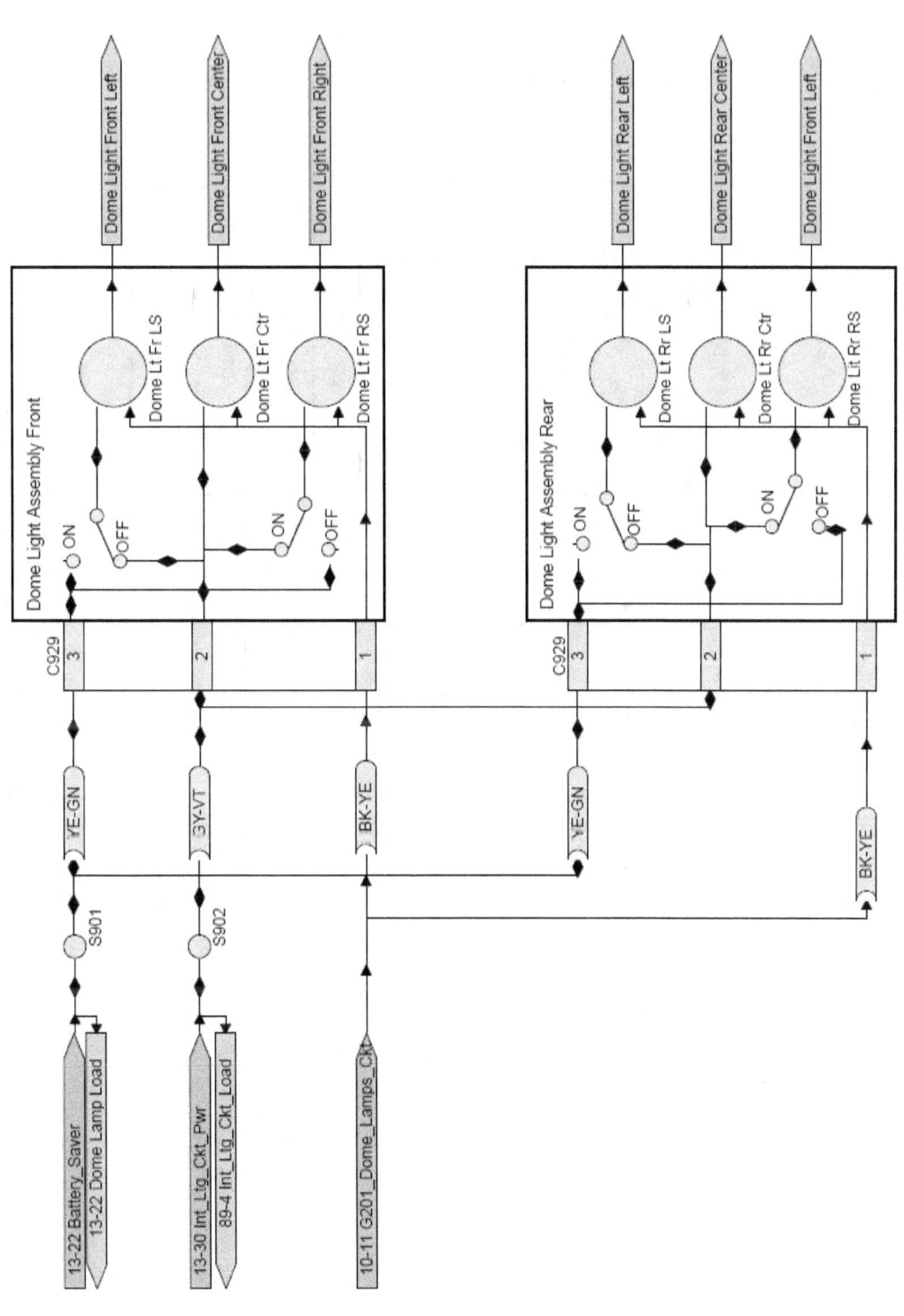

183

89-5 Interior Lamps – Vanity Mirror Lights

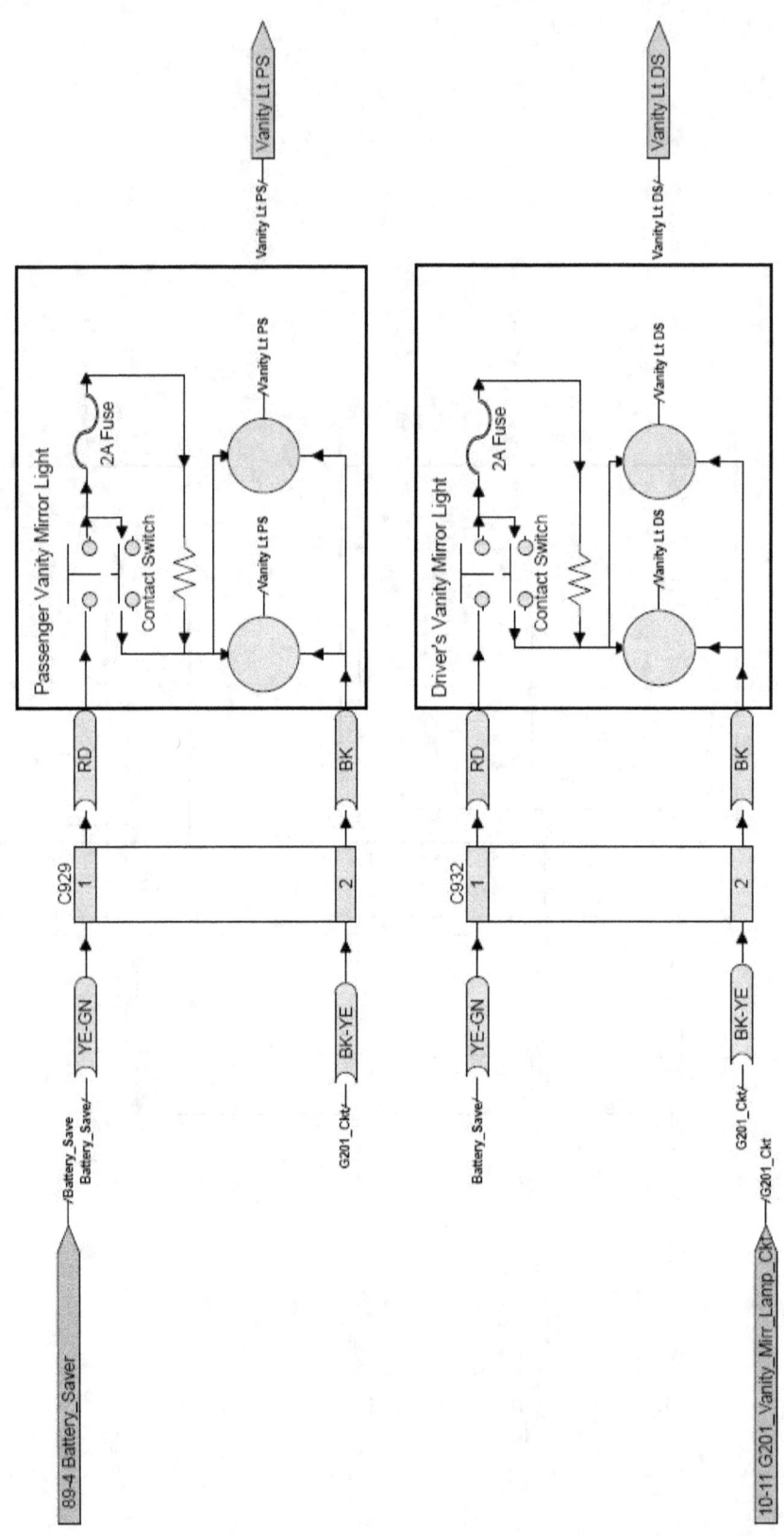

Interior Lamps – Ambient Lighting **89-10**

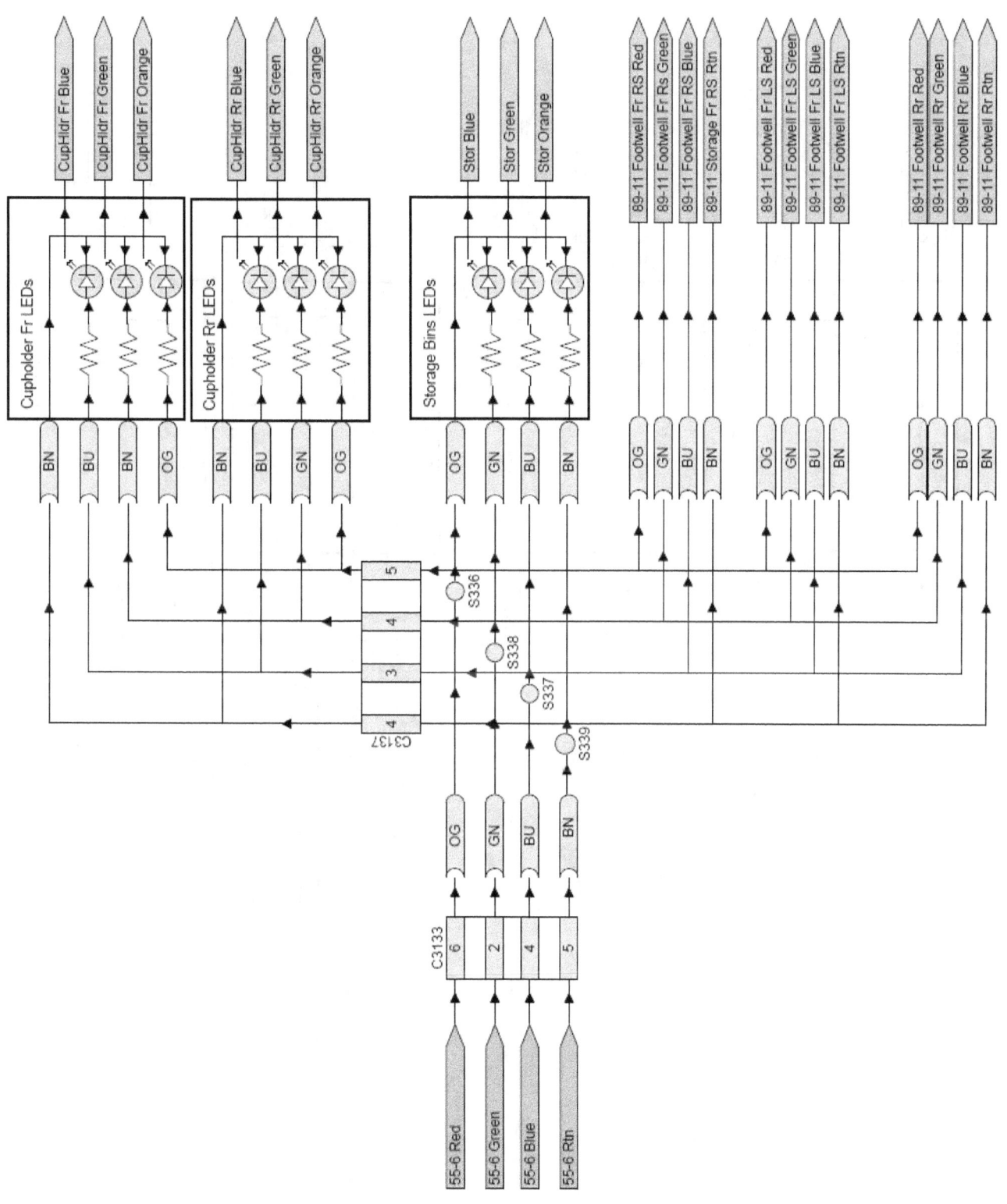

89-11 Interior Lamps – Ambient Lighting

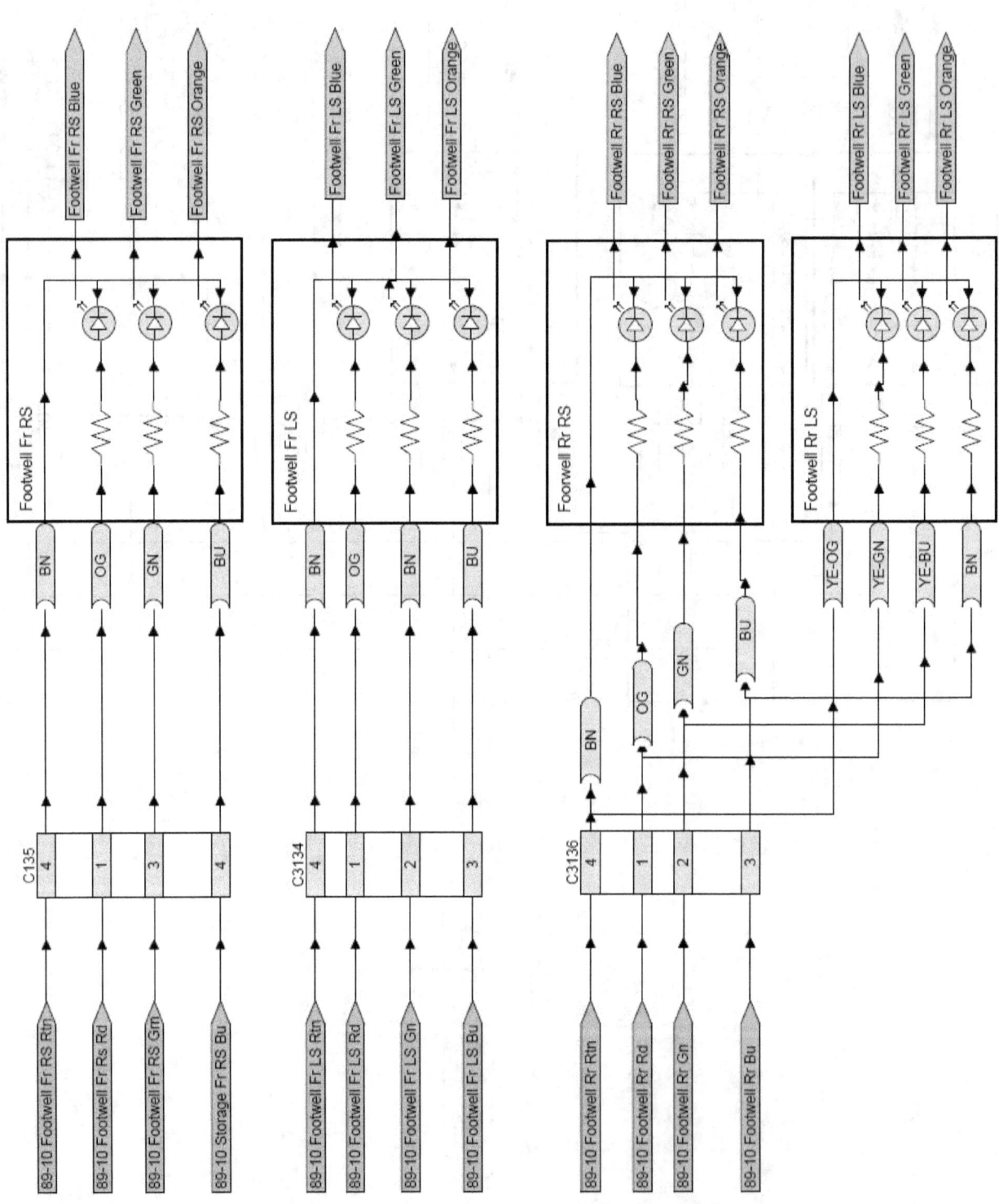

90 - 93 Exterior Lighting
Hi Mounted Stop Lamp Assembly 90-1

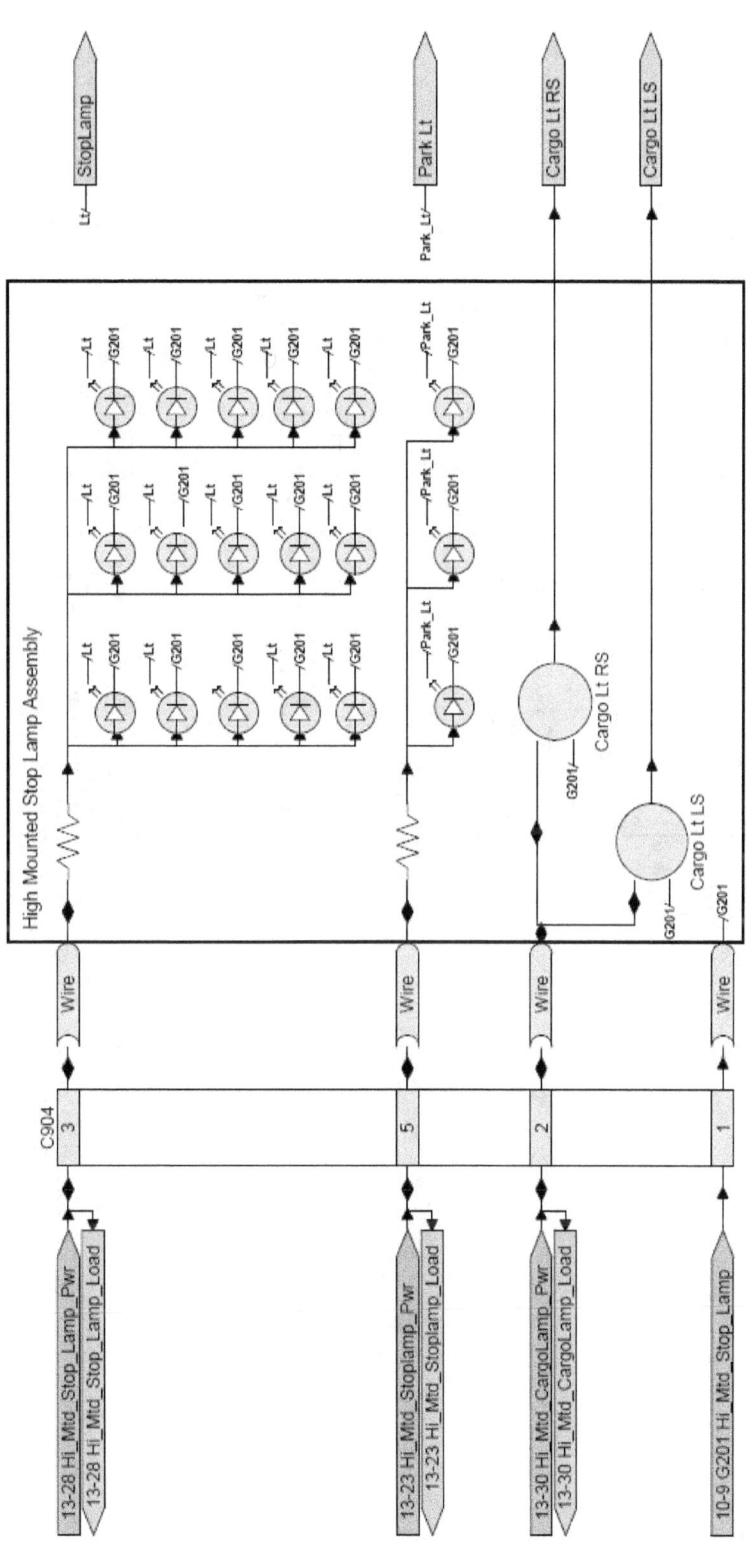

92-2 Exterior Lighting

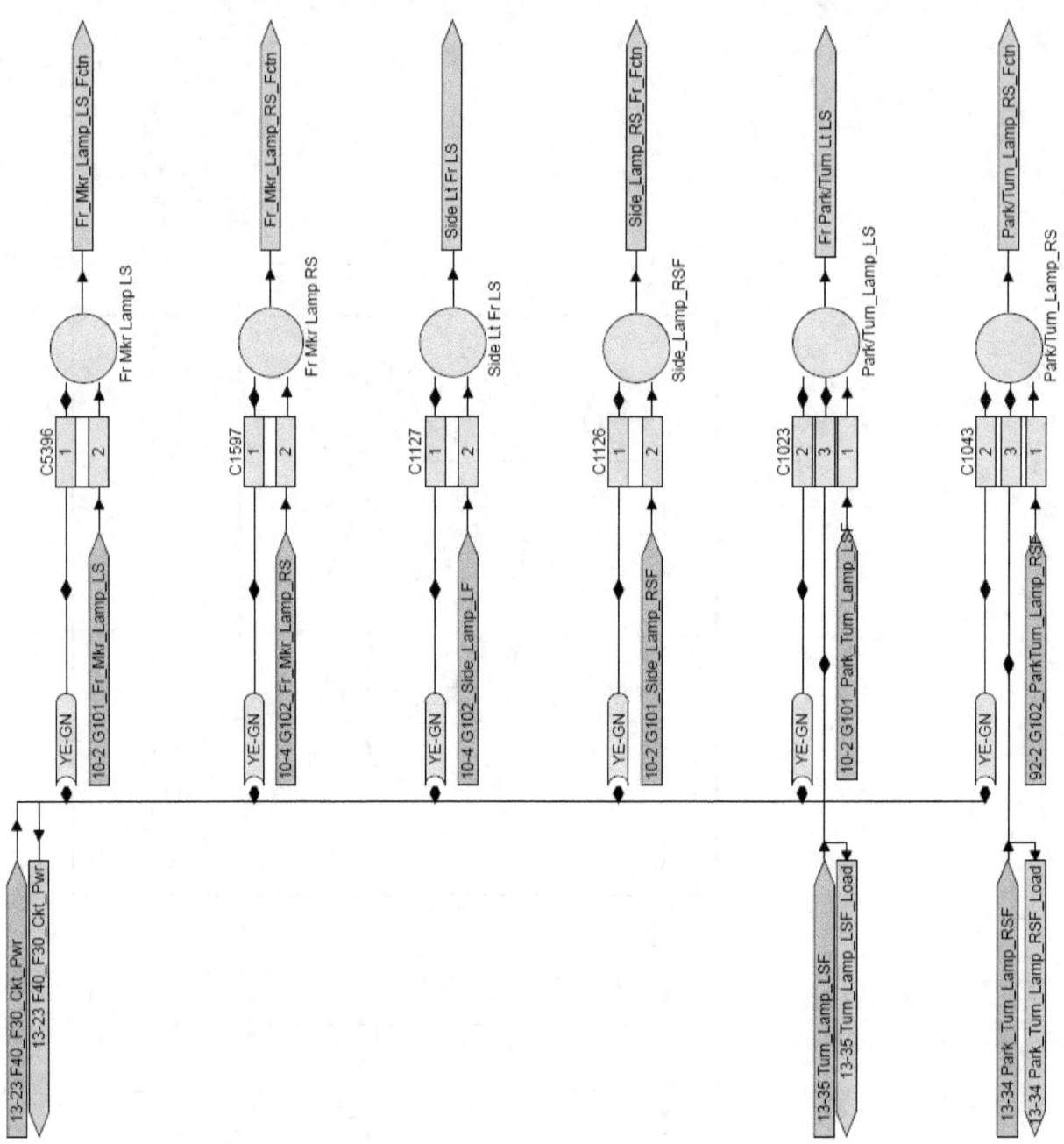

Exterior Lighting **92-3**

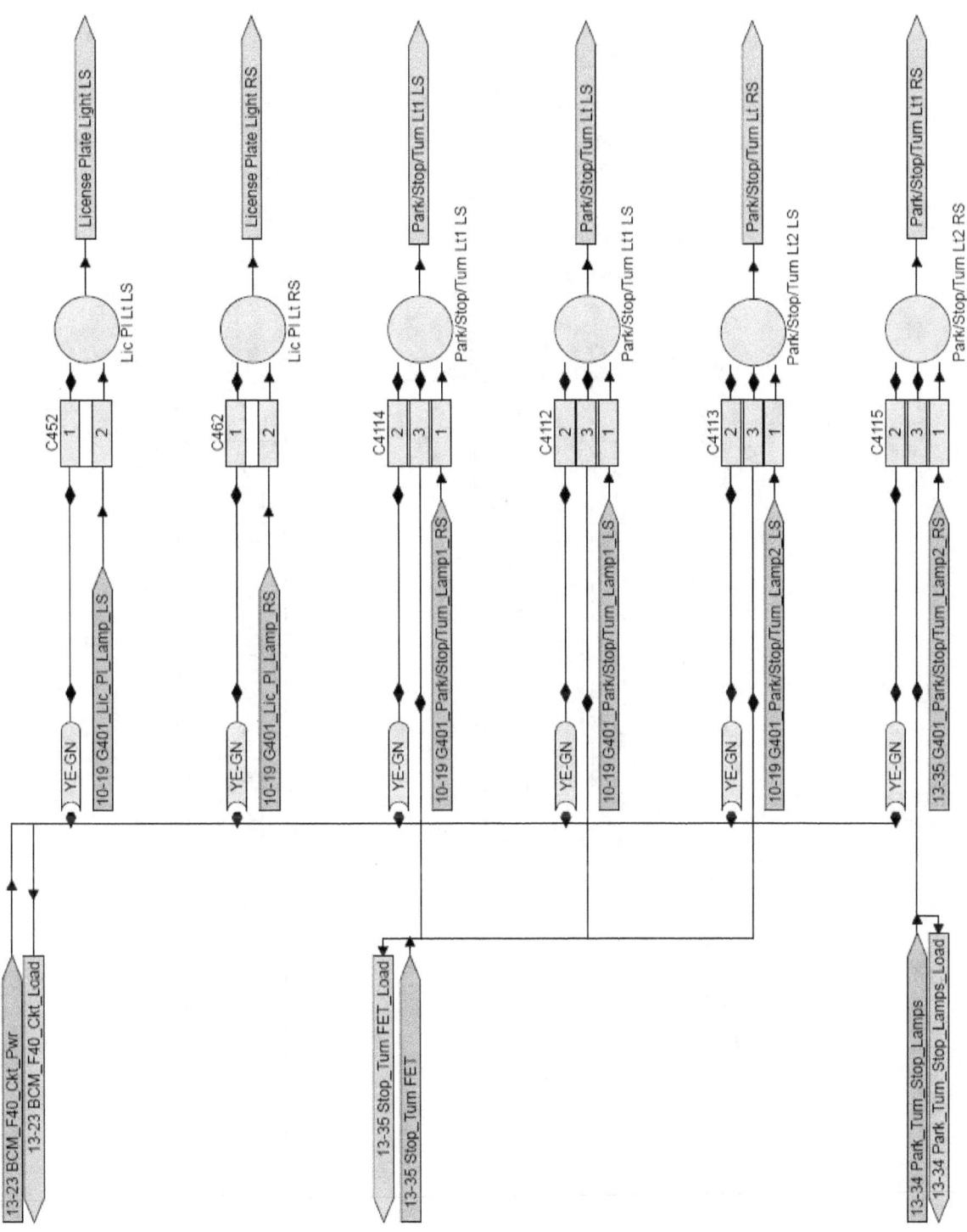

92-4 Exterior Lighting

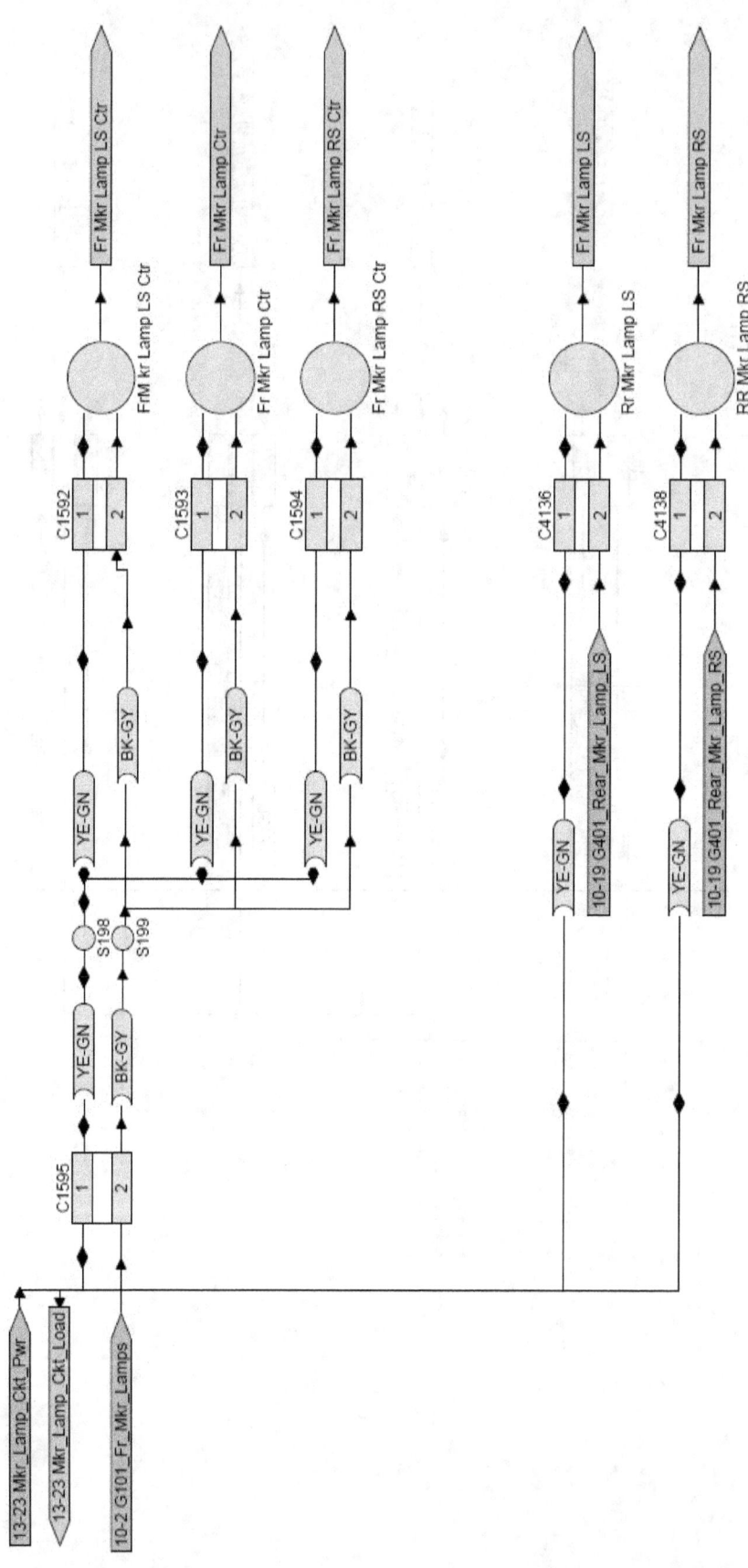

Reversing Lamps 93-1

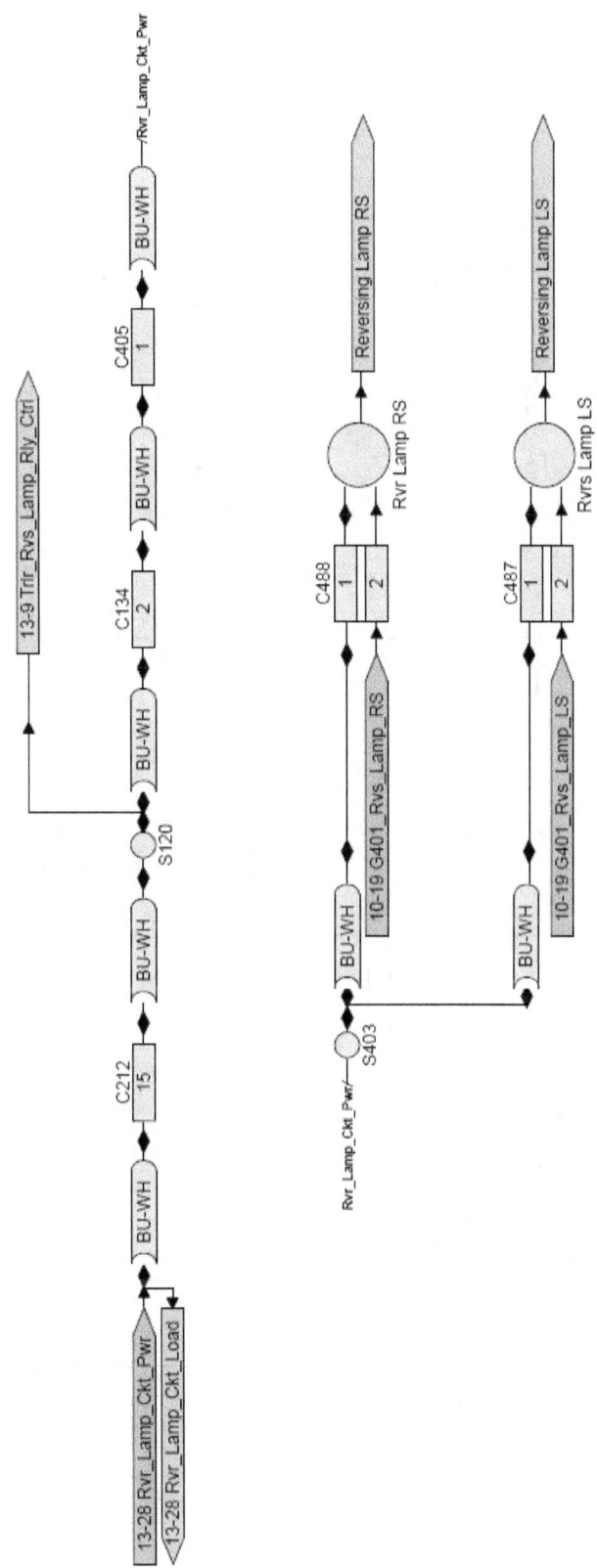

95 Trailer Electrical

95-2 Battery Junction Box – Trailer Relays (Parking, Left & Right Turn)

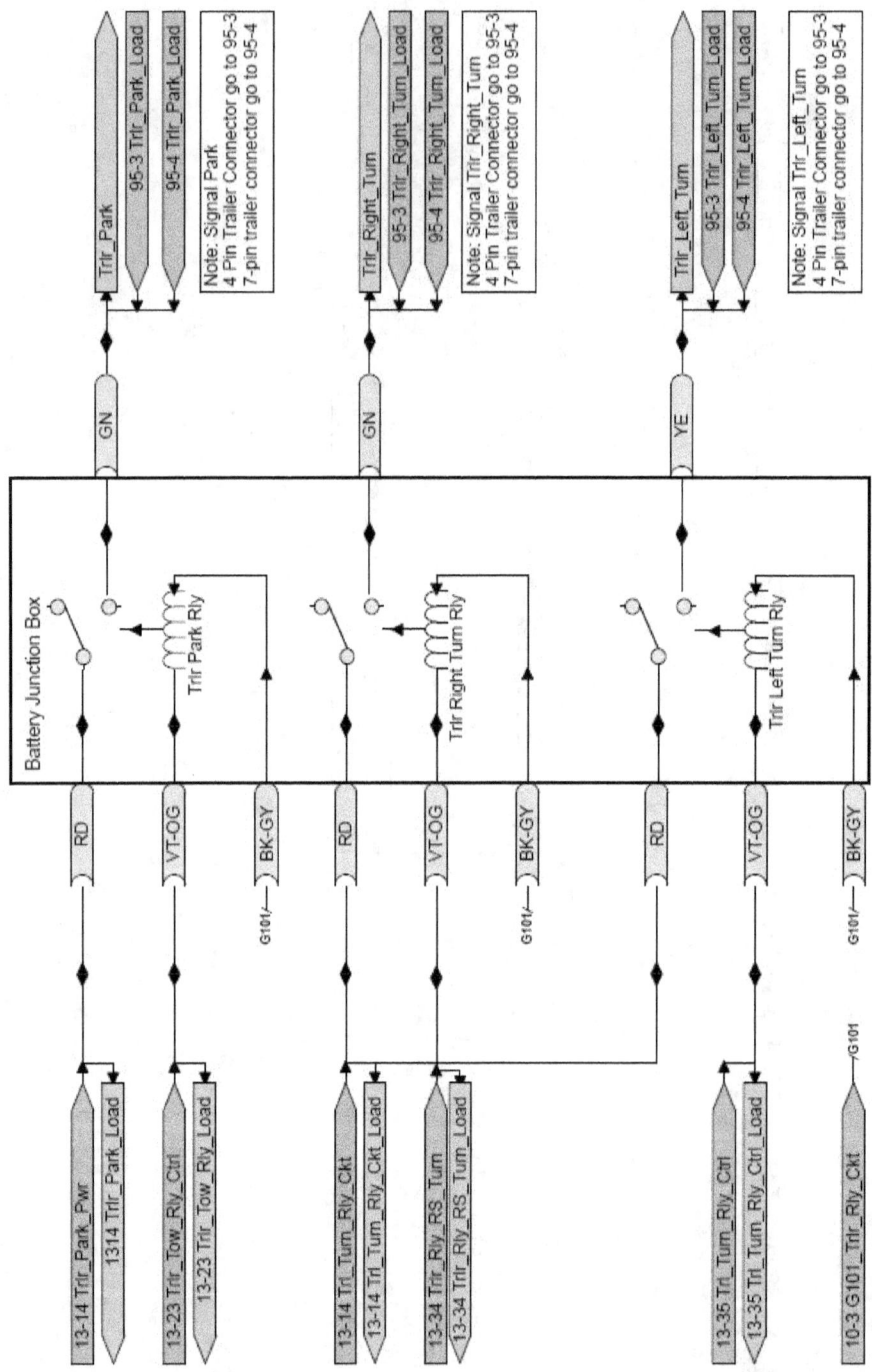

Trailer Connector 4- Pin **95-3**

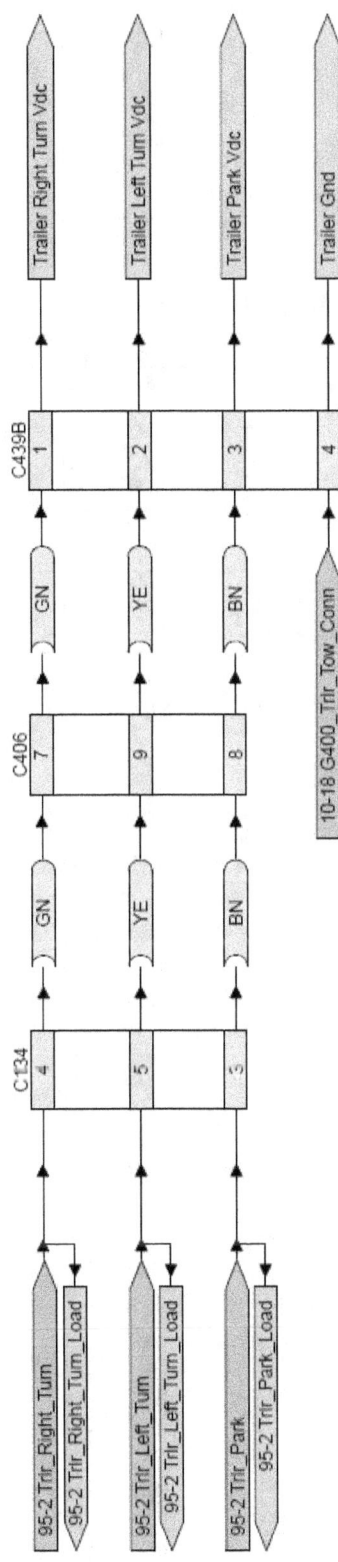

95-4 Trailer Connector 7-Pin

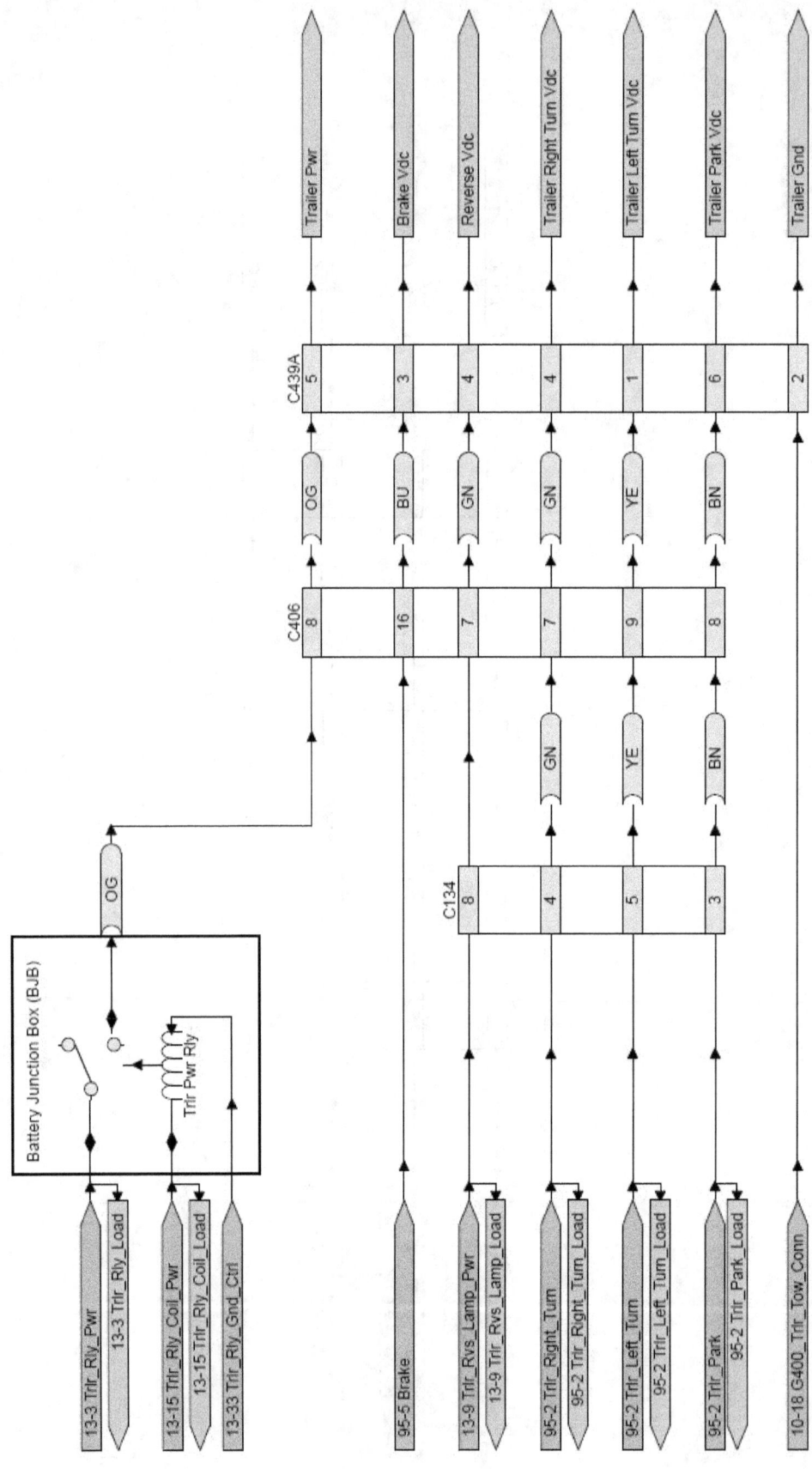

194

Trailer Brake Control Module (TBCM) Power and Ground 95-5

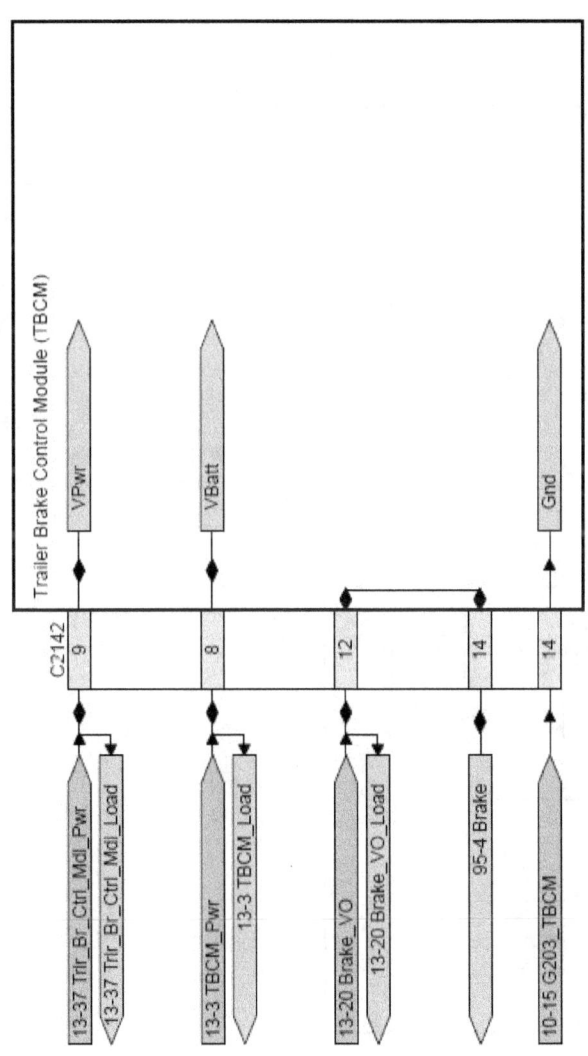

100 Power Windows

100-1 Power Windows – Regular Cab

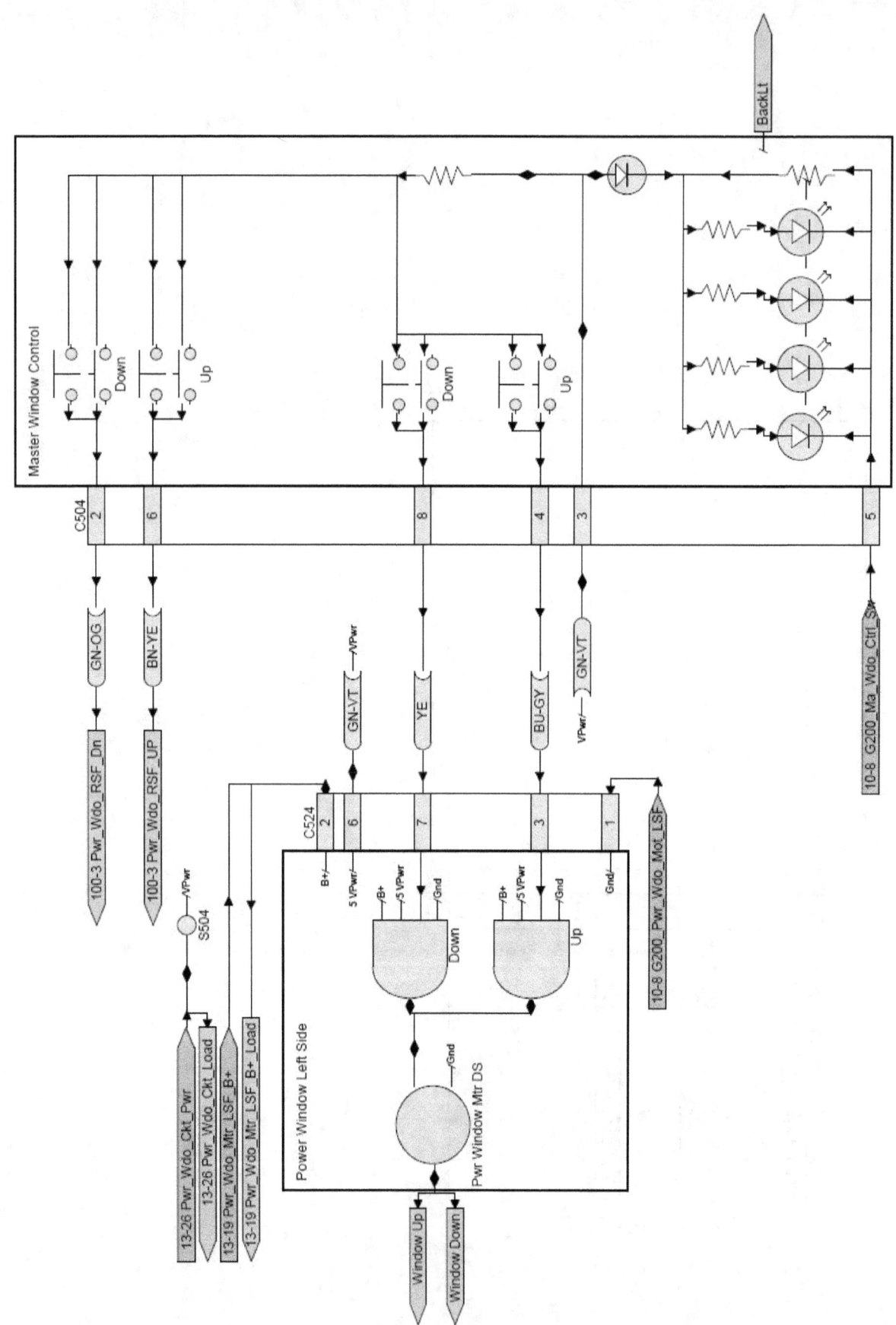

Power Windows – Super Crew, Super Cab 100-2

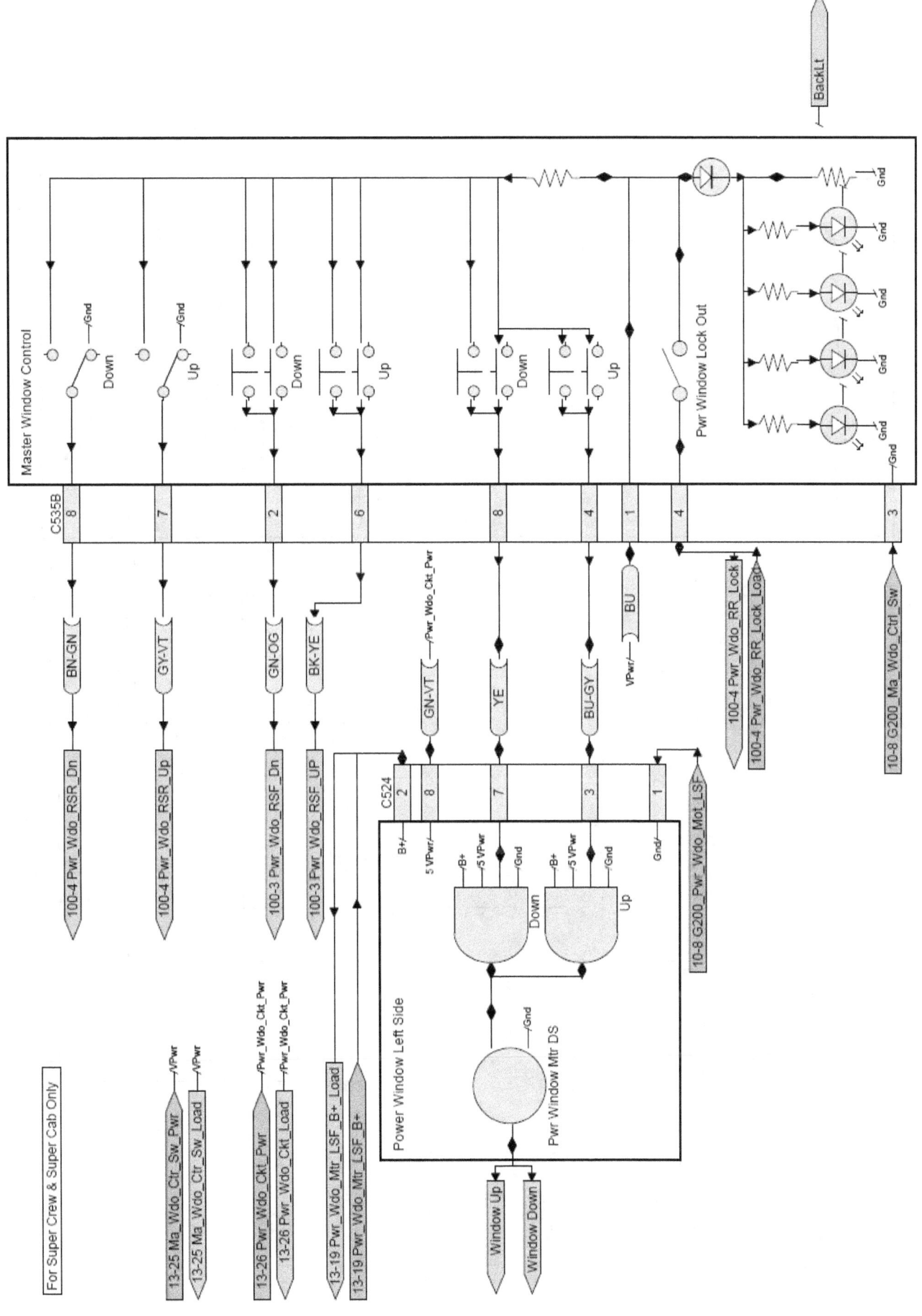

100-3 Power Windows – Passenger Side Switch Control and Motor

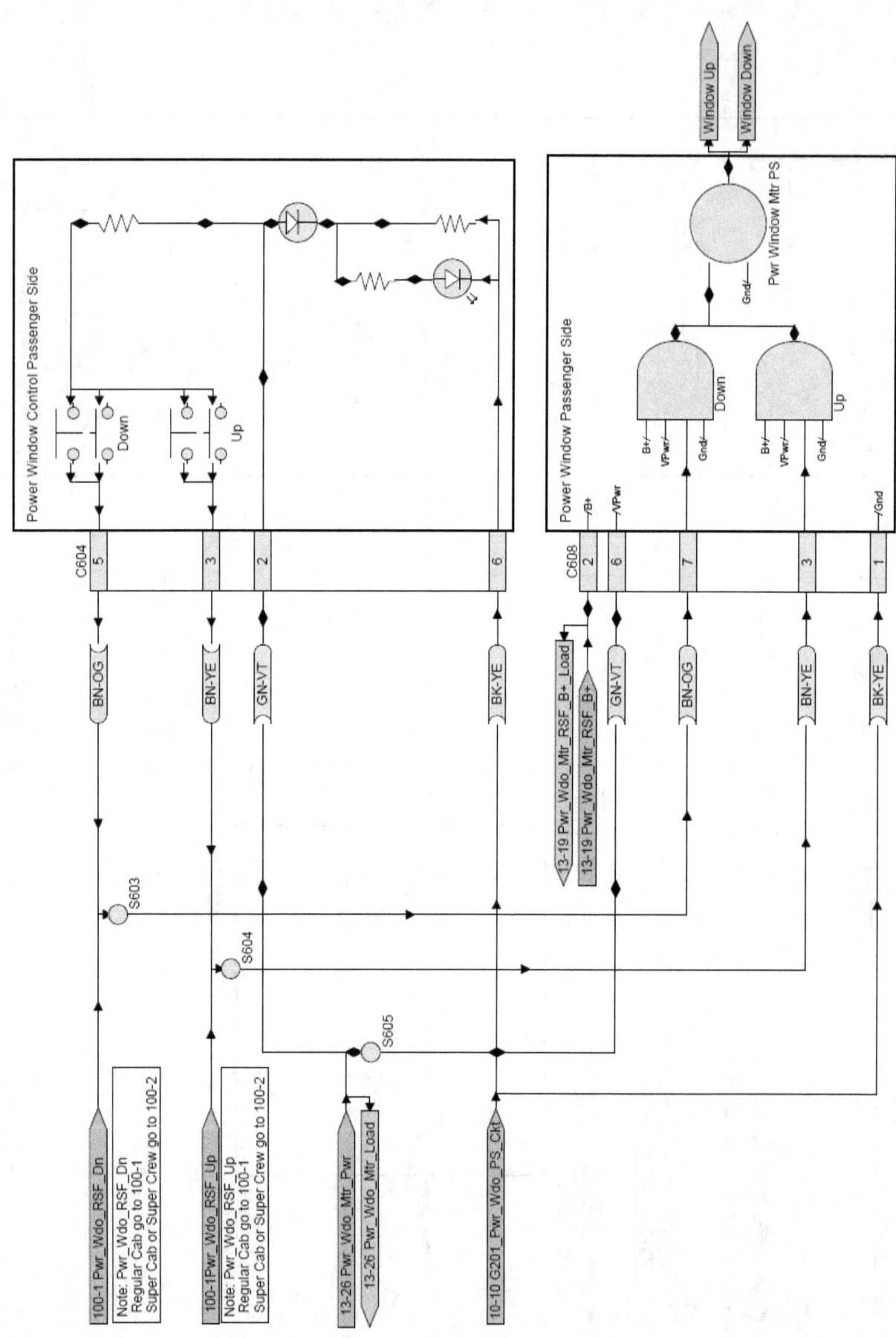

Power Windows – Rear Window Control and Motor Assemblies 100-4

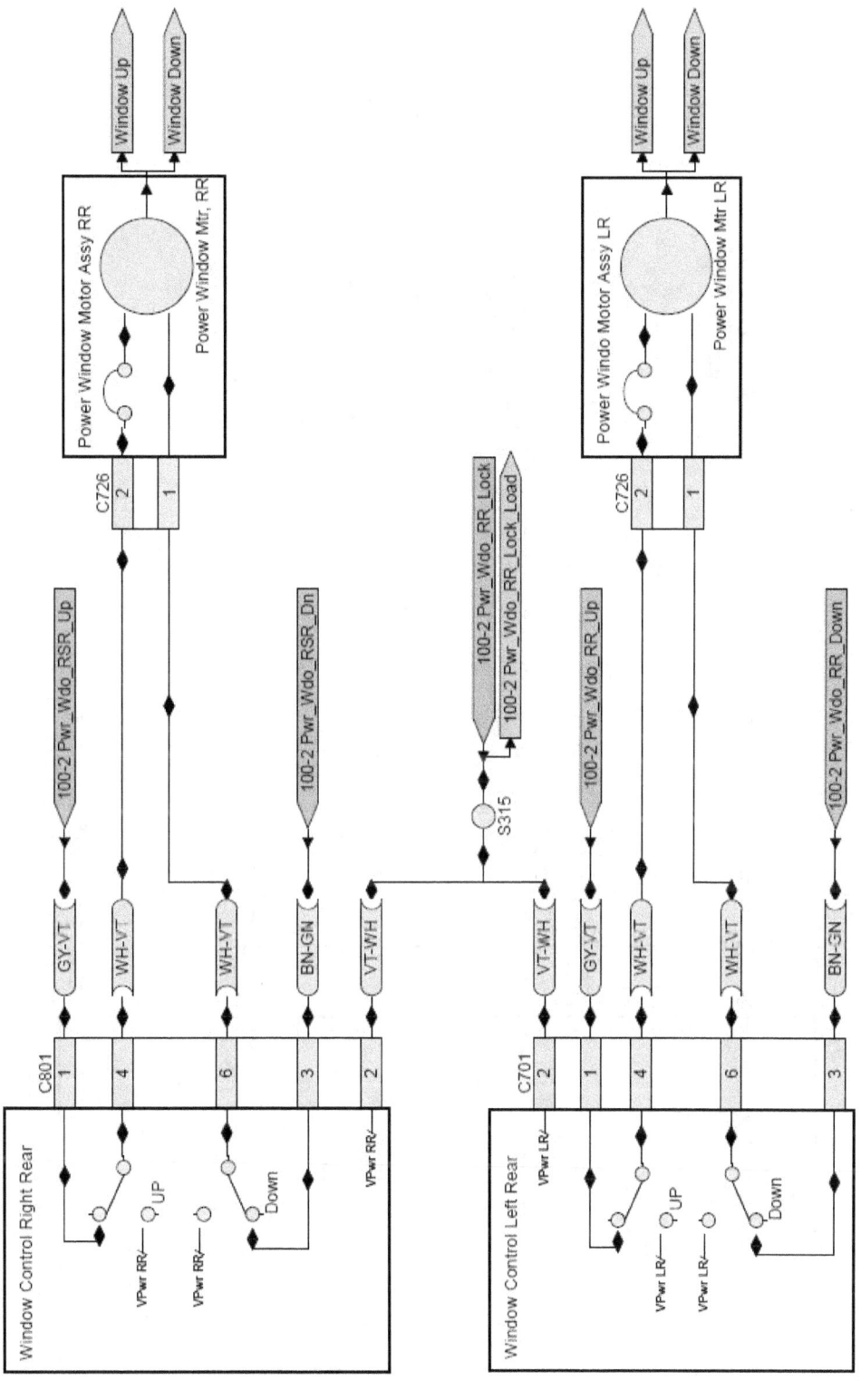

199

100-5 Power Windows – Overhead Switch Console and Power Rear Sliding Window

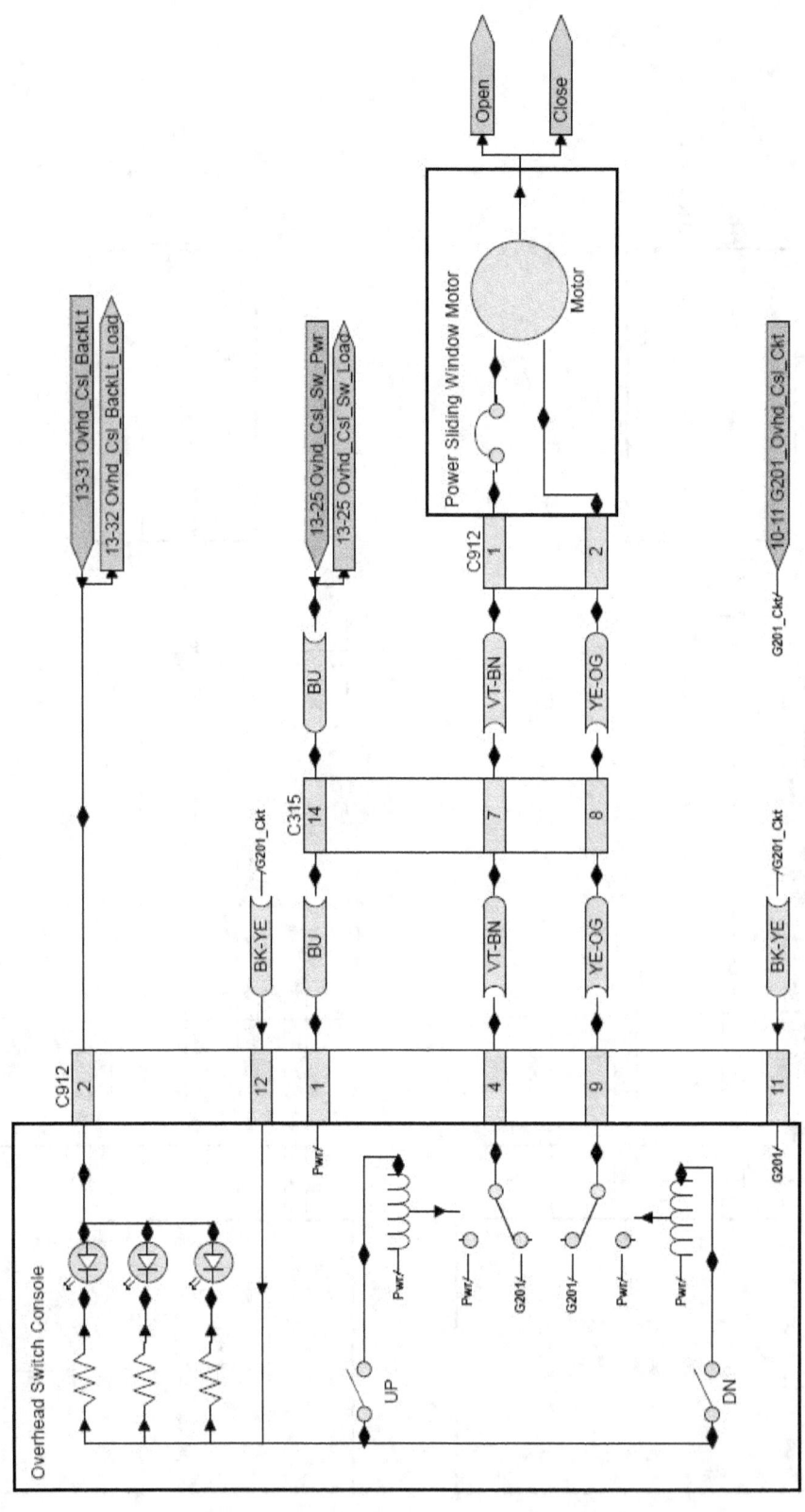

101-1 Overhead Switch Console and Roof Opening Module

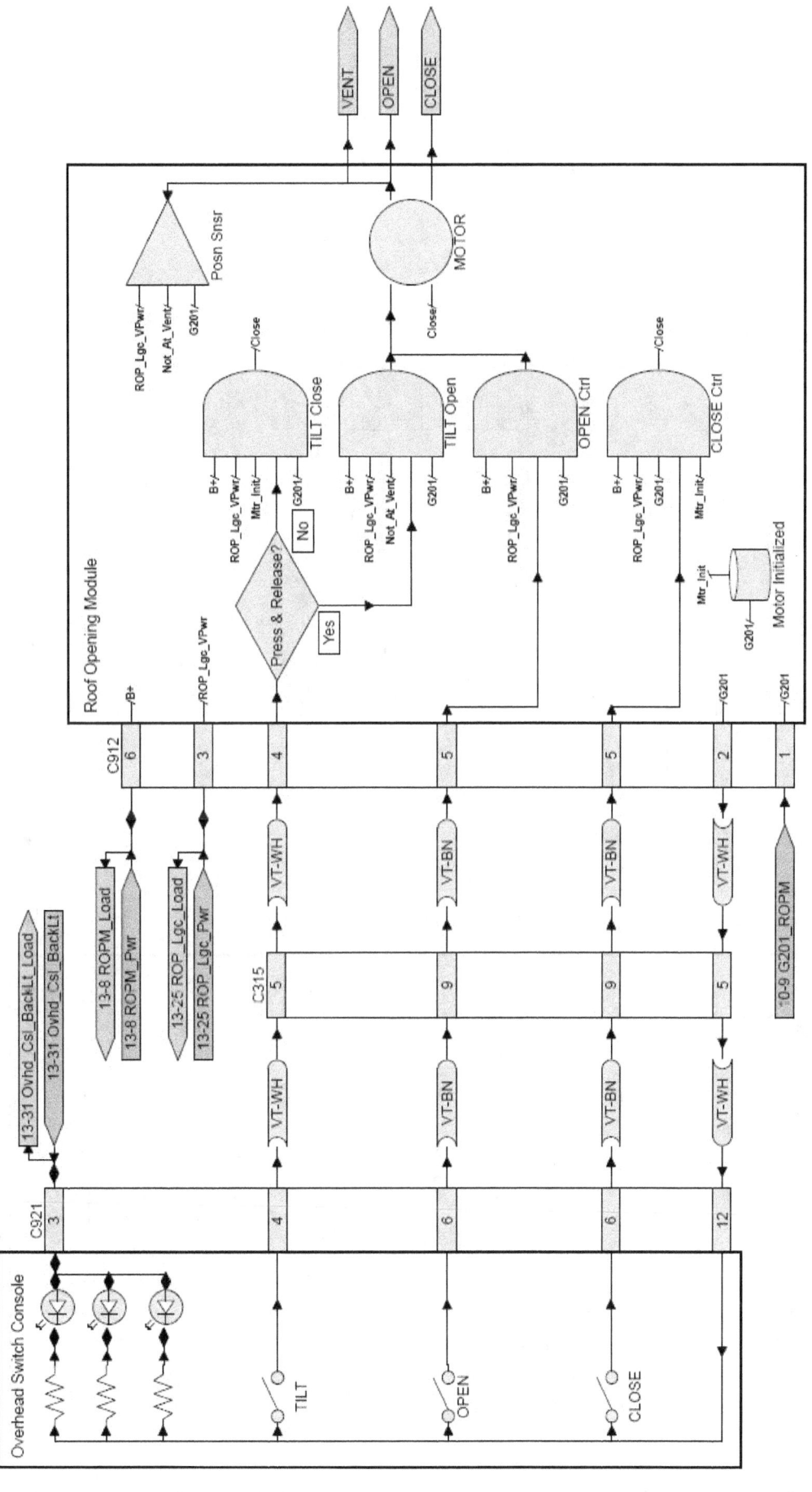

201

109-1 Power Running Board Module and Motors

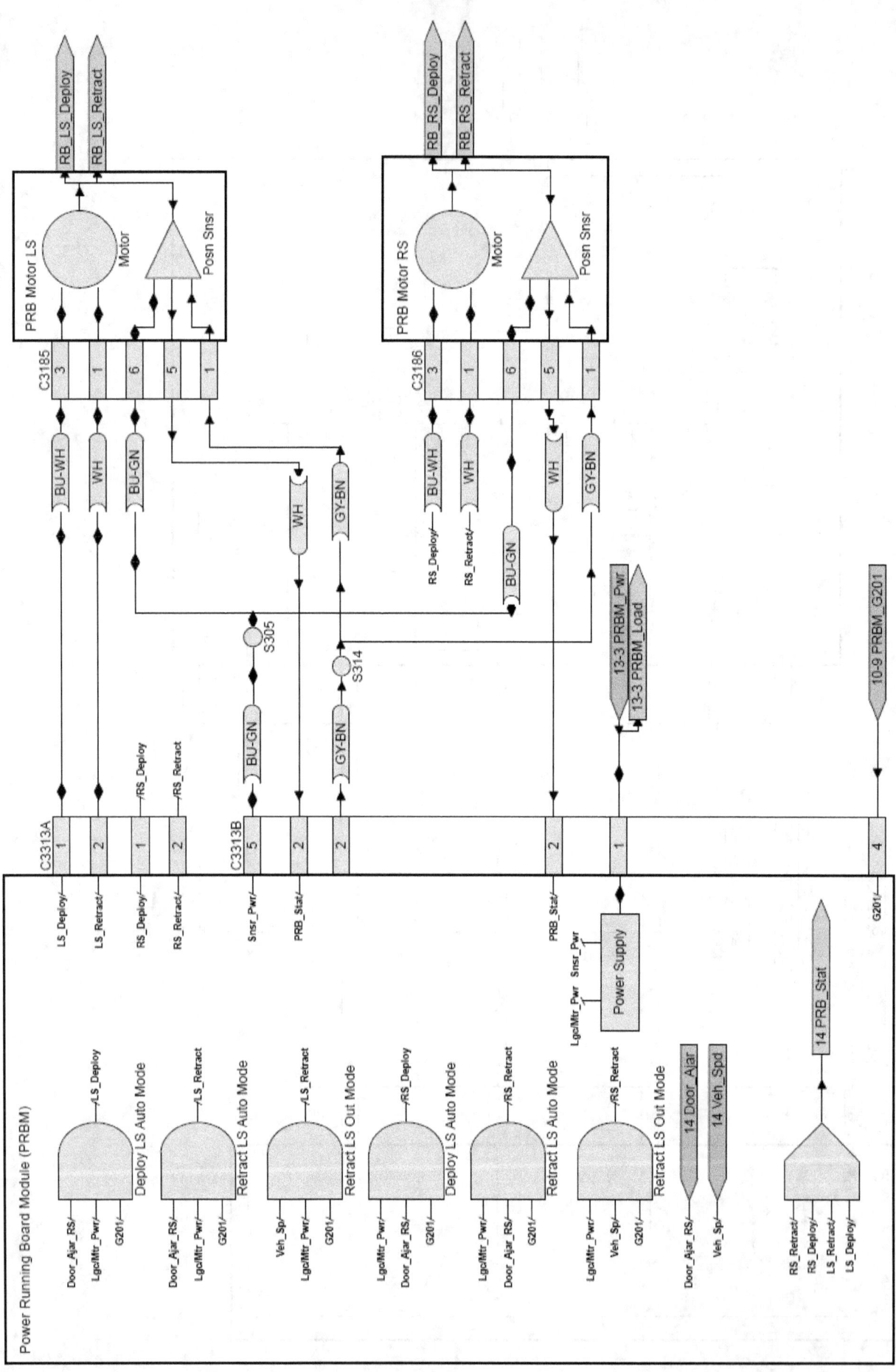

110 Power Door Locks

Power Door Locks – Lock Switches 110-1

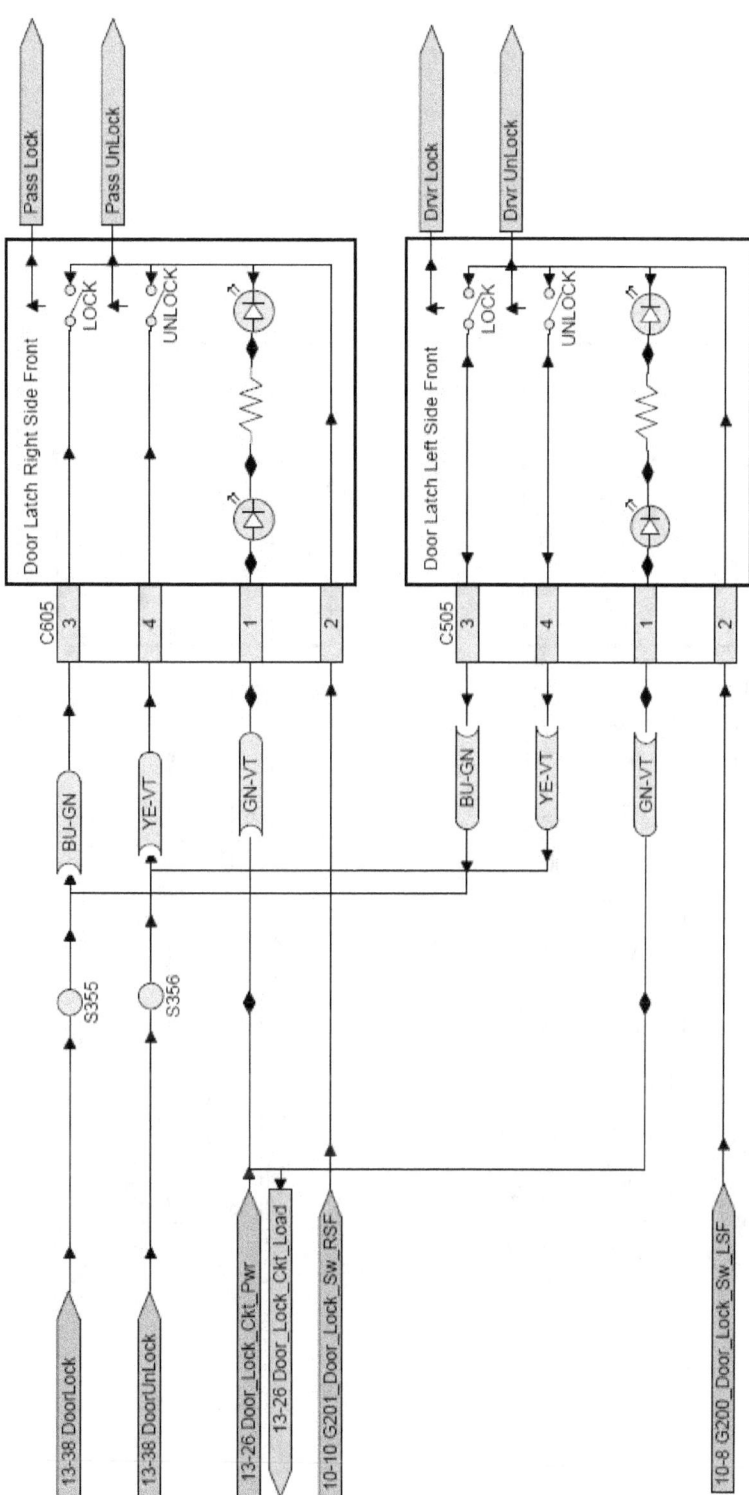

110-2 Power Door Locks – Motors & Ajar Switches

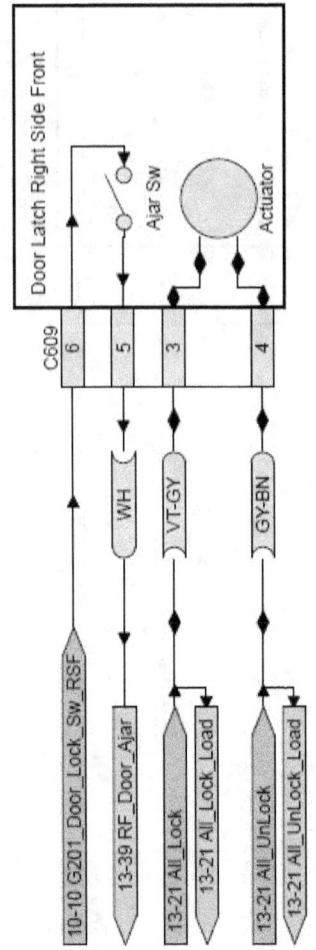
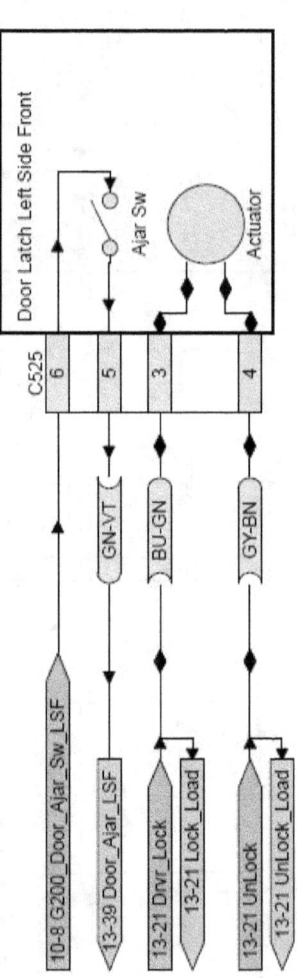

Power Door Locks – Motors & Ajar Switches 110-3

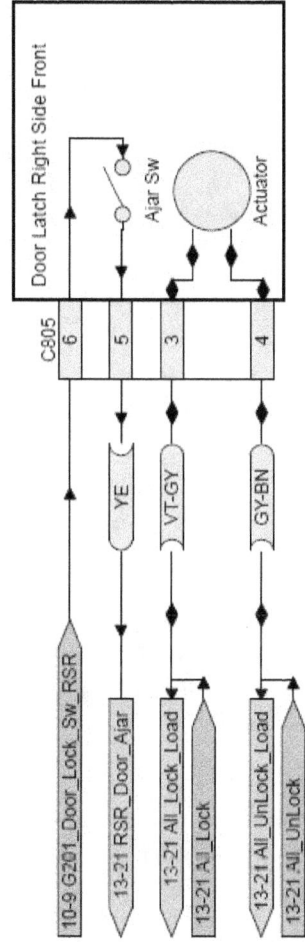
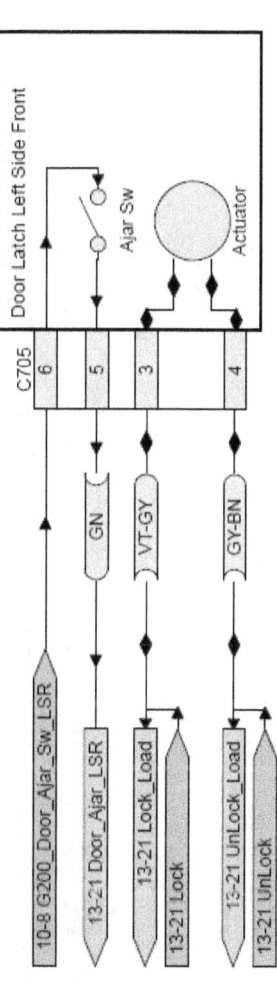

Super Crew Only

110-4 Power Door Locks –Ajar Switches

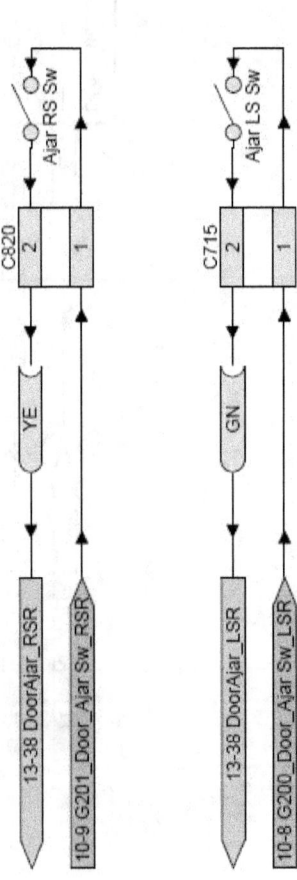

112-1 Passive Anti-Theft Transceiver

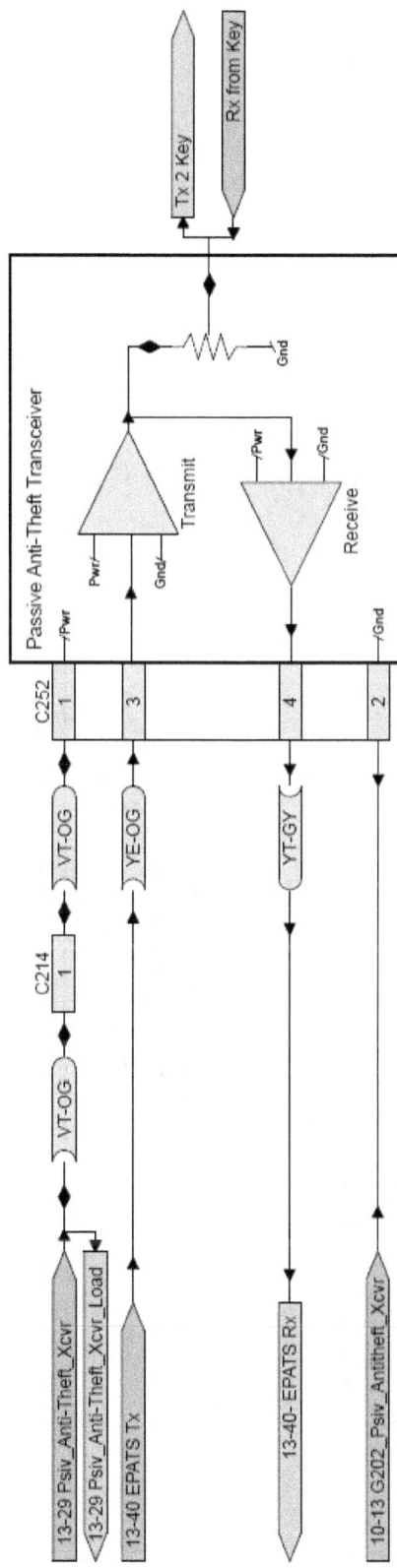

207

118-1 Tire Pressure Monitor Module (TPMM)

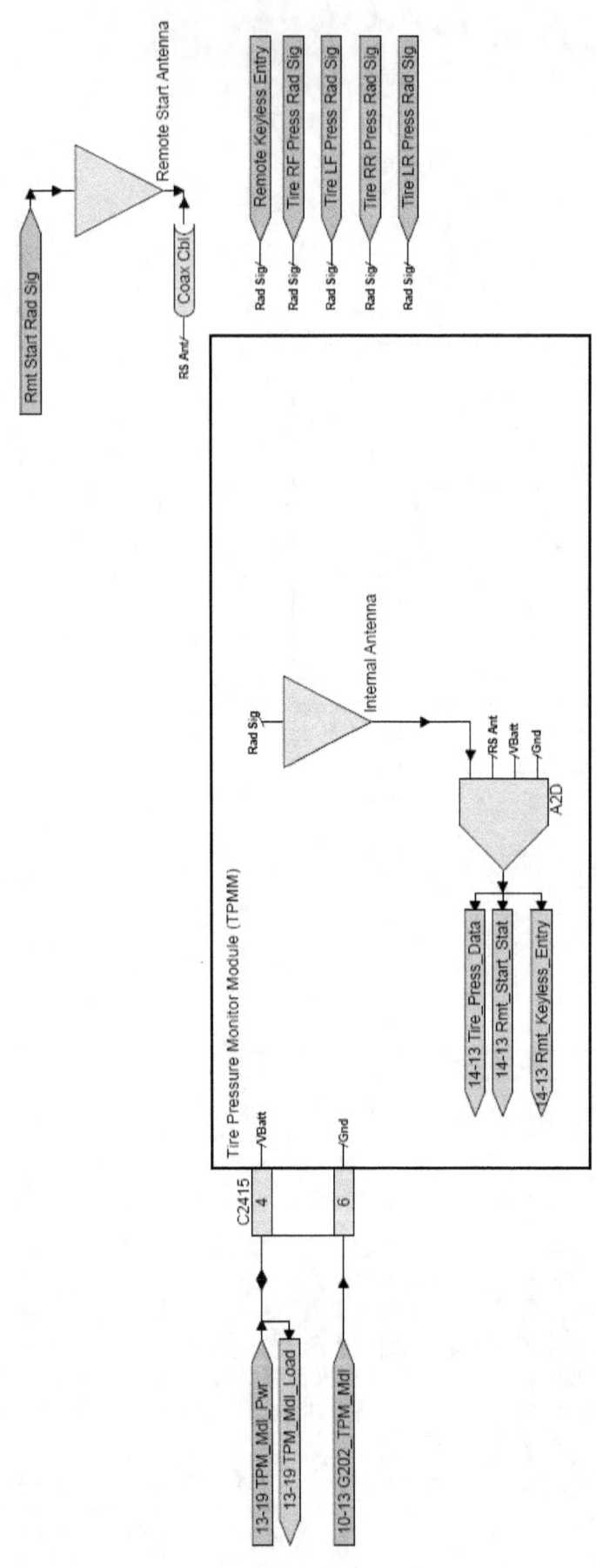

119 Climate Control Seating
Climate Controlled Seats – Driver and Passenger 119-2

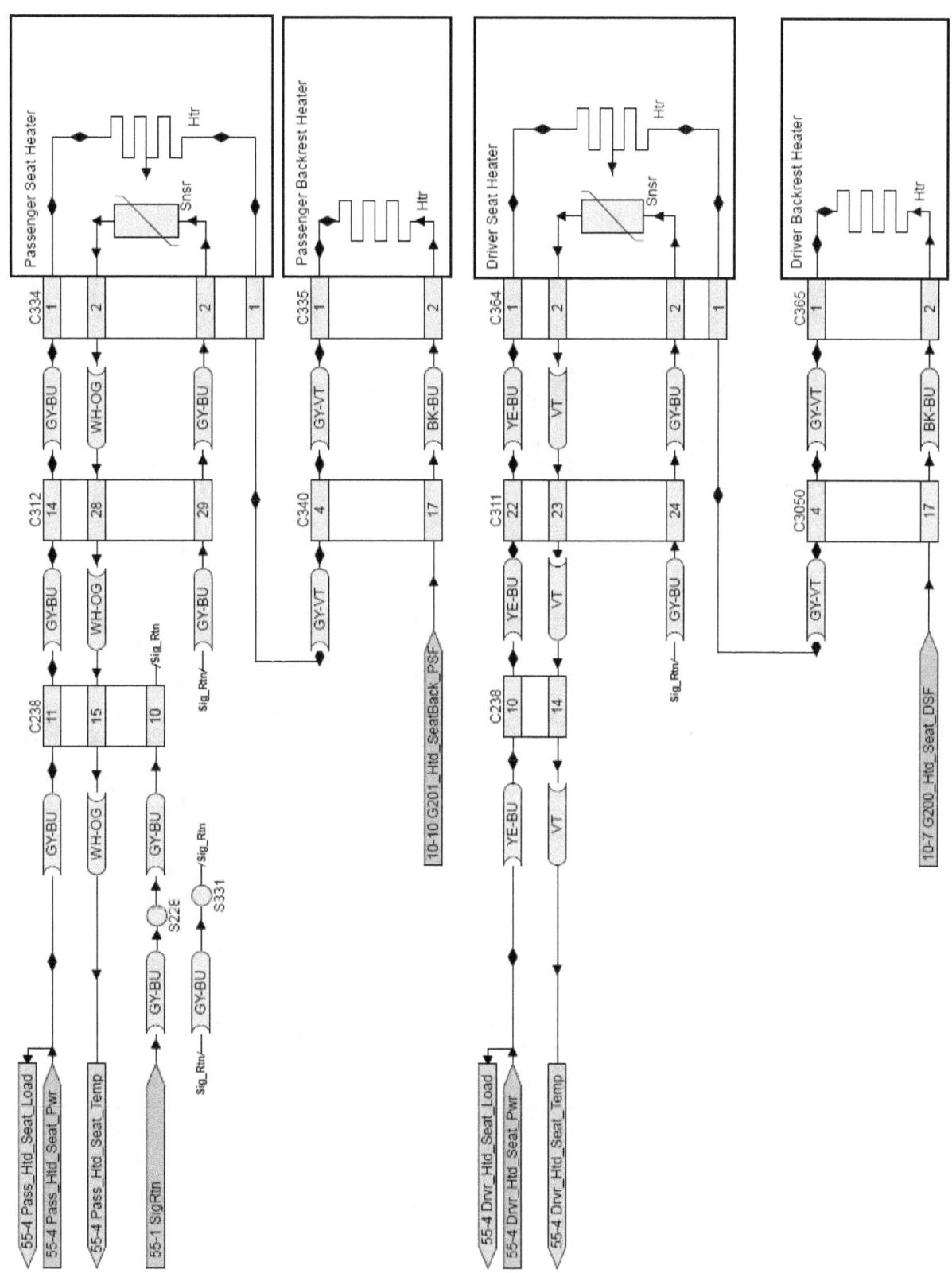

119-3 Dual Climate Control Seat Module – Power, and Ground

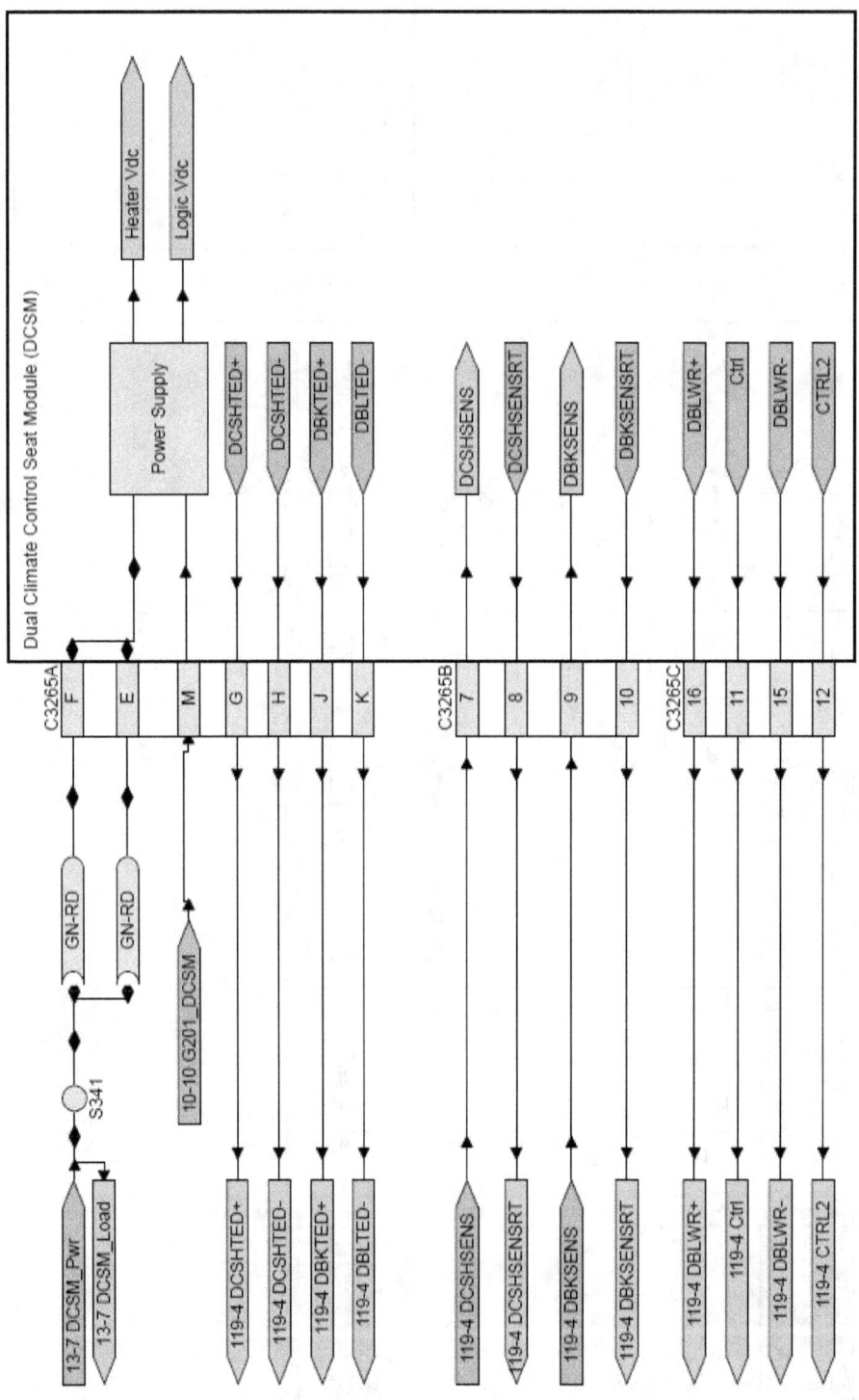

Climate Controlled Seats – Driver's Climate Controlled 119-4

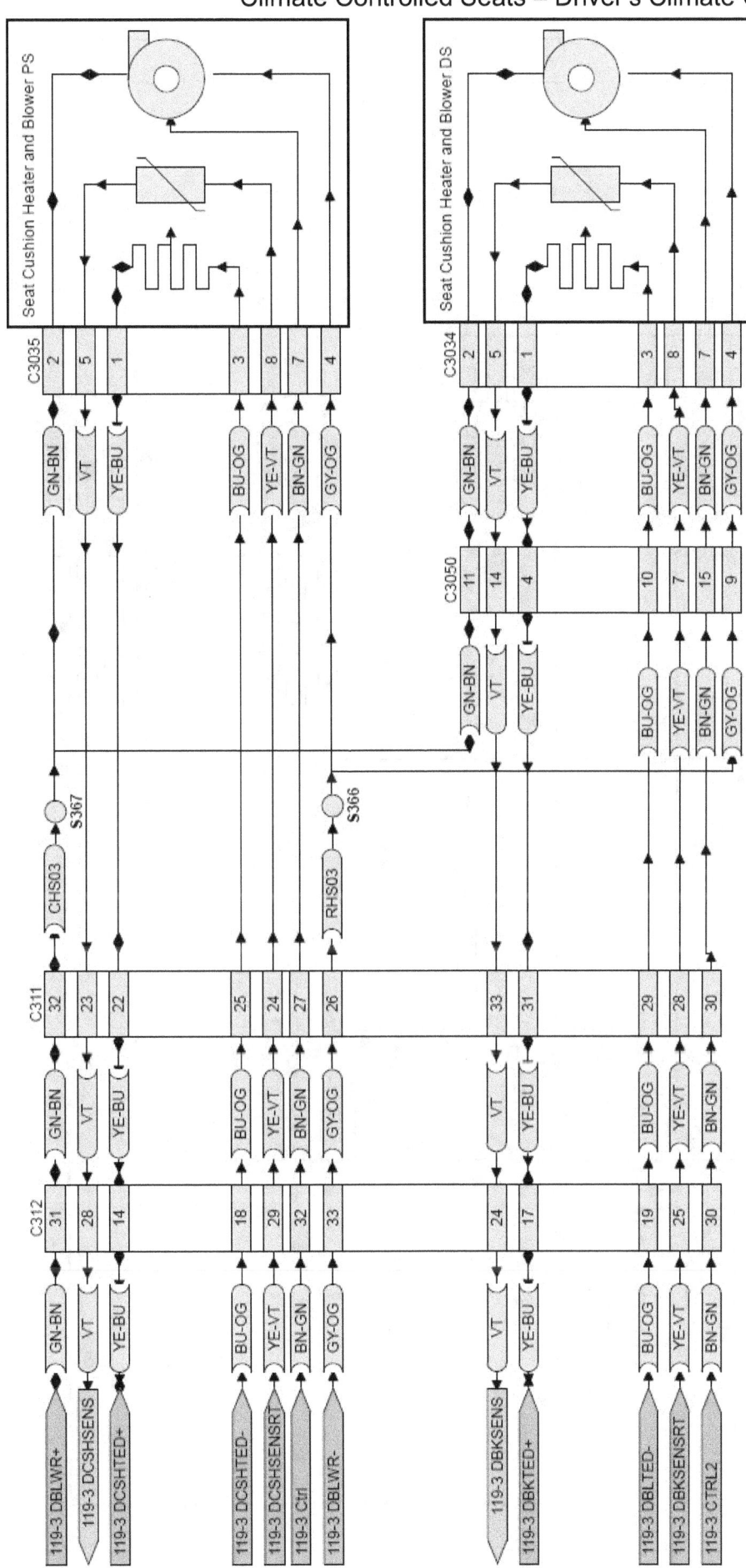

119-5 Climate Controlled Seats – Passenger's Climate Controlled

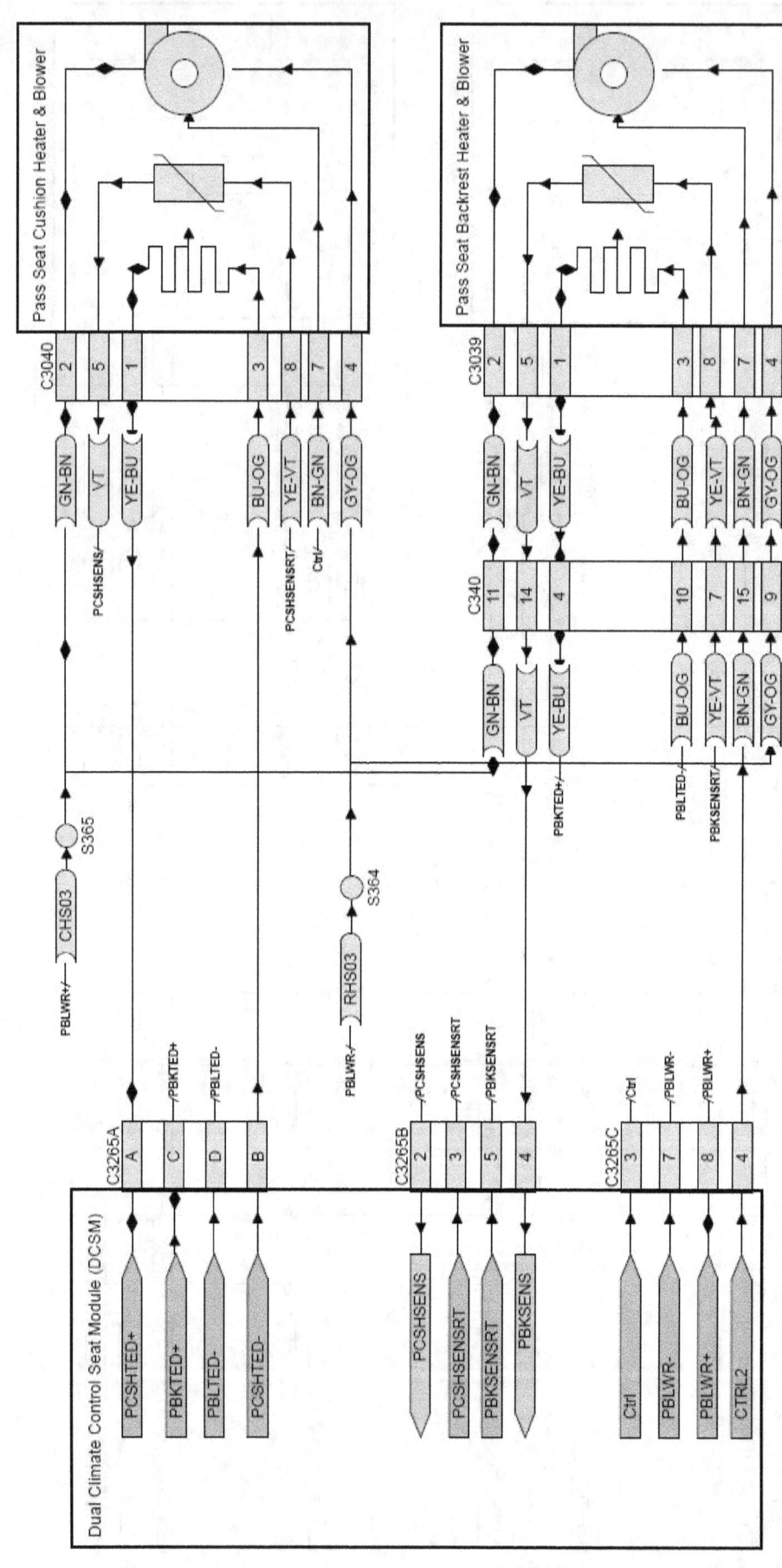

Climate Controlled Seats – Heated Seat Module Left Rear 119-6

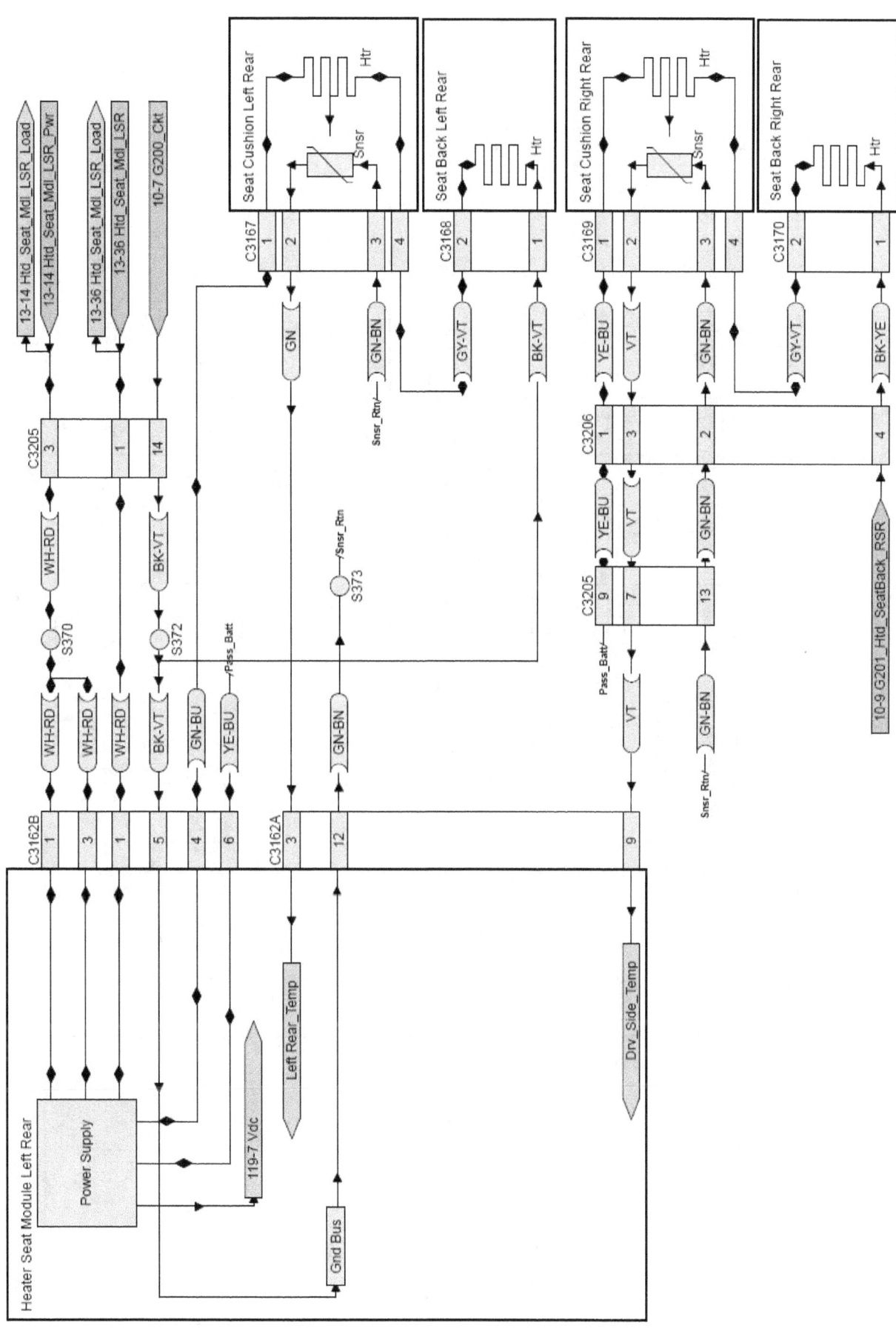

119-7 Climate Controlled Seats – Heated Seat Module Left Rear SUPER CREW

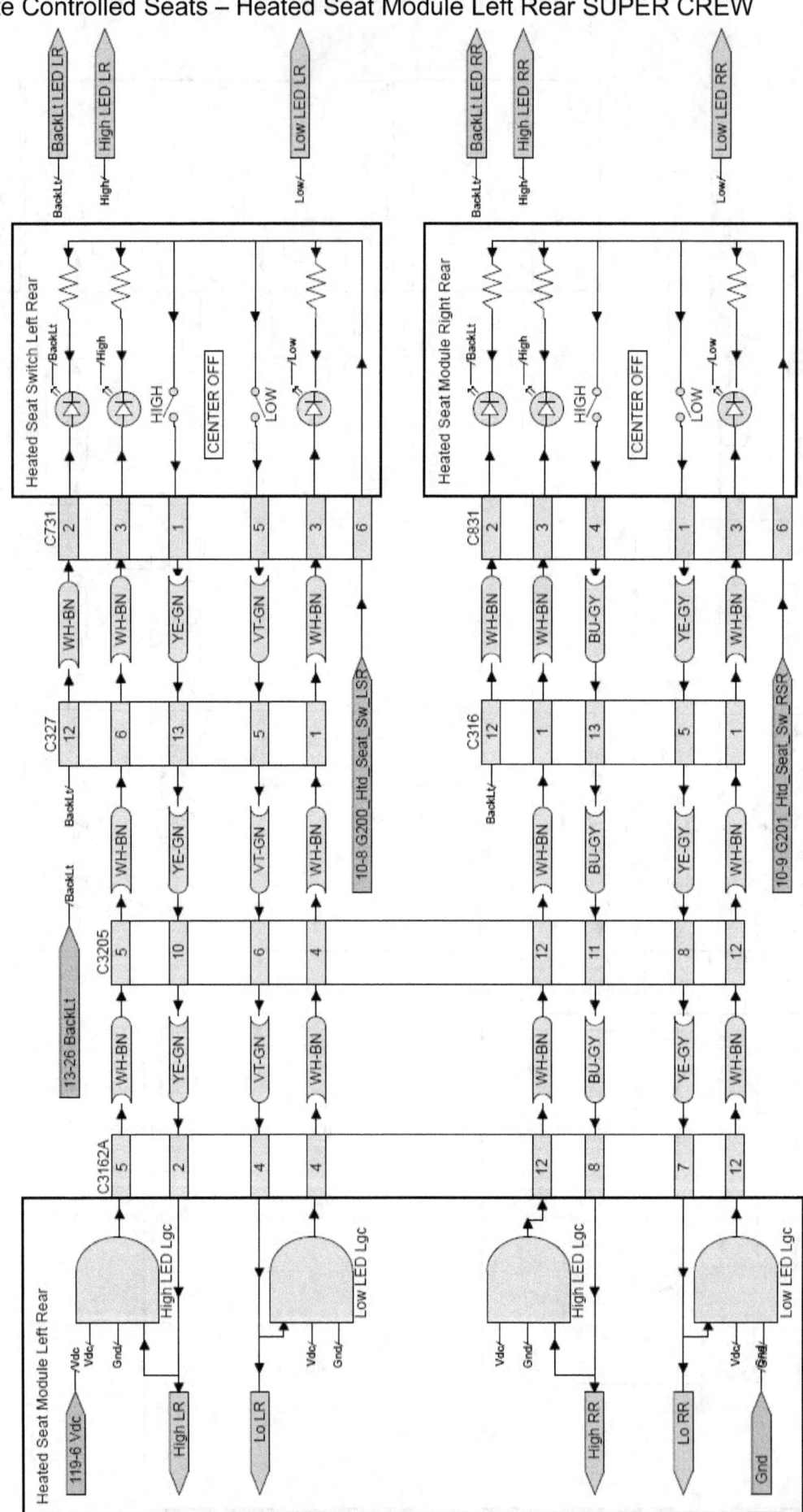

120 Power Seats
Power Seats – 6 Way Driver Seat with Memory 120-1

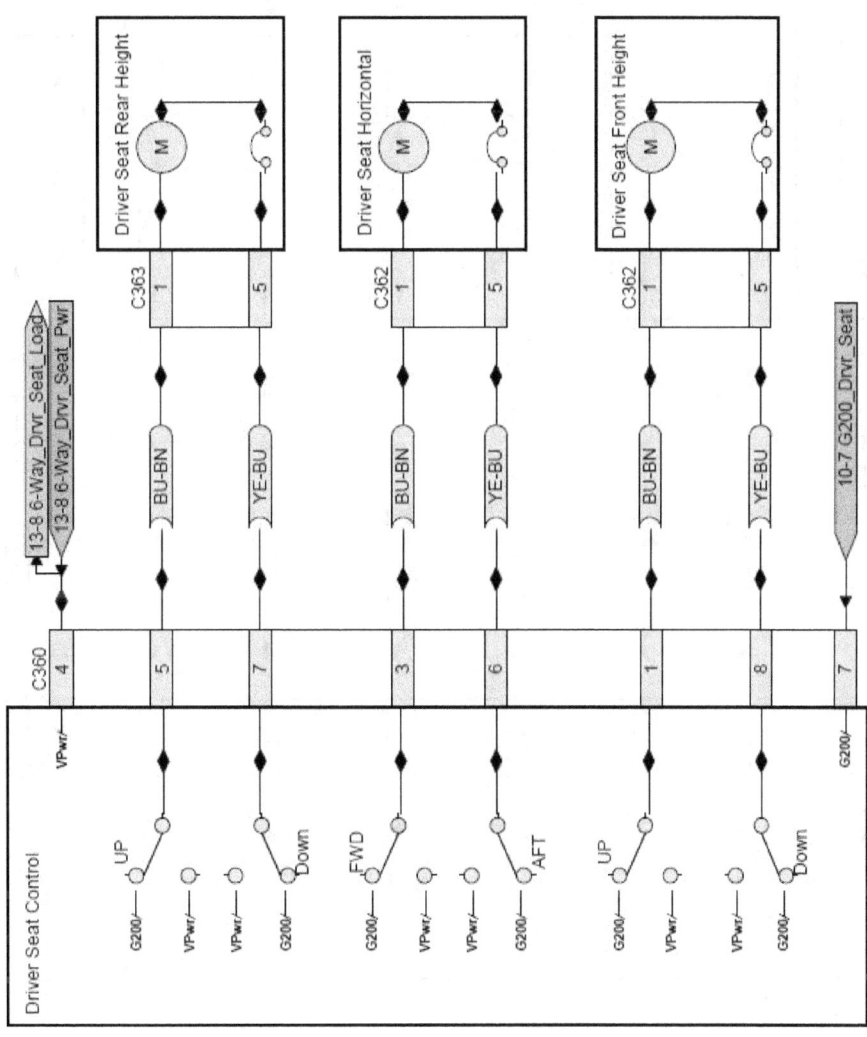

120-2 Power Seats – 10 Way Passenger Seat with Memory

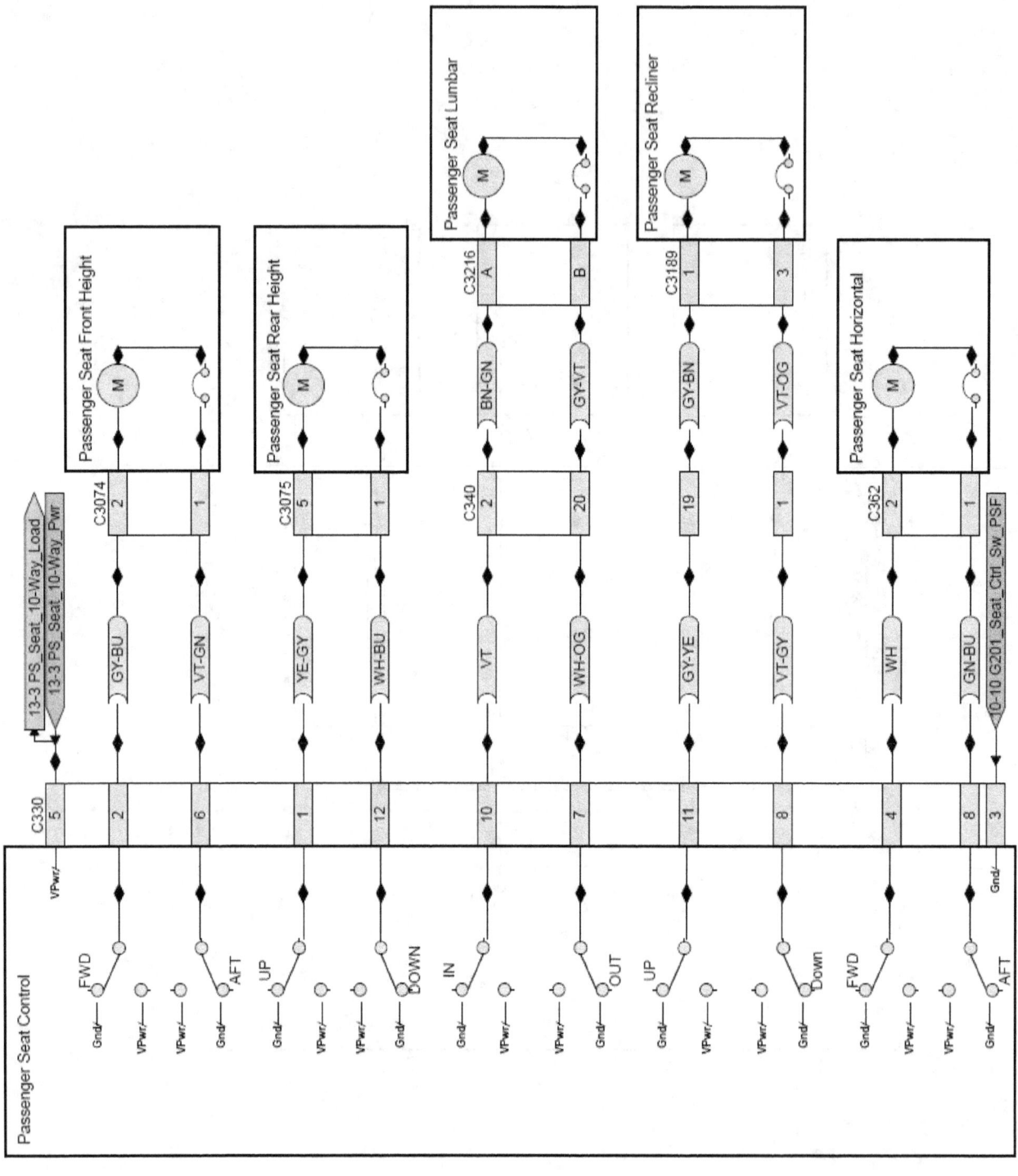

123 Memory Settings

Memory Settings – Driver Seat Module and Memory Set Switch 123-1

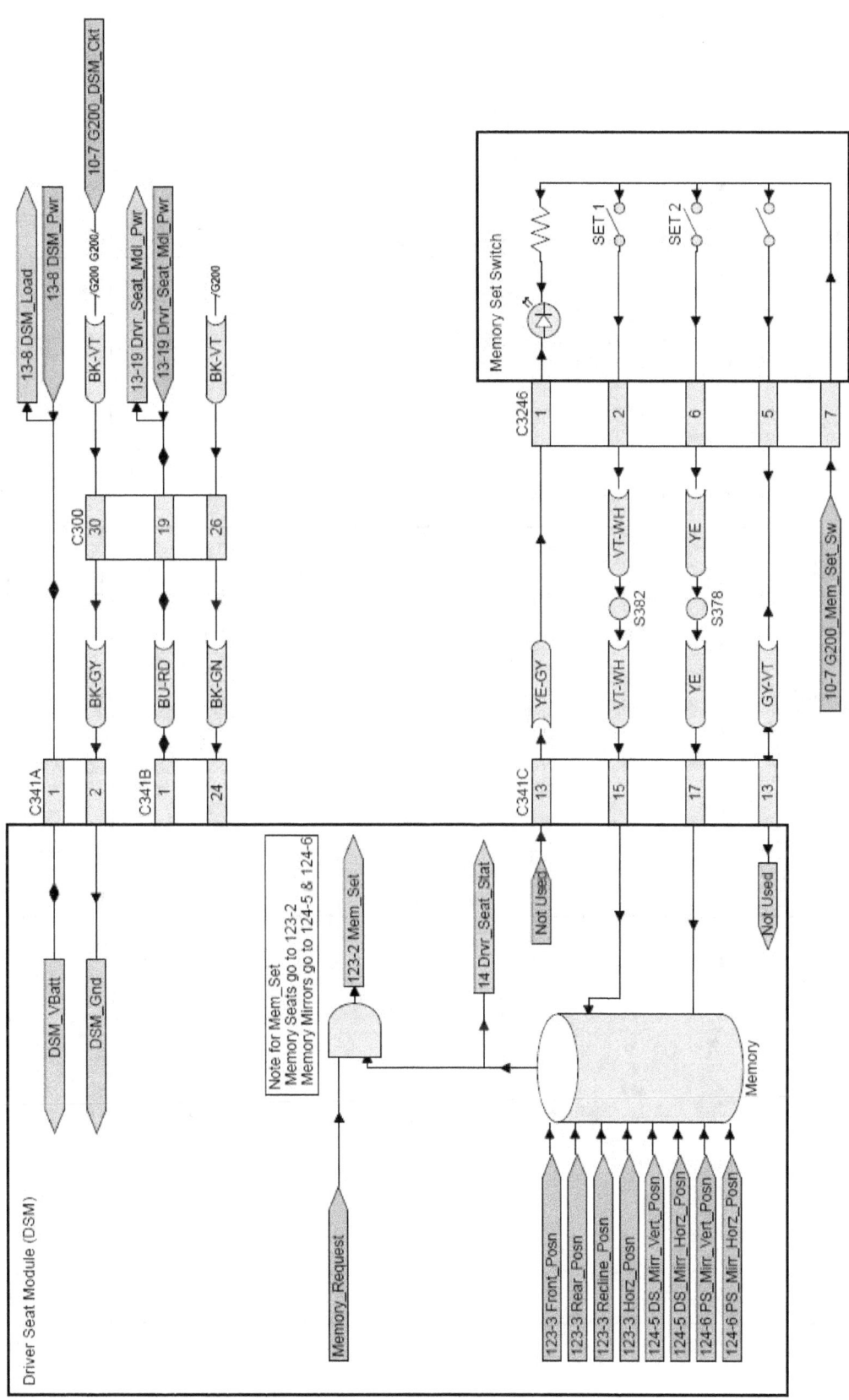

123-2 Memory Settings – Driver's Seat Control Switch Panel

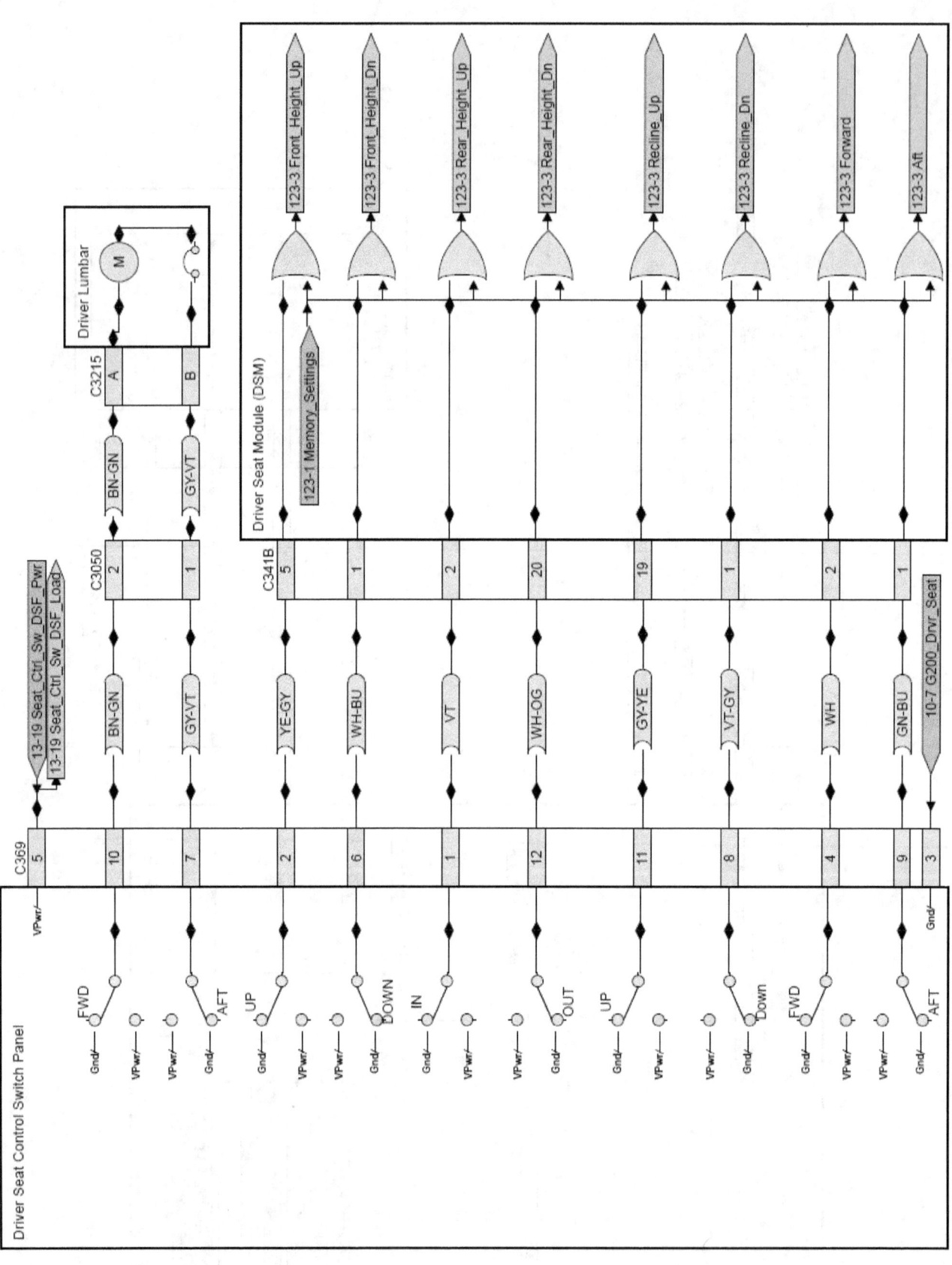

Memory Settings – Driver's Seat Module Control 123-3

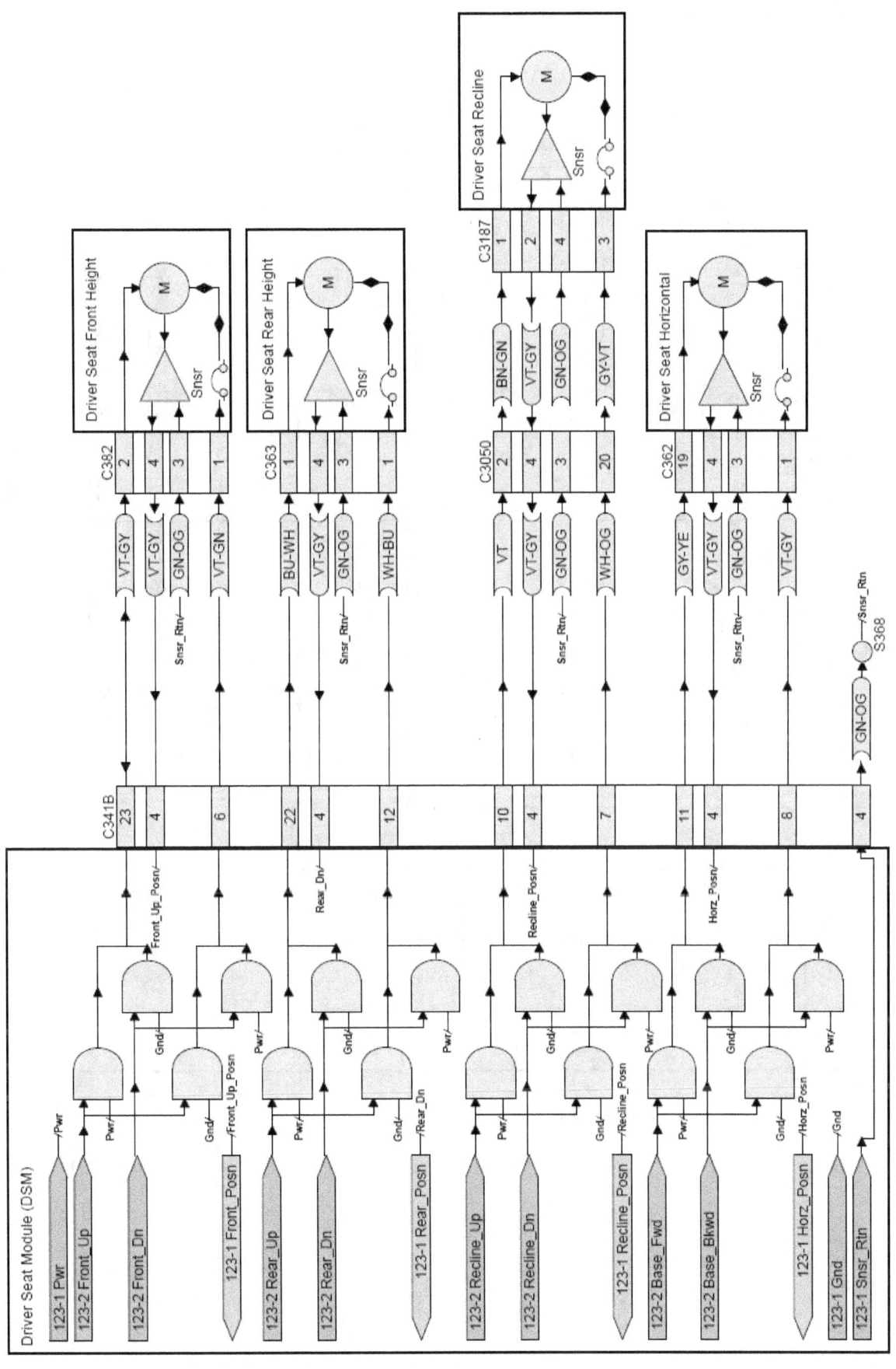

219

123-4 Memory Settings – Driver's Seat Module & Driver Side Rear View Mirror

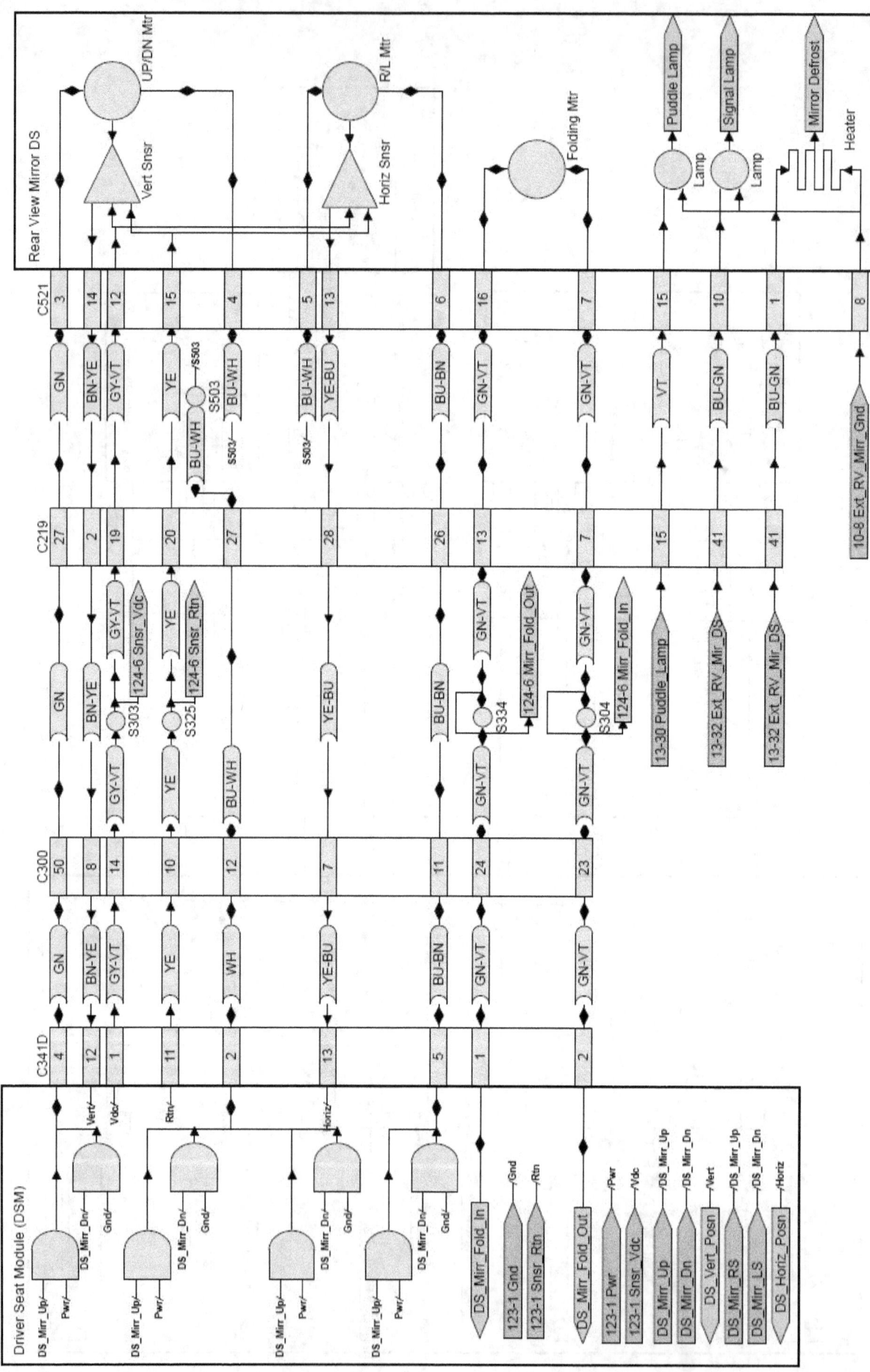

Memory Settings Driver Seat Module & Passenger Side Rear View Mirror 123-5

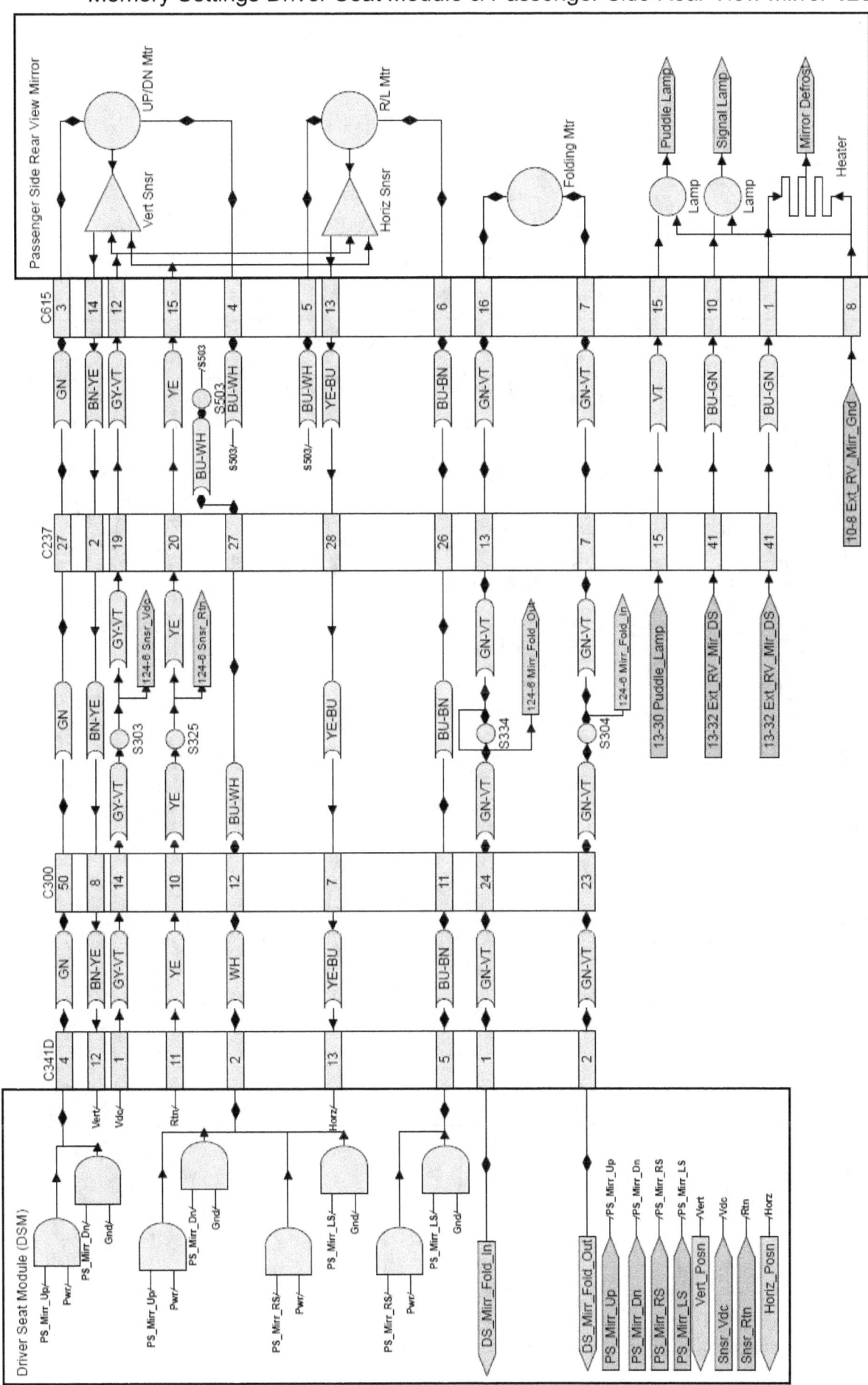

124, 127 Power Mirrors

124-2 Power Mirrors – Rear View Mirror Switch and Controls

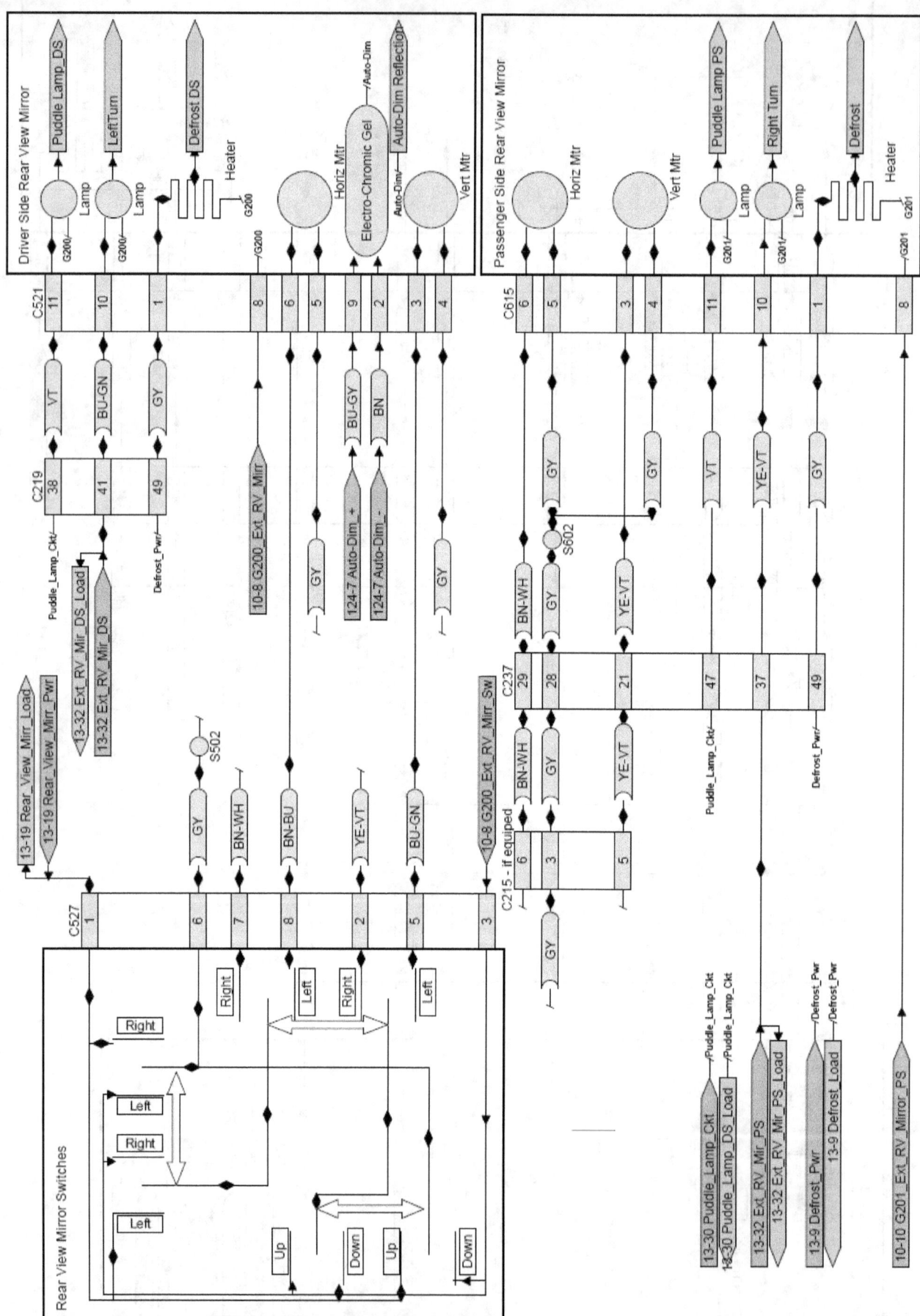

Power Mirrors – Driver Seat Module, Rear View Mirror Switch with Memory Settings 124-4

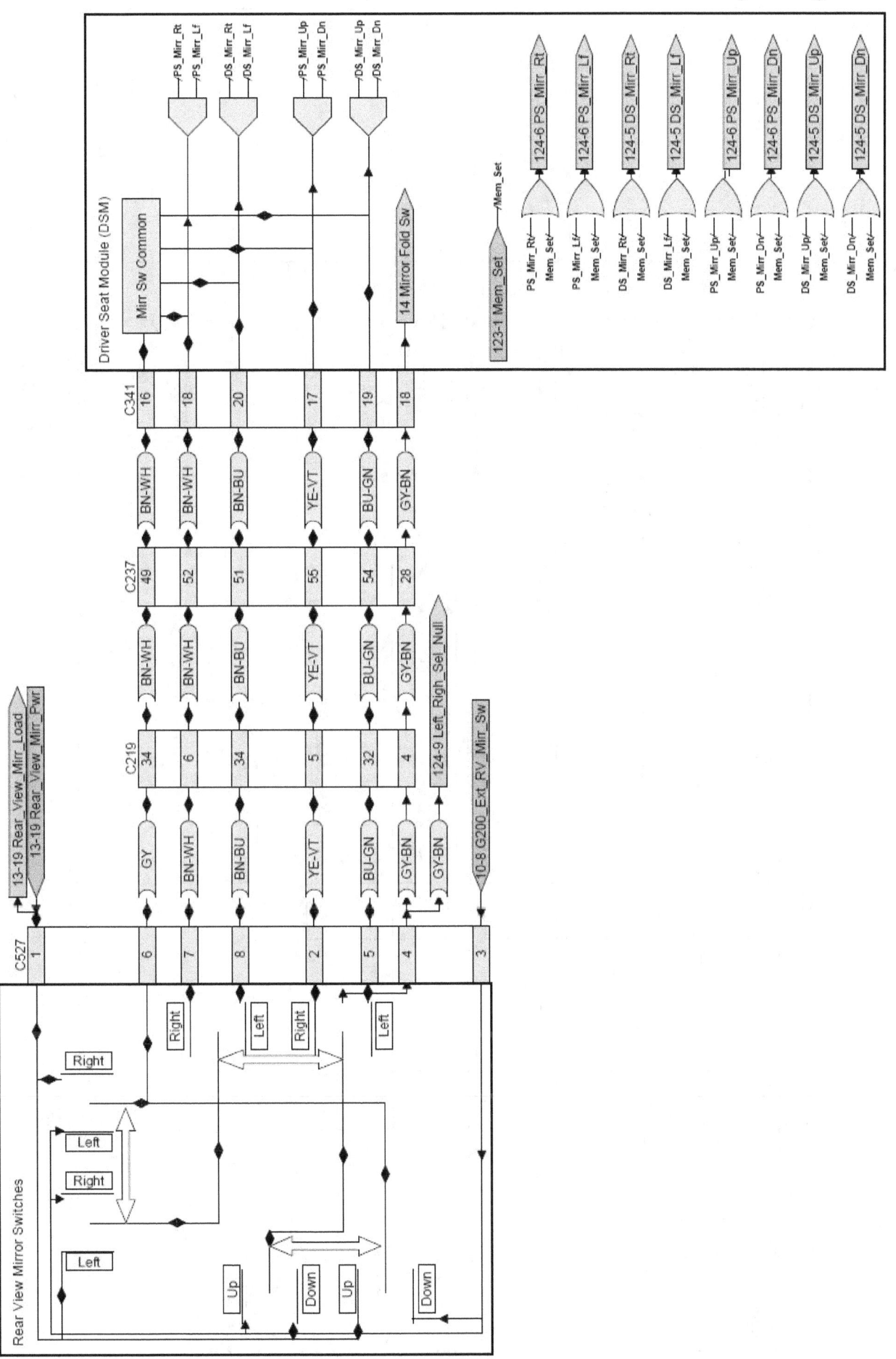

124-5 Power Mirrors – Driver Seat Module, Rear View Mirror Switch with Memory Settings

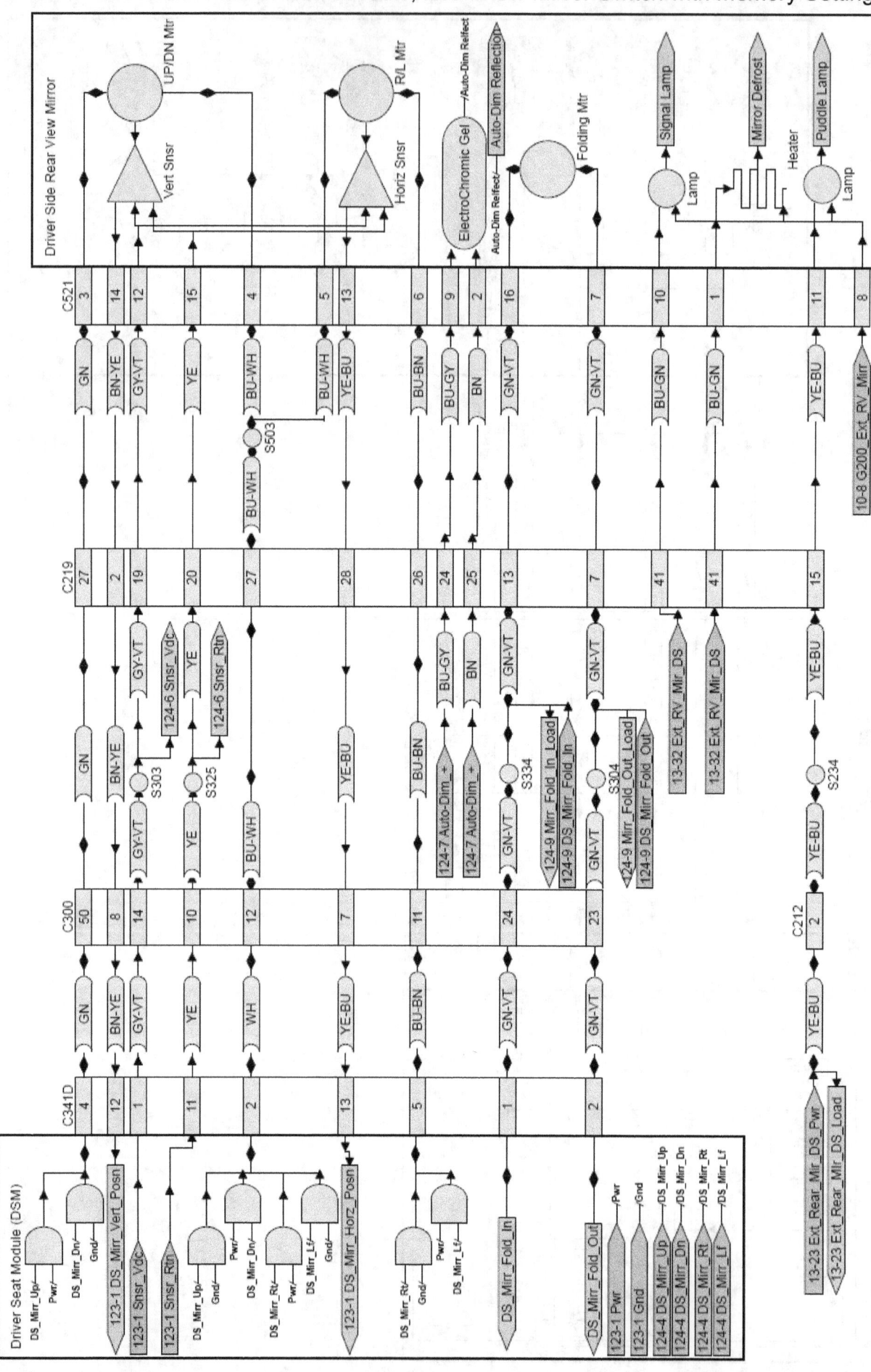

Power Mirrors – Driver Seat Module, Rear View Mirror Switch with Memory Settings 124-6

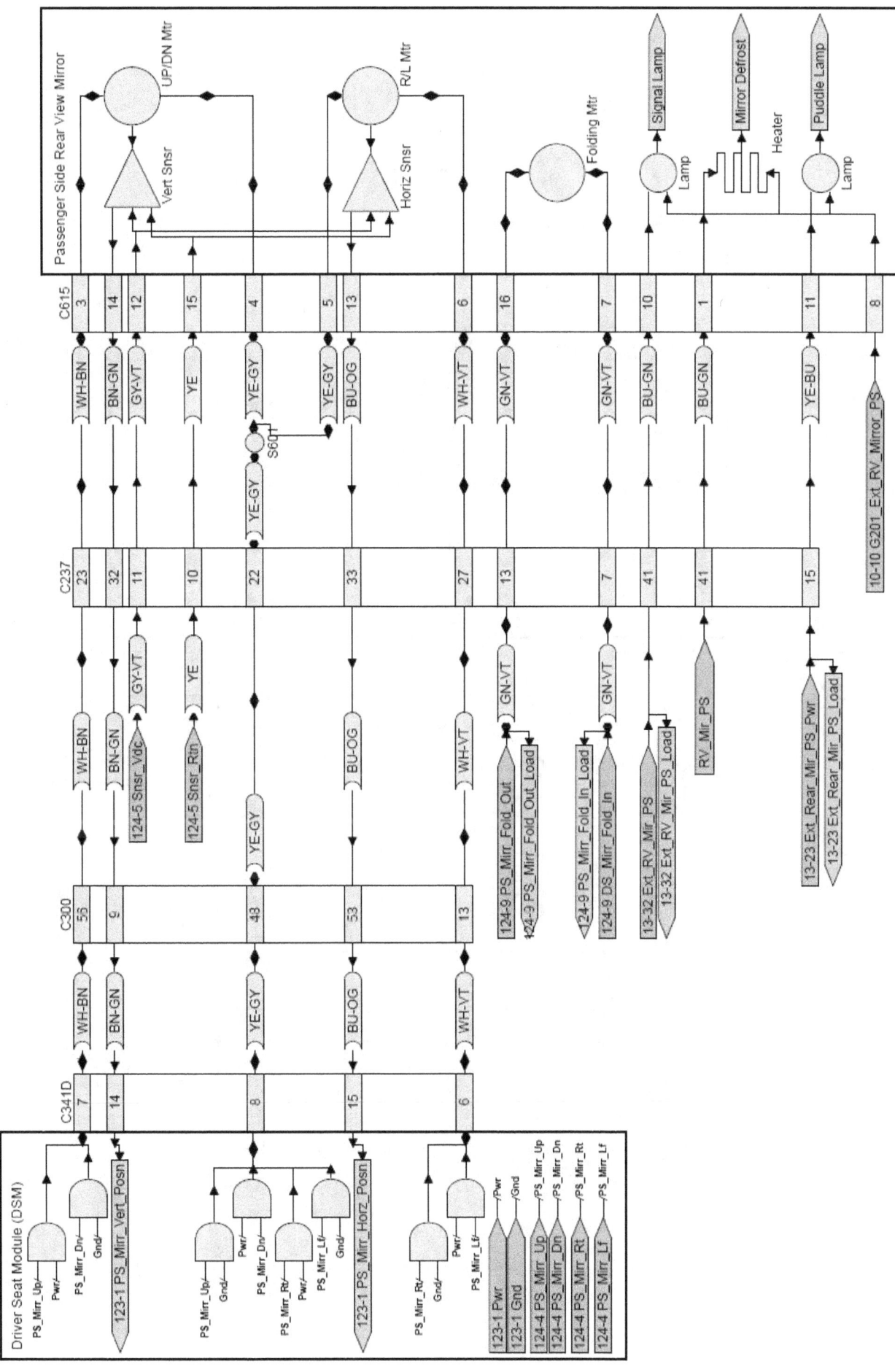

124-7 Auto-Dimming Rear View Mirror

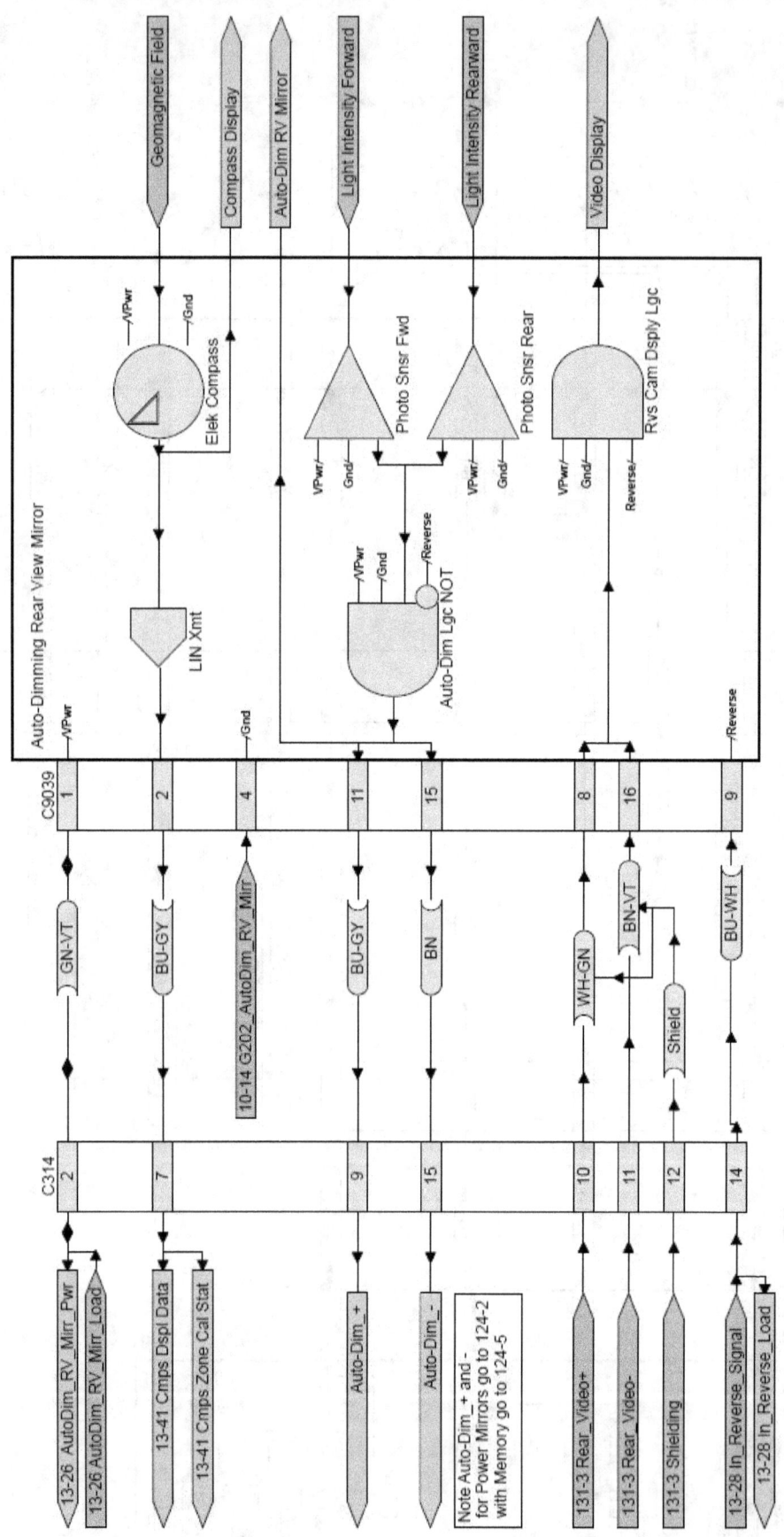

Power Mirrors Folding Switches 124-8

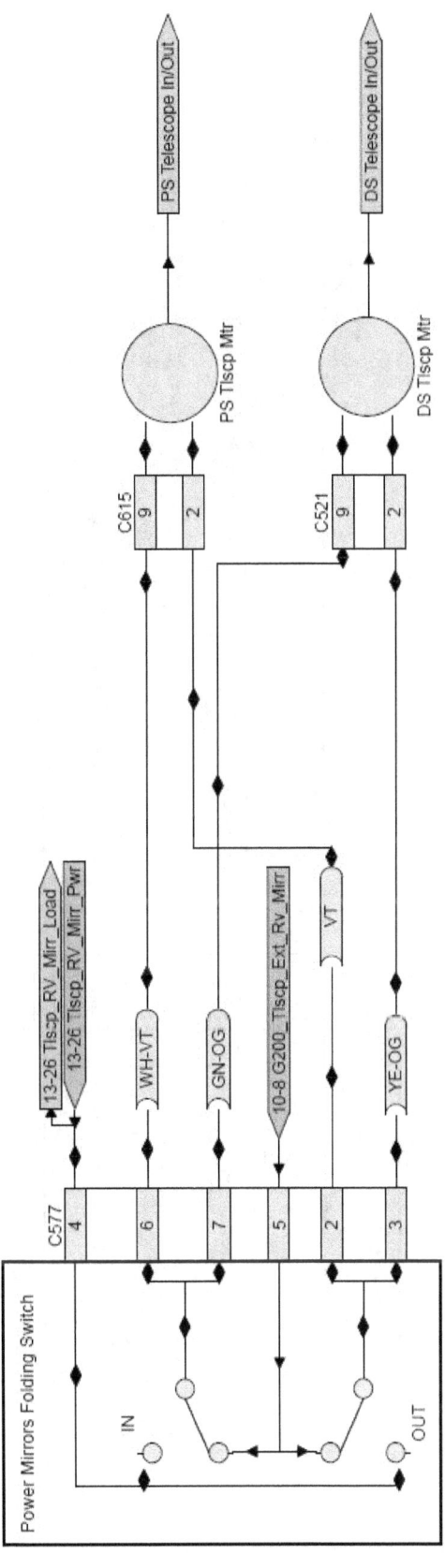

124-9 Folding Mirror Module

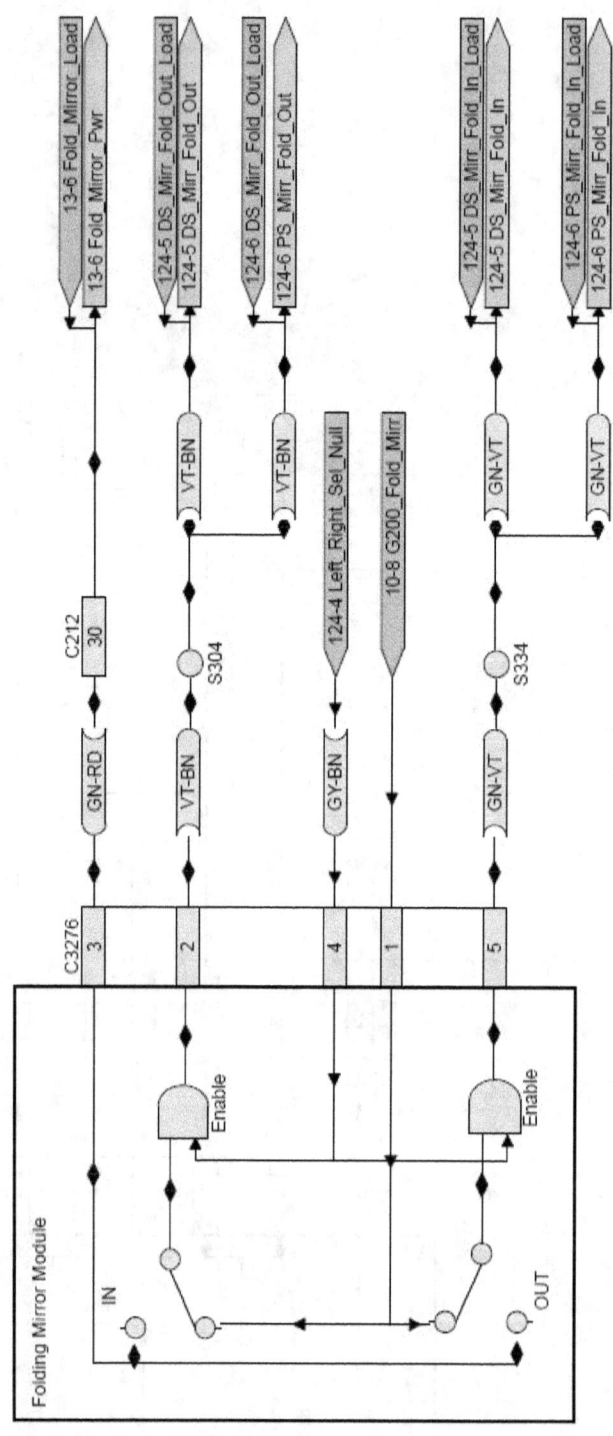

Adjustable Pedal **127-3**

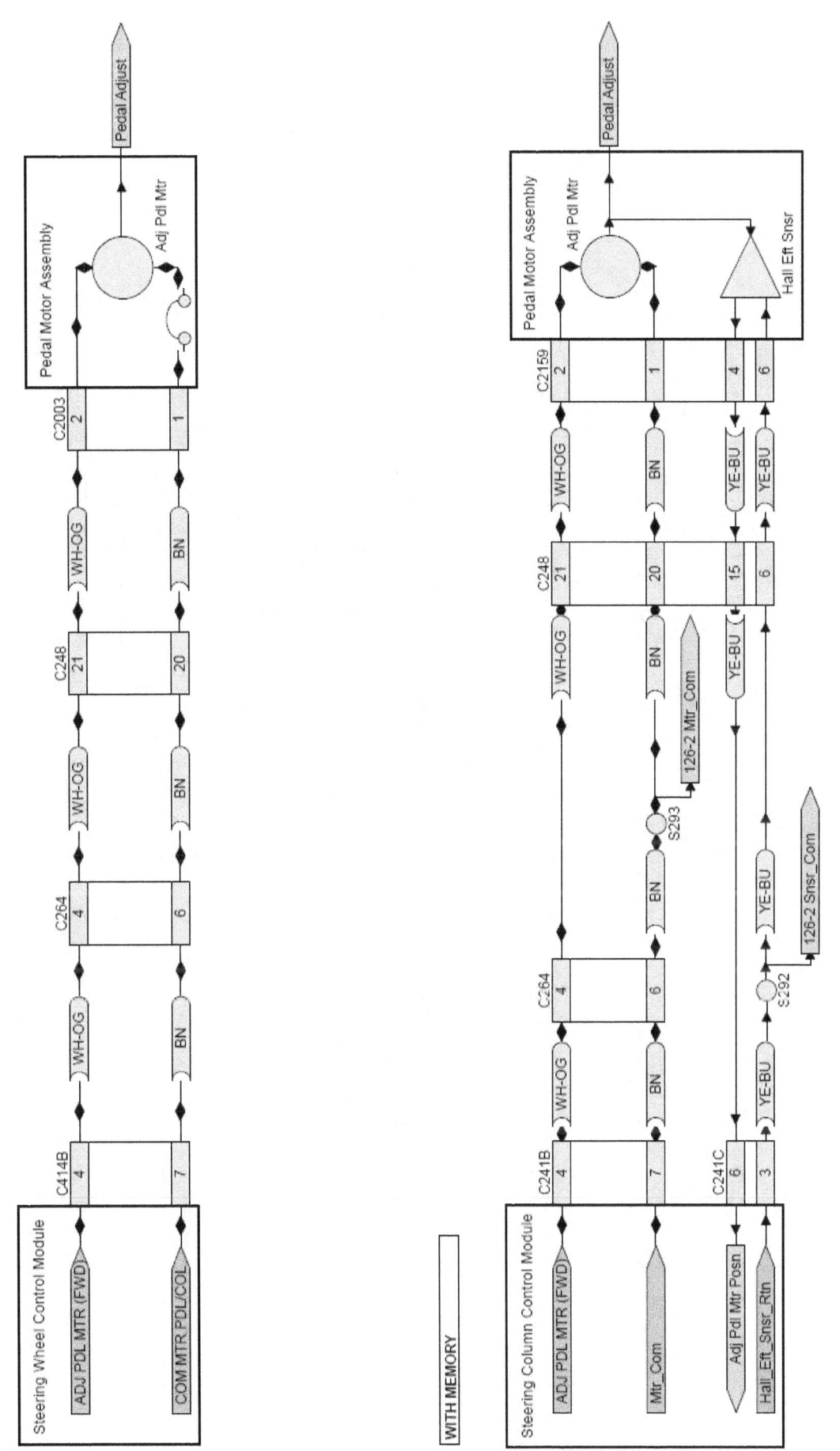

128-2 Steering Column Tilt and Telescoping Motors

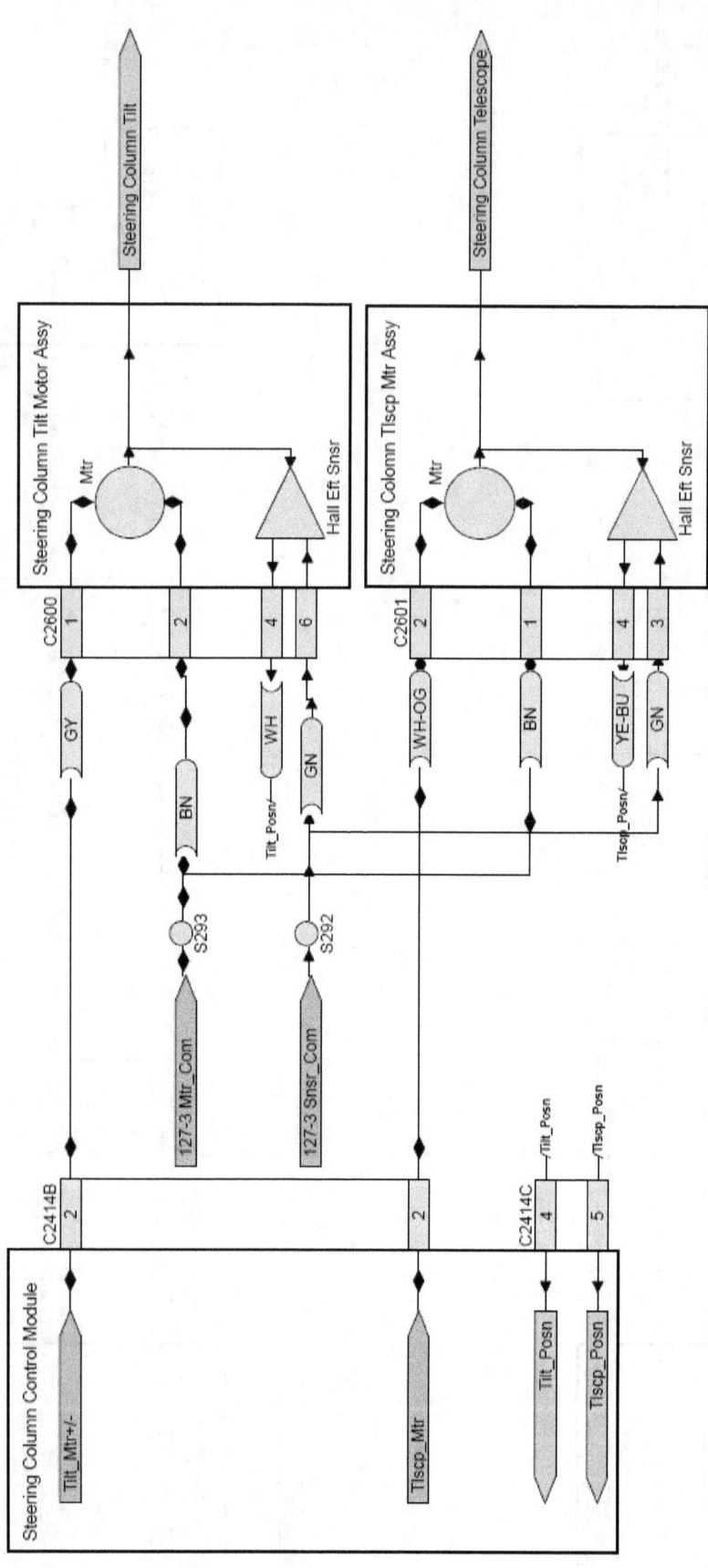

130 Audio Control Module (ACM)
ACM – Base Audio 130-1

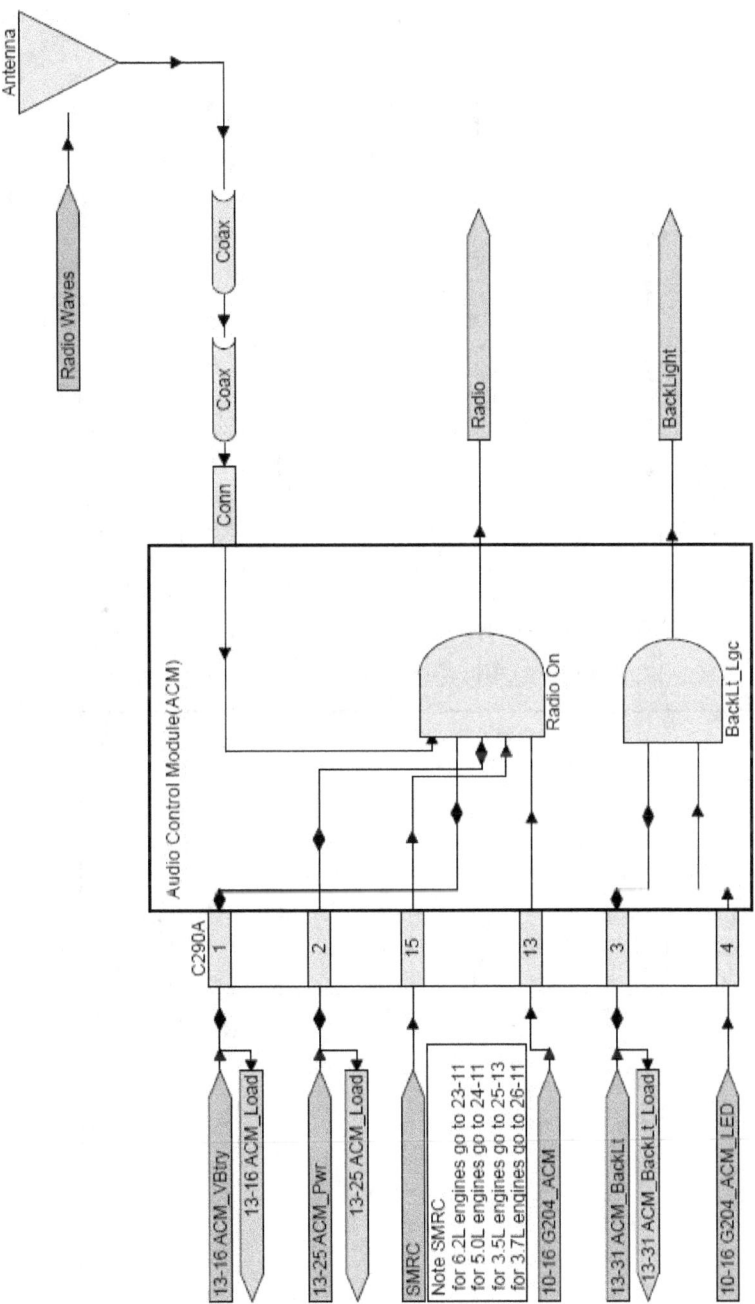

130-2 ACM – Mid Level Audio

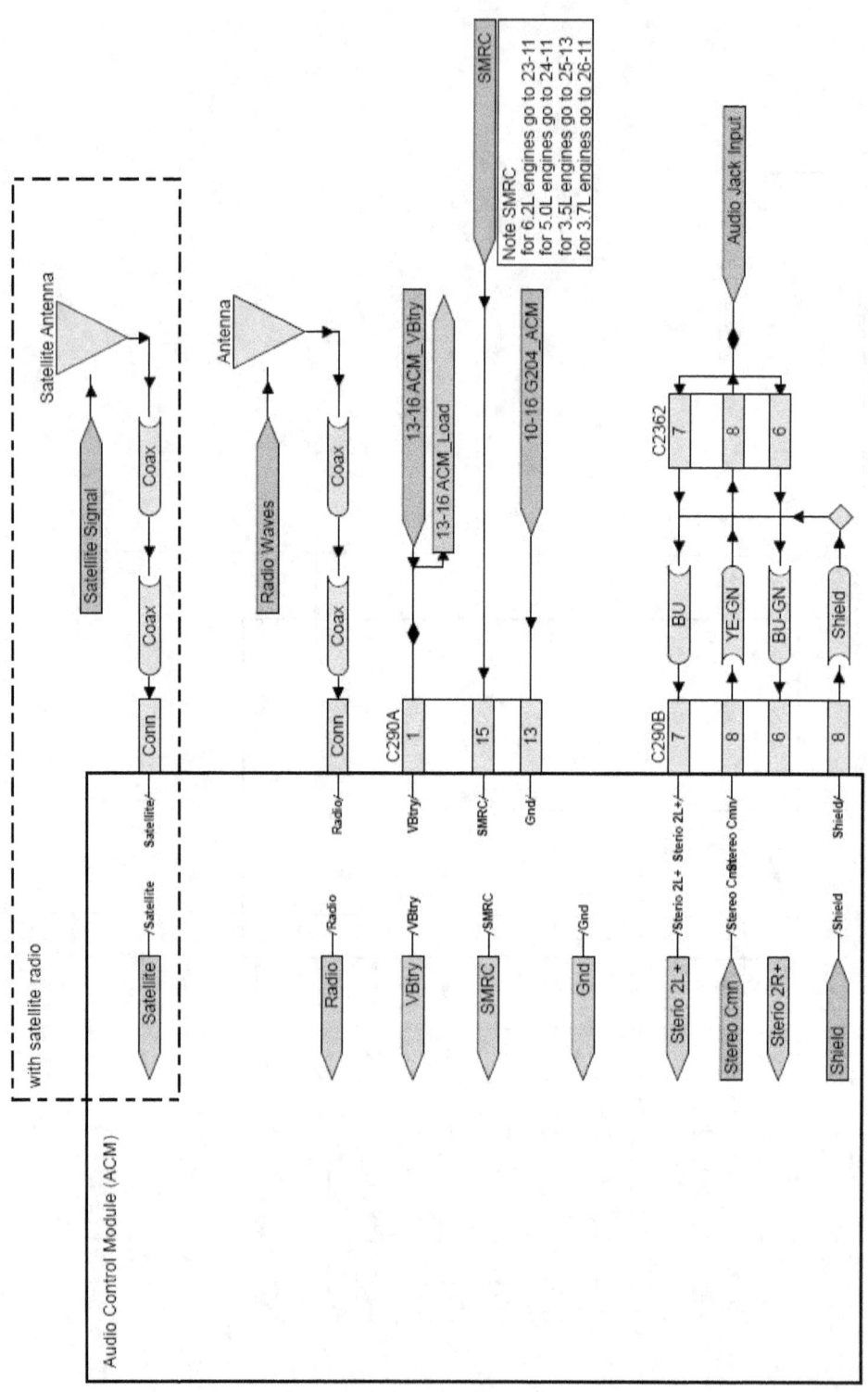

ACM – Premium, Premium Plus and Sony © Sound 130-3

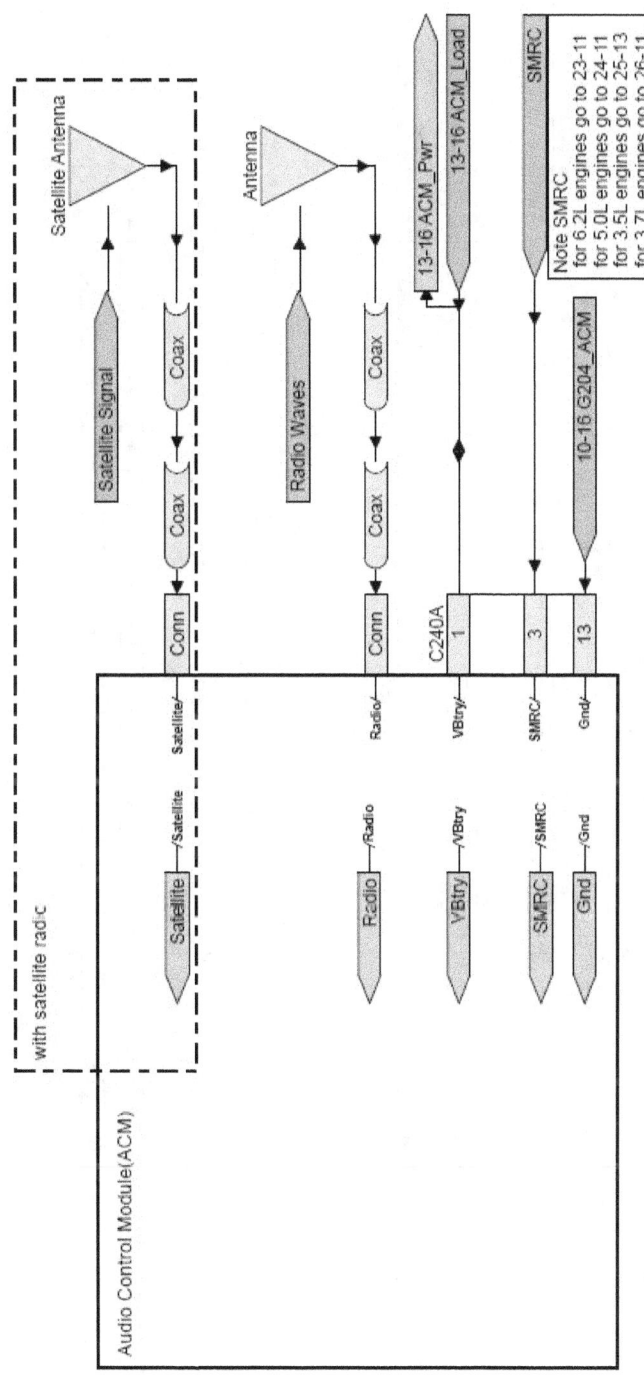

130-4 ACM – Premium, Premium Plus and Sony © Sound

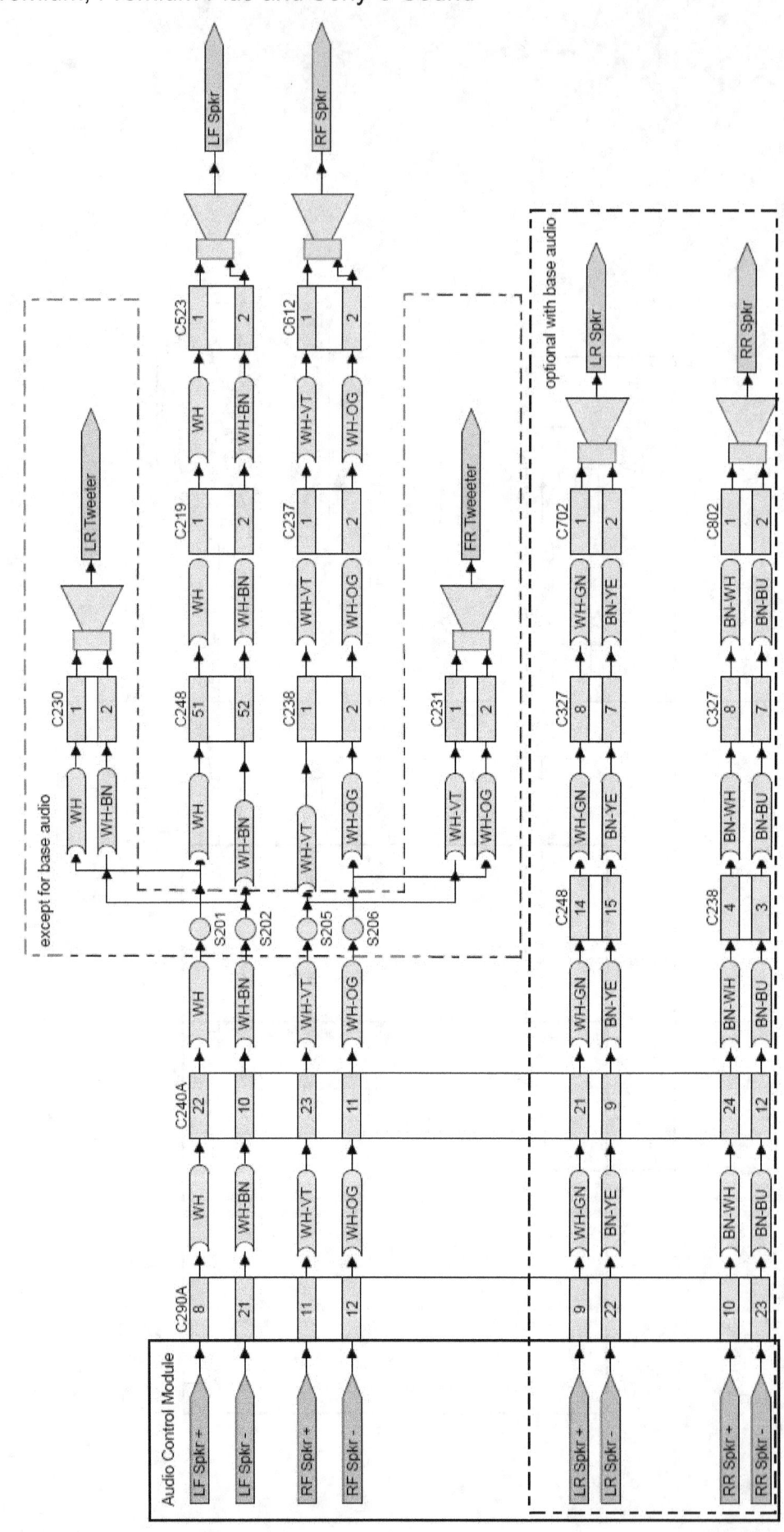

ACM – SYNC 130-5

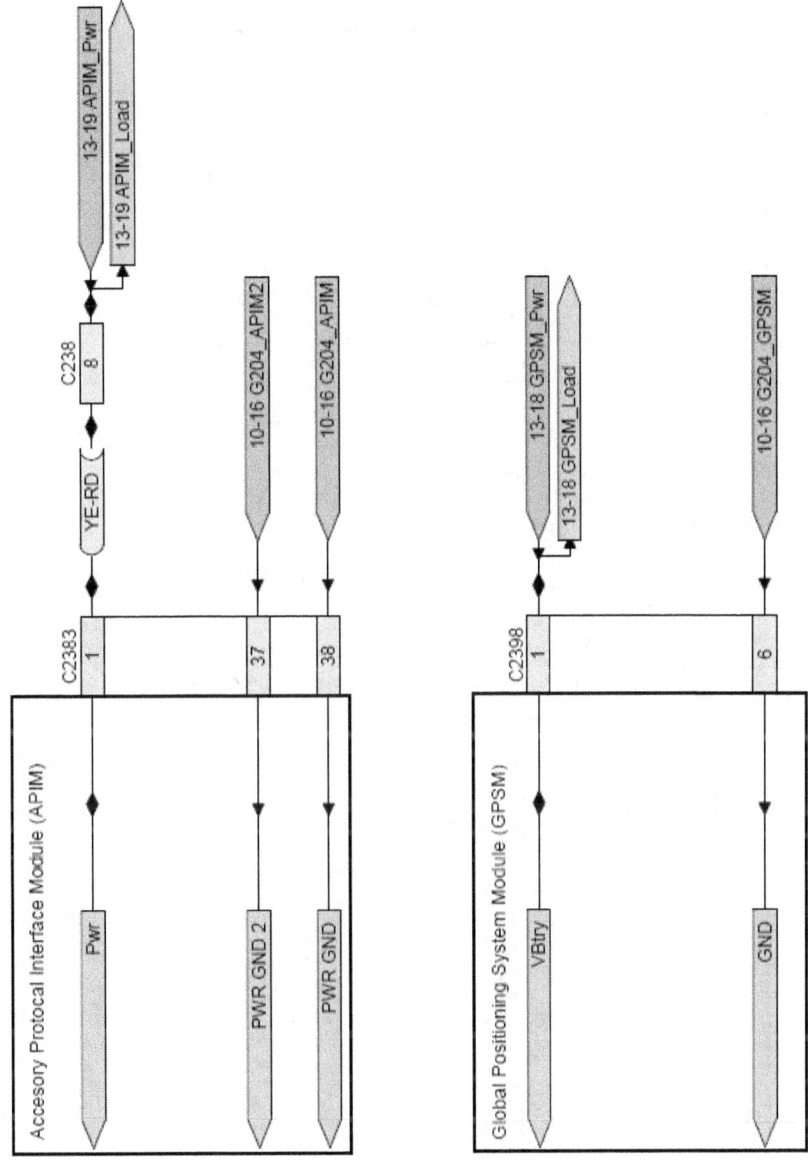

235

130-6 ACM – SYNC Gen 1

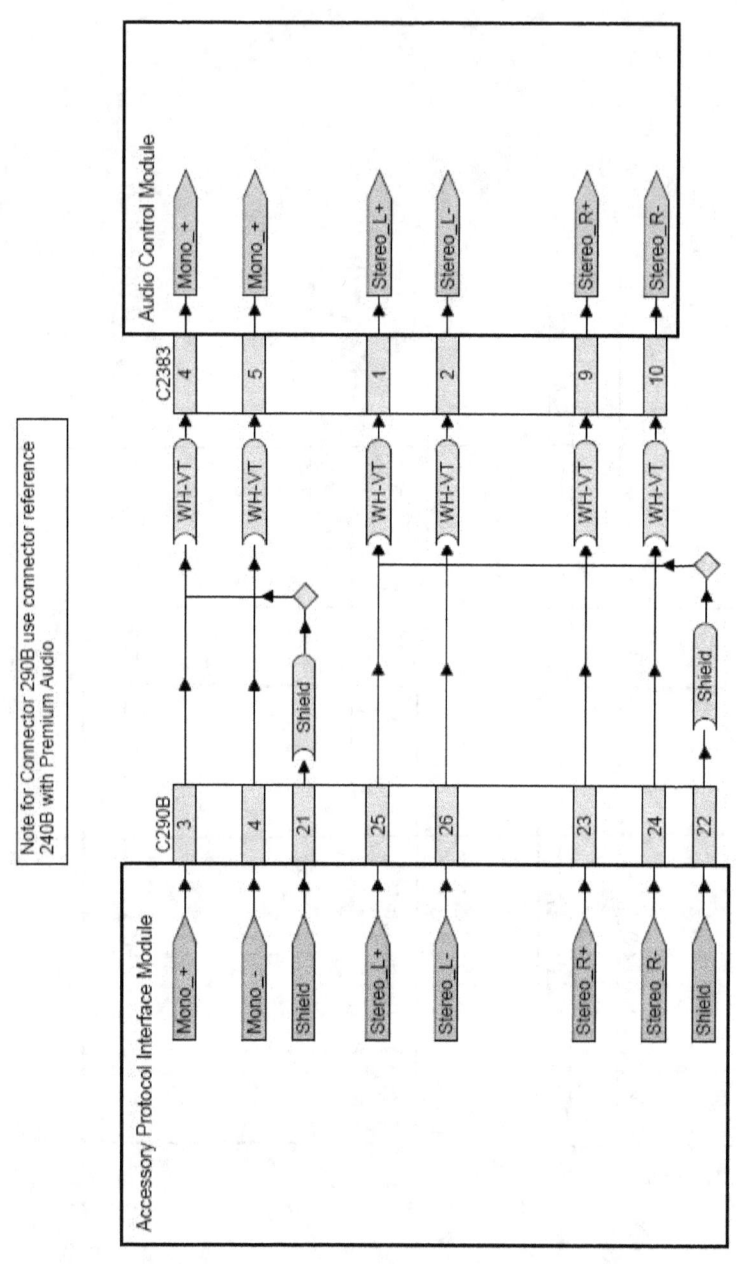

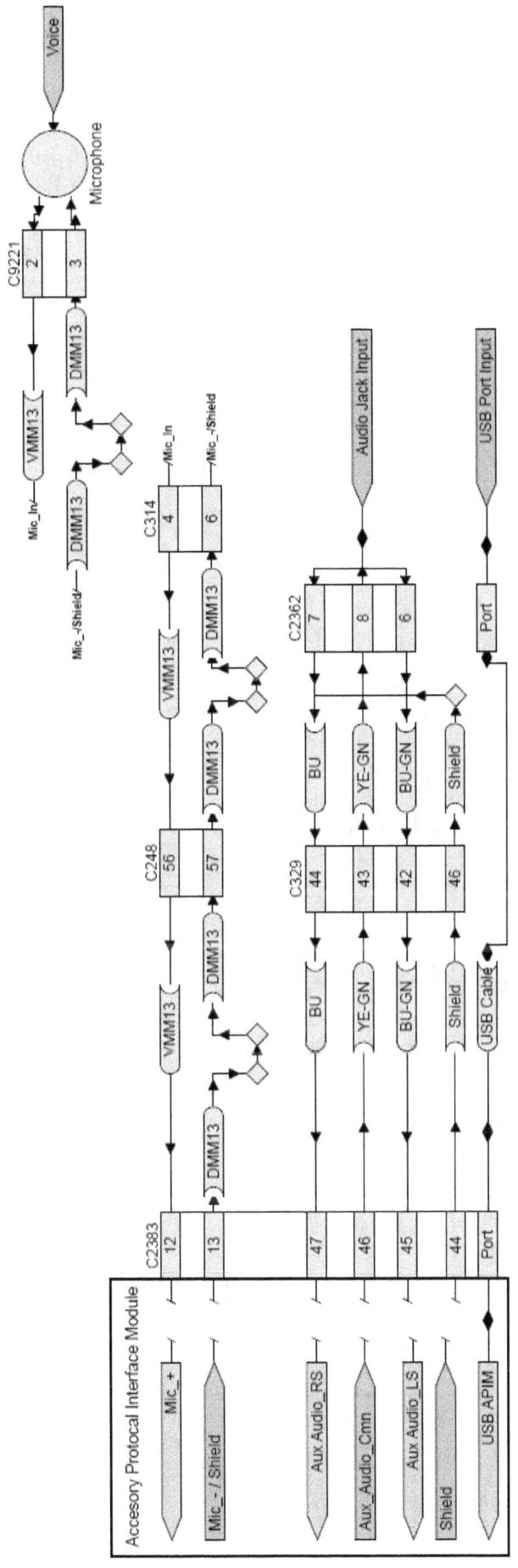

130-8 ACM – Sony © Sound

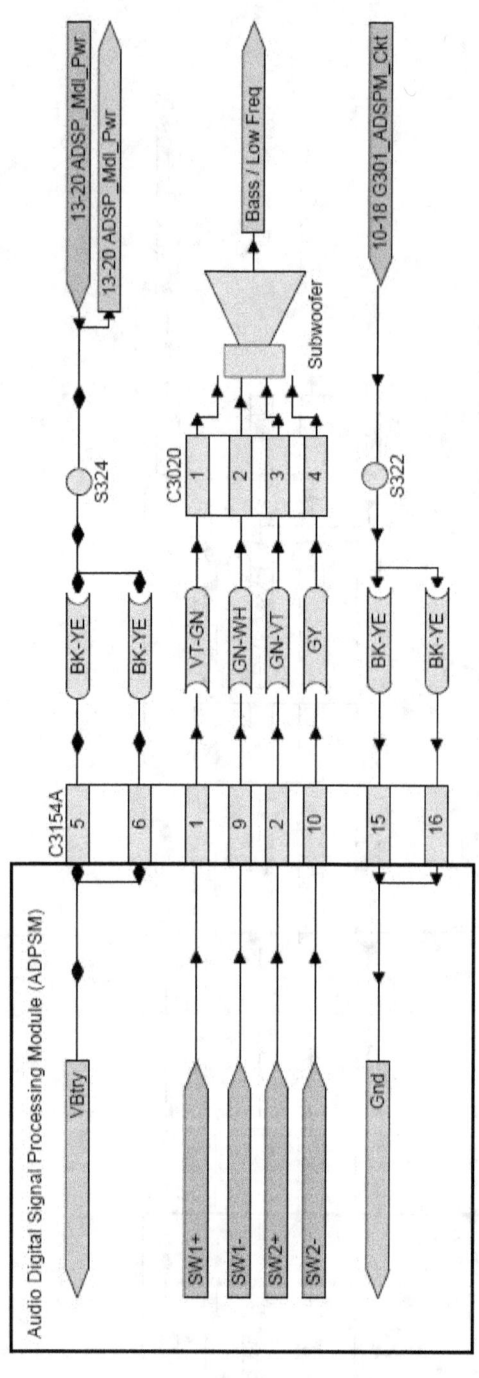

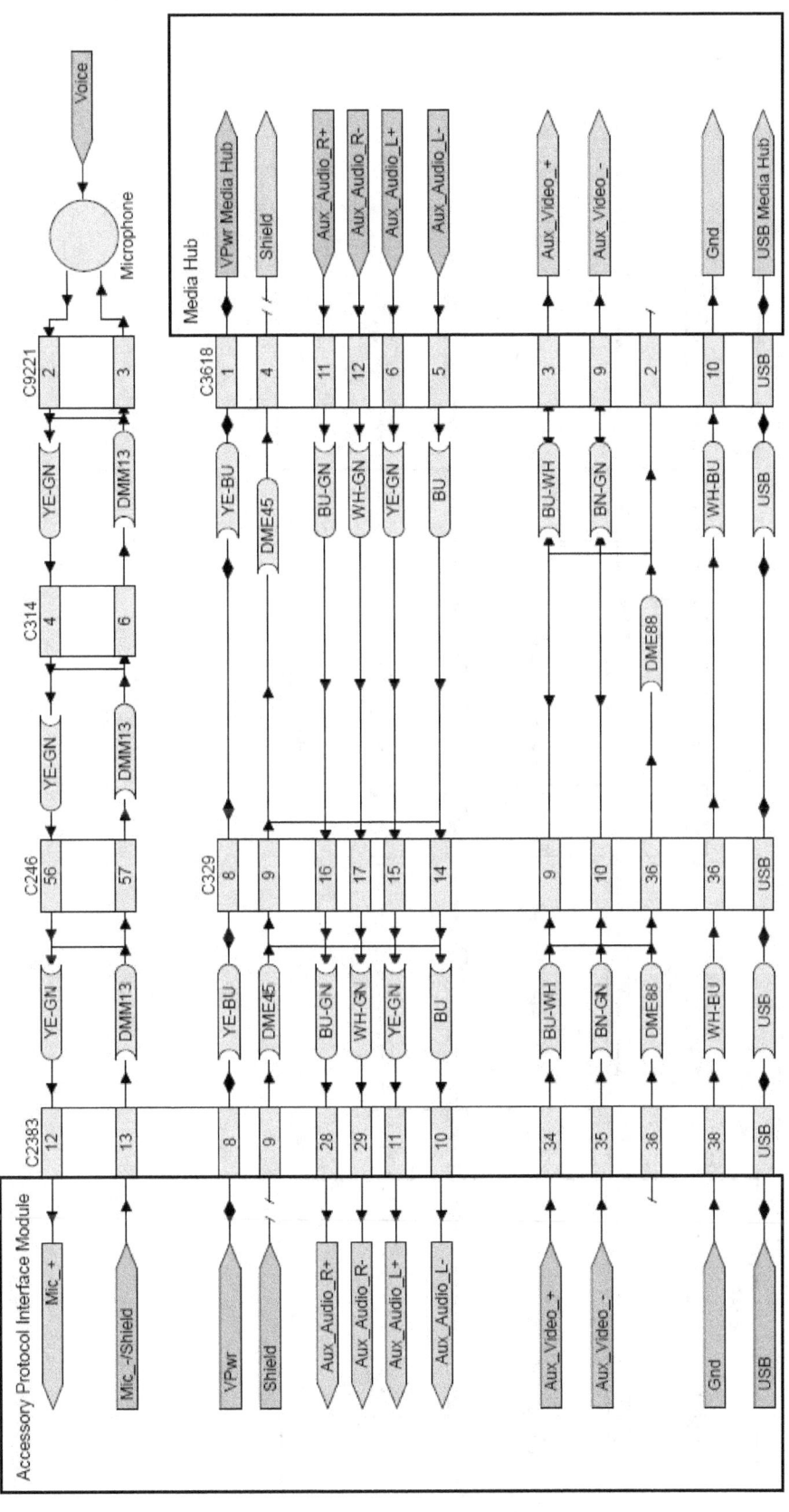

130-10 ACM – Sony © Sound

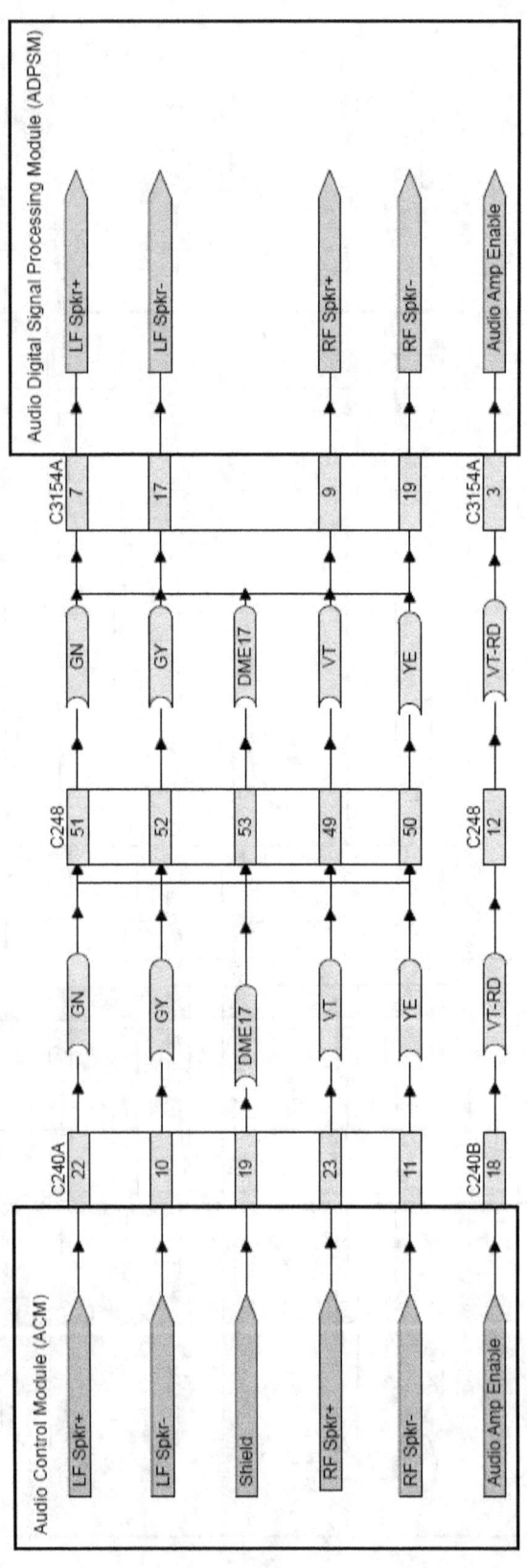

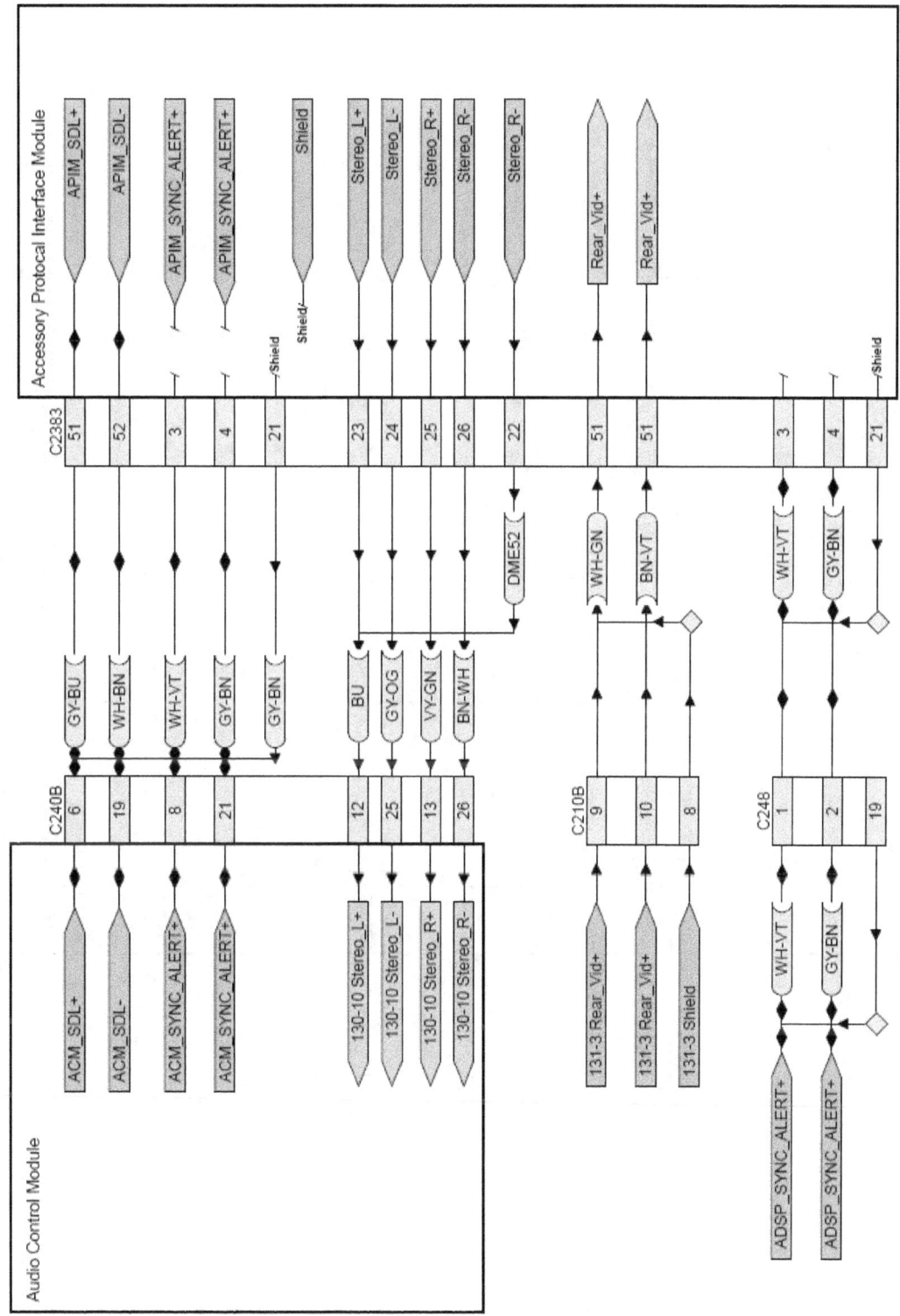

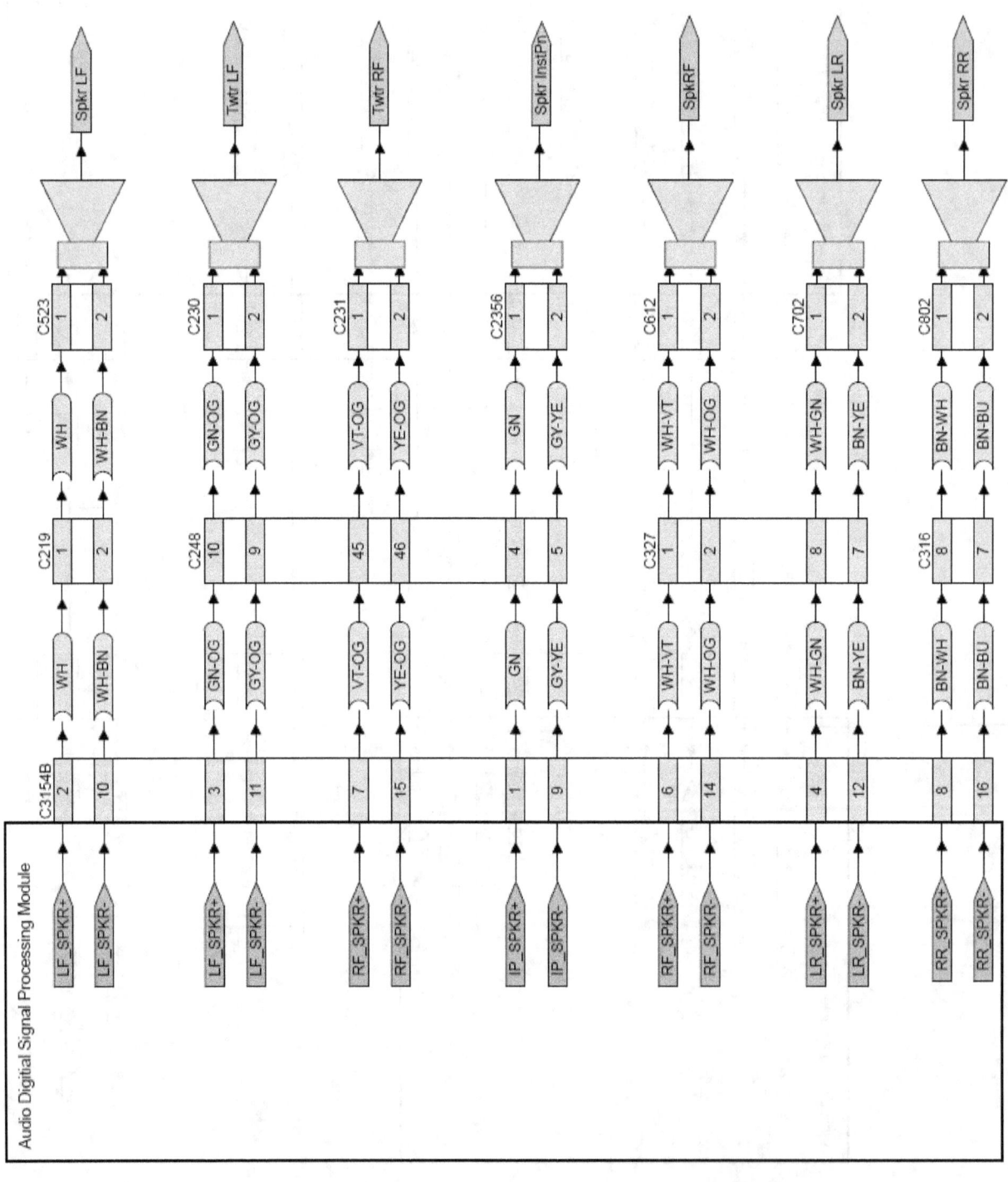

Front Control Display Interface Module (FCDIM) 130-13

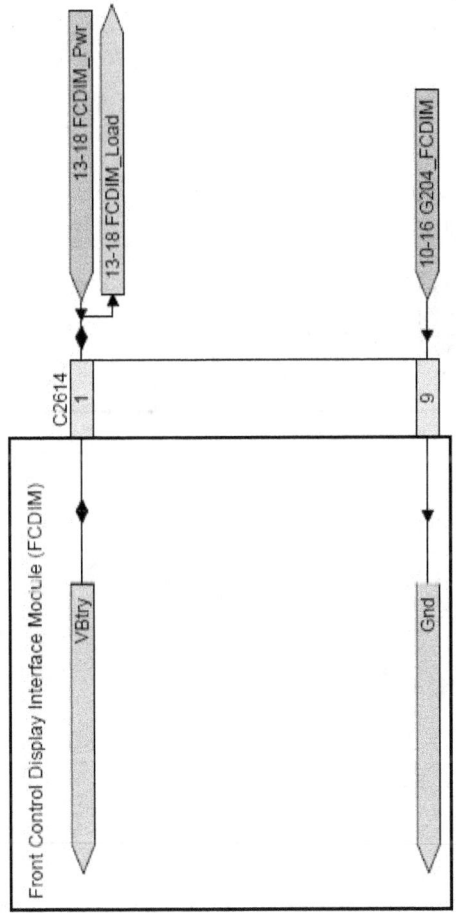

130-14 Front Control Display Interface Module & Front Display Interface Module

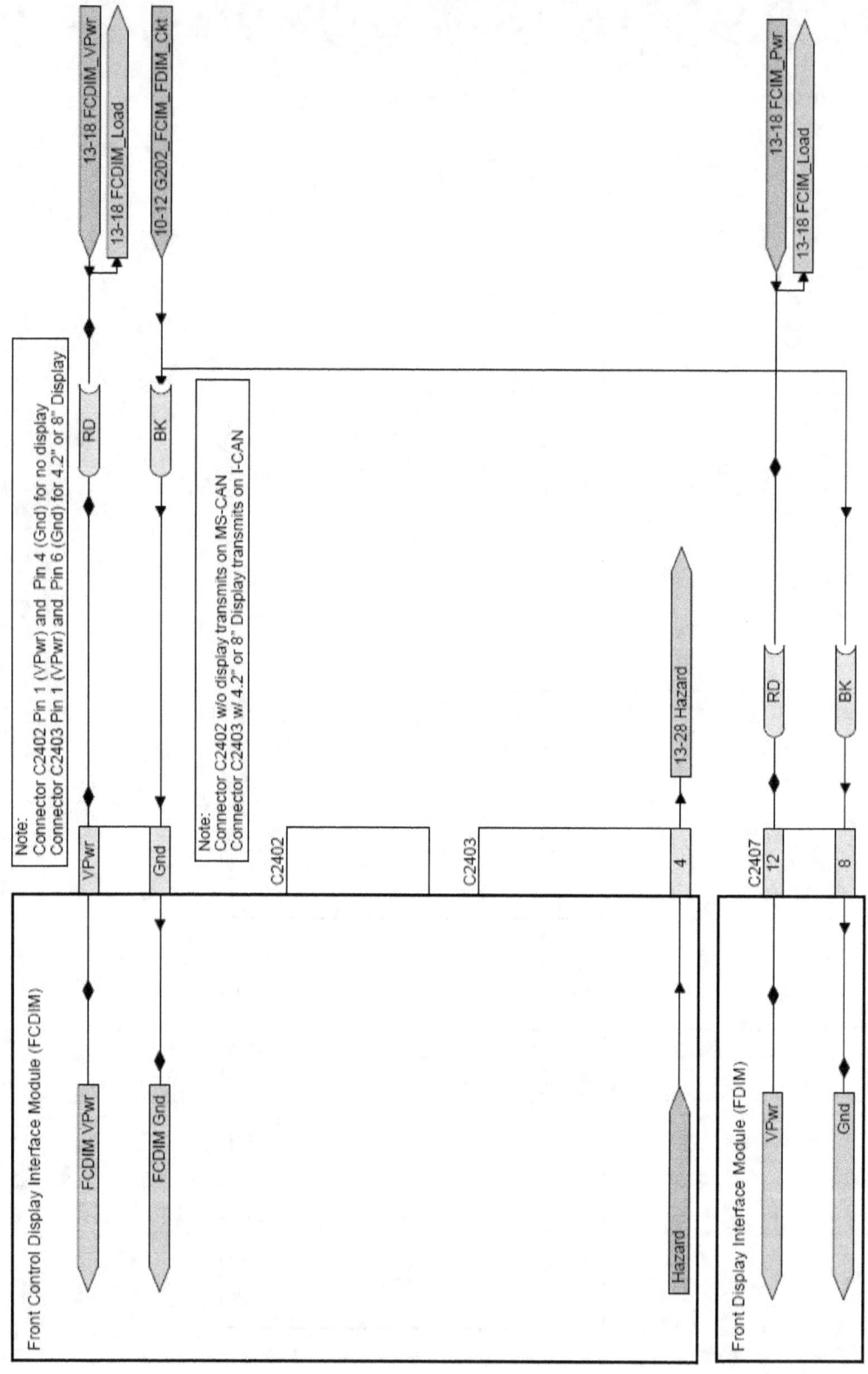

Steering Wheel Switch Right Side Sync Gen 1 and Sync Gen 2 130-15

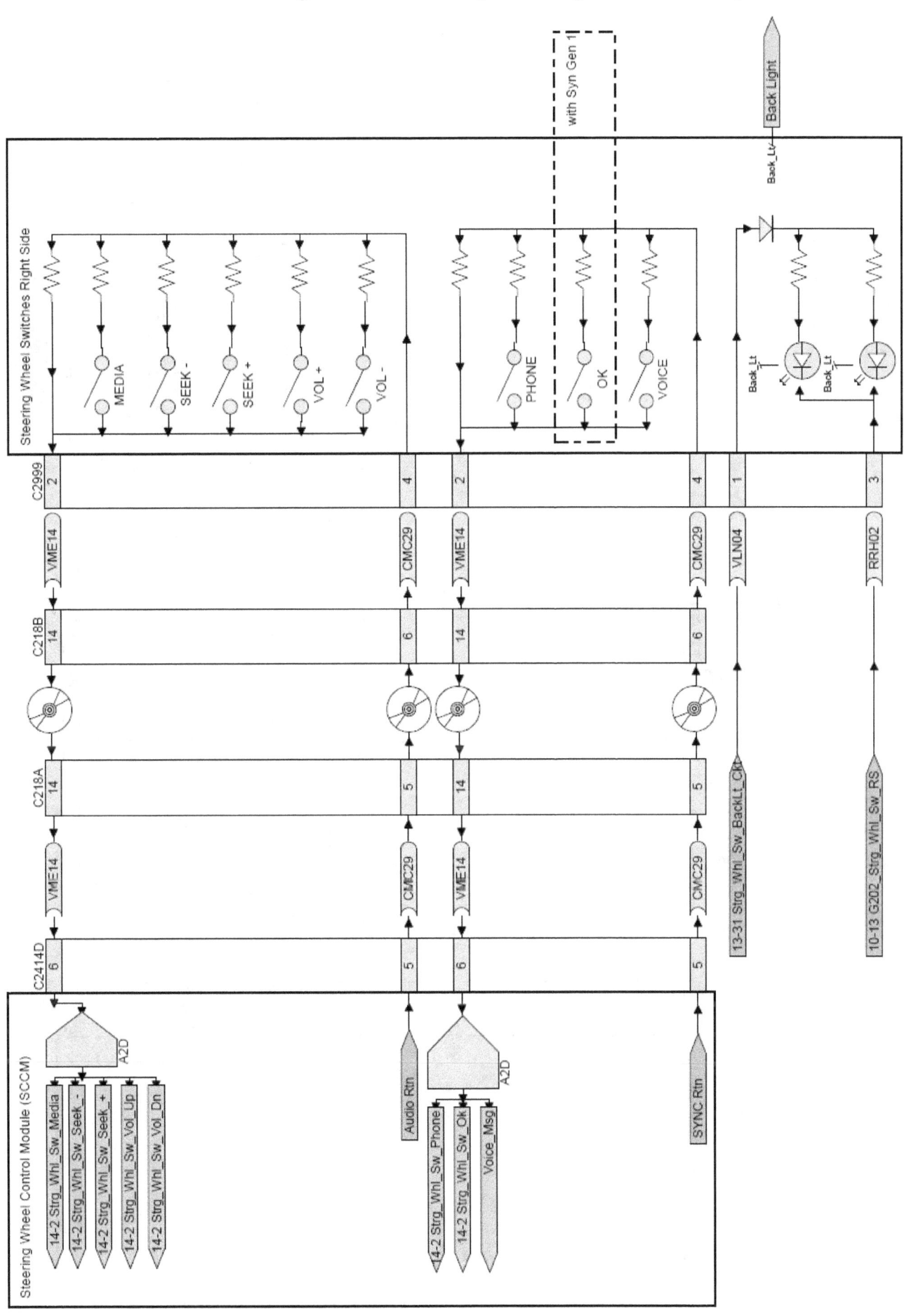

131 Parking Aid Module (PAM) & Cameras
131-1 PAM & Sensors

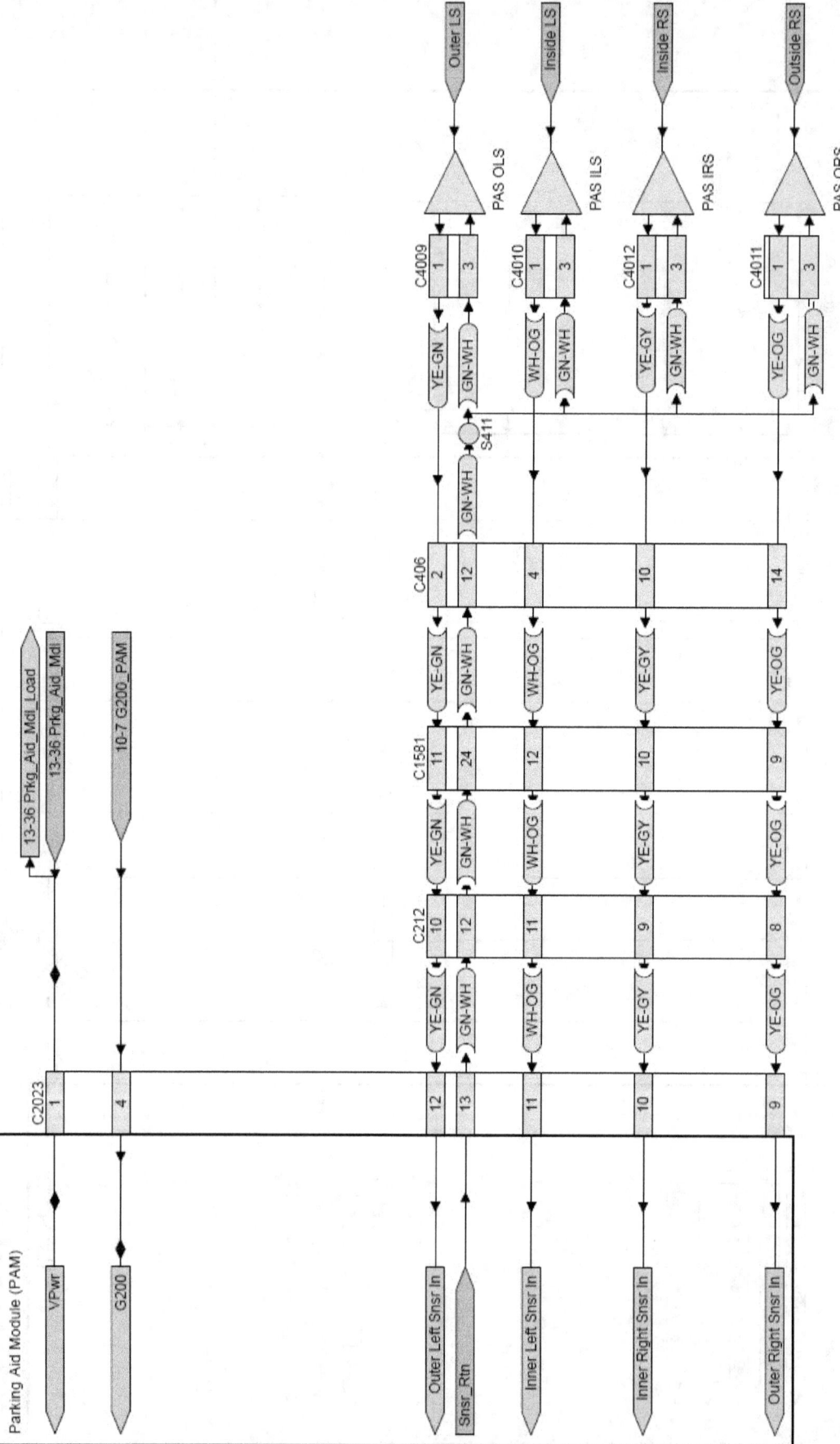

Rear Video Camera 131-3

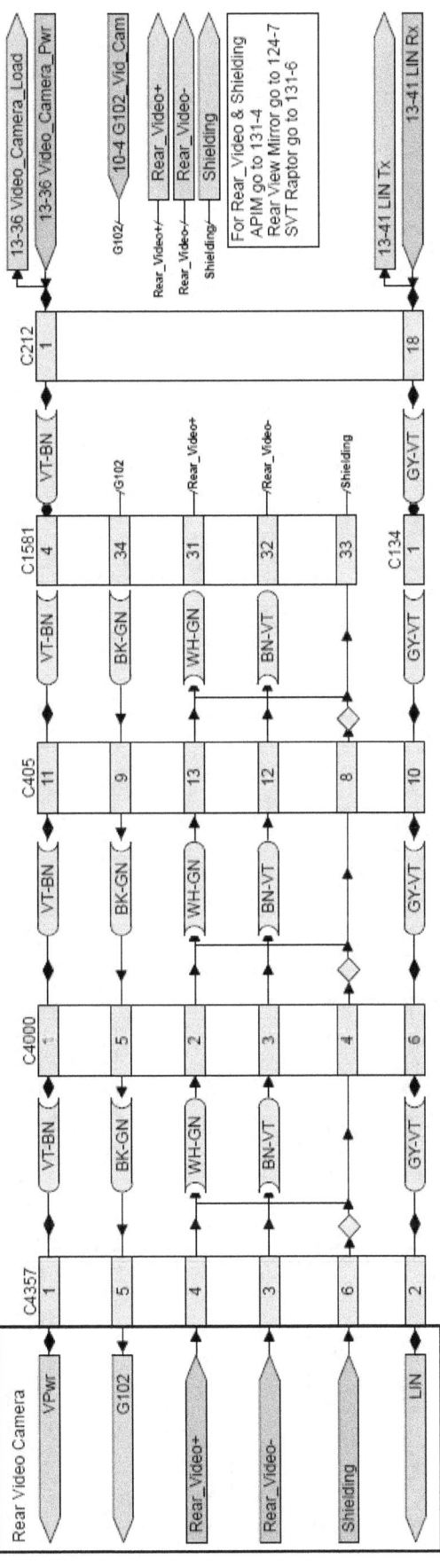

131-6 SVT Raptor Only Front Video Camera

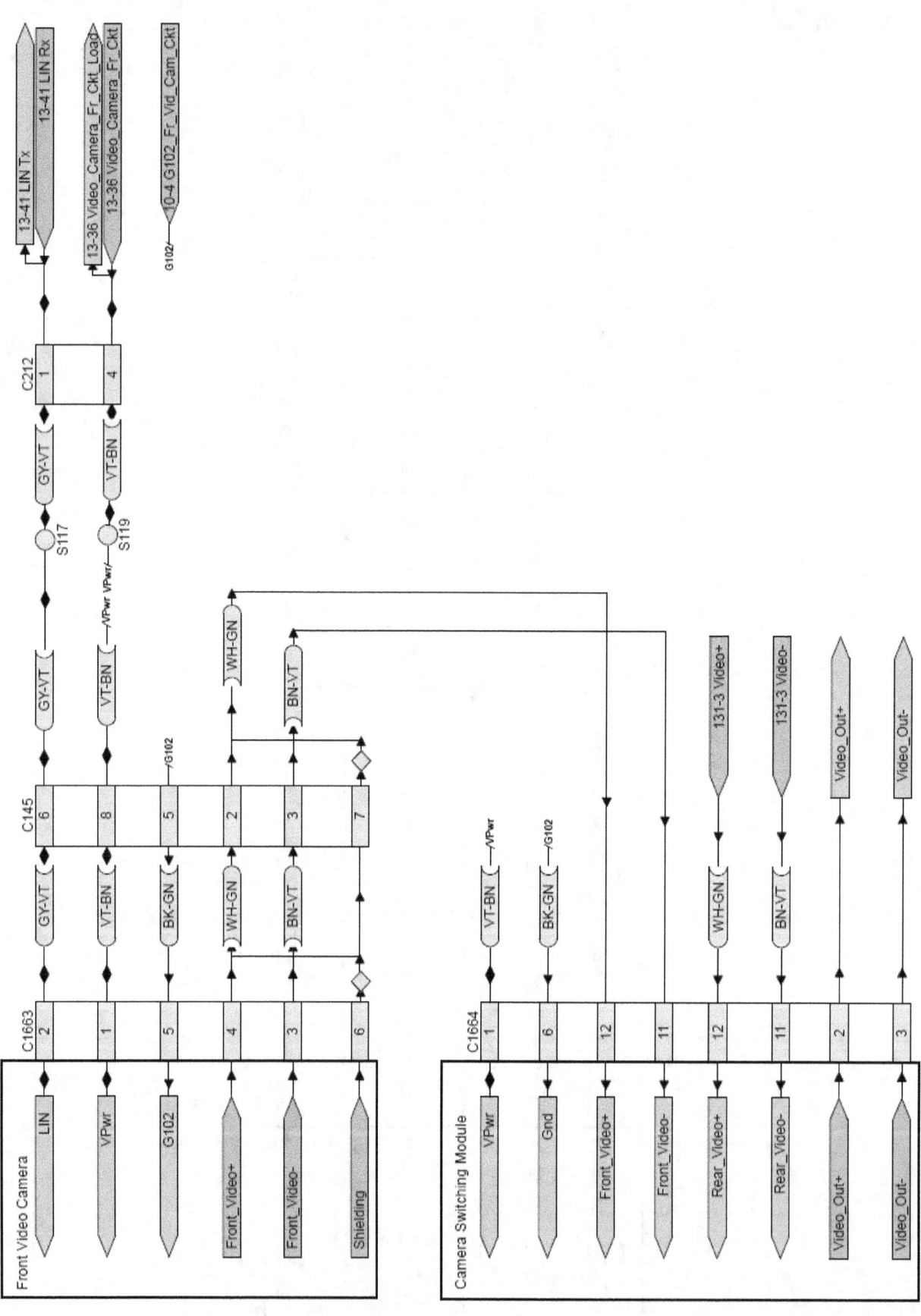

140 SVT Raptor
UpFitter Switch Assembly SVT RAPTOR 140-1

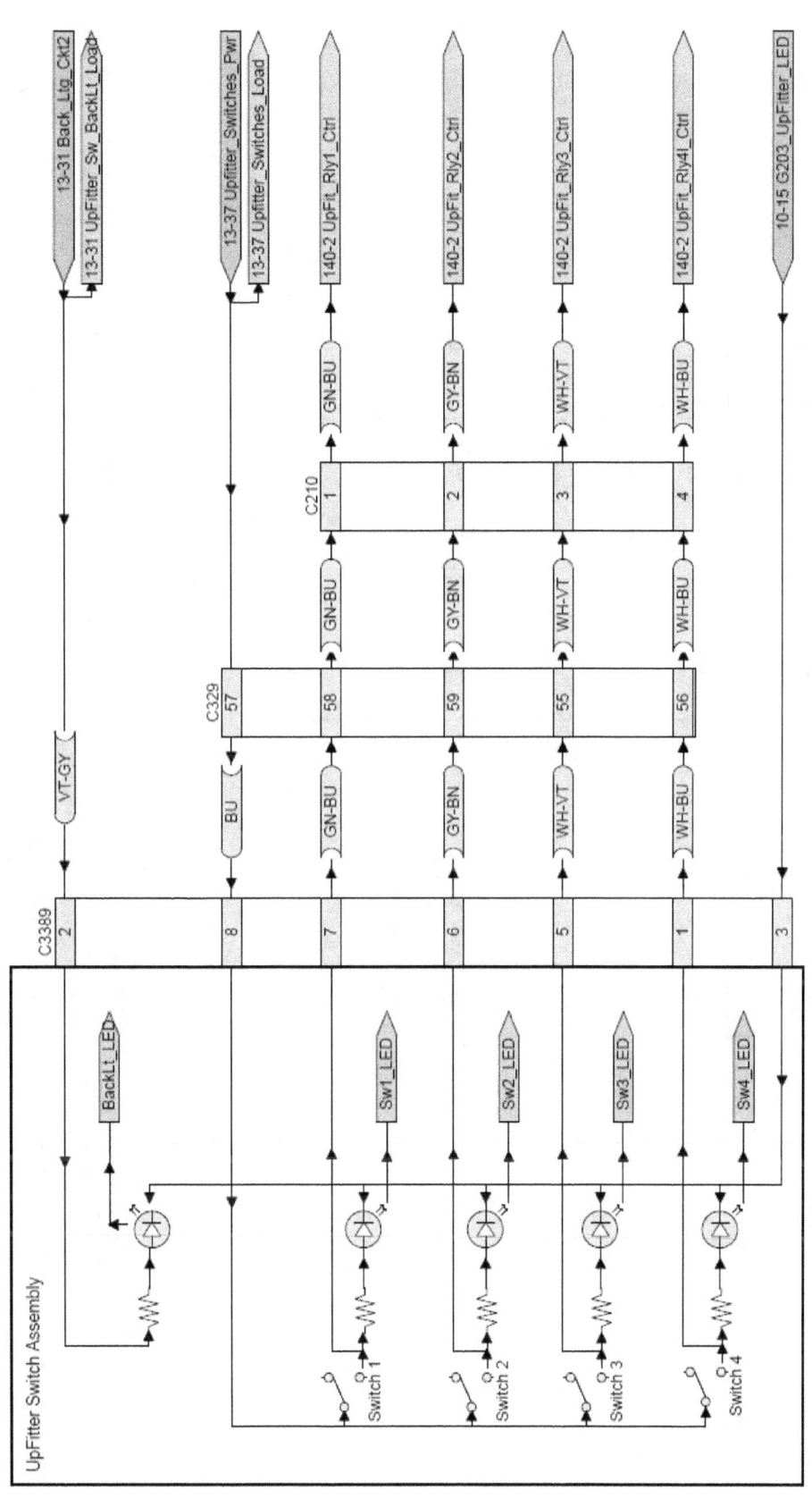

140-2 SVT Raptor Only Battery Junction Box UpFitter Relays

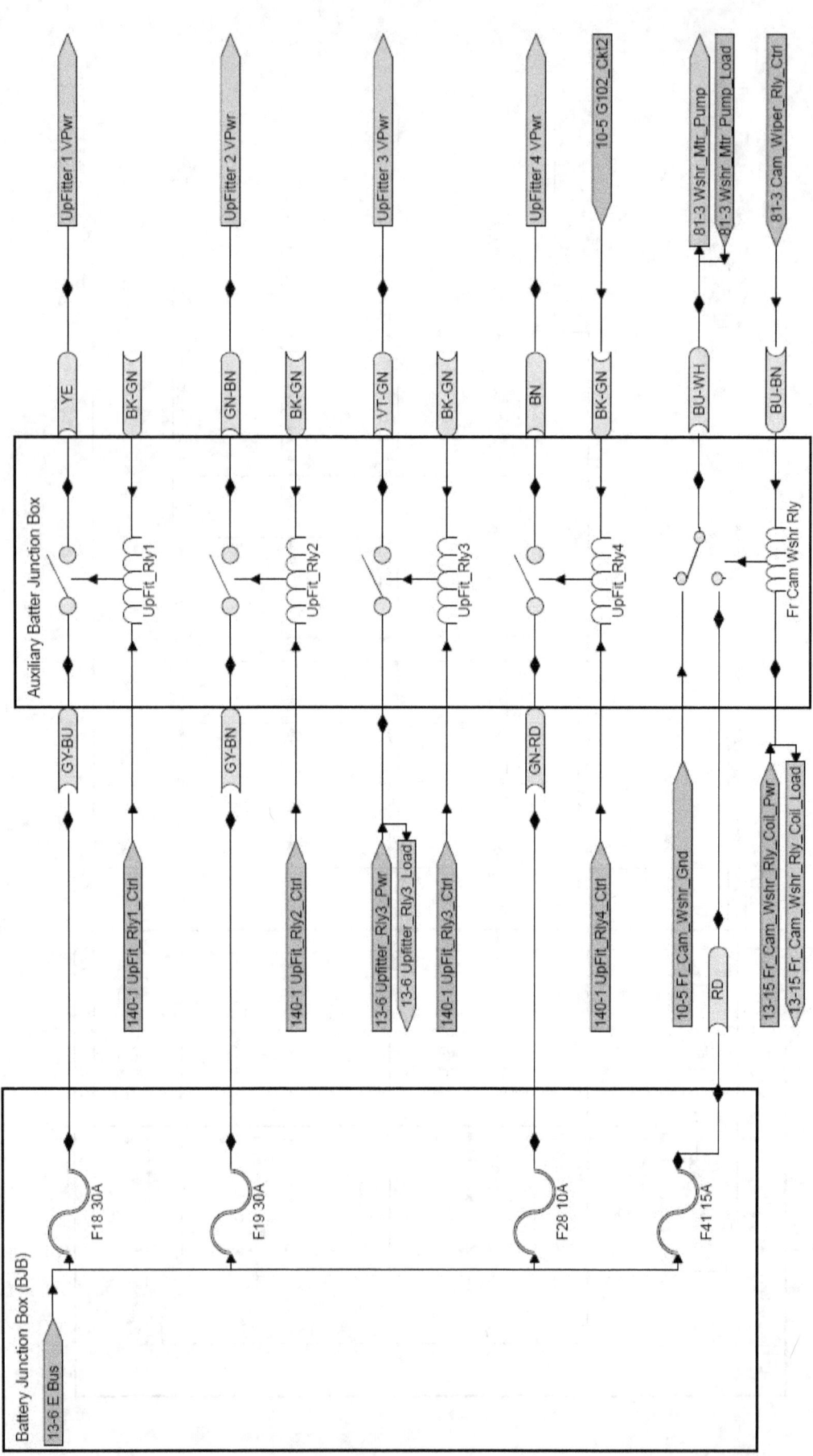

141-2 Telematics Module

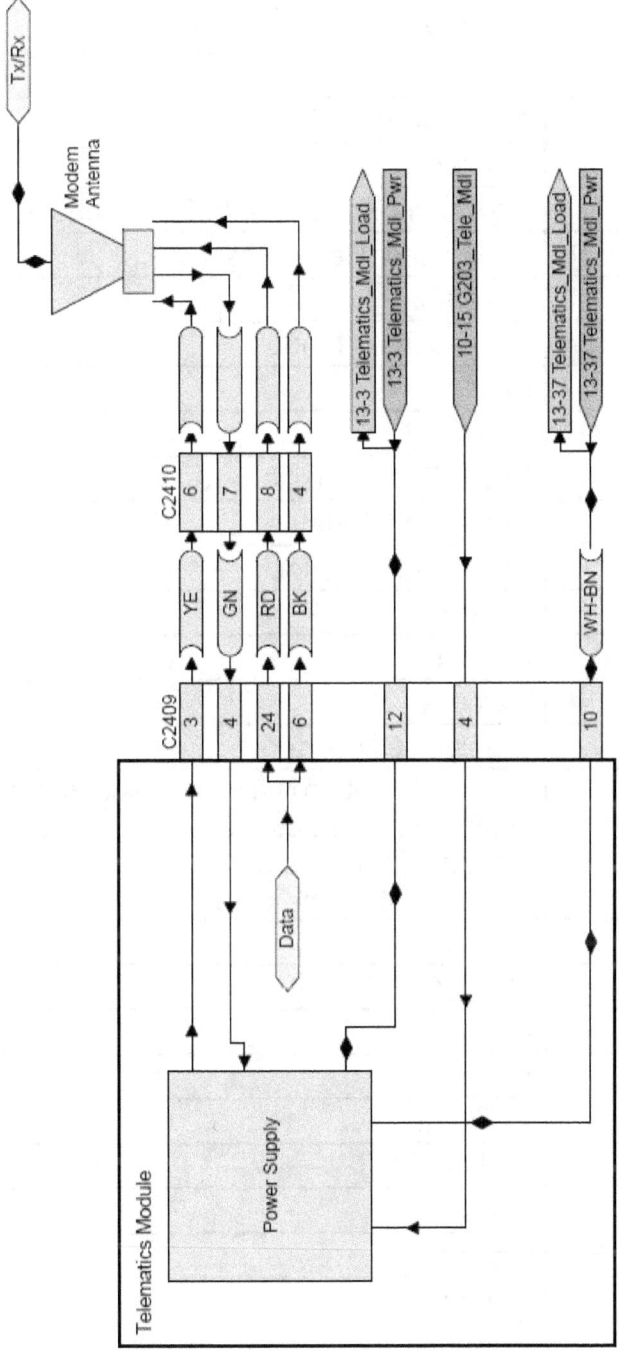

Abbreviations

Abbreviations	Description
6R80	Transmission Model 6R80
A/C	Air Conditioning
A2D	Analog to Digital
AAT	Ambient Air Temperature
ABSM	Anti-Lock Braking System Module
ACC	Accessory
ACM	Audio Control Module
Amb	Ambient
APIM	Accessory Protocol Interface Module
APP	Accelerator Pedal Position
Assy	Assembly
BCM	Body Control Module
BK	Black
Brk	Brake
BPP	Brake Pedal Position
BPS	Brake Pedal Status
BSI	Brake Shift Interlock
Btry	Battery
BYPV	ByPass
Cam	Camera
Cat	Catalytic Converter
Ckt	Circuit, this abbreviation is used with multiple components are using the signal, otherwise the signal name is descriptive of the component on the path.
Cl	Clutch
Clg	Cooling
Cmpnt	Component
Cmps	Compass
Conv	Converter
COP	Coil On Plug
Csl	Console
Ctr	Center
Ctrl	Control
Cur	Current
Cyl	Cylinder
DC/AC	Direct Current / Alternating Current
DCSM	Dual Climate Control Seat Module
Dfr	Differential
Dly	Delay

Abbreviations	Description
DRL	Daytime Running Lights
Drvr	Driver
DSPM	Digital Signal Processing Module
EATC	Electronic Automatic Temperature Control
ELD	Electronic Locking Differential
Elek	Electronic
EMTC	Electronic Manual Temperature Control
Eng	Engine
ETC	Electronic Throttle Control
EVAP	Evaporative
Exh	Exhaust
Ext	Exterior
F##	Fuse and reference number
FCDIM	Front Control Display Interface Module
FCIM	Front Control Interface Module
FET	Field Effects Transistor
Fld	Fluid
Flr	Floor
FP	Fuel Pump
FPCM	Fuel Pump Control Monitor
Fr	Front
Fsbl	Fusible
G###	Ground and reference number
Gen	Generator
GN	Green
Gnd	Ground
GO	Ground Open
GPSM	Global Position System Module
Haz	Hazard
Hdlamp	Head Lamp
Hi	High
HID	High Intensity Discharge
Hmd	Humidity
HMI	Human Machine Interface
HO2S	Heated Oxygen Sensor
HS CAN Rcv	High Speed Controller Area Network Receive
HS CAN Xmt	High Speed Controller Area Network Transmit
Htd	Heated
HVAC	Heating Ventilation Air Conditioning
Hydr	Hydraulic
IAT	Intake Air Temperature

Abbreviations	Description
Ign	Ignition
IKT	Integrated Keyhead Transmitter
Inj	Injector
INJPWRM	Injector Power Monitor
InstPn	Instrument Panel
Int	Interior
Intk	Intake
Intlk	Interlock
Inv	Inverter
IPC	Instrument Panel Cluster
ISPR	Integrated Starter Generator Powertrain
IWE	Integrated Wheel End
Lgc	Logic
Lic	License
LS	Left Side
LSF	Left Side Front
LSR	Left Side Rear
Ltg	Lighting
Lvl	level
Ma	Master
MAF	Mass Air Flow
Mdl	Module
Mem	Memory
Mir	Mirror
Mkr	Marker
Mon	Monitor
Mot	Motor
Msg	Message
Mtd	Mounted
O2	Oxygen
OCS	Occupant Classification Sensor
OCSM	Occupant Classification Sensor Module
Opng	Opening
Out	Output
Ovhd	Overhead
PAD	Passenger Airbag Deactivation
PCM	Powertrain Control Module
Posn	Position
PRBM	Powered Running Board Module
Press	Pressure
Pretnsn	Pretensioner
Prim	Primary

Abbreviations	Description
Prkg	Parking
PrkgBr	Parking Brake
PS	Passenger Side
PSCM	Power Steering Control Module
Psiv	Passive
Pt	Point
PWM	Pulse Width Modulation
Pwr	Power
RCM	Restraint Control Module
Recirc	Recirculating
Retr	Retractor
RKE	Remote Keyless Entry
Rly	Relay
Rng	Range
ROPM_Gnd	Opening
RV	Rear View
Rvr	Reversing
S###	Splice and reference number
Saf	Safety
SCCM	Steering Column Control Module
Sel	Select
Sft	Shaft
Sftw	Software
Shf	Shift
Sig	Signal
SigRtn	Signal Return
SMC	Starter Motor Control
SMRC	Starter Motor Relay Control
Snsr	Sensor
SoC	State of Charge
Sole	Solenoid
Sp	Speed
SST-D	Shift Select Down
SST-U	Shift Select Up
Stat	Status
Stk	Stack
Strg	Steering
Sw	Switch
TBC	Trailer Brake Control
TBCM	Trailer Brake Control Module
TCCM	Transfer Case Control Module

Abbreviations	Description
Temp	Temperature
Tlscp	Telescoping
TOWS	Tow haul Switch
TPM	Tire Pressure Module
Trlr	Trailer
Trq	Torque
Turb	Turbine
USB	Universal Serial Bus
VBatt	Voltage Battery, directly from the battery
VCT	Variable Camshaft Timing
Vdc	Voltage Director Current
Veh	Vehicle
Vid	Video
VO	Volt Open
VREF	Voltage Reference
Wdo	Window
WGV	Waste Gate Valve
Whl	Wheel
Wshld	Windshield
Wt	Weight
Xmsn	Transmission

www.ingramcontent.com/pod-product-compliance
Lightning Source LLC
Chambersburg PA
CBHW051148290426
44108CB00019B/2645